Also in the Variorum Collected Studies Series:

ROGER E. REYNOLDS
Clerics in the Early Middle Ages
Hierarchy and Image

ROGER E. REYNOLDS
Clerical Orders in the Early Middle Ages
Duties and Ordination

ROGER E. REYNOLDS
Law and Liturgy in the Latin Church, 5th–12th Centuries

JAMES A. BRUNDAGE
The Profession and Practice of Medieval Canon Law

H.A. KELLY
Inquisitions and Other Trial Procedures in the Medieval West

JAMES MULDOON
Canon Law, the Expansion of Europe, and World Order

RICHARD KAY
Councils and Clerical Culture in the Medieval West

PAUL FREEDMAN
Church, Law and Society in Catalonia, 900–1500

JEAN GAUDEMET
La doctrine canonique médiévale

JOHN GILCHRIST
Canon Law in the Age of Reform, 11th–12th Centuries

ROBERT SOMERVILLE
Papacy, Councils and Canon Law in the 11th–12th Centuries

STEPHAN KUTTNER
Medieval Councils, Decretals and Collections of Canon Law

STEPHAN KUTTNER
Studies in the History of Medieval Canon Law

VARIORUM COLLECTED STUDIES SERIES

Studies on Medieval Liturgical and Legal Manuscripts from Spain and Southern Italy

Roger E. Reynolds
Corpus Christi Procession in Toledo, Spain
Photo by Lioubov Alexeevna Tarasova

Roger E. Reynolds

Studies on Medieval Liturgical and Legal Manuscripts from Spain and Southern Italy

Routledge
Taylor & Francis Group
LONDON AND NEW YORK

First published 2009 by Ashgate Publishing

2 Park Square, Milton Park, Abingdon, Oxfordshire OX14 4RN
711 Third Avenue, New York, NY 10017

Routledge is an imprint of the Taylor & Francis Group, an informa business

First issued in paperback 2018

British Library Cataloguing in Publication Data
Reynolds, Roger E. (Roger Edward), 1936–
Studies on medieval liturgical and legal manuscripts from Spain and southern Italy.
– (Variorum collected studies series ; 927)
1. Catholic Church – Liturgy – History – Middle Ages, 600–1500.
2. Manuscripts, Latin (Medieval and modern) – Spain.
3. Manuscripts, Latin (Medieval and modern) – Italy, Southern.
4. Liturgies (Canon law) – History – Sources.
I. Title II. Series
264'.02–dc22

ISBN 978-0-7546-5997-6 (hbk)
ISBN 978-1-138-37535-2 (pbk)

Library of Congress Control Number: 2009927951

VARIORUM COLLECTED STUDIES SERIES CS927

CONTENTS

This volume contains xiv + 314 pages

PUBLISHER'S NOTE

The articles in this volume, as in all others in the Variorum Collected Studies Series, have not been given a new, continuous pagination. In order to avoid confusion, and to facilitate their use where these same studies have been referred to elsewhere, the original pagination has been maintained wherever possible.

Each article has been given a Roman number in order of appearance, as listed in the Contents. This number is repeated on each page and is quoted in the index entries.

PREFACE

To the casual reader, it may not immediately be obvious why Visigothic and Beneventan topics should be placed together in the same volume. But a reading of the articles will show that they are indeed very closely related. Although the areas involved, the Iberian Peninsula and the south Italian peninsula, are far removed geographically, they shared many things in common. First, each area had its distinctive liturgical rite, especially in the early Middle Ages. Christians in the Iberian peninsula worshipped according to the Visigothic rite, sometimes called the Mozarabic or Old Spanish rite. Only in Catalonia, largely under the control of the Carolingians and their successors from the ninth century on, were rites from the north celebrated. But even then, these northern rites were not simply Roman, but an amalgam of the Roman and ancient Gallican. Moreover, even when these northern rites were introduced, Christians in Catalonia continued to use elements of their own rites. Further, even with the 'official' conciliar suppression of the Old Spanish rite in 1080 and the suppression of the use of the Visigothic script for liturgical books in 1090, elements of the Old Spanish rite continued to be used in the Iberian peninsula into the sixteenth century and were carried abroad by the Spanish, where they are still used throughout the world by Philippino Christians.

In Italy, in the old southern Lombard duchy of Benevento, another indigenous rite was used in the early Middle Ages, the so-called Beneventan rite or Beneventan use. This rite, related in part to the Milanese rite of the 'northern' Lombards, was an ancient one that borrowed from multiple sources, even Byzantine liturgies. The Beneventan chant used in this liturgical rite was distinguished by its florid, melismatic character, seen in the distinctive Beneventan notation, and the texts by the inclusion of saints of the region and peculiarities in the offices and Mass. As was the case with the Old Spanish rite, there was an attempt to suppress at least the chant used in the Beneventan rite by reforming popes of the second half of the eleventh century. And as was the case in the Iberian peninsula, these attempts at suppression were only partially successful inasmuch as we know from existing manuscripts or fragments – forty-nine of them – that the Beneventan chant was used in select areas into the late thirteenth century at least, and the Beneventan rite texts were often put to the Gregorian music brought from Rome and the north.

Beyond this similarity of indigenous liturgical rites used in the Iberian and southern Italian peninsulas, both areas had their own distinctive forms of writing: in the Iberian peninsula, the so-called Visigothic script, used primarily but not exclusively for liturgical texts, and in the Beneventan zone, the bold and beautiful Beneventan or Langobardic script, also used primarily for liturgical texts. (Over 70% of all manuscripts and fragments in Beneventan script are liturgical.) In both areas, there were attempts to suppress these indigenous scripts. At the Synod of Leon of 1090 the writing of liturgical books in the *littera Toletana* was forbidden. And in the Constitutions of Melfi of 1231, the emperor Frederick II forbade the use of the Beneventan script. But again, it was difficult to suppress completely indigenous scripts, and we know that the Visigothic was used in Spain into the thirteenth century and the Beneventan into the late sixteenth (and in a 'pseudo' form even in the eighteenth century).

Manuscripts in both scripts made their way across the Mediterranean to the other peninsula. Visigothic script manuscripts were very early taken to the Italian peninsula by Christians fleeing Muslim domination, and some of our finest examples of the ancient Old Spanish liturgy are found in codices now in Italian depositories. So also, in the case of Beneventan-script manuscripts, these were taken to the Iberian peninsula, although not as early as the Visigothic script manuscripts came to Italy. Hence, we find examples of Beneventan script manuscripts and fragments in Catalonia as early as the twelfth century. Moreover, it is clear that texts from southern Italian sources found their way into Catalonia by the eleventh century, as is witnessed by the manuscript from Santa Maria de l'Estany, and by a much later Catalan Ordinal of Christ with its typical south Italian peculiarities.

As has been the case with my earlier volumes in the Variorum series, the concentration of the articles is on liturgy and canon law. As one can see from the articles devoted to 'Visigothica,' it is perhaps bending the term to call them all 'Visigothica.' They also deal with Mozarabic, Catalan, and 'Spanish' topics. They begin with an important canonistic text attributed to the great doctor of Visigothic Spain, Isidore of Seville, followed by an article on the persistence of the Visigothic rite in the Carolingian empire. An article dealing with the Reconquista follows, and then a number of articles on Visigothic script remains in manuscripts from Lucca, Venice, and Utrecht. Particularly significant is the one on baptismal rites in which the Visigothic script is used for a 'Roman' rite of baptism. A final article is based on a manuscript from Catalonia that reflects texts from southern Italy. In the section devoted to 'Beneventana' the articles are grouped first according to liturgy, and second, to canon law.

As in my earlier volumes in the Variorum series, a number of individuals who have contributed in major ways to the articles here must be singled out. First, there is my dear colleague, Virginia Brown, whose unparalleled mastery of the Beneventan script has stimulated and inspired me in my work on that script, be it in canon law or liturgy, a field in which she has now become a noted expert. We have worked together closely for over two decades in our major research project, Monumenta liturgica beneventana, generously sponsored by the Social Sciences and Humanities Research Council of Canada and the Pontifical Institute of Mediaeval Studies. In that project we have also enjoyed the assistance, support, and friendship of two of my talented former doctoral students, Professors Richard F. Gyug and Charles Hilken, both experts in aspects of the liturgy of the Beneventan zone. Also of great help has been our musicologist colleague, Professor Thomas Forrest Kelly, to whose colorful volume on the cathedral of Benevento we contributed a number of chapters. Several other colleagues have inspired articles on the genesis and progress of the project, Dr Ritva Jacobsson of Stockholm, Dr Miguelina Girao y Ortega of Beunos Aires, and Dr Marica Cuncic and Dr Hana Breko of Zagreb, all of whom invited me to talk about this project in their universities and institutes. Don Faustino Avagliano, archivist and prior of Montecassino, and his Benedictine confrère, Don Mariano Dell'Omo, have been especially helpful and welcoming as we have spent many a summer in the archive of that great abbey. Then there is Dr Maria Crescenza Carrocci and her family and Dr Lena Massi and Don Mario Iadanza, who have made our lives so pleasant as we have worked in southern Italy. In Dalmatia Dr Jasko Belamaric has opened many a door for us, and as a result new manuscripts and pieces of Beneventana have come to light.

I owe a heavy debt of gratitude to many others. Professor Robert Somerville has for many years shared with me the riches of his own research, especially as they touch my areas of specialization, and he generously continues to do so. Professor Giles Constable saw to it that I enjoyed a memorable and productive year of research and writing at the Institute for Advanced Study at Princeton as the George William Cottrell Jr. Member of the School of Historical Studies, a membership generously endowed by Mrs Annette Merle-Smith. Monsignor Miguel Pujol Gros of Vic encouraged me to complete the study of the rich and fascinating manuscript from Santa Maria de l'Estany and kindly saw it through publication in the periodical of the Societat Catalana de Estudis Litúrgics, to which we both belong. In Toledo I received a generous and warm welcome from the members of the Cofradia Internacional de Investigadores when I was invested in that confraternity in Ferdinand and Isabella's church of San Juan de los Reyes and joined them in the festooned streets of Toledo, in the solemn procession of the feast of Corpus Christi, a feast whose liturgy has for so long engaged me.

Then there are the many talented students whose licentiate or doctoral theses I have directed, including Drs Susan Keefe, Ronald Zawilla, Brian Bethune, Jonathan Black, Renate Amstutz, Daniel Taylor, John Douglas Adamson, Kathleen Cushing, Barry Graham, and Neil Roy, all of whom have been a great stimulus and help in my own research.

Many colleagues have been especially generous in sending me offprints and copies of their own works and information valuable to me in my research: Horst

Fuhrmann, Hubert Mordek, Raymund Kottje, Peter Landau, Rudolf Schieffer, Herbert Schneider, Martin Bertram, Eric Palazzo, Paul De Clerck, Martin Brett, Uta-Renate Blumenthal, and Richard Pfaff. Then, of course, there are the many colleagues and friends, whose kindness is cited in the articles in this volume.

I end this preface with a 'happy irony.' In the very month my last two volumes in the Variorum series appeared, both lovingly dedicated to my wife of forty years, she separated from me and filed for divorce. Since that time, Providence has seen to it that another beautiful, intelligent, and talented woman has come into my life. She has accompanied me as I have done research in southern Italy and Dalmatia on Beneventan topics and in Spain on Spanish topics, and best of all, she has been of significant assistance to me as a facilitator and translator as I worked in manuscript depositories in Russia and Poland. Moreover, she has introduced me to a generous and lovely circle of her friends in Russia and the Ukraine, all of whom have enriched my life and widened my vision to a new and fascinating area of the world. It is to her, my dear wife, Lioubov Alexeevna Tarasova of Kaliningrad, Russia, that this present volume is dedicated.

ROGER E. REYNOLDS

Toronto
May 2009

ACKNOWLEDGEMENTS

Grateful acknowledgement is made to the following institutions and publishers for their kind permission to reproduce the articles included in this volume: Verlag Ferdinand Schöningh GMBH and Co., Paderborn (for article I); the Gesellschaft für mittelrheinische Kirchengeschichte, Mainz (II); the Pontifical Institute of Mediaeval Studies, Toronto, ON (III, IV, V, VI, XI, XVI, XVII, XVIII); the Institut d'Estudis Catalans, Barcelona (VII); Egbert Forsten Publishing, Groningen (VIII); Jan Thorbecke Verlag, Ostfildern (IX); Jacqueline Hamesse, Fédération Internationale des Instituts d'Etudes Médiévales, Louvaine-la-Neuve (X); the Biblioteca Apostolica Vaticana, Vatican City (XII); the Medieval Academy of Ireland (*Peritia*), Cork (XIII, XV); and Pierre-Maurice Bogaert (*Revue Bénédictine*), Abbaye de Maredsous (XIV).

ACKNOWLEDGEMENTS

[illegible]

I

The ‚Isidorian' Epistula ad Massonam on Lapsed Clerics: Notes on its Early Manuscript and Textual Transmission[1]

One of the hallmarks of the scholarship of Peter Landau has been his ability to blend careful manuscript research with medieval legal theory. Nonewhere is this better exemplified than in his study, *Officium und Libertas christiana.*[2] In that work one of the early medieval texts and its manuscript tradition examined was the ‚Isidorian' *Epistula ad Leudefredum.*[3] While this epistle enumerated the duties of clerical officers, another epistle attributed to Isidore, the *Epistula ad Massonam* (hereafter EM), dealt with the restoration of lapsed clerics.[4] At least from the middle of the ninth century these two Isidorian epistles were often combined in manuscripts, especially canon law manuscripts. The present article has as its focus the EM, the ‚travelling companion' of the *Epistula ad Leudefredum,* whose influence and manuscript diffusion Peter Landau examined with such care in his work on the development of the concept of *officium.*

Virtually from the seventh century when it was likely written, the letter of Isidore to the Visigothic bishop of Mérida, Massona, has been cited in whole or in part for many reasons, especially in canonical collections and the manuscripts in which they are found. The letter, dated on the last day of February in the third year of the reign of the Visigothic king Witteric (603-610), is directed to Massona († ca. 600), whose age or health is of some concern to Isidore. Massona, it seems, had contacted Isidore regarding a canonical problem: whether or not a cleric who had lapsed by sinning and who

---

1 Portions of the research for this article were conducted for the program ‚Monumenta Liturgica Beneventana' supported by the Social Sciences and Humanities Research Council of Canada.

2 P. LANDAU, Officium und Libertas christiana, SB.BayAkadWiss., Phil.-Hist. Kl., 1991, H. 3; Munich 1991.

3 On this epistle see R. REYNOLDS, ‚The ‚Isidorian' *Epistula ad Leudefredum:* An Early Medieval Epitome of the Clerical Duties,' Mediaeval Studies 41 (1979), 252-330. In his Officium und Libertas Christiana,. 46 f., Peter Landau makes the valuable and important addendum to this study that a lost manuscript of Ivo's *Decretum* is reported as having the additional verse for the archpresbyter found in Gratian's version of the *Epistula ad Leudefredum* (303). While this may have indeed been the case with the manuscript, one would want to verify that the addition was actually entered as part of the text rather than being a marginal addition or an addition in the printed text depending on Gratian's version.

4 Epistle 4, PL 83, 899-902; and see the ‚edition' (taken from Arévalo's edition in the PL) and English translation by G. FORD, The Letters of St. Isidore of Seville, Amsterdam ^{2}1970, 22-27.

had repented and done adequate penance might be allowed to return to his rank and ministry. The problem seems in part to have arisen out of what Isidore later in the epistle calls an ancient and authoritative canon of the Council of Ancyra (314), which appears to allow for the restoration of a penitent sinner. The canon is unnamed and unnumbered in the EM itself, but given the repetition of the word ‚*pristine*' – ‚*pristinos officii gradus*,' ‚*statum pristinum*,' ‚*pristinae dignitatis*,' and ‚*pristinum gradum*'– and the reference to Maria, the sister of Aaron, being cast out of the camp for seven days – ‚*id est extra collegium sanctae Ecclesiae septem annis*' – it is most probable that the citation is to c. 20 of the council, although that canon does not mention clerics as such: ‚*Si cuius uxor adulterata fuerit vel si ipse adulterium commiserit, septem annorum penitentia oportet eum perfectionem consequi secundum pristinos gradus*.'[5] On the other hand, Massona also appears to have known other canons that forbid the restoration of lapsed clerics. Isidore attempts to solve the problem of divergent canonical directives primarily by divine authority citing biblical, especially Old Testament, passages that seem to support the more lenient treatment of the lapsed cleric. In concluding the epistle Isidore adds a comment that when conciliar canons appear to be contradictory, the opinion of that whose authority is older and stronger is to be preferred.

The EM assumes its special importance for the early Middle Ages in the context of patristic teaching on the status of lapsed clerics. As Raymund Kottje has shown in his masterful treatment of the EM, the majority position of patristic canons appears not to allow restoration.[6] In the canons of the oriental and African churches some cases speak of deposition with no mention of restoration, leading to the conclusion that restoration was not allowed. Other canons deny restoration outright. What is true of these oriental and African canons is also largely true of the canons of the Visigothic and Gallican churches, which at times speak of perpetual deposition. By the sixth and certainly by the seventh centuries the strict position was beginning to erode. This is seen in several Visigothic councils, such as Lerida and XIII Toledo, in the early Irish *Poenitentiale Vinniani*, and in Gallican territories themselves. It is in this context that the EM was written to support a more lenient position.

As is the case with its sister Isidorian *Epistula ad Leudefredum*, the Isidorian authenticity of the EM has at least since the sixteenth century been frequently contested and defended by scholars.[7] Holding it to be authentic have been such eminent scholars as Friedrich Maassen,[8] Bernhard Poschmann,[9]

[5] PL 67, 155.

[6] R. KOTTJE, Die Bussbücher Halitgars von Cambrai und des Hrabanus Maurus: ihre Überlieferung und ihre Quellen, =Beiträge zur Geschichte und Quellenkunde des Mittelalters 8, Berlin-New York 1980, 216-240.

[7] See the discussion in Faustino Arévelo, PL 81, 496-498.

[8] F. MAASSEN, Geschichte der Quellen und der Literatur des canonischen Rechts, 1, Graz 1870 ND 1956, 381.

[9] B. POSCHMANN, Die abendländische Kirchenbusse im Ausgang des christlichen Altertums, =Münchener Studien zur hist. Theologie 7; Munich 1928, 296.

Charles Henry Beeson,[10] Gabriel Le Bras,[11] José de Aldama,[12] Charles Munier,[13] Manuel Díaz y Díaz,[14] and the newest edition of the *Clavis Patrum Latinorum.*[15] On the other hand an equally impressive array of scholars has questioned its authenticity, including Joseph de Ghellinck,[16] Paul Fournier,[17] Paul Séjourné,[18] Horst Fuhrmann,[19] Hubert Mordek,[20] and most recently Roger Collins, who has studied the career of Massona.[21] Among the objections advanced against Isidore's authorship are that the style, content, and formal epistolary elements in the letter seem alien to the other letters of Isidore, and that the lenient position in the EM contradicts the position of Isidore in his *De ecclesiasticis officiis*, his letter to Helladius, and a canon of the IV Council of Toledo, over which Isidore presided.[22] Since Massona died ca. 600 and Witteric reigned from 603-610, that is, very early in Isidore's career as bishop of Seville, it is possible that the EM represents an early position that Isidore later changed. But in view of his position consistently held later, this is unlikely. On balance, then, it seems preferable to doubt Isidore's authorship, although there are no major reasons to doubt that it was composed in areas under Visigothic domination – except for the fact that its earliest appearance in texts and manuscripts lies outside those regions. But when was the EM composed and what is its terminus post quem non?

---

10 C. Beeson, Isidor-Studien, =Quellen und Untersuchungen zur lateinischen Philologie des Mittelalters, 4.2, Munich 1913, 60.

11 G. Le Bras, ‚Sur la part d'Isidore de Séville et des Espagnols dans l'histoire des collections canoniques,' Revue des sciences religieuses 10 (1930), 224 f.

12 J. De Aldama, ‚Indicaciones sobre la cronología de las obras de S. Isidoro,' in Miscellanea Isidoriana: homenaje a S. Isidoro de Sevilla en el XIII centenario de su muerte 636 – 4 abril 1936, Rome 1936, 88.

13 C. Munier, Les sources patristiques du droit de l'Église du VIIIe au XIIIe siècle, Muhlhouse 1957, 108 f.

14 M. Díaz y Díaz, Index scriptorum latinorum medii aevi hispanorum, =Acta Salamanticensia, Filosofía y letras, 18; Salamanca 1958-59, 42, nr. 124.

15 Clavis, 407, nr. 1209.

16 J. De Ghellinck, Le mouvement théologique du XIIe siècle: sa préparation lointaine avant et autour de Pierre Lombard, ses rapports avec les initiatives des canonistes: études, recherches et documents, =Museum Lessianum, section historique 10; Bruges-Brussels-Paris [2]1914, 482 f.

17 P. Fournier, ‚Le premier manuel canonique de la réforme du XIe siècle', Mélanges d'archéologie et d'histoire de l'École française de Rome 14 (1894), 189.

18 P. Séjourné, Le dernier Père de l'Église, Saint Isidore de Séville: son rôle dans l'histoire du droit canonique, Paris 1929, 74-77.

19 H. Fuhrmann, Einfluss und Verbreitung der pseudo-isidorischen Fälschungen von ihrem Auftauchen bis in die neuere Zeit, =MGH Schriften 24.1, Stuttgart 1972, 91, n. 92, with a massive bibliography on the importance of this text.

20 H. Mordek, Kirchenrecht und Reform im Frankenreich: Die Collectio Vetus Gallica, die älteste systematische Kanonessammlung des fränkischen Gallien. Studien und Edition, =Beiträge zur Geschichte und Quellenkunde des Mittelalters 1, Berlin-New York 1975, 227 f., n. 62.

21 R. Collins, ‚Merida and Toledo: 550-585,' in Visigothic Spain: New Approaches, ed. E. James, Oxford, 1980, 201 and 206, n. 2, who suggests the EM was written in Toledo in the late seventh century.

22 See Kottje, Die Bussbücher Halitgars von Cambrai, note 6, 219, n. 257.

Until recently the earliest evidence cited for the existence of the EM has been the *Collectio canonum hibernensis*,[23] generally dated to the early eighth century and at least before ca. 763, the date of the earliest extant manuscript of the *Hibernensis*, Cambrai, Bibliothèque municipale, 679 (763x790, north-eastern France, Peronne?).[24] If one looks to the *Hibernensis* it is true that the EM is quoted in L. XI, cc. 4-6,[25] but it is in a strange form, broken into snippets under rubrics and arranged in an order not found in the full text of the letter. In the EM as found in the best-known manuscript of the ‚B family' of the *Hibernensis*, Rome, Biblioteca Vallicelliana, Tom. XVIII, there is additional material not found in the text printed in Wasserschleben's edition.[26] For example, after the citation of Apoc. 2.5 in L. XI, c. 4a, there are added the words ‚*Hireneus et Primasius hec dicunt de cadentibus sub gradu*,' probably references to the *Commentarius in Apocalypsin* by Primasius,[27] and the *Adversus Iovinianum* of Jerome (Hieronymus),[28] where Apoc. 2.5 is cited. Further, after the word ‚*movebo*' in L. XI, c. 9, the Vallicelliana text reads: ‚*et reliqua. Item notandum quod filii Aaron peccantes ita et filii Heli non degradati sunt*.' How the EM reached the compilers of the *Hibernensis* is not certain, but if they were indeed working in Ireland, it is known that works attributed to Isidore had reached there by the late seventh century.[29]

There is now another piece of manuscript evidence from the early eighth century for the existence of the EM. It is found in an uncial manuscript written by several different scribes, Copenhagen, Kongelike Bibliotek, Ny Kgl. Saml. 58$^{8°}$, whose script E. A. Lowe placed in southern France in the early eighth century.[30] This suggests a region of scribal activity not far from Visigothic influence, and indeed the manuscript shows signs of Visigothic-script traditions. But since the appearance of Lowe's date in the *Codices Latini Antiquiores*, Paul Meyvaert has reported to the author of this present article that Bernhard Bischoff once told him that Lowe had never actually seen the manuscript and that he was not certain of Lowe's location of the manuscript in southern France or Septimania. Rather, he leaned toward northern Italy, a position supported by Meyvaert's own study of the textual family of the *Libellus responsionum* of Gregory I, also found in the Copenhagen codex.[31]

In any event, the EM does appear in the Copenhagen manuscript on fols. 73r-77v. While the complete text of the letter is wanting, the substantial ex-

23 See, e.g. L. MAIR DAVIES, ‚Isidorian Texts and the *Hibernensis*, Peritia 11 (1997), 240 f.

24 If the terminus post quem non is difficult to establish on the basis of extant manuscript evidence, the question of the terminus post quem, author(s), and place of compilation are fully as difficult, on which see DAVIES, Isidorian Texts, note 23, 209 – 216.

25 Die irische Kanonensammlung, ed. H. WASSERSCHLEBEN, Leipzig ^{2}1885 ND Aalen 1966, 31f.

26 fol. 67r-v.

27 Clavis 873.

28 Clavis 610.

29 See J. HILLGARTH, ‚Old Ireland and Visigothic Spain,' in: Old Ireland, ed. R. MC NALLY , New York 1965 212 f.

30 CLA 10, Oxford 1963, nr. 1568.

31 I am very grateful to Dr. Meyvaert for this information. The task of editing the Gregorian *Libellus responsionum* has now been undertaken by Dr. Rob Meens.

cerpt follows the sequence of text commonly met elsewhere in later manuscripts, not that found in the *Hibernensis.* And not unlike the Vallicelliana codex of the *Hibernensis,* the Copenhagen manuscript has an addition, albeit a different one, at the conclusion of the text. After the words ‚timore iudicii divini committit' of c. 12, there are added the words ‚*Hucusque sermo efficio dom. episcopi de penitentia sacerdotali quem ecitius ad Mosonem episcopum portavit. Et nosciendumque in hoc lectione episcopus, presbiter, et deinceps reliquos gradus sacerdotum nomine conprehendat.*' It is also interesting that slightly before the EM, Apoc. 2.5 in a form unlike that in the *Hibernensis* is presented,[32]after which are added the words, ‚*Eneus et Primasius hoc denuntiat de sub gradu cadentibus,*' resembling the insertion in the Vallicellicana text of the EM. It has been pointed out by Franz Asbach that the Copenhagen manuscript contains extracts from the *Hibernensis,*[33] and these do in fact surround the EM.[34] But the form of the EM itself does not follow the *Hibernensis* suggesting 1) that the florilegium of texts seemingly from the *Hibernensis* may represent a source used by the compilers of the *Hibernensis,* not an extract therefrom, 2) that the compiler had a different form of the *Hibernensis* as his model differing from the common A and B forms,[35] or 3)

32 fol. 72v.

33 F. ASBACH, *Das Poenitentiale Remense und der sogen. Excarpsus Cummeani* Diss. Regensburg 1975 [1979], 24.

34 In this section of the manuscript there is a florilegium of texts, a few from the Bible and many attributed to patristic sources, including Augustine, Jerome, Origen, a Roman synod, an unidentified synod, Gregory, Patrick, an Eneus and Primasius, Isidore, and a council of Nicea. Many of these canons have rubrics and texts from or similar to those in the *Hibernensis*, especially the B tradition found in the south Italian manuscript, Rome, Biblioteca Vallicelliana, Tom. XVIII: XVII [= XV in A]. 8 (Augustine), 8 (Jerome) (Vallicelliana, fol. 72v); XV. 1 (Origen), 2c (unidentified ecclesiastical decree, said in the *Hibernensis*, Form A, to be a ‚Sinodus Romana'), 2b (Augustine); XVII. 8 (Gregory) (Vallicelliana, fol. 72v); XV. 3c (Gregory), 3d (Gregory); XLVII. 5b (Jerome); XII (= XI in A). 1 (Origen) (Vallicelliana, fol. 67r); XI. 1b (Patrick), 1a (Jerome), 2 (Augustine), 4a (Apoc. 2.5), 3 (unidentified synod, said in the *Hibernensis,* Form A, to be a ‚*Synodus Hibernensis*'); the Isidorian *Epistula ad Massonam*; XV. 6a (Jerome), 6b (Jerome), 6c (Jerome); XIII. 8 (Jerome and Augustine, said to be Jerome alone in the *Hibernensis*, Form A); XLVII. 13b (Augustine); and XLVIII (= XLVII in A). 8 (Nicea, said to be Arles in the *Hibernensis,* Form B) (Vallicelliana, fol. 123v); XLVII.22 (Vallicelliana, fol. 125v attributed to an unidentified synod); XLVII. 22 (Vallicelliana, fol. 125v attributed to a ‚*Synodus Hibernensis*'); XLV. 4b, 4a, 4c, 4d; XLV.5.

35 One of the most vexing problems in studies on the *Hibernensis* has been the number of versions of the collection contained in the manuscripts. It has long been recognized that there are two major recensions, a short form traditionally called A by scholars and Alpha by the late Maurice Sheehy, and a long form traditionally called B by scholars and Beta by Sheehy. But controversy begins as to which manuscripts contain which form. Moreover, there are other forms or families related to each of these groups. It can be hoped that Sheehy's study and edition, if it is eventually published, can help clear up these problems; here it is only possible to present what scholars have said to this point.
There are several manuscripts of the full collection, which by general agreement contain the long or B form. Chief among these is the codex, Rome, Biblioteca Vallicelliana, Tom. XVIII, an eleventh-century manuscript from southern Italy written in both Carolingian and Beneventan scripts. Also containing the B form is the codex, Oxford, Bodleian Library, Hatton 42, which Bernhard Bischoff dated to the middle of the ninth century, Ludwig Bieler to the late

that on reaching the texts from the EM of the *Hibernensis* he returned to a earlier or purer ordering of the text which he possessed. Beyond this connection with the Irish *Hibernensis,* there is, however, a connection in the manuscript with Spain inasmuch as the *Epitome hispana,* found in other early

ninth century, and Neil Ker placed first in Brittany in the ninth or tenth century and taken later to Worcester. Sheehy has further refined the differences between these two B manuscripts, suggesting that the Vallicelliana text was based on the Oxford text or a near relative by a copyist who did not properly understand the Irish origins or meaning of the text and who hence altered it to a ‚more sober, less contentious version.' In Sheehy's Beta recension he would also include a codex with excerpta of the collection, Montecassino, Archivio della Badia, 297, a manuscript written in Beneventan script at the beginning of the eleventh century.
Beyond the two full manuscripts of the B version of the *Hibernensis*, there are other full manuscripts or excerpta that have been included in this version by scholars. First, there is the fragment of the collection in Karlsruhe, Landesbibliothek, Aug. XVIII (saec. IX^{in}, Reichenau). According to MORDEK, *Kirchenrecht und Reform,* note 20, 256, this is a B form manuscript, but Sheehy has included it under his Alpha form. Likewise, the full manuscript of the collection in Livorno, Biblioteca Labronica, sin. num., an eleventh- or twelfth-century codex written probably in northern Italy and containing also the Pseudo-Isidorian Decretals and *Excerpta Bobbiensis,* is classified by Mordek as a B form codex, not the Alpha form as Sheehy would have it.
There are far greater numbers of manuscripts of the short or A form of the *Hibernensis.* Several of the full manuscripts are extraordinary because they appear to have been written in Brittany: Orléans, Bibliothèque municipale, 221 (saec. IX^{in}, Brittany [Bischoff], saec. VIII, Fleury [Bieler]); Paris, BN, lat. 3182 (saec.$^{2/2}$, Brittany [Bischoff], saec. $X^{1/2}$ [Bieler]); and Paris, BN, lat. 12021 (saec. X^{in}, Brittany). Beyond these manuscripts generally recognized as belonging to the A or B families, the categories grow slippery. London, British Library, Cotton Otho E XIII (saec. X^{in} [Bieler]) contains two parts; part 1 is a corrected version of the Alpha form according to Sheehy; and part 2 is uncategorized. Everyone agrees that the codex St. Gall, Stiftsbibliothek, 243 (saec. $IX^{1/2}$, St. Gall), used by Wasserschleben for his text, is of the A type, but Sheehy has noted peculiarities in it that make it inappropriate as a base text for an edition of the A form.
Beyond these manuscripts there are several groups that have been classified as either A or B versions, but that are in short or modified forms. First, there are several manuscripts that contain a form whose canons go only as far as L. 38, c. 18: among these are the oldest-known codex of the collection, Cambrai, Bibliothèque municipale, 679 (763x790, northeastern France, Peronne?) and a now destroyed manuscript, Tours, Bibliothèque municipale, 556 (saec. $IX^{4/4}$, prov. Marmoutiers). Also, the codex, Cologne, Erzbischofliche Diozesan-und Dombibliothek, 210 (saec. VIII^{ex}, northeastern France) has this same configuration and is sometimes called the *Collection in 450 Chapters.* In a sense, this manuscript is not really a pure example of a partial manuscript of the *Hibernensis.* Not only has the traditional division of the *Hibernensis* texts into books and chapters been broken down, but many of the canons themselves have been reduced and many non-*Hibernensis* texts have been added. These additions include a host of canons from Greek, African, and Gallican councils, including Epaon, Clermont, and Orléans V, and several papal decrees.
Finally there are several manuscripts or fragments of manuscripts that scholars, including Sheehy, have not classified: a codex destroyed in 1944 at Chartres, Bibliothèque municipale, 124 (saec. XI^{in}, prov. Notre Dame, Chartres); Munich, Bayerische Staatsbibliothek, Clm 29051(b) (saec. VIII-IX, written in an Irish-influenced Continental scriptorium); and Trier, Stadtbibliothek, 137/50 (saec. VIII^{ex}, Irish hand). For other versions of the *Hibernensis,* see R. REYNOLDS, ‚*Unity and diversity in Carolingian canon law collections: The case of the Collectio Hibernensis and its derivatives,*' in *Carolingian essays: Andrew W. Mellon Lectures in early Christian studies*, ed. U.-R. BLUMENTHAL, Washington, D.C. 1983, 99-135.To be added to these manuscripts with portions of the *Hibernensis* are: Münster, Staatsarchiv MSC VII.5201 (saec. $X^{2/2}$, Corvey); Bern, Burgerbibliothek 89 + A 26 (saec. IX^{in}, Alsace?); Munich, Bayer. Staatsb, Clm 14468 (ca. 821, St. Emmeram); New Haven, Yale University, Beinecke Library 413 (ca. 875, Rheims); Vatican, BAV, Pal. lat. 577 (saec. VIII/IX, Germany with insular symptoms); and Vienna, ÖNB 2232 (saec. X^{in}, southern Germany).

northern Italian manuscripts,[36] is also found in the Copenhagen manuscript.[37] In any event, the terminus post quem non for the composition of the EM can now be pushed back securely to the early eighth century.

After the appearance of parts of the text of the EM in the Copenhagen manuscript and the *Hibernensis*, its next appearance is in manuscripts of the *Collectio vetus gallica*. In his study of the *Vetus Gallica* Hubert Mordek noted that the EM appears as an addendum to the *Vetus Gallica* in five manuscripts dating from the late eighth to the the early tenth centuries:[38] Paris, BN, lat. 1603 (saec. VIII-IX, northeastern France),[39] Cologne, Erzbischöfliche Diözesan- und Dombibliothek, 91 (saec. VIII-IX, Burgundy?),[40] Stuttgart, Württembergische Landesbibliothek, HB.VI.113 (saec. VIII^{ex}, Chur area),[41] Paris, BN, lat. 10588 (saec. IX^{1}, Burgundy or southern France),[42] and Stuttgart, Württembergische Landesbibliothek, HB.VI.112 (saec. X, Bodensee area, perhaps Constance).[43] Further, he made the keen observation that the text of the EM is followed by the words: ‚*Kanon Anquiritane hr XX. Si quis vel si qua adulterium commisserit, VII annos oportet perfectionem consequi secundum pristinus gradus;*' that is, an identification of the unnamed and unnumbered canon of Ancyra mentioned in the EM.[44]

One of the major derivatives of the *Vetus Gallica* was the *Collectio Herovalliana*, compiled in the second half of the eighth century. While the edition of the collection in the *Patrologia Latina*,[45] based on the manuscript Paris, BN, lat. 13657 (saec. XI^{2}, France), does not contain the EM, it is, in fact, an integral part of the collection.[46] And like the five manuscripts of the *Vetus Gallica* noted earlier, after the EM there is the text from the Council of Ancyra: ‚*Canon Anquiritani hr XVIIII. Si quis vel si qua adulterium commiserit, VII annos oportit perfeccionem consequi secundum pristinos gradus.*'[47]

One of the most interesting of Mordek's observations is the number of manuscripts of the *Vetus Gallica* in which the EM is associated with several genuine or pseudonymous texts on lapsed clerics.[48] Chief among these is the pseudo-Hormisdas *Ecce manifestissime*,[49] which takes the more ancient strict

---

36 Lucca, Biblioteca Capitolare Feliniana, 490 (saec. VIII-IX, Lucca); Merseburg, Archiv des Domkapitels, 104 (saec. IX/X, northern Italy or southern France); Vatican, BAV, Vat. lat. 5751 (saec. IX^{ex}, upper Italy, Verona or Bobbio?); Verona, Biblioteca Capitolare, LXI [59] (saec. VII-VIII, Verona).

37 fols. 52r-69v.

38 MORDEK, Kirchenrecht und Reform, note 20, 221.

39 fols. 149v-152v.

40 fols. 80v-82v.

41 fols. 191r-193r.

42 fols. 72r-73v.

43 fols. 65v-67r.

44 MORDEK, Kirchenrecht und Reform, note 20, 227.

45 PL 99, 989-1026.

46 See, e.g., Paris, BN, lat. 2400 (saec. XI$^{1/3}$, Angoulême), fol. 112r-v; and Paris, BN, lat. 4281 (saec. IX$^{1/4}$, Burgundy, eastern France), fols. 19r-20v.

47 Paris, BN, lat. 4281, fol. 20v.

48 MORDEK, Kirchenrecht und Reform, note 20, 220 f.

49 IBID. 225, n. 56, notes that the *Ecce manifestissme* is first assigned to Hormisdas in the *Vetus Gallica*.

position regarding clerical restoration, and the Gregorian *Libellus responsionum* met already in the Copenhagen manuscript. Beyond these texts, Mordek notes yet another text on the restoration of lapsed clerics in combination with the EM, the Gregorian or pseudo-Gregorian *Epistula ad Secundinum* (hereafter GS).[50] It is this letter in combination with the EM that Kottje describes so thoroughly in his study of Rabanus Maurus's *Poenitentiale ad Otgarium* and *Poenitentiale ad Heribaldum*, in which the combination is found.[51] The GS has long been known to exist in two forms: a genuine form and an interpolated form, in the latter of which a lapsed cleric is allowed to be restored. Using the work of Horst Fuhrmann, Kottje notes that this interpolation in the genuine letter was made by at least 769[52] and can be found in two forms, one in which the interpolation begins the letter, and one in which it is fitted into the body of the letter. It is not known whether the interpolation was inspired by the EM, but it is interesting that it was precisely at the time that the EM was finding its way into multiple manuscripts of canonical collections that the interpolation of the Gregorian letter took place. In any event, it appears that a crisis in clerical and penitential discipline in the late eighth or ninth-century led to the combination of the two letters to bolster a position allowing lapsed clerics to be restored after appropriate penance.

Kottje locates that crisis to the time of the depositions and restorations of Ebo of Rheims and places the combination in the context of the penitentials of Rabanus Maurus and manuscripts with the Penitential of Halitgar of Cambrai. Kottje begins by noting that Rabanus in his penitentials deals with the question of what one is to do with clerics in higher orders who have sinned. A distinction is to be made between those who have committed serious public sins and those whose have committed occult sins.[53] The former are not to be restored; the latter may be restored after appropriate penance. To support the case for restoration Rabanus is the one, according to Kottje, who was responsible for combining the EM and interpolated GS, and his part in this is reflected in the early manuscripts where they are combined.

From 822 to 842 Rabanus was abbot of Fulda and from 834 to 840 the deposed Ebo of Rheims was at Fulda doing penance there in a way common for deposed highly-placed clerics in the ninth century.[54] It seems that both Rabanus as abbot of Fulda and Otgar of Mainz, to whom one of Rabanus's penitentials was dedicated, were keenly interested in the question of the re-

---

[50] IBID. 226, n. 60.

[51] Poenitentiale ad Otgarium, c. 1, PL 112, 1400-1404, and Poenitentiale ad Heribaldum, c. 10, PL 110, 476-480.

[52] KOTTJE, Die Bussbücher Halitgars von Cambrai, note 6, 220.

[53] In a paper entitled ‚What was Public about Public Penance. Paenitentia publica and justice in the Carolingian world,' delivered at the Spoleto Settimane, 1996, that she has kindly allowed me to read M. DE JONG makes the point that the expression *paenitentia privata* became current only in the twelfth century and that for the Carolingians the standard expression was *paenitentia occulta* or *secreta*. [Meanwhile published, in: La Giustizia nell'alto medioevo, 44.Sett.Spol., Spoleto, 1997, 863 – 902]

[54] This practice is nicely described by M. DE JONG in the paper cited in the previous note.

storation of lapsed higher clerics. Hence, sometime between 835 and 839 Rabanus undertook to collect a variety of texts dealing with this issue, including the pseudo-Hormisdas text, an extract from the work of Julianus Pomerius entitled ,*Ex libro Prosperi*,' the GS, and the EM. This florilegium of texts is found together in a group of related manuscripts that Kottje designates as the ,mainzisch-lotharingische Gruppe.' While none of these was written at Fulda where Rabanus was in the 830s, they do appear in a manuscript written at Mainz in the middle of the ninth century, Wolfenbüttel, Herzog-August Bibliothek, Helmst. 656, to which Rabanus's *Poenitentiale ad Otgarium* is attached, and Kottje suggests that this manuscript was based on a model from Fulda brought to Mainz when Rabanus became archbishop in 847.

Not only was Rabanus keenly interested in the question of the restoration of lapsed clerics, but also another important Carolingian cleric, Grimald, abbot of Wissembourg (809 – 839 and from 847), chancellor for Louis the German (833-837, and 837-840), and abbot of St. Gall (841-843). Kottje suggests that on one of his visits to Fulda Grimald obtained a copy of the Rabanus's florilegium of texts and had it copied in the manuscript St. Gall, Stiftsbibliothek, 277, written at Wissembourg, saec. $IX^{2/4}$. The florilegium can also be found in two other manuscripts, St. Gall, Stiftsbibliothek, 570, written in Lotharingia or eastern France, saec. IX^{med}, and Vatican, BAV, Pal. lat. 973, written in the vicinity of Rheims, saec. IX^{2}.

The combination of the EM and GS was clearly of interest, also, to canonistic compilers and scribes in many parts of the Carolingian realm. The influential Penitential of Halitgar of Cambrai would naturally attract this combination of texts dealing with the penance of lapsed clerics, and three of the manuscripts of Kottje's ,mainzisch-lotharingische Gruppe,' Wolfenbüttel, Herzog-August Bibliothek, Helmst. 656, and St. Gall, Stiftsbibliothek, 277 and 570, contain both the EM and GS and Halitgar's Penitential. Kottje also notes the presence of the combination in a ,south German group' of manuscripts, including Munich, Bayerische Staatsbibliothek, Clm 14540, written in Regensburg, saec. $IX^{3/4}$, and Vatican, BAV, Reg. lat. 407, written in the vicinity of St. Gall, saec. IX^{med}.[55] Kottje suggests that the Regensburg manuscript may have been based on one from Fulda. The Reginensis manuscript contains the Salzburg canonical *Collection in Two Books*, some of whose texts are also found in the codex Vatican, BAV, Pal. lat. 973 of the ,mainzisch-lotharingische Gruppe.'[56] It is a pity that the earlier Salzburg manuscript of this canonical collection, Paris, BN, n.a., lat. 452, written at Salz-

---

[55] This dating and location was kindly given me by Professor BISCHOFF in a letter of 24 August 1970.

[56] R. REYNOLDS, ,Canon law collections in early ninth-century Salzburg,' Proceedings of the Fifth International Congress of Medieval Canon Law: Salamanca, 21-25 September 1976, edd. S. KUTTNER and K. PENNINGTON, =MIC, C, 6, Vatican 1980, 20, n. 28; and MORDEK, Kirchenrecht und Reform, note 20, 121, n. 87, and H. MORDEK, Bibliotheca capitularium regum Francorum manuscripta. Überlieferung und Traditionszusammenhang der fränkischen Herrschererlasse, =MGH Hilfsmitttel 15; Munich 1995, 804.

burg itself at the time of Adalramnus (821-36), has lost the last part of the second book of the collection and what might have been the additional texts found in the Reginensis manuscript of the collection.[57]

The connection between the *Collection in Two Books* and St. Gall suggests that clerics in Salzburg may have been interested in the subject of the restoration of lapsed clerics, and there is manuscript evidence that they indeed were. In the codex, Vienna, Österreichische Nationalbibliothek, 934, written in Salzburg, saec. IX^{in}, and containing the *Collectio Pauli* of the Gregorian letters, including the GS, the Salzburg master Baldo has written next to the interpolation: ‚Consolatio optima de officio sacerdotali resumendo post lapsum.'[58] More significant perhaps is the codex Vienna, Österreichische Nationalbibliothek, 1322, written in Salzburg, saec. IX$^{2/4\text{-med}}$, which contains precisely the texts found in Kottje's south German manuscripts, Munich, Bayerische Staatsbibliothek, Clm 14540 and Vatican, BAV, Reg. lat. 407 following its text of the Salzburg *Collection in Two Books*. Given the close connections between Salzburg and St. Gall and Regensburg,[59] this may suggest that the south German tradition of the combination of the EM and GS could as well have extended to Regensburg from these centers as from Fulda.

While Rabanus may have been responsible for combining the EM and GS at Fulda, there is manuscript evidence that the combination was also being made elsewhere. Kottje has noted that the combination is in three Italian manuscripts: Vatican, BAV, Reg. lat. 1997, Vat. lat. 5751, and Rome, Biblioteca Vallicelliana, Tom. XVIII. This group of manuscripts is interesting for several reasons. Vatican, BAV, Vat. lat. 5751, written in northern Italy and containing the Penitential of Halitgar and the preface to the *Collectio Dacheriana*, also contains the *Epitome Hispana* like the early Copenhagen manuscript with the EM.[60] The Vallicelliana manuscript, written in both Caroline and Beneventan scripts in the eleventh century,[61] is interesting in that it contains the EM once in its text of the *Collectio canonum hibernensis*, seen earlier, and a second time, in the normal form, later in the manuscript preceding the GS, not following it as it the usual pattern.[62] Perhaps the most significant of Kot-

---

57 On this see REYNOLDS, ‚Canon law collections in early ninth-century Salzburg,' note 56, 31.

58 fol. 59r.

59 On this see REYNOLDS, ‚Canon law collections in early ninth-century Salzburg,' note 56, 18, 30 f.; and J. FLECKENSTEIN, Die Hofkapelle der deutschen Könige, I. Grundlegung, Die karolingische Hofkapelle, =MGH Schriften 16.1, Stuttgart 1959, 179.

60 Vatican, BAV, Vat. lat. 5751 (saec. IX^{ex}, upper Italy, Verona or Bobbio?); and KOTTJE, Die Bussbücher Halitgars von Cambrai, note 6, 73.

61 R. REYNOLDS, ‚Odilo and the *Treuga Dei* in Southern Italy: A Beneventan Manuscript Fragment,' Mediaeval Studies 46 (1984), 454, n. 25.

62 fol. 151r-152r. H. MORDEK, ‚Die historische Wirkung der Collectio Herovalliana,' ZKG 81 (1970), 238f., n. 87; and Kirchenrecht und Reform, note 20, 134, n. 172, states that a citation of the Ancyra canon, ‚*Canon Anquiritani hr XX*,'in the Vallicelliana manuscript derives not so much from the *Herovalliana*, which picked up the text from the *Vetus Gallica*, but from the *Vetus Gallica* itself, which is known to have been in southern Italy where the Vallicelliana manuscript was written, on which see R. REYNOLDS, ‚A Beneventan Monastic Excerptum from the *Collectio Vetus Gallica*, RB 102 (1992), 298-308.

tje's three manuscripts for its age is the Reginensis manuscript, written at Chieti and containing the canonical *Collectio Theatina*. A variety of dates has been assigned to this manuscript. According to E. A. Lowe[63] and Bernhard Bischoff,[64] it was written in the late eighth or early ninth century in a hand that Lowe describes as resembling Beneventan script and Bischoff as a hand on the verge of Beneventan script. It is significant that the combination of the GS and EM, although written in a more normal Carolingian hand, is in the quire of the manuscript, fols. 150-157, containing the ‚near Beneventan' hand. Kottje himself dates the codex to the second quarter to mid-ninth century,[65] and Paola Supino Martini dates it the the mid-ninth century and describes the hand as an old Italian one.[66] If the earlier date of Lowe and Bischoff is accepted, then this becomes the earliest example of the combination of the GS and EM thus far noted. But whether or not this combination was made in Chieti itself is not certain. In fact, the manuscript likely had northern models, perhaps from Metz,[67] and it contains a text of the Romano-Gallican rite of clerical ordination found in manuscripts of the *Gelasian Sacramentary of the Eighth Century*[68] and a text of the *Laudes regiae*.[69]

While the combination of the EM and GS appears in the many manuscripts just described, the influence of their combination reached another plateau when Rabanus Maurus included them in his *Poenitentiale ad Otgarium* and *Poenitentiale ad Heribaldum*. That the combination was included in the former, compiled ca. 841/842, is not surprising given Otgar's interest in the problem of lapsed clerics. Nor was its inclusion in the penitential dedicated to Heribaldus of Auxerre (compiled 853), inasmuch as Heribaldus was called upon to preside at the Council of Soissons (853) in which the validity of the ordinations of the deposed Ebo was debated. In any event, the texts of the EM in Rabanus's penitentials are somewhat different: in the *Poeniten-*

63 CLA 1, nr. 113; and V. BROWN, The Beneventan Script: a History of the South Italian Minuscule, 1, Rome ²1980, 208.

64 B. BISCHOFF, ‚Panorama der Handschriftenüberlieferung aus der Zeit Karls des Grossen, in Karl der Grosse. Lebenswerk und Nachleben. 2, Das Geistige Leben, ed. B. BISCHOFF, Düsseldorf, 1965, 253.

65 KOTTJE, Die Bussbücher Halitgars von Cambrai, note 6, 220, n. 266.

66 P. SUPINO MARTINI, ‚Per lo studio delle scritture altomedievali italiane: la collezione canonica chietina (Vat. Reg. lat. 1997),' Scrittura e Civiltà, 1 (1977), 148.

67 MORDEK, Kirchenrecht und Reform, note 20, 11, n. 41.

68 R. REYNOLDS, ‚The Ritual of Clerical Ordination of the Sacramentarium Gelasianum saec. viii: Early Evidence from Southern Italy,' in: Rituels: Mélanges offerts au Père Gy O.P., eds. P. DE CLERCK and E. PALAZZO, Paris 1990, 440 f.

69 E. KANTOROWICZ, Laudes Regiae. A Study in Liturgical Acclamation and Mediaeval Ruler Worship, Berkeley-Los Angeles 1958, 86, 104, 182, n. 10, 235. Other manuscripts containing the Penitential of Halitgar with the EM beyond manuscripts in Kottje's ‚mainzisch-lotharingische Gruppe,' ‚south German' group, and Italian group are: Gent, Centrale Bibliotheek der Rijksuniversiteit, 506 (551) (saec. IX$^{3/4}$, western Rhine region), pp. 155-156; Oxford, Bodleian Library, Can. Pat. lat. 49 (saec. XII, prov. Ravenna), fols. 53v-55r; Paris, BN, lat. 3878; Weimar, Hauptstaatsarchiv, Depositum Hardenberg, Fragm. 9 (saec. X/XI, southern Germany or Brixen?), fols. 93v-95v; and Zürich, Zentralbibliothek, Car. C.176 (D.64) (saec. IX$^{med-3/4}$, eastern France, Alsace?), fol. 84r-v.

tiale ad Otgarium the addition dealing with disconcordant canons is included whereas in the *Poenitentiale ad Heribaldum* it is not.

Because of the fame of Rabanus and influence of his penitentials, the EM and GS were repeated in later penitential literature borrowing from Rabanus. Chief among these was Burchard's *Decretum*, where two canons with the EM, cc. 43 and 73 in the *Corrector sive Medicus*, L. XIX,[70] are based on Rabanus. Given the wide distribution of the *Decretum* and its sometimes independent *Corrector* and given the influence of Burchard's work on later collections, it is not surprising that the combination of the EM and GS as based on Rabanus's penitentials was widely known. For example, in his *Decretum*, P. XV, c. 57,[71] Ivo of Chartres borrows from the Burchardian version of the EM, while in P. VI, cc. 397-398, he bases his text on Rabanus's *Poenitentiale ad Otgarium.*[72]

While the EM and GS often appeared in combination from the late eighth century on, the EM alone frequently found its way into of a plethora of early manuscripts and codices containing various early medieval canonical collections. Among the former are a fragment in a late eighth-century manuscript in Anglo-Saxon pre-Caroline minuscule probably from Corbie, Cologne, Erzbischöfliche Diözesan- und Dombibliothek, s.n.;[73] in a Bodensee manuscript of the early ninth century whose provenance is Murbach, Oxford, Bodleian Library, Junius 25;[74] in Munich, Bayerische Staatsbibliothek, Clm 6407 written in Verona, ca. 800;[75] and in the famous codex of the letters of St. Boniface of Fulda, written in Mainz, Vienna, Österreichische Nationalbibliothek 731, saec. IX$^{1\text{- med}}$. Among early canonical collections the EM has been added to are manuscripts containing the *Breviatio canonum* of Fulgentius Ferrandus,[76] *Collectio ecclesiae Thessalonicensis,*[77] *Collection of the Manuscript of Lorsch,*[78] *Collectio canonum Cresconii,*[79] *‚Gallican Cresconius,'*[80] *Collectio Dionysiana,*[81] *Collectio Dionysio- Hadriana,*[82] *Collection of St.*

[70] PL 140, 991 f., 1000.

[71] PL 161, 872 f.

[72] PL 161, 529 f.

[73] CLA 8, nr. 1164.

[74] fol. 76r-v.

[75] fols. 114v-117v.

[76] Vercelli, Biblioteca Capitolare, CLXV (saec. IX$^{1/4}$, France), fol. 214r.

[77] Vatican, BAV, Vat. lat. 5751 (saec. IX^{ex}, upper Italy, Verona or Bobbio?), on which see above, note 60.

[78] Gotha, Forschungsbibliothek, Memb. I 85 (saec. VIII/IX, upper Alsace, perhaps written in Wissembourg), fols. 104v-106r; Vatican, BAV, Pal. lat. 574 (saec. VIII/IX, upper Rhein region).

[79] Roma, Biblioteca Vallicelliana, Tom. XVIII (saec. XI; southern Italy), fols. 151r-152r, on which see above, nn. 25, 61.

[80] Paris, BN, lat. 4280A (saec. IX^{ex}, Rheims), fol. 81r.

[81] Paris, BN, lat. 3848 (saec. XIII).

[82] Florence, Biblioteca Medicea Laurenziana 16.15 (saec. XI-XII), fols. 85v-87r (extract from the Dionysiana); Freiburg im Br., Üniversitätsbibliothek, 8 (saec. IX^{2}, Bodensee area), fols. 3r-4r; Paris, BN, lat. 1453 (saec. IX$^{1/4}$, probably Orléans), fol. 150v; Vatican, BAV, Ottob. lat. 312 (saec. XI-XII), fols. 14r-15r, with the Ancyra canon appended (Hera XVIII); and Vercelli, Biblioteca Capitolare, CLXV (saec. IX$^{1/4}$, France), fol. 214r.

Amand,[83] *Collectio Herovalliana,*[84] *Collectio Quesnelliana,*[85] *Ambrosian Collection in Two Books,*[86] *Collectio Hispana Systematica,*[87] and *Collectio Dacheriana.*[88]

Nowhere in the Carolingian realm would the question of the restoration of lapsed clerics have been of more interest than in the archdiocese of Rheims, where sides had been taken in the struggle between Ebo and Hincmar of Rheims. Already noted has been the appearance of the combination of the EM and GS in the manuscript, Vatican, BAV, Pal. lat. 973, saec. $IX^{2/2}$, written in the vicinity of Rheims. But the combination of the EM and GS came to play an even larger role in the Pseudo-Isidorian forgeries, compiled most likely by an équipe working at the behest of Hincmar of Laon, locked in a bitter feud with his uncle Hincmar of Rheims. In fact, as early as 865 the GS and EM were briefly cited together in connection with the forgeries in the ‚Propagandaschrift' of the deposed Gunthar of Cologne (850-863). In an important manuscript from Soissons written in the tenth or eleventh century, Berlin, Staatsbibliothek zu Berlin, Phill. 1764, there is a florilegium of texts, many from the Pseudo-Isidorian Decretals, into which is inserted material, including the GS and EM, used in Gunthar's treatise.[89] In the third part of the Pseudo-Isidorian Decretals themselves the interpolated version of the GS appears among the letters of Gregory I.[90] This letter has often been published in editions of the Decretals. Unfortunately, the role of the EM in the Decretals has largely been ignored because editors of the Decretals have not included it in their editions. Nonetheless, it is found in many manuscripts of the Decretals, some, like New Haven, Yale University, Beinecke Library 442, dating back almost to the origins of the Decretals.[91] While it was a simple matter to insert the GS among the letters of Gregory I, it was not so simple to insert a letter attributed to Isidore among the decrees of popes and canons of councils. But perhaps it could have been rationalized inasmuch as the Decretals themselves were attributed to an Isidore Mercator

[83] Vatican, BAV, Ottob. lat. 312 (saec. XI-XII), fols. 14r-15v, with the Ancyra text appended (Hera XVIII).

[84] Vercelli, Biblioteca Capitolare, CLXXV (saec. $IX^{1/4}$, France or southern Germany), fols. 34v-37r.

[85] Paris, BN, lat. 1454 (saec. $IX^{3/4}$, probably Paris region), fols. 246r-247v; and Vienna, ÖNB, lat. 2141 (39) (a. 780, Lorsch region, prov. Fulda), fols. 170r-171r.

[86] Milan, Biblioteca Ambrosiana, A.46.inf. (saec. IX^{ex}, northern France, Rheims area; prov. San Dionigi, Milan), fols. 58r-59v.

[87] Paris, BN, lat. 1565 (Colbert 468; Reg. 3887) (saec. X-XI, southern France, perhaps Lyons) (with the *Epistula ad Leudefredum*), fol. 232r.

[88] Montecassino, Archivio della Badia, 541 (saec. XI^{in}, southern Italy), p. 8; Vatican, BAV, Reg. lat. 849 (saec. X, France), fols. 11v-12v.

[89] H. FUHRMANN, ‚Eine im Original erhaltene Propagandaschrift des Erzbischofs Gunthar von Köln (865)', AfD, 4 (1958) 43 f.; and DERS., Einfluss und Verbreitung , MGH Schriften 24.3; Stuttgart 1974, 735 f.

[90] P. HINSCHIUS, Decretales Pseudo-Isidorianae et Capitula Angilramni, Leipzig 1863, ND Aalen, 1963, 735-738.

[91] fol. 240r-v, (saec. $IX^{3/4}$, Rheims or Paris region, sent saec. IX^{ex} by Bishop Frotarius of Périgueux to the monastery of Charroux in the diocese of Poitiers).

or Peccator, which could have been identified with Isidore of Seville. Be that as it may, the EM was paired with the Isidorian *Epistula ad Leudefredum*, as a useful epitome of the duties of the ecclesiastical officers, and placed in many manuscripts of the Decretals.[92] Not only did manuscripts of the Decretals themselves contain the EM; in one manuscript with some of the forged *capitularia* of Benedictus Levita there is added a fragment of the EM.[93]

Given the swift and wide diffusion and enormous influence of the Decretals, it is no surprise that the EM in whole or in part was included in multiple collections to the time of Gratian, although not all citations of the EM were borrowed from the Decretals. Among the many collections later to use the EM are the *Collection of Montecassino 439,*[94] *Collection in Nine Books* of Vat. Lat. 1349,[95] *Collection in Five Books,*[96] *Collection of Santa Croce,*[97] the south-Italian *Collection of Madrid Biblioteca Nacional, lat. 373,*[98] *Collectio canonum Regesto Farfensi inserta,*[99] Farfa excerptum of Vallicelliana, Biblioteca Vallicelliana, Tom. XVIII,[100] *Collectio Angelica,*[101] *Collection in Seventy-Four Titles,*[102] *Collection canonum* of Anselm of Lucca,[103] *Collection in Four*

---

92 Among the manuscript of the Decretals containing the EM and *Epistula ad Leudefredum* are: Avranches, Bibliothèque municipale, 146 (saec. XII, Rheims area), fol. 160r; Florence, Biblioteca Nazionale, Panciatichi 135; Cologne, Erzbischöfliche Diözesan- und Dombibliothek, 113 (olim Darmst. 2112) (saec. X, Cologne?, prov. Cologne); London, BL, Royal 5.A.VIII (saec. XIII); Montecassino, Archivio della Badia, 1 (saec. XI^{ex}, Abruzzi or Montecassino), p. 441; New Haven, Yale University, Beinecke Library, 442 (saec. IX$^{3/4}$, Paris or Rheims?), fol. 240r-v; Oxford, Bodleian Library, Hatton 6 (saec. XIII, northwestern France), fol. 187r-v; Paris, Bibliothèque de l'Arsenal, 679 (6.J.1) (saec. XIV); Paris, BN, n.a., lat. 2253 (saec. XI, Cluny), fol. 142r-v; Paris, BN, lat. 5141 (saec. XIV, France), fol. 197v; Paris, BN, lat. 15391 (olim Sorbonne 729) (saec. XV), fol. 279v; Paris, BN, lat. 16897 (olim Navarre 7) (saec. XII), fol. 283r; Rennes, BM, 134 (112) (saec. IX-X, Rheims or Rouen), fol. 224v; Rouen, BM, E.27 (702) (saec. XI, Angers, prov. Rouen); Toulouse, BM, I.9 (365) (saec. XIII, France, prov. Toulouse); Vatican, BAV, Vat. lat. 1344 (saec. XII, France), fols. 113r-v; Vatican, BAV, Vat. lat. 3791 (saec. XI^{ex}, northern France), fols. cclxxxiii^{r} – cclxxxiii (bis)^{r}; and Venice, Biblioteca Nazionale Marciana, lat. IV.47.

93 Vatican, BAV, Reg. lat. 1023 (saec. IX$^{2/2}$, Rheims?), fol. 133v.

94 Montecassino, Archivio della Badia, 439 (saec. X, southern Italy), pp. 240-244.

95 Vatican, BAV, Vat. lat. 1349 (saec. XI^{med}, southern Italy), fols. 69r-70r.

96 L. II, c. 100. Also in L. II, c. 103 there is a snippet from the EM attributed to a Synodus Romana. See M. FORNASARI, Collectio Canonum in V libris (Lib. i-iii) (CCCM 6) ; Turnhout, 1970, 238-242.

97 Florence, Biblioteca Medicea Laurenziana, 4.4 (saec. XI, central Italy), fols. 43r-45r.

98 Madrid, Biblioteca Nacionale, lat. 373 (saec. XI/XII, southern Italy), fol. 35v.

99 L. III, c. 33; T. KÖLZER, Collectio canonum Regesto Farfensi inserta, =MIC, B, 5, Vatican City 1982, 229f.

100 Rome, Biblioteca Casanatense, 2010 (saec. XI^{ex}, Farfa), fol. 147v.

101 L. III, c. 43; Rome, Biblioteca Angelica, 1447 (saec. XI, central Italy), p. 16 (the snippet from the EM attributed to a Synodus Romana found in the Collection in Five Books, L. II, c. 103, after which is a canon attributed to Isidore concerning *sacerdotes*).

102 c. 202, J. GILCHRIST, Diversorum patrum sententie sive Collectio in LXXIV titulos digesta. (MIC, B, 1) Vatican City, 1973 127-130, where the reference to the Ancyra canon is worked into the text itself: ‚*id est in canone Anquiritano capitulo XVIIII (or XVIII).*'

103 F. THANER, Anselmi episcopi Lucensis: Collectio canonum una cum collectione minore iussu Instituti Saviniani, Innsbruck 1906-1915, ND Aalen 1965, 453-456.

Books,[104] *Collection of Assisi*,[105] *Collection of Vat. lat. 4977*,[106] *Collection in Seven Books of Turin*,[107] Ivo's *Decretum*,[108] *Panormia*,[109] and *Tripartita*,[110] the *De misericordia et iustitia* of Alger of Liège,[111] and finally Gratian's *Decretum*.[112].

Beyond the canonical collections the EM continued to be copied from the ninth century well into the later Middle Ages. Among the manuscripts containing the EM are: Berlin, Staatsbibliothek zu Berlin, Hamilton. 89 (saec. XII, France);[113] Cambridge, Emmanuel College, 243 (saec. XV);[114] London, British Library, Royal 5.A.VIII (saec. XIII);[115] London, British Library, Royal 5.E.I (saec. XIII);[116] London, British Library, Royal 5.E.IV (saec. XII^{ex});[117] London, British Library, Royal 8.F.X (saec. XIII^{ex}); London, British Library, Arundel 201 (saec. XII);[118] London, British Library, Additional 18400 (saec. X);[119] London, British Library, Additional 10973 (saec. XII);[120] London, Lambeth Palace, 380 (saec. XIII);[121] Munich, Bayerische Staatsbibliothek, Clm 52; Munich, Bayerische Staatsbibliothek, Clm 144426 (saec. IX^{2});[122] New York, Hispanic Society of America, 380/819 (saec. XI, Catalonia, Vic?)[123] Paris, BN, n.a., lat. 1615 (ca. 900, Auxerre);[124] Paris, BN, lat. 2833A (saec. X, southern France);[125] Paris, BN, lat. 13765; Prague, Národní Knihova Ceské Republiky, III.G.1 (saec. XII-XIII), Stuttgart, Württembergische Landesbibliothek, HB I.31 (1456);[126] Troyes, Biblio-

---

104 London, BL, Arundel 173 (saec. XII), fols. 108v-109v.

105 Assisi, Biblioteca Comunale, 227 (olim F.337) (saec. XII; provenance St. Francis convent, Assisi), fol. 126r-v.

106 Vatican, BAV, lat. 4977 (saec. XI-XII), fol. 46r.

107 Turin, Biblioteca Nazionale Universitaria, D.IV.33 (Pasini 239; Mazzatinti 507) (saec. XI-XII), fols. 49r-50r.

108 P. VI, cc. 397-398 (on which see above, n. 71), and P. XV, c. 57, 86; PL 161, 872 f., 882.

109 L. III, c. 149 (omitting cc. 7-11 of the EM); PL 161, 1163 f.

110 Oxford, Bodleian Library, d'Orville 46 (saec. XII).

111 Praef. dict. c/can. c, and L. II. c. 43; R. KRETZSCHMAR, Alger von Lüttichs Traktat ‚*De misericordia et iustitia*'. Ein kanonistischer Konkordanzversuch aus der Zeit des Investiturstreits. Untersuchungen und Edition, =Quellen und Forschungen zum Recht im Mittelalter 2, Sigmaringen 1985, 189, 291-293.

112 D. 50, c. 28 (using the text found in Ivo's *Panormia*), A. FRIEDBERG, *Corpus iuris canonici*, 1, Leipzig 1879, 188-190.

113 fol. 51r-v.

114 fols. 1-2.

115 fols. 17v-19r.

116 fols. 2r-4r.

117 fols. 4r-5r.

118 fol. 16r.

119 fols. 2r-3r.

120 fols. 22r-23r.

121 fols. 1r-2v.

122 fols. 148r-150v.

123 fols. 3r-4v.

124 fols. 190v-191v.

125 fols. 52v-54v.

126 fols. 156v-157v.

thèque municipale, 854 (saec. XIII); Vatican, BAV, Ottob. lat. 14 (saec. XII);[127] and Wolfenbüttel, Herzog-August Bibliothek, Weiss. 75 (saec. X).[128]

Over the course of the early Middle Ages the significance of the EM was two-fold. First, it allowed for a more lenient treatment of lapsed clerics than many of the strict canons of the patristic church. In justifying this more lenient position the EM rested on biblical texts, that is, texts that antedated the old canons and could be said to represent divine rather than human authority. Further, inasmuch as the Isidorian author of the EM was attempting to harmonize seemingly disconcordant ancient canons, the EM took on another significance. In its concluding addition the epistle provided one criterion for choosing between two conciliar decisions, that the older and more authoritative council should be preferred. While later canonists and theologians would elaborate on this principle and widen it to other types of canonical decisions,[129] the EM remains as one of the earliest medieval attempts in canonistic discussion to bring harmony from dissonance.

---

127 fols. 78r-80r.

128 fol. 123v.

129 On this see J. De Ghellinck, Le mouvement théologique, 472-499; H. Fuhrmann, Einfluss und Verbreitung, 1, note 19, 90f., n. 92; and R. Somerville and B. Brasington, Prefaces to Canon Law Books in Latin Christianity. Selected Translations, 500-1245, New Haven 1998/68.

II

THE VISIGOTHIC LITURGY IN THE REALM OF CHARLEMAGNE

Lex orandi lex credendi is an old saw formerly thought to have been uttered by Pope Celestine I in the fifth century. Indeed, neither was it Pope Celestine who used this saw, nor were these the exact words written by their probable author, Prosper of Aquitaine[1]. In any event, they have at times been used, especially by liturgical specialists, to signify that liturgy is or causes the belief or theology of the Church. From the context in which this adage was originally uttered – and has been used since by popes – this was clearly not its meaning. But at the very least, most scholars would say that *lex orandi lex credendi* signifies that liturgy can be used as one of the principal witnesses to the faith of the Church[2].

One of the best-known examples in the early Middle Ages where liturgical texts were cited to support a theological position was in the Adoptionist Controversy of the late eighth and early ninth centuries. It was this controversy that the participants at Frankfort in 794 addressed in the very first canon of their conciliar decrees:

»Wherat (i.e., Frankfort) in the first capitulum, there arose the matter of the impious and wicked heresy of Elipandus, bishop of the see of Toledo, and Felix, bishop of Urgel, and their followers, who in their erroneous belief concerning the Son of God assert adoption: this heresy did all the most holy fathers above mentioned (i.e., bishops and priests of the kingdom of the Franks, of Italy, and of Aquitaine and Provence) repudiate and with one

1 H.A.P. Schmidt, *Introductio in liturgiam occidentalem*, Rome 1960, 131.

2 As to how this adage has been used and misused and how it might again function in its original sense, see P. de Clerck, *»Lex orandi, lex credendi«, the Original Sense and Historical Avatars of an Equivocal Adage*, in: *Studia Liturgica* 24 (1994) 178-200.

voice denounce, and it was their decision that it should be utterly eradicated from the Holy Church«[3].

In the defense of his position Elipandus had earlier summoned the authority of some of his great Toledan predecessors of the past, Eugenius, Ildefonsus, and Julianus, among others, and had bolstered his position by citing portions of prayers of the Visigothic or Old Spanish liturgy[4]. He had even attributed some of them to these same three Toledan doctors. In responding to Elipandus, a letter of the bishops of France challenged the authority not only of these doctors, but also the prayers used in the Old Spanish liturgy:

»It is better to give credit to the testimony of God the Father as to His own Son than to your Ildefonsus, who composed such prayers for you in your Mass as the holy and universal Church of God knows not. Nor do we think God listens to you when you say them. And if your Ildefonsus in the prayers he wrote called Christ "adoptive", our Gregory, Pope of the Roman See and Doctor renowned throughout the world, in his prayers never hesitated always to call Him the Sole-begotten One«[5].

With the condemnation of Elipandus and Felix in its first canon, the Council of Frankfort in 794 perhaps implied that not only the errors of Elipandus but also their liturgical sources should be utterly eradicated.

Even if canon 1 of Frankfort did not call directly for a systematic eradication of the Visigothic liturgy itself, one of the principal aims of the so-called Carolingian religious reforms could be seen to have the same effect: the establishment of the Roman liturgy (the Roman prayers of St. Gregory) as the universal and ancient liturgy to be followed in the realm of Charlemagne. In short, the combination of the condemnation of Adoptionism and the imposition of the Roman rite would have the effect of suppressing the Old Spanish rite in those areas controlled by the Carolingians.

It is understandable that the Old Spanish rite persisted in the parts of the Iberian peninsula not under the control of Charlemagne, but the question has always been to what extent it continued in the Carolingian realm itself. Historians

---

3 *Cap. Francf.*, 165.

4 See G. Mercati, *More »Spanish Symptoms«*, in: *Liturgica Historica: Papers on the Liturgy and Religious Life of the Western Church*, ed. by E. Bishop, Oxford 1918, repr. 1962, 204f. On the term »Old Spanish« as applied to the rite called Visigothic, Gothic, Toledan, Isidorian, or Mozarabic, see R.E. Reynolds, *The Ordination of Clerics in Toledo and Castile after the Reconquista according to the »Romano-Catalan« Rite*, in: *Estudios sobre Alfonso VI y la Reconquista de Toledo.* Actas del II Congreso International de Estudios Mozárabes, Toledo, 20-26 Mayo 1985, IV (*Instituto de Estudios Visigótico-Mozárabes de Toledo. Serie Historica* 5), Toledo 1990, 47, n. 1.

5 *Ep. episc. Fr.*, 145. Also see Alcuin, *Adversus Elipandum* (*PL* 100, 264-267), written for Leidrad and his companions on the occasion of their journey to Spain.

of liturgy, as far back as Edmund Bishop, used to speak of »Spanish Symptoms« in parts of the liturgy in the Carolingian realm[6]. But as research has continued since his time, it is abundantly clear that there were more than simply »Spanish Symptoms«: there was a virtual flood of influence of the Old Spanish liturgy in the Carolingian realm, despite the condemnation of Adoptionism and the imposition of the Roman rite. It is the purpose of this paper to illustrate at least in part the persistence and role of the Visigothic liturgy in the Carolingian realm, first in terms of manuscripts with the Old Spanish rite texts; second, in terms of the use of Old Spanish liturgical forms, rituals, and prayers; and third, in terms of use of Old Spanish legal texts and commentaries reflecting or alluding to that rite. In illustrating this persistence, manuscripts written in the ninth century and before will be examined, but in case of the persistence of the ceremonies and rites themselves, practices of the late eighth and ninth centuries are reflected often only in documents written beyond this time.

I.

Looking first to the manuscripts of the ninth century and before reflecting on the persistence of the Old Spanish rite in the Carolingian realm, we find that they are written both in Visigothic and Carolingian scripts or a mixture of the two. While codices containing the Old Spanish liturgy written in the Iberian peninsula not under the control of the Carolingians are virtually all in Visigothic script, it is understandable that in the Carolingian realm there should be a mix of the two scripts. Let us look at these extant codices chronologically to see what types of liturgical texts are represented.

From the period before Charlemagne only four manuscripts with elements of the Old Spanish rite have been identified by scholars, two of which were written in the northeast corner of Spain, one perhaps in southern France, and the fourth in northern Italy. The oldest codex has pericope notes in the margins indicating that it was used liturgically. The manuscript, now Autun, Bibl. mun. 27, was written in Visigothic script in the second half of the seventh century, probably in Urgel[7]. Virtually as old is the renowned *Orationale* of Verona, Bibl. cap., LXXXIX. This manuscript contains prayers for use outside the Mass, especially for Matins and Vespers, and is in a sense comparable to the collectars of the

6 See his *Spanish Symptoms*, in: *Liturgica Historica* (cf. n. 4) 165-202.

7 A. Millares Carlo, *Tratado de Paleografía Española*, I: *Texto*, Madrid ³1983, nr. 345; and K. Gamber, *Codices liturgici latini antiquiores*, Fribourg/S 1968, nr. 369.

Roman rite. The manuscript was written in Visigothic script ca. 700 A.D., probably in Tarragona, and was taken by refugees fleeing the Muslim invasions after 711. It was carried first to Sardinia, then according to some scholars to Pisa or Lucca, and then on to northern Italy, where it was in Verona by the late eighth century[8].

In the early eighth century there was written perhaps in southern France an uncial manuscript, now palimpsested, containing a book of prayers for the Mass, Milan, Bibl. Amb. M 12 sup. Although most liturgical specialists designate this book as a Gallican-rite sacramentary because the titles of the prayers are in Gallican style, many of the prayers themselves are found in Old Spanish liturgical books. Hence, the manuscript is at times designated as an Old Spanish *Manuale*, or Mass book for a priest[9]. Also, from the early eighth century is the famous *Bobbio Missal*, written in northern Italy. It is also generally classified as a Gallican-rite or even Celtic-rite Mass book, but it clearly contains a number of texts of the Old Spanish rite, including texts for a Mass to be said for a priest and for a burial service[10].

The next group of four manuscripts with elements of the Old Spanish rite date to the late eighth or early ninth centuries, the very period in which Spanish Adoptionism was under attack. First, by way of caution, it should be noted that the well-known composite manuscript, Lucca, Bibl. cap. 490, written in part in Visigothic script of the late eighth century and containing Old Spanish liturgical commentaries and canon law texts, does not have Old Spanish rite liturgical texts proper. Rather, the antiphonary fragments in the codex, containing chants for the Mass and Office of Advent Sundays, are of a Roman type[11]. Again, by way of caution, it must be noted that of late eighth- or early ninth-century manuscripts with Old Spanish texts said to be written in Visigothic script in Septimania, one, Montpellier, BIM 55, has been shown recently to have been written in Carolingian script and to have come from Autun[12]. Nonetheless, the manuscript, a *Passionarium*, does contain the passion of St. Fructuosus of Tarragona. Also, in

---

8 Millares Carlo (cf. n. 7) nr. 185; and Gamber (cf. n. 7) nr. 330.

9 Gamber (cf. n. 7) nr. 205; and J.M. Pinell, *Los Textos de la antigua liturgia hispánica. Fuentes para su estudio*, in: *Estudios sobre la liturgia mozárabe*, Toledo 1965, nr. 65.

10 Bishop (cf. n. 6) 178f.

11 Gamber (cf. n. 7) nr. 1302.

12 R. Guerreiro, *Le rayonnement de l'hagiographie hispanique en Gaule pendant le haut Moyen Age: circulation et diffusion des Passions hispaniques*, in: *L'Europe héritière de l'Espagne wisigothique*. Colloque international du C.N.R.S. tenu à la Fondation Singer-Polignac, Paris, 14-16 Mai 1990 (*Collection de la Casa de Velázquez* 35), Madrid 1992, 149.

Carolingian-script, but with clear traces of Visigothic-script influence is a manuscript with the *Epistulae sancti Pauli*, Montpellier, Bibl. mun. 6. This codex written probably at the monastery of Aniane of the Visigoth Witiza or Benedict, has marginal notes for use as a liturgical lectionary[13]. Beyond these Caroline-script codices there are two liturgical manuscripts in Visigothic script written in the late eighth century in Septimania. First is the *Liber comicus* or lectionary of Paris, BN, lat. 2269, from St. Nazarius in Carcassone with its readings from Epiphany to the Sunday of St. Lazarus in Lent[14]. The other manuscript is a *homilarium*, Paris, BN, lat. 12254, with its sermons to be read at Mass[15].

Of fifteen manuscripts of the ninth century with elements of the Old Spanish rite, the majority are in Carolingian script, although some may have Visigothic-script symptoms or even Visigothic-script marginalia. Guerreiro has now shown that the *Passionarium* of Montpellier, BIM 154, is not in Visigothic script but in Caroline[16]. Bibles with a *Capitulare Evangeliorum* for liturgical use, Urgel, Bibl. cap. s. n.[17], and Paris, BN, lat. 894[18], are in Caroline, as is Montserrat, Bibl del Mon. 1042.XXIVb, with Theodulf's processional hymn *Gloria, laus et honor*[19]. One of the most interesting manuscripts with hispanic flavour, a martyrology now in Rome, Bibl. Vallicellicana E 26, was written in Lyons in Carolingian script but with marginal entries in Visigothic added by the Visigoth Agobard[20]. Nonetheless, Visigothic script was used for some liturgical manuscripts: the computistic codex, Paris, BN, lat. 609, written in Aquitaine ca. 819[21]; a manuscript with the *Leges visigothorum* with liturgical notes in Paris, BN, lat. 4667[22]; and a manuscript from Barcelona, ACA s.n., with the *Passio sancti Polycarpi*[23].

There are three extant ninth-century manuscripts containing elements of the Old Spanish rite pertaining to the office as found in the monastic rules of Isidore

13 M.S. Gros, *La liturgie Narbonnaise témoin d'un changement rapide de rites liturgiques*, in: *Liturgie de l'église particulière et liturgie de l'église universelle*. Conférences Saint-Serge 1975, Rome 1976, 135.

14 Gamber (cf. n. 7) nr. 361.

15 Millares Carlo (cf. n. 7) nr. 252.

16 Guerreiro (cf. n. 12) 149.

17 A. Olivar, *Les supervivències litúrgiques autòctones a Catalunya en els manuscrits dels segles XI–XII*, in: *II Congrés litúrgic de Montserrat III: Secció d'Historia*, Montserrat 1967, nr. 196.

18 *Ibid.*, nr. 171. (This manuscript also has a pericope from Mt. 1,1-13 with Catalan neumes.)

19 *Ibid.*, nr. 153

20 Guerreiro (cf. n. 12) 148, n. 47; and E.A. Lowe, *Nugae Palaeographicae*, in: idem, *Palaeographical Papers 1907–1965*, Oxford 1972, 323.

21 Millares Carlo (cf. n. 7) nr. 235.

22 Olivar (cf. n. 17) nr. 177.

23 Millares Carlo (cf. n. 7) nr. 9.

and Fructuosus. The first manuscript, now Paris, BN, lat. 10876/10877, Tours, Bibl. mun. 615, was written in Visigothic script perhaps at Toulouse, the ancient capital of the Visigoths[24]. Written much farther from southern France or centres like Lyons with their concentration of Spanish emigrés are two others: Valenciennes, Bibl. mun. 288, a manuscript from St. Amand, which Guerreiro has shown had hagiographical ties with Spain through Saint-Germain-des-Prés[25]; and Munich, Clm 28118 from Trier, the manuscript of Benedict of Aniane with its collection of rules used to prepare his *Concordia regularum* with its references to the Old Spanish liturgical offices in the rules of Isidore and Fructuosus[26].

II.

The fact that there are marginal notations and additions in many ninth-century manuscripts with texts from the Old Spanish rite is evidence that the manuscripts were put to use. But the question remains to what extent the Old Spanish rite itself was used by itself or in combination with the Roman or Romano-Frankish rite being promulgated by Carolingian rulers and clerics. Recent scholarship has shown that in many liturgical ceremonies and practices the Old Spanish rite continued to be very much alive, especially in the south of France and in the Spanish March. Indeed, what is now designated as the Narbonnaise rite, studied so admirably by Mgr. Gros at Vic and the Abbé Martimort in Toulouse, is shot through with elements of the Old Spanish liturgy. Moreover, the influence of Old Spanish rite texts came to be felt throughout the Carolingian empire through the work of the Visigoth Benedict of Aniane in his supplement to the officially-sanctioned *Sacramentarium Gregorianum*. We turn, then, to a series of liturgical ceremonies and practices in which elements of the Old Spanish rite persisted throughout the ninth century in areas controlled by the Carolingians. We begin with three liturgical rites in which lay people could be involved: baptismal, matrimonial, and burial ceremonies.

It has been pointed out that baptism, the sacrament whereby one enters Christian society, was also the cornerstone of Carolingian society[27]. The impor-

---

24 A.M. Mundó, *I »Corpora« e i »Codices Regularum« nella tradizione codicologica delle regole monastiche*, in: *Atti del 7° Congresso Internazionale di Studi sull'Alto Medioevo*, II, Spoleto 1982, 510.

25 Guerreiro (cf. n. 12) 152f.

26 M.C. Díaz y Díaz, *Aspectos de la tradición de la Regula Isidori*, in: idem, *Vie chrétienne et culture dans l'Espagne du VIIe au Xe siècles*, Aldershot/Hampshire 1992, part. IX, 43.

27 S.A. Keefe, *Carolingian Baptismal Expositions: A Handlist of Tracts and Manuscripts*, in: *Carolingian Essays*, 171.

tance of baptism in the mind and realm of Charlemagne is reflected in an extraordinary letter sent by the emperor in 812 to archbishops demanding that they report to him exactly how they and their suffragans taught the rite of baptism to their priests and the people committed to them. As a result of this demand, scores of small tracts were composed throughout Charlemagne's realm explaining not only the meaning of the different parts of the rite, but also exactly what parts were being used and in what order. Charlemagne presumably expected the Roman rite of baptism to be used in his realm, although his own letter shows that he himself was probably not certain what the Roman rite itself was[28].

While most of the small tracts show that throughout Charlemagne's realm baptisms were being performed containing large admixtures of old Gallican rite practices – and also Ambrosian and Celtic rite practices – there is one response that demonstrates that Visigothic practices were also being used. The text itself is anonymous and is found entirely in only a single manuscript of the thirteenth century, El Escorial, RBSL f.iv. 9. Nonetheless, its first nine lines survive in a Carolingian manuscript from Reichenau, now kept in St. Paul in Carinthia, Stiftsbibliothek 5/1, dated to the second third of the ninth century[29].

The descriptions of the baptismal ceremonies have some Roman features, but there are peculiarities, especially in the pre- and post-baptismal ceremonies, that point to the Old Spanish rite. As to the pre-baptismal material, the compiler first says there are four grades through which a person comes to faith: catechumen, competent (elect), faithful (»fidelis«), and finally Christian. The text is based on Isidore, who said there are three grades, but the fourth, the faithful, is found not in Isidore but in the *Commentary on the Apocalypse* by Beatus of Liébana[30]. Since Beatus's commentary was apparently unknown outside of Spain in the early Carolingian period[31], it appears that the compiler worked in or near the Iberian peninsula. Other features of the rite described differing from the Roman rite in *Ordo Romanus* XI and the *Gelasian Sacramentary* of Vatican, BAV Reg. lat. 316, are that the catechumen receives the Creed, is anointed before becoming a competent, and the enrolment is associated with the competent, not the catechumen. All of these features can be explained by recourse to Old Spanish liturgical books

28 Eadem, *Water and the Word: Baptism and the Education of the Clergy in the Carolingian Empire. A Study of Texts and Manuscripts*, South Bend/Indiana 1995 (forthcoming).

29 Eadem (cf. n. 27) 224. I am grateful to Professor Keefe for having pointed out this text to me and for information on it. It will be considered fully in her forthcoming *Water and the Word*.

30 Beatus, *In Apocalipsin libri duodecim*, ed. H.A. Sanders, Rome 1930, 124.

31 W. Heil, *Der Adoptianismus, Alkuin und Spanien*, in: *Karl der Große* II, 102.

such as the *Liber ordinum* and the *Antiphonary of León* and descriptions of baptisms such as the *De cognitione baptismi* of Ildefonsus of Toledo[32].

The post-baptismal ceremonies described in the text also point to Old Spanish practices. There is a single chrismation immediately after the reception from the font, followed directly by an imposition of hands, and the invocation of the Holy Spirit by a single priest. This ceremony, which is found in the baptismal rite *quolibet tempore* in the *Liber ordinum*, is in stark contrast to the Roman rite with two chrismations, the second being administered by a bishop, who also imparted the Holy Spirit.

Despite these Old Spanish features, the text also has Roman elements that suggest it was composed at a time when the liturgy was being opened to Romanization. One of these elements is the intrusion of and even emphasis on the ceremony of giving salt. In some areas of Spain this ceremony was not traditionally observed, as is clear from the texts of the *Liber ordinum* and *Antiphonary of León*[33]. Indeed, Leidrad of Lyons, a bishop who presided in a see with many Spanish emigrés, in his own tract on baptism went to special pains in emphasizing the giving of salt, presumably to counter Spanish practice[34]. Another non-Spanish element in the text is that while it does allow for a single immersion, as was the custom in some Spanish baptisms, it also allows for a triple immersion. Both the emphasis on salt and allowance for triple immersion in baptism are found in a Narbonnaise rite for baptism published by Mgr. Gros on the basis of later manuscripts having a mixture of Roman and Old Spanish elements[35].

Finally, the small commentary on baptism spends what seems to be an inordinate amount of space explaining why heretics returning to the Church are not to be rebaptized and are to be received with chrismation. Although this could reflect earlier concerns in the Iberian peninsula regarding Arians, it would be more appropriate in the late eighth and ninth centuries regarding the followers of Felix and Elipandus who must have been concerned about the validity of their baptisms by those clerics condemned in 794.

Turning to the rite of matrimony, liturgical scholars have always been fascinated with the Old Spanish rite, unique in the western Church and clearly the

---

32 Keefe (cf. n. 28).

33 On this see R.E. Reynolds, *Baptismal Rite and Paschal Vigil in Transition in Medieval Spain: A New Text in Visigothic Script*, in: *MS* 55 (1993) 261.

34 On this text see Keefe (cf. n. 27) 197f.

35 M.S. Gros, *El Antiguo Ordo Bautismal Catalano-Narbonense*, in: *Hispania Sacra* 28 (1975) 37-107, esp. 38-42.

richest of all ancient rites. (Certain elements still remain even today in the marriage rites among Filipinos). Although a relatively »pure« version of the Old Spanish rite is found first in manuscripts of the eleventh century, numerous scholars have shown that most of the elements of the rites in these manuscripts go back at least to the seventh and early eighth centuries.

Liturgical scholars have traditionally emphasized three unusual features of the Old Spanish marriage rite: the giving of betrothal tokens or *arrae*, the benediction of the wedding chamber; and a special benediction of the couple and presentation of the bride by her father to the groom[36]. In fact, in a recent study by Brian Bethune, it has been demonstrated that there are no less than nine elements of the Spanish rite that make it unique among European rites in the early Middle Ages. With respect to the tokens of betrothal, it must be emphasized that there are two tokens and these are given within the church, emphasizing the mutuality and religious nature of the Spanish ceremony. Then there is the blessing of the bedchamber itself – not the couple in bed as elsewhere – before, not after the wedding. There are also an admonition to sexual purity, additional benedictions before the nuptial Mass, the Mass itself in Visigothic form, the unique mutual veiling of bride and groom and nuptial kiss at the moment of blessing, the *traditio puellae*, and a rite for a second marriage[37].

Again, many of these unusual features of the Old Spanish rite of marriage appear to have been mixed with Roman practices and prayers in the early ninth century, especially in northeastern Spain and the Narbonne region. Our documentation for this is from the late tenth and early eleventh centuries, that is, it is long before the imposition of the Roman rite in the late eleventh century, and hence the mixture of the rites probably came from the early ninth century. Indeed, some of the Old Spanish texts can be found even before that time in the *Bobbio Missal* and the somewhat later tenth-century *Fulda Sacramentary*[38]. Our documentation from northeastern Spain comes especially from the *Pontifical of Roda* (ca. 1000), a closely related ritual, Montserrat, Bibl. de Mon. 72 (s. XII), and the *Sacramentary of Vic* (1038). If the texts of these are carefully compared, it is clear that Romanization is not as advanced in the *Sacramentary of Vic* as in *Roda*[39]. In any event, both the sacramentary and pontifical contain a mixture of Old Spanish

36 See, e.g., M. Gros, *Les Wisigoths et les liturgies occidentales*, in: *L'Europe héritière* (cf. n. 12) 130f.

37 B. Bethune, *The Text of the Christian Rite of Marriage in Medieval Spain*, diss. Toronto 1986, 12-38.

38 See K. Stevenson, *Nuptial Blessing. A Study of Christian Marriage Rites*, London 1982, 56-58, giving the date of *Bobbio Missal* as ninth century.

39 Bethune (cf. n. 37) 54.

material and texts especially from the *Gregorian Sacramentary*. It is especially in the pre-Mass ceremonies that the Old Spanish are maintained, in the *arrae* ceremony and blessing of the bedchamber. Nonetheless, even in the former some of the Visigothic flavour has disappeared with the removal of the »Amen« after each petition in several benedictions. Further, in the blessing of the bedchamber, which follows the Old Spanish rite, one of the ancient Visigothic prayers has been omitted in the *Sacramentary of Vic*. In the Mass itself the influence and structure of the Roman rite is far more clear, where the Gregorian prayers, collect, and the like appear together with the proper preface and *Hanc igitur*. Nonetheless, with the *Pax* a group of Old Spanish practices appears, such as a prayer with the Visigothic »Amens«, just before the *Pax* and after it, the presentation of the bride to the priest and the veiling, the *traditio puellae*, and the admonition to sexual purity.

In his famous article *Spanish Symptoms*, Edmund Bishop pointed out that texts from the Old Spanish rites of death and burial had been used in the Supplement to the *Gregorian Sacramentary* sent to Charlemagne by Pope Hadrian I as well as the English *Book of Cerne*[40]. In Bishop's day it was thought that Alcuin had compiled the Supplement, and hence Bishop was forced to trace the influence of the Old Spanish rite from Spain to the Insular churches and back to the Continent. Since Bishop's time it has been demonstrated that the Supplement was the work of the Visigoth, Benedict of Aniane, and hence Old Spanish influence is almost to be expected[41].

As to the ceremony of the Old Spanish rites of death and burial, one depends on the late eleventh-century manuscripts of the *Liber ordinum*, and as a result there is debate among scholars regarding the exact nature of the early rite in Visigothic times. In any event, it is widely recognized that among the most unusual aspects was a ceremony, following the anointing of the sick, for deathbed penance in which the sick person was tonsured, given communion, and covered with sackcloth and signed with ashes[42]. When Benedict of Aniane compiled his Supplement to the *Gregorian Sacramentary* this peculiarity of the Old Spanish rite was not taken over into his rites of death and burial. Perhaps it was too distinctive

---

40 Bishop (cf. n. 6) 167.

41 This was the brilliant demonstration of Dom Jean Deshusses, on which see R.E. Reynolds, *The Portrait of the Ecclesiastical Officers in the Raganaldus Sacramentary and its Liturgico-Canonical Significance*, in: *Speculum* 46 (1971) 438, n. 33.

42 See F.S. Paxton, *Christianizing Death. The Creation of a Ritual Process in Early Medieval Europe*, Ithaca 1990, 73-78.

for a person like Benedict, who had taken part in the battle against Adoptionism, to add it to a sacramentary as »official« as that sent by Pope Hadrian to Charlemagne. Thus, in his prayers for the visitation of the sick, Mass for the sick, prayers for the return of health, and reconciliation of a penitent at death he used prayers from the Gregorian and Gelasian sacramentaries. He continued to borrow from these sources for the prayers in *agendum mortuorum*, but surprisingly he inserted three prayers from the Old Spanish liturgy. At the conclusion of this rite, he introduced the *Requiem aeternam*, also found in the Old Spanish rite. Although this verse probably had origins predating the Old Spanish liturgy, Sicard in his study on early medieval funerary rites attributes Benedict with the introduction of this verse into the standard western death rituals[43].

Beyond these Old Spanish prayers and verses said after the death of a person, Benedict used Old Spanish texts alone for after the washing of the corpse and the grave before burial. In these ceremonies, then, Benedict seems to have had no hesitation in taking over entirely texts from the Old Spanish rite. Finally, among the prayers said after burial, one Old Spanish text is intruded among five from the *Gelasian Sacramentary*[44].

The fact that Benedict could use prayers exclusively from the Old Spanish rite for the washing of the corpse and at graveside within his Supplement to the *Gregorian Sacramentary* suggests that when necessary he had no hesitation in using texts from the rite whose prayers had provided Elipandus with material to support his Adoptionism. Even so, the texts forming the majority of his rites for the sick, dying, and dead in the Supplement are clearly more Roman than Old Spanish, reflecting Benedict's general position as a liturgical reformer under Charlemagne and Louis the Pious.

Many of the decrees of the Carolingians had insisted on the institution of anointing of the sick, but the Roman rite had no such rite. The Old Spanish did, however, and it was this rite which came to be inserted into several manuscripts of the *Gregorian Sacramentary*. Some years ago Boone Porter drew attention to this text, which appears in the *Sacramentary of Rodradus*, Paris, BN, lat. 12050, written at Corbie ca. 853, and in the *Sacramentary of Noyon*, Paris, BN, lat. 12051, written also at Corbie in the second half of the ninth century[45]. Because of its dependence on Old Spanish sources it was suggested that the author of the text was working in

43 D. SICARD, *La liturgie de la mort dans l'Église latine des origines à la réforme carolingienne*, Münster/W. 1978, 72-74, 76-78.

44 For a summary table of these texts see PAXTON (cf. n. 42) 141.

45 H.B. PORTER, *The Origin of the Medieval Rite for Anointing the Sick or Dying*, in: *JTS* n.s. 7 (1956) 211-225.

the south of France. In his recent study Paxton has now called this ceremony the reformed rite for the anointing of the sick and has shown that the antiphons, verses, and prayers are nearly all drawn from the Old Spanish rite. In some cases they have been modified, especially in their invocation of Christ, to avoid possible Adoptionist implications, and these modifications all point to Benedict of Aniane as the author[46].

In the subsequent development of this rite of anointing during Carolingian times, Paxton has shown that Benedict's rite was mixed with other material that looked not so much for restoration of health as to spiritual purification. A prime example is found in the *Sacramentary of Sens*, Stockholm, KB Holm A. 136, written in St. Amand in the 870's. It is interesting, however, that in one of the prayers the original address to Jesus rather than »Dominus Deus« has been restored to its Old Spanish original.

We turn now to a number of ceremonies largely clerical in nature in which elements of the Old Spanish rite were combined with Roman or Romano-Frankish rites in the early ninth century, and here the research especially of Mgr. Gros has revealed the extent to which the Old Spanish rite persisted in the Carolingian realm.

First, there is the rite of clerical ordination. By Charlemagne's time the rite of ordination accepted virtually throughout his realm was thoroughly Gallicanized and hence called the Romano-Gallican rite[47]. Included among the ordination rites were those for the psalmist, doorkeeper, lector, exorcist, acolyte, subdeacon, deacon, presbyter, and bishop. By the late eighth century this rite completely dominated the realm of Charlemagne and had even reached southern Italy[48] and perhaps even Rome itself[49]. The Old Spanish liturgy, however, had its own rites. These are presented primarily in the *Liber ordinum* and include ordination ceremo-

46 PAXTON (cf. n. 42) 151.

47 See, e.g., R.E. REYNOLDS, *The Ordination Rite in Medieval Spain: Hispanic, Roman, and Hybrid*, in: *Santiago, Saint-Denis, and Saint Peter. The Reception of the Roman Liturgy in León-Castile in 1080*, ed. by B.F. REILLY, New York 1985, 139.

48 See IDEM, *The Ritual of Clerical Ordination of the Sacramentarium Gelasianum saec. VIII: Early Evidence from Southern Italy*, in: *Rituels*. Mélanges offerts à Pierre-Marie Gy, o.p., edd. P. DE CLERCK/E.. PALAZZO, Paris 1990, 437-445.

49 See J.ST. H. GIBAUT, *The Cursus Honorum: A Study of the Early and Medieval Development of the Clerical Cursus and its Significance for the Contemporary Church*, diss. Toronto 1993, 202-207, and its fascinating discussion of the account of the eighth-century ordination of »Pope« Constantine in the Lateran according to the Romano-Gallican cursus reported in the tenth-century canon law manuscript Wolfenbüttel, HAB 454 Helmst., fol. 43.

nies for the clerical state, sacristan, overseer of books and scribes, subdeacon, deacon, archdeacon, primiclericus, presbyter, archpresbyter, and bishop[50].

Remnants of the old Roman rite of ordination for the higher grades were combined in the *Gregorian Sacramentary* supplemented by Benedict of Aniane with the Romano-Gallican ceremonies and prayers for the lower grades. Given the almost immediate domination of this rite throughout the Carolingian empire, it could be expected that the Old Spanish ordination rite in northeastern Spain and the Narbonne region would quickly disappear. But in fact, there is evidence in an eleventh-century manuscript from Vic, BC 104, that elements of the Old Spanish rite continued to be copied and used. In this ordination text there are clearly ordination ceremonies for a number of grades from the supplemented *Gregorian Sacramentary*. But one is surprised to find that ceremonies and prayers for a number of the grades in the Old Spanish rite have been intruded. There are ceremonies for the clerical state, tonsuring, doorkeeper, lector, exorcist, acolyte, subdeacon, archdeacon, primiclericus, sacristan, overseer of books and scribes, archpresbyter, deacon, presbyter, and bishop. While Mgr. Gros would date this particular text to the late ninth or early tenth century primarily because of the late date of the Vic manuscript and restoration of the see of Vic only in 888[51], it is fully conceivable that a rite like this containing the unusual Old Spanish grades could have been composed much earlier as the Romano-Gallican and Old Spanish rituals confronted each other.

One of the most interesting of the pontifical rites with a mixture of Old Spanish and Roman or Romano-Frankish elements is found in the ceremony for the dedication of churches. It was discovered and reported by Mgr. Gros in his Paris doctoral thesis and called the Narbonne Romano-Hispanic *ordo*[52]. The text itself is found in the *Pontifical of Roda* (ca. 1000); in a manuscript now lost which Martène dated to ca. 1100 and called a Pontifical of Narbonne; the *Pontifical of Vic 104* with its ordination rite just treated; a fragment from Ripoll in Barcelona, ACA Ripoll 40 (ca. 1100); a gradual from Narbonne, Paris, BN, lat. 780 (s. XII); and a fragment with antiphons in Vic, BC 46 with musical notation. At base for the order for the dedication of a church is a Romano-Frankish *ordo* found in many sacramentaries of the ninth century from the ecclesiastical provinces of Reims and

50 See Reynolds (cf. n. 47) 132.

51 M.S. Gros, *Las ordenes sagradas del Pontifical MS. 104 (CV) de la Bib. Cap. de Vic*, in: *Hispania Sacra* 17 (1964) 99-133.

52 Idem, *El Ordo romano-hispánico de Narbona para la consagración de iglesias*, in: *Hispania Sacra* 19 (1966) 321-340.

Sens. The text itself, however, goes back to the mid-eighth century. What the compiler did was to add antiphons and propers from an Old Spanish order to a Romano-Frankish base. The antiphons come from a text like the *Antiphonary of León*. One might expect the prayers to be found in the *Liber ordinum*, but they are not; rather they are solely in the *ordo* of Narbonne. In any event, the rite shows the combination of Romano-Frankish texts with the Old Spanish antiphons and prayers in the Narbonne region.

The *Roda Pontifical* and the *Pontifical of Vic 104* contain yet another Narbonne ceremony in which the Old Spanish rite as found in the *Liber ordinum* is reflected. This is the blessing of oils on Holy Thursday. The ceremony itself is based largely on the old *Ordo Romanus XXIV* into which prayers from various rites have been worked. The *Roda Pontifical* draws largely from the *Gregorian Sacramentary* sent to Charlemagne, whereas the Vic text relies more on the *Gelasian Sacramentary of the Eighth Century*, many of whose manuscripts could be found in southern France in Carolingian times. Nonetheless, a benediction for the oil of the sick from the Old Spanish *Liber ordinum* has been worked into the ceremony. While the manuscripts containing this *ordo* are later than the ninth century, Mgr. Gros places it at the beginning of the ninth century when the Old Spanish rite was succumbing to the Romano-Gallican[53].

There is one Old Spanish liturgical ceremony in which bishops were involved that entered the Carolingian realm and became the standard for centuries thereafter: the rite for the celebration of ecclesiastical councils. This *ordo* was developed in Spain at least during the time of Isidore and is reflected in the canons of the IV Council of Toledo in 633. Later, probably under Julian of Toledo, it was augmented and is found in several tenth-century manuscripts in a form called the Visigothic Order for the holding of Councils (OCW). This particular form is interesting in that there is a provision for the attendance of the king, which would have been the case in Visigothic national councils.

A variant form of this *ordo* was in Francia by 787 in the famous Racchio manuscript in Strasbourg, destroyed in 1870, perhaps reflecting the presence of Visigothic emigrés in Alsace[54]. Not long thereafter the *ordo* appeared in a canon law manuscript written in eastern Francia at the turn of the century, now Vienna ÖNB 411. The version of the *ordo* in these manuscripts is called by scholars the

53 Idem, *L'Ordre Catalano-Narbonès per a la Benedicció dels Sants Olis*, in: *Revista Catalana de Teología* 1 (1976) 231-258.

54 See Guerreiro (cf. n. 12) 151. And for the Racchio manuscript see G. Martínez Díez, *La colección canónica hispana*, I: *Estudio*, Madrid 1966, 171f.

Frankish Order for the holding of Councils (OCF), and it differs from the Visigothic version in that there is no provision for the king's presence and multiple metropolitans, that is, it is for a provincial council. According to some scholars this Frankish version antedated the Visigothic version, but the exact sequence of the version will be clarified in the forthcoming edition of the conciliar *ordines* to be published by Herbert Schneider in the *Monumenta Germaniae Historica*. An abridged form of the Frankish version was added to the canonical *Collectio Dionysiana Bobbiensis* in the codex Milan, Bibl. Amb. S 33 sup. written in northern Italy in the second half of the ninth century[55]. Also, another version of the *ordo* for the holding of a provincial council appears in a codex written in the first quarter of the ninth century at Mainz and now kept in Cologne, DB 138[56].

That versions of the Visigothic *ordo* itself were known outside the Iberian peninsula in the ninth century is certain; portions appear in the ninth-century *Gregorian Sacramentary* of Mainz, Seminarbibl. 1[57], written in the late ninth century either in Mainz or St. Gall, and in the early tenth-century manuscript, Vatican, BAV lat. 5845, written in Beneventan script by Cassinese monks at Capua[58]. But it was the Frankish version that was most popular in the ninth century inasmuch as it appeared in Pseudo-Isidorian Decretal manuscripts as well as the Pseudo-Isidorian canonical *Collectio hispana gallica Augustodunensis*[59]. The existence of this *ordo* originating in Visigothic Spain in multiple manuscripts written throughout the Carolingian realm is one of the most striking examples of the persistence of elements of the Old Spanish rite in the highest circles of the Carolingian church, in synods themselves. Moreover, it is not likely that conciliar participants and their assistants were unaware of its connections with the Spanish church because it was most often attached to manuscripts of the canonical *Collectio hispana* and its derivatives with their canons from the Spanish councils.

Turning to the celebration of the Mass, scholars have often noted that while the Credo was not used in the Mass at Rome until the early eleventh century, it

---

55 On which manuscript see F. MAASSEN, *Geschichte der Quellen und der Literatur des canonischen Rechts*, Graz 1870, 471-476.

56 On which see M. KLÖCKENER, *Eine liturgische Ordnung für Provinzialkonzilien aus der Karolingerzeit: Der Ordo romanus qualiter concilium agatur des Cod. 138 der Dombibliothek Köln liturgiegeschichtlich erklärt*, in: *AHC* 12 (1982) 109-182.

57 See *Le Sacramentaire Grégorien: ses principales formes d'après les plus anciens manuscrits*, III, ed. J. DESHUSSES, Fribourg/S 1982, 274f.

58 On which see R.E REYNOLDS, *Rites and Signs of Conciliar Decisions in the Early Middle Ages*, in: *Segni e riti nella chiesa altomedievale occidentale, Spoleto 11-17 aprile 1985* (*Settimane* 33), Spoleto 1987, 242.

59 Vatican, BAV lat. 1341, fol. 3v (s. IXex., Corbie).

appeared in the Roman rite as practiced in the Carolingian realm as early as the late eighth century. They point out, however, that long before this a version of the Niceno-Constantinopolitan creed of 381 had been used in the Old Spanish Mass. As early as the III Council of Toledo (589) it was directed that the creed, with the *Filioque* (actually *et Filio* in Spanish sources), be said before the *Pater noster*. According to many scholars the practice of using the creed at Mass spread from Spain to Ireland, where without the *Filioque* it is found in the early ninth-century *Stowe Missal* before the offertory. Then, so goes the theory, the practice spread to England where Alcuin would have known it. It was he who encouraged Charlemagne and Paulinus of Aquileia to introduce the practice in reaction to Adoptionism – strange, since it was from the Old Spanish rite used in Toledo that the practice grew. In any event, Walafrid Strabo notes that the creed was introduced by Charlemagne as a result of the heresy of Felix[60], and a number of ninth-century Mass commentaries note its existence in the Mass. In any event, beyond the commentaries the use of the creed in Mass is not consistently represented in late eighth- and ninth-century sources.

Yet another variant theory by Hesbert has it that the use of the creed in the late Carolingian period did not come from Spain at all[61]. Indeed, he correctly notes that the canons of Frankfort in 794 make no reference to the creed, that in the liturgical commentaries of the late eighth century there is no mention of the creed, and that the text and position of the creed were different in Spain and in Charlemagne's churches. Hence, he speculates that the creed in its Carolingian form and in its position after the Gospel came from Beneventan territories and was brought to the court of Charlemagne by Paulinus of Aquileia, whose Friuli synod of 796/97 had included it in its acta[62].

Beyond the introduction of the creed into the Mass, there is other evidence of the Old Spanish rite in special Masses in the Carolingian period. In his Supplement to the *Gregorian Sacramentary* Benedict of Aniane added a *Missa specialis sacerdotalis*, all of whose prayers are drawn from the Masses said for the priest alone, which were extremely popular in the Old Spanish rite[63]. In most cases the texts of the prayers are very close to their Old Spanish originals, but in others

60 See *De exordiis et incrementis quarundam in observationibus ecclesiasticis rerum*, ed. A. Knoepfler, Munich 1899, 62.

61 R.-J. Hesbert, *L'»Antiphonale Missarum« de l'ancien rite bénéventain*, in: *Ephemerides liturgicae* 52 (1938) 36-40.

62 MGH *Conc.* II 1, 187.

63 Bishop (cf. n. 6) 169.

Benedict has modified them, especially the *Alia oratio*[64]. But it is especially interesting to see how he took prayers from the parts of the Old Spanish Mass and placed them in a Roman framework. His first two collects are from the first of two different Masses. The *Super oblata* is drawn from the Old Spanish *Ad pacem*, the *Praefatio* from the Old Spanish *Illatio*, and the *Ad complendum* from the *Completuria* of yet another Old Spanish Mass[65].

The introduction of Old Spanish material into Carolingian liturgical practices is further evident in elements of the office and in private devotion. Earlier, it was noted that the monastic rules of Isidore of Seville and Fructuosus of Braga with their materials on the office were known in manuscripts in the Carolingian realm. Moreover, Isidore's treatment of the office in his *De ecclesiasticis officiis* II 19-23 found its way into the *Institutio canonicorum* of 816, the *De institutione clericorum* of Rabanus Maurus, and the *Liber de divinis officiis* attributed to Alcuin. Further, in the tract on the office more properly attributed to Alcuin, the *Beatus igitur David*, there is material that corresponds to that in Fructuosus[66].

In the establishment of a uniform and ancient monastic rule in the Carolingian realm, the *Rule of St. Benedict* played a role comparable to the *Gregorian Sacramentary* in the liturgy or the *Collectio Dionysiana* in canon law. But just as these two texts were quickly augmented with Gallican and Old Spanish texts, so the office practices by Carolingian Benedictines were augmented with Old Spanish material. For example, Psalter collects from the Spanish cathedral office were taken into the Benedictine office[67]. These collects, actually collected in Carolingian times[68], were taken from the large repertory of Psalter collects – the *Liber psalmographus* – used in the Old Spanish office since the end of the sixth century[69]. Yet another influence of the Old Spanish office is found in the New Hymnal used in the Romano-Frankish and Benedictine offices. This hymnal had developed from the one used in the eighth-century Gallican and Spanish office[70].

64 *Le Sacramentaire Grégorien* (cf. n. 57) I, 428, nr. 1281.

65 *Ibid.*, 428f., and *Le Liber ordinum en usage dans l'église wisigothique et mozarabe d'Espagne du cinquième au onzième siècles*, ed. M. FÉROTIN, Paris 1904, 234, 297f., 280.

66 J.G. BLACK, *The Daily Cursus, the Week, and the Psalter in the Divine Office and in Carolingian Devotion*, diss. Toronto 1987, 278, n. 39.

67 *Ibid.*, 438.

68 *Ibid.*, 267.

69 *Liber Orationum Psalmographus*, ed. J. PINELL (*Monumenta Hispaniae Sacra*, series liturgica 9), Barcelona 1972, 241.

70 BLACK (cf. n. 66) 431.

The existence of manuscripts of the Old Spanish *passionarium* has earlier been noted, but it is appropriate here to comment on the Hispanic saints honoured in the Carolingian realm in the *Vitae*. Recently, Rosa Guerreiro has studied the distribution of these saints' lives in a number of regions in the Carolingian realm: Septimania and Aquitaine, the Rhone valley and Burgundy, Paris and the north, and the eastern Frankish empire[71]. Her conclusions are especially interesting in that they show that with the exceptions of the universally honoured Vincent and Leocadia, and the Cordoban saints, the saints most often honoured are those from the Catalan region: Eulalia of Merida under the name of Eulalia of Barcelona, Cucuphatus of Barcelona, Felix of Gerona, and Fructuosus of Tarragona. In part, their popularity was due to the importation of relics – something easier to accomplish from an area under the control of the Carolingians – but it was also due, especially in Septimania and Aquitaine, to ties there with the Iberian hagiographical tradition.

One of the Old Spanish influences in prayerbooks used in the Carolingian realm has recently been brought to light by Patrick Sims-Williams[72]. It is a prayer called in some manuscripts the *Oratio sancti Isidori pro omnibus Christianis*. This is the title in the so-called *Fleury Prayerbook*, Orléans, Bibl. de la Ville 184, and in the Pseudo-Alcuinian *Officia per ferias*; elsewhere it is anonymous. In its diction the prayer is very much like that of several Spanish texts, including the *Synonyma* of Isidore, but most important, it is a version of one of the invariable prayers, *Dei omnipotentis misericordia*, of the Old Spanish *Missa omnimoda* found in the *Liber ordinum*[73]. In the Old Spanish rite the prayer continued the intercessory content of the prayers of the faithful, that is, it is an extremely ancient relic of the universal prayer of the early Church. When this prayer was brought into the prayerbooks of the Carolingian realm, it was adapted to private use, and perhaps it was at this time that it may have assumed its attribution to Isidore, just as Elipandus of Toledo, out of a concern for prestige, had attributed other prayers in the Old Spanish liturgy to his Toledan predecessors.

One of the best-known prayerbooks of the ninth century, but outside the realm of Charlemagne, is the *Book of Cerne*, Cambridge UL Ll.1.10, written in Mercia. It was Edmund Bishop who long ago pointed out that not only prayers for the dead from the Old Spanish liturgy are contained in the book, but also a

---

71 Guerreiro (cf. n. 12) 142-155.

72 P. Sims-Williams, *Oratio sancti Isidori pro omnibus Christianis*, in: *Mélanges François Kerlouégan. Annales Littéraires de l'Université de Besançon n. 515* (*Série Institut Félix Gaffiot* 11), Besançon 1994, 579-601.

73 *Le liber ordinum* (cf. n. 65) 234f.

modified prayer which the priest says for himself in the Old Spanish liturgy[74] has been changed to form an *Oratio penitentis* in the *Book of Cerne*[75]. Whether these prayers came to England directly from Spain or through Continental routes is unclear since some of the prayers are in the supplemented *Gregorian Sacramentary*[76].

III.

We turn now to a third major area in which the Old Spanish liturgy played a major role in the realm of Charlemagne: in the liturgical law known in the Carolingian church and in the commentaries on the liturgy. Liturgical specialists often concentrate their studies on the euchological and ritual texts alone and ignore these areas, yet they are exceedingly rich and often illuminate sometimes obscure ordinary liturgical texts.

Before dealing with the transmission of liturgico-legal texts from Spain, two preliminary remarks are appropriate. First, the Hispanic councils are extraordinarily rich in canons dealing with the liturgy. The Spanish councils had decreed liturgical uniformity in the realm of the Visigoths, and councils frequently legislated on liturgical matters. One need only consult the *Indice Doctrinal* in the edition of the councils by Vives to see the large number of canons devoted to liturgical matters[77]. Second, it is often forgotten that many of the so-called Gallican and Merovingian councils were held in territories in southern France where the Visigoths lived and worshipped. Hence, when the Visigoths included canons from these Gallican and Merovingian councils in their collections of canon law, liturgical practices of the Visigoths are often reflected in them.

Of all the collections issuing from the Spanish church, the best-known is the *Collectio hispana*. But several Spanish collections antedated this one, and it is notable that the manuscripts of these collections are all found outside Spain in the Carolingian realm. The earliest of these is the *Collection of Novara*, so called because it was first found in a manuscript from Novara in northern Italy. The collection itself, compiled between 546 and 589, contains the canons of oriental

74 *Ibid.*, 266f.

75 BISHOP (cf. n. 6) 167-169.

76 On the other hand, the Old Spanish prayers might have come to Ireland and England directly since a burial prayer from the Old Spanish rite, also found in the *Gelasian Sacramentary*, appears in a fragment written in Ireland which later came to St. Gall, SB 1395, on which see GAMBER (cf. n. 7) nr. 106, and PAXTON (cf. n. 42) 79.

77 *Concilios visigóticos e hispano-romanos*, ed. J. VIVES, Barcelona/Madrid 1963, 541-548.

councils together with Gallican and Spanish councils. The collection (and excerpta) is still found in nine manuscripts of which six come from northern or central Italy and six date to the late eighth and ninth centuries. That manuscripts of this Spanish collection should be concentrated in northern Italy is probably not surprising in light of the bonds between these two regions, as reflected in the travels of the *Orationale* of Verona. The influence of this collection of canons on Carolingian collections of canon law was especially strong at the end of the ninth century when it was heavily used in the compilation of the *Collectio Anselmo dedicata*[78].

The second Spanish collection antedating the *Collectio hispana* is called the *Epitome hispanica* because the texts of conciliar canons and papal decretals are abbreviated. The collection itself was compiled, perhaps by a bishop of Galicia, at the beginning of the seventh century (ca. 598–633). The canons of councils are strictly separated from papal decretals, and among the former are oriental, Gallican and Spanish councils. Like the *Collection of Novara*, there are among its eleven manuscripts none from Spain. It has generally been thought that its major manuscript witnesses are from northern and central Italy. Two in particular are still found in locations with close ties to Spain, Lucca, BC 490, and Verona, BC LXI. But it is now known that its earliest witness is from southern France in the early eighth century, København, KB 58.8°, and that several other examples come from Germany, especially southeastern Germany, with its close connections in Carolingian times with northeastern Italy.

Most specialists in canon law hold that the lack of Spanish manuscripts of the *Collection of Novara* and the *Epitome hispanica* is due to the fact that they were soon replaced in Spain by the greatest of the Spanish collections, the *Collectio hispana* in its various forms. The collection itself is found in several redactions, and most of the manuscripts were written in Spain in Visigothic script. There is, however, one manuscript fragment in Visigothic script, discovered in the summer of 1994 in Lucca, again illustrating the bonds between this Italian city and Spain. But for our purposes, it is important to emphasize that this great collection, containing canons of oriental, Gallican, and Spanish councils and papal decretals, all arranged historically, was taken into the realm of Charlemagne in several forms. One is called the *Collectio hispana gallica* (found in the codex Vienna, ÖNB 411, mentioned earlier). Another Gallican redaction is found in the destroyed Racchio manuscript at Strasbourg, two ninth-century manuscripts in Carolingian minus-

78 On this see R.E. Reynolds, *Law, Canon, before Gratian*, in: *Dictionary of the Middle Ages* 7 (1986) 401.

cule, Vatican, BAV Pal. lat. 575, and Rome, Bibl. Angel. 1091, and in a tenth-century manuscript in Carolingian minuscule with Visigothic-script influence, Rome, Bibl. Vallicelliana D 18. Beyond these Gallican versions of the *Collectio hispana*, there is a Catalan redaction represented in post-Carolingian manuscripts at Seo de Urgel, BC 2005, and Gerona, BC 4.

One of the most interesting forms of the *Collectio hispana* to have reached the Carolingian realm is a systematized version, called the *Collectio hispana systematica*. Liturgical material is concentrated in Book I on clerics, their ordination, and duties, and in Book IV where the construction of churches and altars is treated together with the office, Mass, fasting, baptism, and funerals. Because the three Latin manuscripts of the collection are from southern France, it has been thought by some scholars that it was a Frankish systematization of the *Collectio hispana*. But a fourth manuscript and several fragments in Arabic are now known to exist, suggesting a Spanish origin. In any event, there are two manuscripts written in Carolingian minuscule at Lyons in the early ninth century, but most interestingly, they bear marginal and interlinear glosses in Visigothic script, and one, Paris, BN, lat. 11709 belonging to Archbishop Leidrad, shows traces of having been copied from a Visigothic-script exemplar[79].

Both the *Collectio hispana* and the *Collectio hispana systematica* came to play major roles in the formation of canon law in the Carolingian realm. The *Systematica* was used heavily to compile the most widely-spread systematic collection of the early Carolingian period, the *Collectio Dacheriana*, compiled almost certainly in Lyons in the early ninth century and still found in over fifty manuscripts, many from the first half of the century. The *Collectio hispana* itself in its Gallican form was then used by the Pseudo-Isidorian atelier in the mid-ninth century to compile the Pseudo-Isidorian Decretals and the so-called *Collectio hispana gallica Augustodunensis*. It has also been claimed that because of the value of the Spanish and Gallican conciliar canons in the *Hispana* it was combined with the quasi-official *Collectio Dionysio-Hadriana* to form a *Collectio Hispana-Hadriana*, but because of the late date of its manuscripts this claim is now disputed[80].

The heavy influence on the Carolingian church of the Spanish canon law collections with their liturgical canons has a parallel in liturgical commentaries originating in Spain. Manuscripts of these commentaries were repeatedly copied

---

79 See IDEM, *The »Isidorian« Epistula ad Leudefredum: An Early Medieval Epitome of the Clerical Duties*, in: *MS* 41 (1979) 277; and LOWE (cf. n. 20) 323.

80 See REYNOLDS (cf. n. 78) 404.

in the realm of Charlemagne, and of the commentaries written in the ninth century in this realm, hardly any is without the influence of Spanish texts.

First, the Carolingian manuscripts of the Spanish liturgical commentaries. The earliest of the commentaries is a tract often attributed to Jerome entitled in most manuscripts *De septem ordinibus ecclesiae*. For years it was believed that this tract, in which the officers of the Church and their liturgical duties are described, was composed in southern Gaul in the fifth century. More recently, scholars believe it to have been compiled sometime before the sixth century in Catalonia or the Pyrenees inasmuch as there are echoes of biblical texts in the Old Spanish antiphonaries[81]. While there are no Spanish manuscripts with this tract, there is abundant manuscript evidence from the late eighth and ninth centuries in codices written throughout the Carolingian realm. In an abbreviated form it very early was added to the *Epitome hispanica* in the Verona and Lucca manuscripts of that collection already mentioned. Yet another abbreviated form is found in early ninth-century manuscripts from St. Gall and Würzburg[82]. In a fuller or long form it then appears in many late eighth- and early ninth-century codices from Bavaria and Salzburg, including manuscripts of the canonical *Collectio Frisingensis prima* and the *Collection of Diessen*[83]. Fragments also appear in the Salzburg *Collectio duorum librorum*[84]. In an early ninth-century manuscript written perhaps in Rhaetia the *De septem ordinibus ecclesiae* is found together with the *Concordia canonum Cresconii* and *Breviatio Fulgentii Ferrandi*, and thereafter in northern Italy in manuscripts with the *Collection of Novara* and Pseudo-Isidorian Decretals. From these northern Italian manuscripts it then entered into the late ninth-century *Collectio Anselmo dedicata*[85].

The ecclesiastical orders listed in the *De septem ordinibus ecclesiae* are unusual in that the hierarchy begins with the grade of gravedigger, an officer rarely found in western European tracts on orders[86]. Despite this oddity, the tract came to play an important role in Spain as a source for the first of Isidore's major liturgical

81 See Idem, *The Pseudo-Hieronymian »De septem ordinibus ecclesiae: Notes on its Origins, Abridgments, and Use in Early Medieval Canonical Collections*, in: *RBen* 80 (1970) 252; and idem (cf. n. 47) 150, n. 31.

82 Idem, *The »De officiis VII graduum«: its Origins and Early Medieval Development*, in: *MS* 34 (1972) 124, n. 47.

83 See idem, *Canon Law Collections in early ninth-century Salzburg*, in: *Proceedings of the Fifth International Congress of Medieval Canon Law*. Salamanca 21-25 September 1976, edd. S. Kuttner/K. Pennington (*Monumenta Iuris Canonici*, Ser. C, Subsidia 6), Vatican 1980, 21, n. 33, and idem, *The Ordinals of Christ from their Origins to the Twelfth Century* (*BGQMA* 7), Berlin/New York 1978, 32, n. 24.

84 Idem, *Canon Law Collections* (cf. n. 83) 29.

85 Reynolds (cf. n. 79) 274, n. 121.

86 Idem, *Ordinals of Christ* (cf. n. 83) 43, 48, 50.

commentaries, the *De ecclesiasticis officiis*. The first book of this work is concerned largely with the components of the Mass, office and the ecclesiastical year, while the second book describes the clerical officers and their duties and the liturgy of baptism. The manuscript diffusion and influence on later liturgical commentaries of the *De ecclesiasticis officiis* would be enormous.

In the recent edition of the *De ecclesiasticis officiis* by the late Christopher Lawson, a substantial but not complete list of the early manuscripts of the tract is given and a stemma developed. Of the forty-seven manuscripts assigned *sigla* for the edition, twenty-two date from the seventh through the ninth century[87]. Relatively few were written in the Iberian peninsula; rather the vast majority come from Charlemagne's realm to its farthest reaches. There is one notable manuscript, already mentioned, that seems to have been based on a Visigothic exemplar, Lucca, BC 490. Also, one »hyparchetype« may have originated in Verona[88], yet another place of contact between Spain and Carolingian scribes and books.

The influence of the *De ecclesiasticis officiis*, Lawson shows, was extraordinary. Even before Carolingian times its liturgical sections had been worked into no less than eight important texts outside Spain, including the *Liber scintillarum* of Defensor of Ligugé, the *Expositio antiqua liturgiae Gallicanae*, and the *Collectio canonum hibernensis*, which in its turn spawned multiple derivative collections in the Carolingian period[89]. The influence of the *De ecclesiasticis officiis* in the late eighth and early ninth centuries was even greater, and Lawson lists eighteen texts written in the Carolingian realm (including the Spanish March in the *Commentary on the Apocalypse* by Beatus of Liébana) which used liturgical sections of the *De ecclesiasticis officiis*. Chief among these are the major liturgical commentaries of Amalarius and Rabanus Maurus[90]. One of the most interesting uses made of the *De ecclesiasticis officiis* was that by Benedict of Aniane in the *Institutio canonicorum*. In this compilation of older texts, which is found in dozens of manuscripts[91], Benedict first dealt with the clerical grades and he used the descriptions of the *De ecclesiasticis officiis*. He rearranged their order, however, to correspond to the Romano-Gallican hierarchy widely recognized in the Carolingian realm: doorkeeper, lector, exor-

87 Sancti Isidori Hispalensis *De ecclesiasticis officiis*, ed. C.M. Lawson (*CCSL* 113), Turnhout 1989, 137-141.

88 *CCSL* 113, 130#.

89 See R.E. Reynolds, *Unity and Diversity in Carolingian Canon Law Collections: The Case of the Collectio Hibernensis and Its Derivatives*, in: *Carolingian Essays*, 99-135.

90 *CCSL* 113, 146#-159#.

91 Reynolds (cf. n. 79) 254, n. 3; and *CCSL* 113, 141f.

cist, acolyte, subdeacon, deacon, and presbyter. But the *De ecclesiasticis officiis* lacked a description of the acolyte, and hence Benedict inserted a text from Isidore's *Etymologies*. The effect of this was double. First, the wide diffusion of the *Institutio canonicorum* assured that the hierarchy of orders in the Western Church, even down to 1972, would be that represented in its text. Second, because the text on the acolyte had been intruded into the *Institutio canonicorum*, it came to be inserted into ninth-century manuscripts of the *De ecclesiasticis officiis* itself, often on tiny scraps of parchment[92].

After Isidore had completed his *De ecclesiasticis officiis*, he used parts of the text in his *Etymologies* or *Origines*, and hence this great encyclopedia of knowledge came to have sections on the liturgy, especially in Books VI and VII dealing with the office, baptism, and clerics. There exist relatively few Spanish manuscripts of the *Etymologies*, and for his edition of the text Lindsay used only four from the eighth century, none Spanish[93]. The manuscripts of the *Etymologies* and their families have been studied by Walter Porzig, Bernhard Bischoff, and Marc Reydellet in preparation for a new edition[94]. Also, Manuel Díaz y Díaz has listed early manuscripts and fragments in his *Index scriptorum latinorum medii aevi hispanorum* by date: seventh century, one; eighth century, ten; late eighth or early ninth century, seven; ninth century, forty-six; and late ninth or early tenth century, three[95]. Beyond the family of Spanish manuscripts, the codices fall basically into two families, the Italian and French. Notable among the former are those written in the north of Italy, again demonstrating the ties of that area with Spain. Another codex, this time in Visigothic script, El Escorial RBSL P.I.8, was written in the Narbonne region in the early ninth century and is a type of bridge among all the three major families of manuscripts written in Carolingian times[96].

---

92 See R.E. Reynolds, *Excerpta from the Collectio hibernensis in three Vatican manuscripts*, in: *Bulletin of Medieval Canon Law*, n.s. 5 (1975) 8, n. 57.

93 Isidor Hispanensis, *Etymologiarum sive Originum libri XX*, ed. W.M. Lindsay, Oxford 1911, VII-XVI.

94 W. Porzig, *Die Rezensionen der Etymologiae des Isidorus von Sevilla*, in: *Hermes* 72 (1937) 129-170; B. Bischoff, *Die europäische Verbreitung der Werke Isidors von Sevilla*, in: idem, *Mittelalterliche Studien. Ausgewählte Aufsätze zur Schriftkunde und Literaturgeschichte*, I, Stuttgart 1966, 171-194; M. Reydellet, *La diffusion des Origines d'Isidore de Séville au haut Moyen Age*, in: *Mélanges d'Archéologie et d'Histoire publiés par l'École Française de Rome* 78 (1966) 383-437; and idem, *Compte rendu du Colloque isidorien tenu à l'Institut d'Études latines de l'Université de Paris, le 23 juin 1970*, in: *Revue d'histoire des textes* 2 (1972) 282-287.

95 *Acta Salmanticensia iussu Senatus Universitatis edita*, I (*Ser. Filosofía y Letras* 13/1), Salamanca 1958, 40f.

96 See M.C. Díaz y Díaz, *Problemas de algunos manuscritos hispánicos de las Etimologías de Isidoro de Sevilla*, in: *Festschrift Bernhard Bischoff zu seinem 65. Geburtstag*, dargebracht von Freunden, Kollegen und Schülern, edd. J. Autenrieth/F. Brunhölzl, Stuttgart 1971, 76.

Earlier, Charlemagne's questionnaire on baptism was mentioned. In many of the responses both the *De ecclesiasticis officiis* and *Etymologies* were used, and it is often difficult to know precisely which is being used as a source. But the important fact is that Isidorian texts provided the major source for these texts. In her Toronto thesis and in a forthcoming monumental study now in press Susan Keefe has studied these texts and their Isidorian content[97]. While only a few of the texts have been recognized and published in the past, Keefe has turned up nearly seventy separate tracts. What is even more extraordinary is the number of times Isidore's texts are used to describe the constituent parts of baptism. In her work Keefe has studied twenty-two parts of the Carolingian baptismal rite (of which thirteen parts use Isidore) and has listed how many of the nearly seventy texts use Isidore in their descriptions of individual parts of the baptismal process: catechumen (forty-five texts); competent (sixteen texts); renunciation of Satan (nineteen texts); exsufflation (fourteen texts); exorcism (thirty-one texts); salt (twenty-four texts); creed (twenty-nine texts); credulity (seven texts); baptism (thirty-four texts); anointing of head with chrism (one text); episcopal confirmation (thirteen texts); chrism (nineteen texts); and confession of faith through another (three texts). The enormous influence of Isidore in Carolingian times is only fully recognized when it is noted that many of these individual texts appear in dozens of manuscripts written in the ninth century[98]. In short, in the Carolingian explanation of the liturgy of baptism, Isidore was the source above all others that Carolingian writers used and cited.

Given the fact that the Adoptionist controversy had created doubts as to the orthodoxy of Spanish writers and the Old Spanish liturgy, one can rightly ask why Isidore's liturgical work continued to be used so heavily in Carolingian times. It was perhaps because of his stature as what Jacques Fontaine has recently called the *auctor reformationis* of the Carolingian period[99]. Even though his works had been cited by Elipandus as containing Adoptionist texts, Isidore was far too important a model for Carolingian authors to discard. In fact, at times, as Keefe has shown in her study of baptismal texts, they even attributed to the Sevillian doctor texts that were not his but which needed his authority.

The use by the Carolingians of texts attributed to but not necessarily by Isidore is seen in a text on the clerical officers and their duties clearly reflecting

---

97 See KEEFE (cf. n. 28).

98 This is very clear in the list of manuscripts (which will be augmented in her *Water and the Word* [cf. n. 28]) in KEEFE (cf. n. 27) 178-218.

99 J. FONTAINE, *La figure d'Isidore de Séville à l'époque carolingienne*, in: *L'Europe héritière* (cf. n. 12) 201.

the Old Spanish liturgical practice gradually being suppressed in the Carolingian realm. This text is a letter supposedly written to Leudefedus of Cordoba. The text came into the realm of Charlemagne as an addendum to the Leidrad manuscript of the *Collectio hispana systematica*, Paris, BN, 11709, mentioned earlier[100]. Despite its hierarchy of orders reflecting Spanish, not Romano-Gallican use and despite its description of Old Spanish elements of the Mass, such as the *laudes* or *preces*, the text was too important to be ignored by Carolingian canonists and was given extremely wide broadcast in the middle of the ninth century through incorporation in Pseudo-Isidorian manuscripts. Long after Carolingian times it was included in the major canonical collections of Burchard of Worms, Ivo of Chartres, and Gratian.

Tracts on the Mass, written in the Carolingian period describing not the Old Spanish but the Romano-Frankish Mass also used the works of Isidore and were indeed on occasion attributed to him[101]. But perhaps the most remarkable visually illustrated commentary on elements of the Mass was written in the Carolingian period and attributed to a bishop, Eldefonsus of Spain. This text, many times published in the past from an unidentified Vatican manuscript, has now been identified as an addendum to the ninth-century Corbie manuscript of the Pseudo-Isidorian *Collectio hispana gallica Augustodunensis*, Vatican, BAV Vat. lat. 1341, already mentioned in connection with conciliar *ordines* and the *Collectio hispana*. The tract also appears in two further tenth-century manuscripts whose provenances are in southern France, Paris, BN, lat. 2077 from Moissac, and BN, lat. 2855 from Le Puy, the latter written in part in Visigothic script and containing the genuine work of Ildefonsus of Toledo[102]. The text is in the form of a revelation on how eucharistic hosts should be made and distributed on the altar according to different patterns. In a way, these patterns are reminiscent of the distribution of eucharistic particles on the altar in the Old Spanish Mass, but the text as a whole, perhaps composed in Aquitaine, appears to be Carolingian.

To conclude, let us skip ahead to the late eleventh century and beyond to a situation parallel to that of the Carolingian period that has been the focus of our attention. Late in the eleventh century during the Reconquista of lands in the Iberian peninsula under the rule of the Muslims, an attempt similar to that during

---

100 Reynolds (cf. n. 79) 285f.

101 See idem, *Pseudonymous Liturgica in Early Medieval Canonical Collections*, in: *Fälschungen im Mittelalter.* Internationaler Kongreß der Monumenta Germaniae Historica, 16.–19. September 1986, II: *Gefälschte Rechtstexte, Der bestrafte Fälscher* (MGH *Schriften* 33/2), Hannover 1988, 71, n. 37.

102 *Ibid.*, 74.

the Carolingian period was made to suppress the Old Spanish – or by now, the Mozarabic – rite by imposing the Roman or Romano-Frankish. Although Pope Gregory VII did not specify Adoptionism by name in his attempts to impose the Roman rite, he did note dangers of »heretical depravity« in Spain and the »superstitio toletana«, and in a letter of 1081 to Alfonso VI mentioned that he had been informed by religious men that some language contrary to the orthodoxy of the Catholic faith existed in the Old Spanish rite[103].

The results of the eleventh-century attempts to suppress the Mozarabic liturgy were much the same as those of the Carolingian period. In some places, notably Toledo, the Mozarabic liturgy continued on – as it does today and in many locations in Spain – and manuscripts of that liturgy continued to be written in Visigothic script into the thirteenth century. In other places the Romano-Frankish rite was accepted, but Mozarabic prayers and ceremonies continued to be intruded into this rite, something very clear in ceremonies as popular as marriage or as ecclesiastical as clerical ordinations. In short, official attempts to suppress completely an indigenous liturgy as rich and beautiful as the Old Spanish or Mozarabic are bound to failure. Twelve hundred years after the Council of Frankfort in 794, churches, both Roman and otherwise, should remember the lessons and results of the condemnation of liturgical sources of what is judged to be a theological heresy and the attempts to suppress them in the worship of the church and her people.

---

103 See J.F. O'Callaghan, *The Integration of Christian Spain into Europe: The Role of Alfonso VI of León-Castile*, and R. Gonzálvez, *The Persistence of the Mozarabic Liturgy in Toledo after A.D. 1080*, in: *Santiago, Saint-Denis, and Saint Peter* (cf. n. 47) 105-113, 160-163.

III

BAPTISMAL RITE AND PASCHAL VIGIL IN TRANSITION IN MEDIEVAL SPAIN: A NEW TEXT IN VISIGOTHIC SCRIPT*

In the rich manuscript collection of the Biblioteca Nazionale Marciana in Venice there is a miscellany of fragments from medieval codices notable for the various scripts in which they are written. The códex, Marc. lat. XIV.232 (4257; olim XCIX.3), was originally in the private collection of Iacopo Morelli, the librarian of the Marciana from 1778 to 1819, and still bears his number 420. On one of the first paper folios prefacing the collection, there is a general description of contents: "Fragmenta Codicum Manuscriptorum Latinorum Graecorumque a seculo VII usque ad seculum XV a me Jacobo Morellio collecta — MDCCCXVII." Morelli either put together the disparate fragments or enlarged an existing collection. His reasons for doing so are not fully clear. Perhaps he intended the volume to be a specimen book of various scripts to help in dating and locating other codices.[1] Or perhaps he did so to conform to the motto written on another folio at the beginning of the volume, "Colligite fragmenta ne pereant." But whatever Morelli's reasons for making the collection, the codex is remarkable not only for the scripts in which the fragments are written but also for the texts they contain.

According to the *elenco* of users attached to the codex, numerous scholars over the years have consulted the fragments for everything from ancient

* The fragment was found on 6 July 1989, during an examination of the Beneventan-script fragments in the codex for the *Monumenta Liturgica Beneventana*, a programme supported by a grant from the Social Sciences and Humanities Research Council of Canada. For their help at various stages in the prepartion of this article I am grateful to James Grier, Miquel S. Gros i Pujol, Michel Huglo, Peter Jeffery, Susan Keefe, Thomas Kelly, Maria Teresa Ramos Rioja, and Barbara Shailor.

[1] Robert G. Babcock, "Two Unreported Uncial Fragments," *Scrittura e civiltà* 9 (1985): 299.

texts in Glagolitic script to texts in Greek.[2] Recently, several fragments in the miscellany that previously seem to have been neglected have attracted the attention of scholars in a variety of fields. First, two uncial fragments were discovered,[3] one a *membrum disiectum* belonging with a Stuttgart fragment, and they were duly entered by Bernhard Bischoff and Virginia Brown in their addenda to E. A. Lowe's *Codices Latini Antiquiores* as written in Italy, one in the seventh century and one in the seventh or eighth century.[4] Then a fragment of the major systematic canon law collection of the Merovingian church, the *Collectio Vetus Gallica*, was discovered.[5] This was of special importance because the text of the Council of Autun of ca. 670, hitherto known only in the *Collectio Vetus Gallica*, is in a fuller form in the Venice fragment than in any of the other manuscripts of the collection.[6] The Marciana codex further contains three parts of manuscripts, two bifolios and one a folio, written in the beautiful Beneventan script of south Italy.[7] One of them is especially notable because it was written not in southern Italy itself but across the Adriatic in Dalmatia and contains liturgical texts and lections in forms hitherto unknown.[8] Among the many other fragments is a badly mutilated one written in the Visigothic script of Spain, significant not only because manuscripts and fragments written in this script are rare, but also because the text shows the liturgical rite in Spain in transition from the Mozarabic or Old Spanish rite to the "Roman" or Romano-Gallican rite used especially in southern France.

The fragment in Visigothic script, originally a complete folio, has been ripped through the centre, and the pieces, the upper and lower halves of the original folio, now form two smaller folios joined together by a paper

[2] For the contents of the manuscript, see Pietro Zorzanello, *Catalogo dei codici latini della Biblioteca Nazionale Marciana di Venezia non compresi nel catalogo di G. Valentinelli*, vol. 3: Classe XIV (Trezzano, 1985), 364–83.

[3] Babcock, "Two Unreported Uncial Fragments," 299, notes the actual discovery by Francis Newton. It is not clear whether Morelli recognized these fragments as having been written in the seventh century, although fol. 29r has "saec. VI" written in the upper right-hand corner.

[4] Bernhard Bischoff and Virginia Brown, "Addenda to *Codices Latini Antiquiores*," *Mediaeval Studies* 47 (1985): 348, 361–62.

[5] See Roger E. Reynolds, "A Beneventan Monastic Excerptum from the *Collectio Vetus Gallica*," *Revue Bénédictine* 102 (1992): 303–4 n. 34.

[6] Hubert Mordek and Roger E. Reynolds, "Bischof Leodegar und das Konzil von Autun," in *Aus Archiven und Bibliotheken: Festschrift für Raymund Kottje zum 65. Geburtstag*, ed. Hubert Mordek, Freiburger Beiträge zur mittelalterlichen Geschichte 3 (Frankfurt/M, Berne, New York, Paris, 1992), 71–92 + 1 pl.

[7] Virginia Brown, "A Second New List of Beneventan Manuscripts (II)," *Mediaeval Studies* 50 (1988): 619–20.

[8] In a forthcoming article a junior associate at the Pontifical Institute of Mediaeval Studies will deal with these texts in Item 44 of the manuscript.

hinge. They bear the folio numbers 37 and (37). Joined together they enclose or are used as a "wrapper" around two other parchment fragments. These two fragments, numbered as folios 38 and 39, are also joined together by a paper hinge and are written in two different humanistic scripts.

The Visigothic-script folios have been trimmed, folded, and mutilated so that not all of the text is visible (see plates). The horizontal dimensions of fol. 37 are 200 mm. and 205 mm., and the vertical are 122 mm. and 140 mm. The horizontal dimensions of fol. (37) are 188 mm. and 180 mm., and the vertical are 159 mm. and 145 mm. The parchment is of medium quality and thickness. At the top of fol. 37 prickmarks, separated by 7 mm. and punctured from hair to flesh side, are visible for the marginal ruling, which is 51 mm. from the vertical edge of the folio. No prickmarks are visible on fol. (37). Lines for text and music ruled in drypoint are 8 mm. apart; fol. 37 has 16 lines visible and fol. (37) has 19 visible. If the upper and lower pieces of the complete folio are joined, the written space from the bottom rule to the headline of minims of the top line of text is 238 mm. Rubrics, in an orangish-red written both over and throughout the text, measure 3 mm. for minims, 5 mm. for ascenders, and 6 mm. for descenders. On fol. 37v there is one large initial uncial *E* for the *Exultet* coloured in green and orangish-red; its dimensions are 21 × 22 mm.

The script of the text, apparently written by a single hand in the late eleventh century, is in brown ink. Minims are 2 mm., ascenders 4.5 mm., and descenders 5 mm. Characteristics of the script point to an origin in northern Spain either in Castile or farther east. The script is not that of León, Silos, or the western section of northern Spain. It bears some features common with manuscripts produced in the Rioja.[9] Many of the letters, abbreviations, and words are similar to those in an undated and apparently as yet unattributed biblical manuscript, Madrid, Biblioteca Nacional 2, which Millares Carlo points out has Carolingian-script influence.[10] In the Venice fragment the double *f*s descend to sharp points, the final *t* sweeps up, *que* consists of a *q* with an almost full suprascript *s*, the loop of *g* is round and extends out with a tail swinging left, and *et* and *omnibus* are similar to those in Madrid. The *r* in *Israel* does not descend as far as the Madrid *r*, but the whole word is similar in Venice and Madrid. In several cases Madrid and Venice are different; for example, in Venice the down stroke of the *x* in *ex* is not the heavier stroke of Madrid, and the final *a* of *tua* or *custodia*

[9] I am grateful to Professor Barbara Shailor for her observations regarding the origins of the script.

[10] Agustín Millares Carlo, *Tratado de Paleografía Española*, 3d ed., vol. 1 (Madrid, 1983), 329.

circles around to meet the backstroke. In the Venice fragment there are occasional diacritical marks over words such as "ímperat" or "réserat." Abbreviations for Nomina Sacra are used for *Israel*, *spiritus*, *deus*, *dominus*, *domine*, and *Jesus Christus*. Plural forms are added in a small hand in brown ink above several words.

As for musical supports, there are no extra rules, clefs, or directs. The sizes of the letters for the musical text are 1.25 mm. for minims, 3 mm. for ascenders, and 4 mm. for descenders. Between some words of the musical text there are short connects in the orangish-red of the rubrics. The musical notation is Aquitanian.

Visigothic script, much like Beneventan script, was preeminently a liturgical one. Although there are far fewer Visigothic-script codices than Beneventan (there are less than 400 extant Visigothic items, as opposed to over 1600 in Beneventan),[11] they share with the Beneventan the fact that they are largely liturgical. But while Beneventan-script codices have a variety of liturgical rites and uses in them—Old Beneventan, Roman, Benedictine, and even Franciscan[12]—Visigothic-script codices generally have only Old Spanish-rite texts, with the exception of a few that have Roman or Romano-Gallican texts.[13] Our Venetian fragment can now be added to this latter category of extraordinary codices.

The liturgical text of our fragment is a portion of a baptismal rite; first, several texts for the making of a catechumen, followed by the *Exultet* sung at the paschal vigil. In the Old Spanish rite the ceremony for the making of catechumens had elements found elsewhere in western rites: the *consignatio*, exorcisms, *effetatio*, and *traditio symboli*. These were ceremonies that would

[11] See the repertory of items in Visigothic script in Millares Carlo, *Tratado*, 323–42; and Manuel C. Díaz y Díaz, *Códices visigóticos en la monarquía leonesa*, Colección Fuentes y Estudios de Historia Leonesa 31 (León, 1983), 299–480. The following may be added to this repertory: Cava, Archivio della Badia della Santissima Trinità 14; Lyons, Bibliothèque de la Ville 452 and 620; Paris, Bibliothèque Nationale lat. 2832 and 11709; and three newly reported fragments in Braga noted in Miquel S. Gros i Pujol, "Las tradiciones liturgicas medievales en el noroeste de la peninsula," in *IX Centenário da Dedicação da Sé de Braga. Congresso Internacional. Actas. Vol. III: Teologia do Templo e Liturgia Bracarense* (Braga, 1990), 111 n. 20, citing Avelino de Jesus da Costa, *A Biblioteca e o Tesouro da Sé de Braga nos séculos XV–XVIII* (Braga, 1984), particularly 279–80, 302–15, esp. est. 25, 31, 32.

[12] On rare Franciscan rubrics in Beneventan script, see Virginia Brown, "Boccaccio in Naples: The Beneventan Liturgical Palimpsest of the Laurentian Autographs (MSS. 29.8 and 33.31)," *Italia medioevale e umanistica* 34 (1991): 41–126 and plates 2–7.

[13] The following items in the repertory of Millares Carlo are Roman rite: 17, 18, 19, 22, 26, 27, 28, 31, 32, 34, 35, 38, 88, 106, 108, 116, 126, 202, 230, 230a, 276, 289, 298, and 318. On the Roman-rite manuscripts, see Jorge M. Pinell, "Los textos de la antigua liturgia hispánica: Fuentes para su estudio," *Estudios sobre la liturgia mozárabe* (Toledo, 1965), 154–57, esp. nos. 224–36, 242–45, 247–53, 255.

be used in the process of baptisms done at anytime of the year, and these were followed by the baptism itself, including chrismation, imposition of hands in the confirmation, and communion.[14] In the Old Spanish rite, baptisms might also be performed during the paschal vigil, and here again, there are elements like those of the Roman or Romano-Gallican rite. Lights and a paschal candle were blessed, once in a sacristy and then in the congregation. The latter blessing consisted of long poetic songs analogous to but not very like the *Exultet* of the Beneventan, Gallican, and finally the Roman paschal services.[15] As in the Roman rite, there followed in the Old Spanish paschal vigil a series of lessons and prayers, and then the baptismal ceremonies themselves, after which there was a eucharistic celebration.[16]

Despite the similarities of the Old Spanish and the Roman or Romano-Gallican baptismal ceremonies, there were distinctive features in the former that at times were frowned upon both inside and outside Spain, such as an omission of placing of salt on the tongue of the catechumen and a single rather than triple baptismal immersion.[17] Moreover, the formulae and prayers of the ceremonies, although resembling the Roman rite, were different in the Old Spanish liturgy.

The distinctive features of the Old Spanish liturgy, including baptism, led to a series of attempts to replace it with Roman practices. These attempts began as early as Carolingian times when an endeavour was made to replace the Old Spanish rite with its prayers considered—incorrectly—to be tainted with adoptionism.[18] In his attempt to introduce uniformity of liturgical practice in his realm, Charlemagne introduced a "pure" Roman sacramentary

[14] See, e.g., T. C. Akeley, *Christian Initiation in Spain c. 300–1100* (London, 1967), 123–58.

[15] On the various texts of the *Exultet*, see Jordi M. Pinell, "La benedicció del ciri pasqual i els seus textos," in *Liturgica* 2, Scripta et Documenta 10 (Montserrat, 1958), 1–119. On the *Exultet* in general, see the unedited thesis of Christopher Willcock, *La bénédiction du cierge pascal: Étude littéraire et théologique de ce rite* (Université de Paris-Sorbonne, Thèse de doctorat de IIIe Cycle en Sciences des religions, 1987); and more recently, Eric Palazzo, "Iconographie et liturgie: La mosaïque du baptistère de Kélibia (Tunisie)," *Archiv für Liturgiewissenschaft* 34 (1992): 102–20.

[16] Akeley, *Christian Initiation*, 159–79.

[17] See Susan Ann Keefe, *Water and the Word: Baptism and the Education of the Clergy in the Carolingian Empire: A Study of Texts and Manuscripts* (forthcoming).

[18] Miquel S. Gros, "La liturgie Narbonnaise témoin d'un changement rapide des rites liturgiques," in *Liturgie de l'église particulière et liturgie de l'église universelle (Conférences Saint-Serge 1975)* (Rome, 1976), 151; and Michel Gros, "Les Wisigoths et les liturgies occidentales," in *L'Europe héritière de l'Espagne wisigothique (Colloque international du C.N.R.S. tenu à la Fondation Singer-Polignac [Paris, 14–16 Mai 1990])*, ed. J. Fontaine and C. Pellistrandi, Collection de la Casa de Velázquez 35 (Madrid, 1992), 134.

in the form of the *Gregorian Sacramentary*. And it was this sacramentary which worked its way into the old Visigothic territories that Charlemagne and his successors controlled, especially the Narbonne region of southern France and the Spanish March in the Pyrenees and Catalonia.

Ironically, however, this "pure" Gregorian sacramentary introduced into the old Visigothic territories was itself a sacramentary supplemented by the Visigoth Witiza or Benedict of Aniane with a plethora of Old Spanish- and Gallican-rite texts. And it is in the supplement to this form of the *Gregorian Sacramentary* that one finds most of the texts in our Venetian Visigothic fragment. They are also texts found in many "Gallicanized" Roman Gelasian sacramentaries, called the *Gelasian Sacramentary of the Eighth Century* and represented in manuscripts found in southern France, the *Gellone Sacramentary* and the *Sacramentary of Angoulême*.[19] In short, the Roman rite of the supplemented *Gregorian Sacramentary*, sometimes called the *Gregorian of Aniane*, had become a Romano-Gallican or even a Romano-Gallican-Old Spanish rite.

With pressures by the Carolingian rulers to accept the Roman rite, the churches of Septimania, particularly in the Narbonne region and Catalonia, began to adopt elements of the rite as early as the ninth century. According to José Janini, this seems to have been done rather voluntarily,[20] but in light of Carolingian attempts to suppress Spanish adoptionism—reflected in the wording of Old Spanish-rite prayers—it is more likely that the acceptance of the Roman rite was the result of subtle pressures.[21] In any event, from the ninth century on, the adoption of the Roman rite took at least two forms, and these are reflected in manuscripts of Septimania and Catalonia. First, there could be outright acceptance of books of the new rite. Second, there was conscious mixing of the indigenous Old Spanish and Catalan rites with the Roman, seen, for example, in the ceremonies for clerical ordination in the codex Vic, Biblioteca Capitular 104.[22]

Beyond the Spanish March, acceptance of the Roman rite was far slower. It is often said that it was only in the second half of the eleventh century that this change took place, but the existence of a few earlier manuscripts

[19] *Liber Sacramentorum Gellonensis. Textus*, ed. A. Dumas, CCL 159 (Turnhout, 1981); *Liber Sacramentorum Engolismensis: Manuscrit B.N. Lat. 816. Le Sacramentaire Gélasien d'Angoulême*, ed. Patrick Saint-Roch, CCL 159 C (Turnhout, 1987).

[20] J. Janini, "Liturgia Romana," in *Diccionario de Historia Eclesiástica de España*, vol. 2 (Madrid, 1972), 1321.

[21] Gros, "La liturgie Narbonnaise," 151.

[22] Roger E. Reynolds, "The Ordination Rite in Medieval Spain: Hispanic, Roman, and Hybrid," in *Santiago, Saint-Denis, and Saint Peter: The Reception of the Roman Liturgy in León-Castile in 1080*, ed. Bernard F. Reilly (New York, 1985), 140–41.

with the Roman rite written in Visigothic script suggests that changes of rite or at least an acceptance of Roman-rite books and texts may have come somewhat earlier.[23] It is, of course, possible that scribes writing Visigothic script worked—as they indeed did—outside the confines of the Iberian peninsula,[24] but the presence in Spanish depositories of Visigothic-script codices of the tenth century containing Roman-rite texts suggests that the change of rites or acceptance of Roman-rite books was taking place gradually in Spain itself before the second half of the eleventh century.

In any event, the major transition in the liturgical rite from Old Spanish to Roman came about in the second half of the eleventh century particularly in Aragon and Castile with much bitterness, contention, and even violence. In Aragon the Benedictines brought Roman liturgy into such great monasteries as San Juan de la Peña; and the king, Sancho Ramrez, saw to it that the Roman rite was introduced into cathedral liturgy.[25] Resistance to the introduction of the Roman rite into Castile and León was far more substantial. Under the reforms of Pope Gregory VII, there was a concerted effort—aided especially by the Cluniacs of southern France—to impose the Roman rite in those regions. The forcible imposition of the rite is reflected in the well-known decision of the Synod of Burgos in 1080 to make the Roman rite official in the lands under King Alfonso VI of Castile.[26] A decade later at the Synod of Leon of 1090 the writing of liturgical books in the *littera Toletana* was forbidden.[27]

José Janini, in his magisterial article on the penetration of the Roman rite into Spain in the late eleventh and first half of the twelfth century, has traced the process especially as it is reflected in extant liturgical codices.[28]

23 Among these manuscripts are fragments of a breviary, Cambridge, University Library Add. 5905 (s. x–xi), and Roman homiliaries, Córdoba, Biblioteca Capitular 1 (72) (s. x, San Pedro de Berlangas), Toledo, Biblioteca del Cabildo 33.1 (s. ix–x), Coimbra, Arq. Catedral 2 (s. ix ex.), and Lleida, Arxiu de la Catedral 16 (ca. 1000), which, although written in a Caroline script, displays features of Visigothic script (see Josep Romá Barriga Planas, *El Sacramentari, Ritual i Pontifical de Roda: Cod. 16 de l'arxiu de la Catedral de Lleida, c. 1000* [Barcelona, 1975] 46, 49).

24 See Roger E. Reynolds, "The 'Isidorian' *Epistula ad Leudefredum:* An Early Medieval Epitome of the Clerical Duties," *Mediaeval Studies* 41 (1979): 277, and literature therein.

25 Janini, "Liturgia Romana," 1321.

26 See Joseph F. O'Callaghan, "The Integration of Christian Spain into Europe: The Role of Alfonso VI of León-Castile," in *Santiago, St.-Denis, and St. Peter*, 101–20.

27 Bernhard Bischoff, *Latin Palaeography: Antiquity and the Middle Ages*, trans. Dáibhí Ó Cróinín and David Ganz (Cambridge, 1990), 100, 126; and Antonio García y García, "Reforma gregoriana e idea de la 'Militia sancti Petri' en los reinos ibéricos," in *La Riforma gregoriana e l'Europa (Congresso Internazionale, Salerno, 20–25 maggio 1985)*, Studi Gregoriani 13 (Rome, 1989), 259–60, who deals with the issue as to whether the prohibition extended only to liturgical books or to all books.

28 Janini, "Liturgia Romana," 1321–23.

In Aragon the Romanization of the liturgy went through two phases. First, the Roman rite, with a few concessions to local sensibilities, was simply copied in Visigothic script; the well-known *Sacramentary of San Millan*, now Madrid, Real Academia de la Historia Aemil. 52, reflects this first phase. In the second phase, the Roman rite was copied in manuscripts not written in Visigothic script, and the texts in these are often closely related to Pyrenean and Catalan texts from the ninth century and beyond.

In Castile, where our Venetian Visigothic fragment appears to have been written, the degree of acceptance of the Roman rite is also reflected in extant manuscripts. Because of the fierce opposition to the Roman rite in Castile, it was at first necessary to have monks from southern France copy the rite in their own Carolingian script; an example of this is found in the *Sacramentary of Sahagún* (Madrid, Biblioteca Nacional Vitr. 20.8), a codex possibly taken by the Cluniac Bernard from Sahagún to Toledo when he was made bishop there.[29] On the other hand, there are several Castilian manuscripts, like our fragment, in which the Roman rite was simply copied in the beautiful and traditional Visigothic script of the region. Despite the Leonese condemnation in 1090 of the *littera Toletana* for liturgical manuscripts, the use of the script continued into the middle of the twelfth century. Beyond that, however, the use of the script is generally thought to have been discontinued, except in Toledo, where the Old Spanish liturgy continued in selected parishes.[30] In northern Spain the old Visigothic-script liturgical codices, now difficult to read in liturgical settings, were destroyed or even palimpsested so that precious parchment might be used to copy the newly introduced Roman rite; witness the *breviarium-missale* of Burgos, Archivo Capitular 18.[31]

It is in this context of the imposition of the Roman rite into northern Spain that our Venetian Visigothic fragment finds its place. The texts in our fragment clearly are Roman or Romano-Gallican, not Old Spanish. They can be found in a variety of sacramentaries going back to the eighth century from north of the Pyrenees. But more important, the texts of our fragment are also found in sacramentaries, missals, and pontificals written in Catalonia from the tenth to the twelfth centuries. In this respect the texts in the fragment are not unlike those in the second phase of the Aragonese changes,

[29] See Reynolds, "Ordination Rite," 144. On the relationship between Sahugún and Cluny, see Debra Hassig, "He will make alive your mortal Bodies: Cluniac Spirituality and the Tomb of Alfonso Ansurez," *Gesta* 30 (1991): 144–45.

[30] Ramón Gonzálvez, "The Persistence of the Mozarabic Liturgy in Toledo after A.D. 1080," in *Santiago, St.-Denis, and St. Peter*, 157–85, esp. 179 nn. 89–90.

[31] Millares Carlo, *Tratado*, 324, no. 28.

in which texts in the Aragonese manuscripts were clearly related to Catalan and Pyrenean texts.[32] Among the Catalan texts related to our fragment in Visigothic script are the *Pontifical of Roda*, the *Missale parvum of Vic*, the *Sacramentary of Ripoll*, the *Sacramentary of Osca*, the *Sacramentary-Antiphonal-Ritual of San Romá dels Bons*, and the *Pontifical of Vic*.[33]

Since there is only one mutilated folio containing our texts, it is not clear from what type of book the fragment came. It was probably not a plenary missal because a gospel reading in a full missal is at times inserted between our Texts 4 and 5, as is the case in the *Missale parvum of Vic*.[34] It is possible that our fragment was originally in a pontifical; texts similar to ours appear in such pontificals as the *Pontificale Romano-Germanicum* of the tenth century,[35] and in the pontificals of Roda and Vic. Nonetheless, the closest parallels in sequence, context, and rubrics appear in sacramentaries, and hence, it is probable that our fragment was detached from a sacramentary.

Since the ancient *Gelasian Sacramentary*, the *Gelasian Sacramentary of the Eighth Century*, and the supplemented *Gregorian Sacramentary* contain some of our texts, it is possible that our texts were drawn from a manuscript of one of these. But the closest parallels are in the Catalan manuscripts noted above, and thus it is with these that one should compare our texts, which are printed below.

The arrangement of our texts is interesting for several reasons. First, between Texts 5 and 7 there is the tradition of the Creed and Pater noster. The intrusion of these texts is not found in any of our Catalan texts. Moreover, the texts for the making of catechumens is followed immediately by the *Exultet* sung at the paschal vigil, implying that the texts of the making of catechumens were for the Lenten season. In other sources, including the Catalan, the *Exultet* text usually is found among texts presented earlier for the paschal vigil.[36] But occasionally it does follow the texts for the making of the catechumens. For example, in the *Missale parvum of Vic* a reference to the *Exultet* is made after the catechumen texts, but it refers the user back to the full text of the *Exultet* given before the catechumen texts.[37] In the *Sacramentary of Osca*, however, it is clear that the *Exultet* comes

[32] Janini, "Liturgia Romana," 1321–22.

[33] For the dates, origins, and editions (if existing), see the list of abbreviations below preceding the edition of our texts.

[34] MP 131.419.

[35] PRG 107.17–24.

[36] PRod 42.2, Rp 343.

[37] MP 134.479, MP 37.159.

after the catechumen texts.[38] Nonetheless, in all of these analogous sources there is more to the catechetical texts than appears in ours; that is, the *Exultet* in our fragment follows our catechumen texts, and one would have expected a more complete sequence of texts for the making of catechumens for either Lenten or non-Lenten use. In many manuscripts, going back to the eighth century, the *Exultet* is a "wandering" text not necessarily related to its near neighbours.[39] Hence, it is possible that the unexpected appearance of the *Exultet* immediately after our catechumen texts is another instance of an *Exultet* "dropped into" a sequence of other texts, although here clearly added to related texts.

As for the specific texts in our fragment, the first is an adjuration of Satan. Since our fragment has no rubric over this adjuration, it is not certain over whom the text is said. But it is almost certain that it was to be said over male catechumens (called *infantes*) because in other analogous texts this is the case; further, our Text 2 is said over a female catechumen, implying that Text 1 was said over a male.

Text 2 is a prayer said over a female catechumen followed by a malediction of the devil. In almost all other analogous sources this is the case, but strangely in the *Missale parvum of Vic* the prayer is one said over a male catechumen because it follows our Text 1 without specifying that it is said *super feminam.*[40]

Text 3, the exorcism of an unclean spirit and malediction of the devil, is found in the *Pontificale Romano-Germanicum*, which specifically directs that it be said after a priest signs with a cross the forehead of the male catechumen and places his hand on the catechumen's head. Presumably this was also the case in our text and analogous Catalan sources. Probably this would also have been the case with our Text 4, an exorcism and malediction over a female catechumen, although in the *Missale parvum of Vic* it is probably an alternative prayer for males since females are not specified in the rubric.

In the *Sacramentary of Ripoll* and the *Missale parvum of Vic* there follows at this point a gospel reading.[41] Elsewhere our Text 5 follows immediately. In the *Pontificale Romano-Germanicum* Text 5, a prayer for enlightenment

[38] See Alejandro Olivar, "El sacramentario aragonés ms. 815 de la Biblioteca de Montserrat," *Hispania Sacra* 17 (1964): 74; Olivar also notes that the material for the catechumens in Montserrat, Biblioteca del Monastir 72, pp. 142–49, precedes the *Benedictio cerei*, on pp. 151–54 of the manuscript (see Alexandre M. Olivar, "Serie de *benedictiones lectionum* en *cod. Montserratensis 72*," *Ephemerides liturgicae* 62 [1948]: 232).

[39] E.g., Hsp 1021 and SV 1.

[40] MP 131.416.

[41] Rp 377, MP 131.419.

and purity, is said first for males and then for females after the priest signs with a cross the foreheads of the catechumens and places his hand on their heads. In the Catalan analogues, however, the prayer is given only once, as it is in ours, and is specified for males and females.

At this point our text in the Visigothic fragment differs from all other analogues. The priest delivers the Creed and Pater noster to the catechumen. In the *Pontificale Romano-Germanicum* there is no delivery of the Pater noster, but much earlier in the ceremonies for the making of a catechumen the Creed was given.[42] In any event, the tradition of the Pater noster is a characteristic of the Roman rite.[43] In the Old Spanish rite there is no question as to the tradition of the Creed, but there is a question as to whether or not there was a tradition of the Pater noster.[44]

Where the tradition of the Creed and Pater noster stands in our Visigothic fragment, in both the *Sacramentary of Ripoll* and the *Missale Parvum of Vic* there is a rubric indicating that the following prayers and ceremonies are those taking place on the Saturday evening of the paschal vigil, and it is here that our Text 7, *Nec te latet Satanas*, falls. In the other Catalan analogues this prayer simply follows the prayer above said over males and females.

Following Text 7 there is the *effetatio* ceremony, and here our Text 8 is unique among the Catalan analogues, where the words of the *Effeta* are simply said as a group. In our text and the *Pontificale Romano-Germanicum*, however, the phrases are divided so that the first is said while touching the catechumen's right ear with spittle, the second while touching the nose, and the third while touching the left ear.

Immediately following the *effetatio* ceremony is the *Exultet*, Text 9, under a rubric specifying that it is to be sung on Holy Saturday. The absence of the *Exultet* in the Old Spanish rite and its somewhat unusual placement in our fragment have already been remarked upon, but several more comments must be made. First, despite the fact that the *Exultet* was lacking in the Old Spanish rite, it appears in many of our Catalan analogues.[45] Moreover, it also appears in several other nearly contemporary manuscripts from Castile and other areas where Visigothic script was written. Further, in these manuscripts the notation is not the Mozarabic notation one might expect in these areas—although it must be remembered that our text of the *Exultet* was not used in the Old Spanish rite where one finds Mozarabic

42 PRG 107.3.

43 José Pijuan, *La liturgia bautismal en la España romano-visigoda* (Toledo, 1981), 57.

44 Ibid., 51–52.

45 PRod 42.2, SV 1, MP 134.479, Rp 343, Mont, Mt.

notation most often—but in the Aquitanian notation of southern France. Among these manuscripts are the well-known plenary Roman-rite *Missal of San Millan de la Cogolla* of the last third of the eleventh century, Madrid, Real Academia de la Historia Aemil. 18, itself written in Visigothic script.[46] Then, it appears in the twelfth-century *Missal of Silos*, Salamanca, Biblioteca Universitaria 2637.[47] In our fragment there is nothing especially remarkable about the text of the *Exultet*, but the melody, which resembles Huglo's "type 2" melody found in manuscripts from the west of France,[48] appears to be different from its Castilian analogues where the Aquitanian notation is used for the *Exultet*.[49]

"Colligite fragmenta ne pereant" is the well-known saw Morelli added as a preface to the various fragments in the Venetian manuscript described in this paper. Morelli probably recognized that his fragment in a Visigothic hand, mutilated and scrappy as it was, was nonetheless significant for the script in which it was written; there are, after all, far fewer extant codices in Visigothic script than those of other early medieval "national" scripts such as Beneventan. But probably unknown to Morelli were the unusual liturgical features in the text: a Romano-Gallican baptismal and paschal text written not in Carolingian script but in the ancient script generally used for the Visigothic liturgy; the text of the paschal *Exultet*, unknown in the ancient Visigothic and Mozarabic liturgies, here musically noted in Aquitanian style and with a melody hitherto unknown; and parts of baptismal ceremonies unique among medieval baptismal liturgies. In short, the Venetian Morelli in gathering this fragment into his collection preserved one of the most unusual and precious pieces of evidence documenting the transition in the late eleventh century from the Old Spanish/Mozarabic to the Romano-Gallican rite, mandated by Rome and brought to Spain by the southern French clerics and monks whose own liturgical practices would all but submerge the ancient rites of the Iberian peninsula.

In the presentation below of the individual texts of our fragment, numbers have been assigned to each in square brackets; abbreviations have been

[46] Fol. 123v.

[47] Fols. 95v–96r; on this codex, see Reynolds, "Ordination Rite," 144. An unnoted version of the *Exultet* is found in one of the recently reported fragments from Braga (Avelino de Jesus da Costa, *A Biblioteca*, esp. 315, est. 32). This fragment, although written in a Carolingian hand, has Visigothic-script symptoms.

[48] Michel Huglo, "Exultet," in *The New Grove Dictionary of Music and Musicians* (London, 1980), 6:336.

[49] For this information I am grateful to Maria Teresa Ramos Rioja, who has compared the notation with that of the *Exultet* in the *Missal of San Millan* and the *Missal of Silos*.

expanded; missing or illegible letters, words, and phrases are inserted between pointed brackets; and italics are used for the rubrical directions and rubricized letters, words, or phrases. The interlinear plural forms for words in the manuscript have not been added. The following abbreviations are for analogous (~ = similar) texts:

Va *Gelasian Sacramentary*, Vatican City, Biblioteca Apostolica Vaticana Reg. lat. 316 (s. viii med., Chelles); ed. Leo Cunibert Mohlberg, Leo Eizenhöfer, Petrus Siffrin, *Liber sacramentorum romanae aeclesiae ordinis anni circuli (Cod. Vat. Reg. lat. 316/Paris Bibl. Nat. 7193, 41/56) (Sacramentarium Gelasianum)*, Rerum ecclesiasticarum documenta, ser. maior, fontes 4 (Rome, 1960).

Ge *Gellone Sacramentary*, Paris, Bibliothèque Nationale lat. 12048 (s. viii ex., Meaux; at Gellone by s. ix); ed. A. Dumas, *Liber Sacramentorum Gellonensis. Textus*, CCL 159 (Turnhout, 1981).

En *Sacramentary of Angoulême*, Paris, Bibliothèque Nationale lat. 816 (s. viii/ix, prob. south of Loire); ed. Patrick Saint-Roch, *Liber Sacramentorum Engolismensis: Manuscrit B.N. Lat. 816. Le Sacramentaire Gélasien d'Angoulême*, CCL 159 C (Turnhout, 1987).

Hsp Supplemented *Sacramentarium Hadrianum;* ed. Jean Deshusses, *Le Sacramentaire Grégorien: Ses principales formes d'après les plus anciens manuscrits*, vol. 1, Spicilegium Friburgense 16 (Fribourg/S, 1971).

PRG *Pontificale Romano-Germanicum;* ed. Cyrille Vogel and Reinhard Elze, *Le Pontifical romano-germanique du dixième siècle: Le texte*, 2 vols., Studi e testi 226–27 (Vatican City, 1963).

PRod *Pontifical of Roda*, Lleida, Arxiu de la Catedral 16 (ca. 1000, Catalonia, vicin. Urgel-Roda?); ed. Josep Romá Barriga Planas, *El Sacramentari, Ritual i Pontifical de Roda: Cod. 16 de l'arxiu de la Catedral de Lleida, c. 1000* (Barcelona, 1975).

MP *Missale parvum of Vic*, Vic, Biblioteca Capitular 71 [CXIX] (s. xi$^{4/4}$, Ripoll); ed. Miquel S. Gros, "El 'Missale parvum' de Vic," *Hispania Sacra* 21 (1968): 313–77.

Rp *Sacramentary of Ripoll*, Vic, Biblioteca Capitular 67 (s. xi, Ripoll); ed. Alejandro Olivar, *Sacramentarium Rivipullense*, Monumenta Hispaniae Sacra, ser. lit. 7 (Madrid-Barcelona, 1964).

SV *Sacramentary of Vic*, Vic, Biblioteca Capitular 66 [XLVIII] (1038, Vic); ed. Alejandro Olivar, *El Sacramentario de Vich. Estudio y Edición*, Monumenta Hispaniae Sacra, ser. lit. 4 (Barcelona, 1953).

Mont *Sacramentary-Antiphony-Ritual of San Romá dels Bons*, Montserrat, Biblioteca del Monastir 72 (s. xii, San Romá dels Bons); see Alexandre M. Olivar, "Serie de *benedictiones lectionum* en *cod. Montserratensis 72*," *Ephemerides liturgicae* 62 (1948): 230–34; analogues as reported in PRod.

Vc *Pontifical of Vic*, Vic, Biblioteca Capitular 104 (CV) (s. xi/xii, Vic); see Miquel S. Gros, "Las ordines sagradas del pontifical ms. 104 (CV) de la

Bib. Cap. de Vic," *Hispania Sacra* 17 (1964): 99–133; analogues as reported in PRod.

Mt *Sacramentary of Osca*, Montserrat, Biblioteca del Monastir 815 (s. xi–xii, perhaps San Victoria d'Asan); see Alejandro Olivar, "El sacramentario aragonés ms. 815 de la Biblioteca de Montserrat," *Hispania Sacra* 17 (1964): 61–97; and "Los textos raros o hasta ahora inéditos del sacramentario ms. 815 de Montserrat," *Hispania Sacra* 18 (1965): 365–83; analogues as reported in PRod.

VENICE, BIBLIOTECA NAZIONALE MARCIANA
Marc. lat. XIV.232 (4257), fol. 37–(37)

[fol. 37r]

[1] <saecu>lo tuo et beate inmortalitatis victuro. Da igitur honorem <advenien>ti spiritu sancto, qui ex summa caeli arce descendens , perturbatis frau<dibus tuis,> divino fonte purgatum pectus, id est sanctificatum deo templum et <habitum> proficiat. Et ab omnibus penitus noxiis preteritorum criminum <liberatus> servus dei, gratias perhenni deo referat semper, et benedicat nomen <eius sanctum, in saecul>a saeculorum. AMEN.

Va 294, Ge 405, En 694, Hsp 1075, PRG 107.17, PRod 43.14, MP 131.415, Rp 373, Mont, Vc, Mt

Super feminam

[2] <Deus abraham, deu>s isaac, deus iacob, deus qui tribus israhel de egiptia servitute <liberatas, per> moysen famulum tuum de custodia mandatorum tuorum in <deserto m>onuisti, et susannam de falso crimine liberasti, te supplices <deprecam>ur domine, ut liberes et hanc famulam tuam, il., et perducere <eam digne>ris ad gratiam baptismi tui. *E*rgo maledicte.

Va 295, Ge 406, En 695, Hsp 1076, PRod 43.15, MP 131.416, Rp 374, Mont, Vc, Mt

Super masculum

[3] <Exorcizo> te inmunde spiritus in nomine patris et filii et spiritus sancti, ut <exeas et rec>edas ab hoc famulo dei, il. Ipse enim tibi imperat male<dicte damna>te, qui pedibus super mare ambulavit, et petro mergenti <dexteram p>orrexit. *E*rgo maledicte diabole.

Va 296, Ge 407, En 696, Hsp 1077, PRG 107.19, PRod 43.16, MP 131.417, Rp 375, Mont, Vc, Mt

Super fe<minam>

[4] <Exorcizo> te inmunde spiritus [fol. (37)v] per patrem et filium et spiritum sanctum, ut exeas et <recedas ab hac f>amula dei, ill. Ipse enim tibi imperat maledicte <damnate, q>ui ceco nato oculos aperuit, et quatriduanum lazarum <de mon>umento suscitavit. *E*rgo maledicte.

Va 297, Ge 408, En 697, Hsp 1078, PRG 107.20, PRod 43.17, MP 131.418, Rp 376, Mont, Mt

Super masculum vel feminam

[5] <Aeternam> ac iustissimam pietatem tuam deprecor domine <sancte pa>ter omnipotens aeterne deus luminis et veritatis, super hunc famulum tuum, ill., ut <digne>ris eum illuminare lumine intelligentiae tuae. Munda eum <et sanctifica. D>a ei scientiam veram, ut dignus efficiatur accedere ad <gratiam bap>tismi tui. Teneat firmam spem, consilium rectum, doctrinam <sanctam, ut a>ptus sit ad percipiendam gratiam baptismi tui. Per eumdem.

Va 298, Ge 410, En 700, Hsp 1079, PRG 107.21, PRod 43.18, MP 131.420, Rp 378, Mont, Mt

<Dic>at sacerdos super caput infantis simbolum fidei et oratio dominica.

[6] <Credo in unum> deum. *P*ater noster qui es.

[7] <Nec te l>atet sathanas imi<n>ere tibi penas, <inminere> tibi tormenta, <in>minere tibi diem iudicii, diem supplicii <sempiterni, di>em qui venturus est velut clibanus ardens, in quo tibi <atque uni>versis angelis tuis aeternus veniet interitus. Proinde dam<nate atque> damnande, da honorem deo vivo et vero, da honorem <iesu christo fi>lio eius et spiritui sancto paraclito, in cuius nomine atque virtute [fol. 37v] praecip<io> tibi quicumque es spiritus inmunde, <ut exeas> e<t reced>as ab hoc <famulo> dei, <qu>em hodie deus et dominus noster iesus christus ad suam sanctam gratia<m et ben>edictio<nem> fontemque baptismat<is d>ono voca<r>e <dignat>us est, ut f<iat> eius t<emplum per> aquam regenerationis <in remis>sionem <omnium> pe<ccatorum.> In nomine eiusdem domini nostri iesu christi, qui venturus est iudic<are. . . .>

~ Va 419, ~ Ge 668, ~ En 725, ~ Hsp 1080, ~ PRG 107.23, ~ PRod 43.19, ~ MP 131.421, ~ Rp 379, Vc, Mt

Tunc accipiat sacerdos sputo et dicat ad au<rem dexteram>.

[8] *E*ffeta quod est adaperire. *R. E*ffeta.

Ad nares <In odorem> suavitatis. *R. E*<ffe>ta.
*Ad aurem <sinistram> T*u <autem> effugare <dia>bole appropinqua<bit enim> iudic<ium> dei.

PRG 107.24

SABBATO SANCTO BENEDICTIO CEREI PASCHALI

[9] *E*xultet iam angel<ica turba ce>lor<um, exul>tent div<ina mys>teria, <et pro ta>n<ti reg>is <vict>oria tuba intonet salutaris. *G*audeat se tellus tant<is inradiata> [fol. (37)r] fulgoribus et ae<terni reg>[fol. 37v]is splendore illustrata, tot[fol. (37)r]<ius orbis se sentiat amisi>sse cal<iginem>. Letetur et mater ecclesia <tanti luminis adornat>a fulgoribus <et magnis> populorum vocibus hec aula resultet. Qua<prop>ter <adst>an<tes vos fratr>es carissimi, ad tam <m>iram sancti <huius luminis> claritatem, una mecum quaeso dei omnipotentis mise<ricordiam invocate, ut qui m>e non <meis> m<eriti>s intra levitarum numerum <dignatus est adgregare,> luminis <sui> g<ratia infundente cerei> huius l<audem implere perficiat. Per dominum nostrum iesum christum filium suum cum quo vivit et regnat in unitate spiritus sancti, per omnia saecula saeculorum. R. Amen.> *D*ominus vobiscum. *E*t cum <spiritu tuo. Sursum cor>da. *R.* H<abemus ad dominum.> *G*<ratia>s ag<amus domino deo nostro. R.> *D*ignum et iustum.

Hsp 1021, PRG 99.347, PRod 42.2, [SV 1, without this introductory text of the *Exultet*], MP 134.479, Rp 343, Mont, Mt

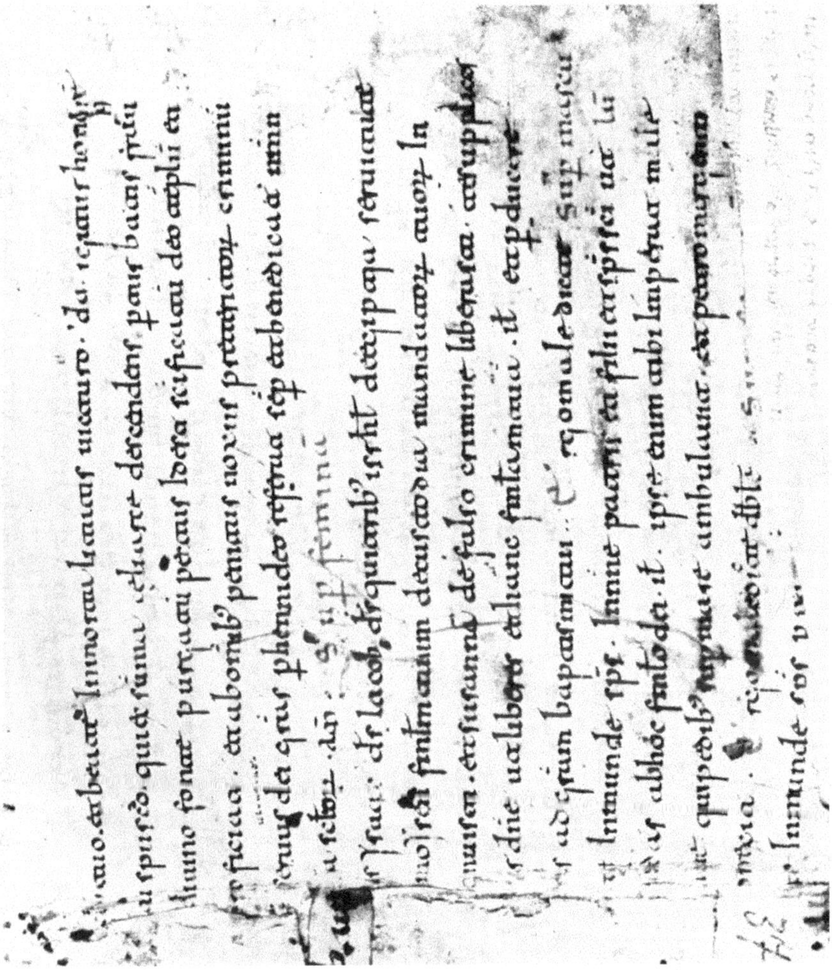

1. Venice, Biblioteca Nazionale Marciana Marc. lat. XIV.232 (4257; olim XCIX.3), fol. 37r.

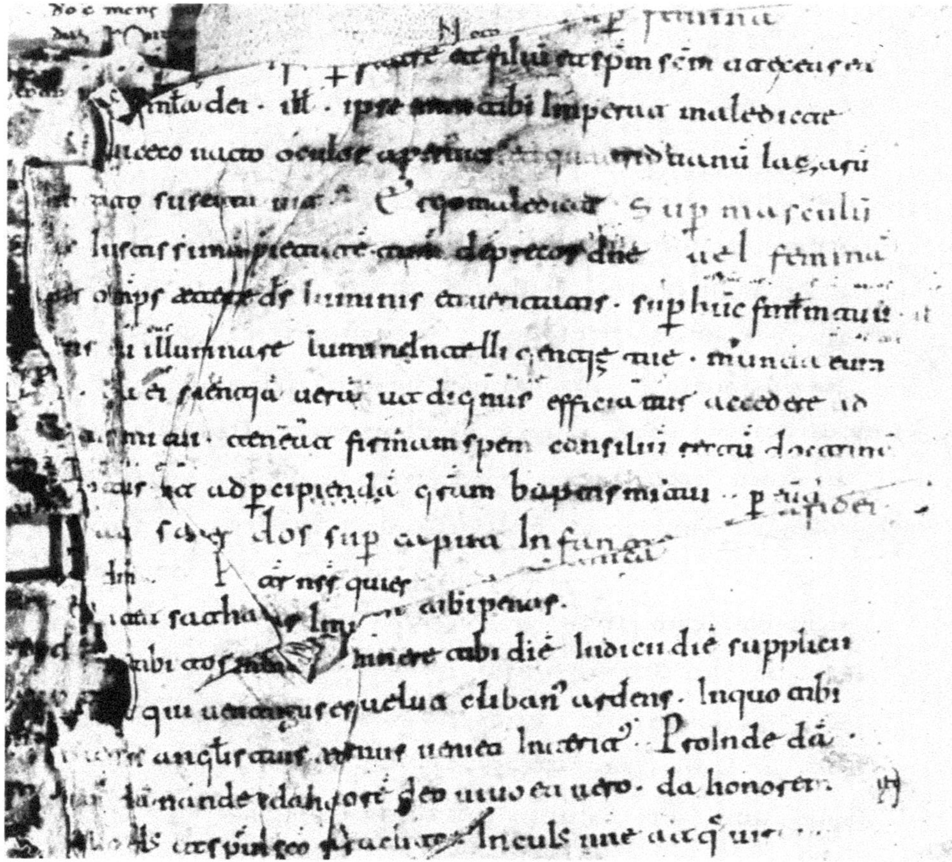

2. Venice, Biblioteca Nazionale Marciana Marc. lat. XIV.232 (4257; olim XCIX.3), fol. (37)v.

3. Venice, Biblioteca Nazionale Marciana Marc. lat. XIV.232 (4257; olim XCIX.3), fol. 37v.

4. Venice, Biblioteca Nazionale Marciana Marc. lat. XIV.232 (4257; olim XCIX.3), fol. (37)r.

VISIGOTHIC-SCRIPT REMAINS OF A PANDECT BIBLE AND THE *COLLECTIO CANONUM HISPANA* IN LUCCA*

ONE of the most famous and important extant early medieval bibles is written in Visigothic script, the so-called Danila Bible now at Cava, Archivio della Badia della Santissima Trinità 1. Written in three columns in the ninth century and bearing later annotations in Beneventan script, it is regarded as one of the great pandect Bibles produced on the Iberian peninsula in the early Middle Ages.[1] How it arrived at Cava is not entirely clear, but it is only one of a number of Visigothic-script manuscripts on the Italian peninsula in the early Middle Ages. Among the other early examples is the renowned *Orationale* of Verona, Biblioteca Capitolare LXXXIX, which was written in the late seventh century in Tarragona and travelled through Sardinia and eventually to Verona.[2] Another famous Italian early manuscript containing Visigothic script is in Lucca: MS 490 of the Biblioteca Capitolare Feliniani in Lucca is well known to palaeographers for its varieties of late eighth-century scripts, including Visigothic. Thus, Lucca seems to have been a location where not only codices in Beneventan script came to rest, but also those in Visigothic.

In May and June of 1994, during a search in the Archivio di Stato in Lucca for Beneventan-script remains used as covers or supports for archival material, four large fragments came to light of what must have been a glorious three-column pandect Bible written in southern Spain in

* These fragments, discovered by Virginia Brown during research for the project Monumenta Liturgica Beneventana in July 1993 and June 1994, would not have come to light without the help of dott. Giorgio Tori, Director of the Archivio di Stato, Lucca, who has granted permission to publish them. The interest and generosity of dott. Tori and his staff is here gratefully acknowledged.

1 See Agustín Millares Carlo, *Tratado de Paleografía Española, I: Texto,* 3d ed. (Madrid, 1983), 326; and E. A. Loew, *The Beneventan Script: A History of the South Italian Minuscule,* Second edition prepared and enlarged by Virginia Brown, vol. 2: *Hand List of Beneventan MSS.*, Sussidi eruditi 34 (Rome, 1980), 30. For the date and later history of this manuscript, see "The Codex Cavensis: New Light on its Later History," in E. A. Loew, *Palaeographical Papers 1907–1965,* ed. Ludwig Bieler, 2 vols. (Oxford, 1972), 2:335–41.

2 See, e.g., Millares Carlo, *Tradado,* 342, no. 345; and Klaus Gamber, *Codices liturgici latini antiquiores* (Fribourg/S, 1968), no. 330.

the late eighth or early ninth century in Visigothic script. These fragments, some of which were attached to archival material in May 1994, have since June of 1994 been separated, placed in a single busta labelled "Codex 517: Frammenti in Visigotica, 3 col. sec. ix–x," and assigned the numbers 1 through 4 by the Archivist.

Fragment 1 was removed from a volume, "Potesta di Lucca 1591," so noted in pencil on the verso. At the top of the recto is written "Cotaib(/) E 1543." The folio, which is cropped in the third column (see plate I), measures 295 × 281 (263 × 247) mm. The fine-quality parchment is of a medium thickness. The flesh side (verso) was outside when used as an archival cover; the hair side is very yellowed with a stain in the upper center. The folio bears prickmarks (holes, not slits) on its hair side between the second and third columns and was ruled in drypoint on the hair side. The measurements of the vertical rules for columns from left to right are 6, 23, 5, 62, 21.5, 6, and 53 mm. apart. The horizontal ruling is across the folio but stops at the inner rule of the outside margin. On this folio there are forty-three written lines, 7 mm. apart. On the recto, the word "Incipit" is in red with blue infill, and the word "Epistula" is in green. These were originally ca. 13 mm. high and were positioned in the columns. Measuring 2.5 mm. are the rubrics over the columns. The word "Argumentum" is in red and "Hebrei" in red over a yellow *H.* The numbers of the *capitulationes* are in alternating green and red with opposing headings in red and green. The large majuscule letters of 13 mm. are in the left margin, and the chapter numbers are in red with dark green, yellow, or blue. The general script, in brown ink with minims of 1.5 mm, and ascenders and descenders of 5 mm., was the work of one scribe, although the *Argumentum* in a smaller script may suggest a second. There are several contemporary intercolumnar annotations. The text begins with the *capitulationes* of the Book of Hebrews and proceeds from Hebrews 1:1 through 7:4.

Fragment 2 formerly served as a loose cover wrapped around "Potesta di Lucca 1698," pencilled on fol. 1v of the fragment, although the date of the volume of records was 1495. The folio, which is cropped off in the third column and at the bottom, measures 422 × 284 (392 × 244) mm. Binding holes are visible on the folio and from top to bottom measure 17, 49, 59, 77, 81, 116, 137, 207, 215, 227, 292, 306, 339, 372, and 422 mm. From flesh to hair side the folio bears 63 vertical prickmarks (holes) in the intercolumnar space between the second and third columns for horizontal ruling 7 mm. apart. Marginal ruling, display scripts, and general script are virtually the same as Fragment 1. The text runs from James 1:19 to 1 Peter 1:7, including the *capitulationes* of 1 Peter.

Fragment 3, labelled as such on the verso side and formerly serving as a cover for "Curia de Fondaco 1587," is a full bifolium measuring 525 × 758 mm. (with a writing space on each folio of 400 × 262 mm.). Since it was used as an archival cover, it was folded and bears stitch marks at the fold from top to bottom measuring 33, 70, 143, 223, 303, 380, 460, and 490 mm. The sequence of the texts indicates that the original folding of the bifolium was the reverse of its present folding. Rectangular pieces have been cut out of the second folio. Vertical prickmarks (holes), 7 mm. apart, made from hair side to flesh side for horizontal ruling are visible between the first and second columns on the left folio and second and third on the right. Prickmarks (holes) for vertical ruling 14 mm. from the top of the bifolium and 21 mm. above the bottom are visible and measure from left to right (fol. 1) 82, 88, 148, 154, 176, 183, 245, 251, 273, 279, 341, 347, and (fol. 2) 415, 421, four missing because of cut in parchment (ca. 483, ca. 489, ca. 512, ca. 517), 578, 584, 605, 611, 671, and 677 mm. Although the vertical prickmarks are for the entire bifolium, the horizontal ruling of sixty-four lines, beginning 44 mm. below the top of the bifolium and ending 81 mm. above the bottom, was made for a single folio at a time; that is, they go to the inner margins of the left and right columns on a single folio but not through the center of the bifolium. The display scripts and general script are like those of Fragments 1 and 2. On fol. 2v is a correction in Visigothic script, and between columns 2 and 3 "almas" is written four times in a later cursive hand. On fol. 1r between columns 1 and 2 are several numbers and a cursive text including "1543 CT Manu $ ADT" and "Antonii de Turribus . . . anni 1543, 1655." The text runs from the prologue to Esther and Esther 1:1 through 4:6 (on fol. 2r–v) and from Wisdom 18:1–2 through the *capitulationes* of Ecclesiasticus (on fol. 1r–v).

Fragment 4 was detached from a document, "Vicario per commissario di Camaiore atti civile / 519," although the date of the contents of the volume is 1543. On the hair side in a late hand is "Curie Camaiorii annorum MDXXXXIII S Io Alusii Cannt"; then in the middle is the subscription "Ioannis Asoisii Antbarini 2 diem 1543"; again in the third column is "1655" in different ink; also on fol. 1v in the center is a large "1543." Although as of June 1994 they were no longer with the fragment, in May 1994 there were pasted to the verso or hair side of the folio two paper labels and two pastedowns in Carolingian script. The folio measures 519 × 365 (399 × 280) mm. with a triangular tear on the right side of fol. 1r. The pricking, ruling, and layout are like those of the bifolium of Fragment 3, the only difference being that in the intercolumnar space are written the Hebrew words "Aleth, Tau," etc. alternating in red and green. In the display script yellow wash has been added to the red, blue, and green. Fol. 1v has a large *E* (29 × 29 mm.) with geometric designs and a bird's-head upper extension. Otherwise, display scripts and general script are like those of the other fragments. The text runs from Lamentations 4:14 through the prologue to Ezekiel and Ezekiel 1:1 through 1:10

Although the fragments were assigned a ninth- or tenth-century date in Lucca, they are indeed earlier. Barbara Shailor has suggested that they were likely written in Toledo or its environs in the late eighth or early ninth century. Moreover, she has pointed out that they are in all respects like a folio bearing Joshua 21:31 through 22:33 now in New York, Columbia University Plimpton 27, which E. A. Lowe dated to the late eighth or early ninth century and placed in the same scriptorium as the famous pandect Vulgate *Codex Toletanus* (Madrid, Biblioteca Nacional Vitr. 13.1 [Tol. 2.1]), the *Etymologies* of Isidore of Seville (El Escorial, Real Biblioteca de San Lorenzo &.I.14), and the *Chronicon* of Isidore Pacensis (London, British Library Egerton 1934 + Madrid, Biblioteca de la Real Academia de la Historia 81).[3] A comparison of the number of columns, lines and bounding lines, punctuation, abbreviations, ink, and other features in the Plimpton and Lucca leaves shows remarkable similarities and confirms Shailor's suggestion.[4] Moreover, the fact that the Plimpton folio has entries in an Italian hand of the sixteenth or seventeenth century ("Procissi de Lorenzi <?> con lazari Ar<nolfino?> <?> Pura Produita presso Vannettio <?> et <?>), as do the Lucca folios, strongly suggests that they were at one time from the same Bible. Consuelo Dutschke, who is currently compiling a catalogue of the Columbia University medieval and Renaissance manuscripts, has further pointed out that the Columbia folio was given the University in 1936 by George Plimpton, who had close connections with a certain Giuseppe Martini of Lucca.[5]

Whether all of the manuscripts and leaves connected by Lowe to the same scriptorium are indeed from Toledo or farther south, perhaps Cordóba, and whether they are all to be dated to the late eighth or early ninth century, as Lowe argued, has been disputed by a number of Spanish scholars.[6] Díaz y Díaz, while accepting Lowe's dating for most of the

[3] See E. A. Lowe, *Codices Latini Antiquiores,* vol. 11 (Oxford, 1966), no. 1654; and "On the Date of the Codex Toletanus," in Loew, *Palaeographical Papers 1907–1965* 1:135–38.

[4] I am very grateful to Professor Shailor for her suggestions and for her connection of the Lucca leaves and the Plimpton leaf.

[5] I am grateful to Dr. Dutschke for this information.

[6] On the manuscripts and their dating, and especially on Plimpton 27, see Agustín Millares Carlo, "Manuscritos visigóticos: Notas bibliográficas," *Hispania sacra* 14 (1961): 337–444, esp. 393; Manuel C. Díaz y Díaz, "Problemas de algunos manuscritos hispánicos de las Etimologías de Isidoro de Sevilla," in *Festschrift Bernhard Bischoff zu seinem 65. Geburtstag,* ed. Johanne

manuscripts, points out that the pricking system in both Plimpton 27 and the Escorial Isidore was common in a number of conservative scriptoria in the ninth and tenth centuries; further, Díaz has contested Lowe's dating of the *Codex Toletanus,* arguing that it was written ca. 950 and retained a number of archaic codicological and palaeographical features, probably out of reverence for the text of the Bible.[7] In any event, the newly found Lucca leaves together with the Plimpton leaf are a significant addition to a small group of great early Spanish pandect Bibles in Visigothic script.

* * *

Since it was compiled in the seventh century, the national collection of canon law on the Iberian peninsula has been the *Collectio canonum hispana.* This large collection of the canons of oriental, African, Gallican, and Spanish councils and the decrees of popes was painstakingly copied on parchment throughout the Middle Ages and continued to be so well into the eighteenth century.[8] Of the twenty-one surviving early medieval manuscripts and fragments of the collection hitherto reported,[9] nine were written in Visigothic script and are all still kept in Spanish depositories. Outside Spain other manuscripts of the *Hispana,* not written in Visigothic script, circulated widely and were modified to conform to the needs of regions and times. By the eighth century there was in circulation in Frankish territories the so-called *Collectio hispana gallica.* This collection was modified in the mid-ninth century by the Pseudo-Isidorian atelier to form the *Collectio hispana gallica Augustodunensis,* named for the city whence the first known manuscript of this version was found.[10] Inserted into the manuscripts of the Pseudo-Isidorian Decretals, this version had wide

Autenrieth and Franz Brunhölzl (Stuttgart, 1971), 70–80, esp. 74; Millares Carlo, *Tratado,* 135 and 335, no. 229; and Jorge M. Pinell, "Los textos de la antigua liturgia hispánica: Fuentes para su estudio," in *Estudios sobre la liturgia mozárabe* (Toledo 1965), 115, esp. no. 17, who calls the Plimpton folio a *Commicus.*

[7] Díaz y Díaz, "Problemas," 74.

[8] See Gonzalo Martínez Díez, *La colección canónica Hispana,* vol. 1, Monumenta Hispaniae Sacra, Serie canónica 1 (Madrid, 1966), 11–13.

[9] To be added to the manuscripts listed by Martínez Díez, ibid., 11 and 104–46, are Florence, Biblioteca Medicea Laurenziana Ashb. 1554 (s. XII$^{1/2}$) [excerpts]; Florence, Biblioteca Riccardiana 258 (s. XII) [excerpts]; Oxford, Bodleian Library Holkham misc. 19 (s. XII in.; Tuscany, perhaps Pistoia); and Paris, Bibliothèque Nationale lat. 4280 (s. XII) [excerpts].

[10] See Horst Fuhrmann, *Einfluß und Verbreitung der pseudoisidorischen Fälschungen von ihrem Auftauchen bis in die neuere Zeit,* Schriften der MGH 24.1 (Stuttgart, 1972), 151.

broadcast throughout the Middle Ages.[11] Another form of the *Hispana* was compiled in Spain, one in which the canons of the historically arranged *Hispana* were ordered according to topic. This *Collectio hispana systematica* is found largely in manuscripts written in Carolingian script in France, although two from ninth-century Lyons with its large population of Visigothic emigrés have Visigothic-script annotations; another manuscript of this collection in a slightly different form was written in Arabic in the eleventh century and has Visigothic annotations.[12]

Antedating these rather full collections of the *Hispana* and *Hispana systematica* are other Spanish canon law compilations that had wide diffusion in northern and central Italy at least from the eighth century and probably before as Spanish travellers, then emigrés, brought their law books with them. One of these collections antedating the *Hispana* is called the *Collectio Novariensis,* so named after a manuscript in Novara. This collection, compiled between the mid- and late sixth century, is now known to exist in nine manuscripts, but none is from Spain.[13] The same is true for another Spanish collection antedating the *Hispana,* the so-called *Epitome hispanica,* now found in eleven manuscripts, many originating in northern and central Italy, and also in southern Germany.[14] Two of the earliest Italian manuscripts of the *Epitome* are located in Verona and Lucca, cen-

[11] See Schafer Williams, *Codices Pseudo-Isidoriani: A Palaeographico-Historical Study,* Monumenta Iuris Canonici, series C, Subsidia 3 (New York, 1971), for a partial list of these manuscripts.

[12] See Roger E. Reynolds, "The 'Isidorian' *Epistula ad Leudefredum:* An Early Medieval Epitome of the Clerical Duties," *Mediaeval Studies* 41 (1979): 276–78. Additional fragments in Arabic can be found in Lisbon, Arquivo Nacional da Torre do Tombo, Sé de Coimbra, segunda incorporação, maço 45, nº 1806 (s. XI); on which see M.-T. Urvoy, "Note de Philologie Mozarabe," *Arabica* 36 (1989): 235–36.

[13] Brescia, Biblioteca Civica Queriniana B.II.13 (s. IX–X; upper Italy); Florence, Biblioteca Medicea Laurenziana Calci 9 (s. $XII^{1/4}$; central Italy) [excerpts]; Lucca, Biblioteca Capitolare Feliniana 124 (probably s. $XI^{4/4}$; central Italy); Monza, Biblioteca Capitolare H-3/151 (s. $IX^{2/2}$; upper Italy); Novara, Biblioteca Capitolare XV [30] (s. $XII^{1/2}$; Italy), XXX [66] (s. $IX^{3/4}$–$X^{1/2}$; Novara), and LXXXIV [54] (s. VIII ex.; upper Italy); Oxford, Bodleian Library Laud. misc. 421 (olim 893) (s. IX ex.; western Germany) [excerpts]; Paris, Bibliothèque Nationale lat. 12448 (olim Sangerm. Harl. 386) (s. IX–X; probably eastern Francia) [excerpts].

[14] Copenhagen, Kongelige Bibliotek Ny Kgl. Saml., 58 8° (s. $VIII^{1/2}$; southern France); Lucca, Biblioteca Capitolare Feliniana 490 (s. VIII–IX; Lucca); Merseburg, Archiv des Domkapitels 104 (s. IX/X; northern Italy or southern France); Munich, Bayerische Staatsbibliothek Clm 3853 (153 Aug) (s. $X^{2/2}$; southern Germany; provenance Augsburg?), Clm 6241 (s. $X^{3/3}$; Freising) [excerpts], and Clm 14468 (a. 821; Regensburg); Paris, Bibliothèque Nationale Baluze 270, fols. 177r–178v + Lyons, Bibliothèque de la Ville 788 [706], fols. 100r–101v (s. IX) [fragment]; Vatican City, Biblioteca Apostolica Vaticana Vat. lat. 5751 (s. IX–X; upper Italy, provenance Bobbio) and Ottob. lat. 3295 (s. $IX^{2/2}$; Mainz) [excerpts]; Verona, Biblioteca Capitolare, LXI [59] (s. VII–VIII; Verona); Vienna, Österreichische Nationalbibliothek 2232 (s. IX in.; southeastern Germany).

ters known for Visigothic-script codices and fragments, as noted above.[15] Hence, it is possible that the extant manuscripts of the *Epitome* in these two cities were copied from Visigothic-script models. These have disappeared, but a folio of a large manuscript of what is probably the full *Hispana* has been uncovered in 1994 in the Archivio di Stato in Lucca, where it was used as a wrapper for archival material.

The large folio has been designated by the Archivist as of June 1994 as "Codex 587" and placed in a busta by itself. In the upper right-hand corner of the recto is "S FI// PPO CHECCHI 1547," next to which in blue ink is "5" (see plate II). In the lower right-hand corner in the same ink is "22/8." The folio, measuring 320 × 224 (290 × 220) mm., has been cropped on the left and right sides and the entire bottom. The parchment of good quality is of medium thickness. The only pricking now visible was done from flesh to hair side with slits between the two columns of text. The ruling for the remaining forty-six lines, 8 mm. apart, is no longer visible. The extant full column measures 290 × 109 mm., and the intercolumnar space is 21 mm. There is a running title at the top of the folio, "CONCILIUM EMERITENSE." Rubrics over the columns in Visigothic script are in orange. Initials in orange of ca. 12 mm. in the left-hand margin are in Visigothic script. The writing, with minims of 2 mm. and ascenders and descenders of 6 mm., is in brown ink. There is only one hand at work, and peculiarities of the script, such as the verticality of the letters, suggest that it was copied in the eleventh century, probably in the north of Spain. Barbara Shailor has also suggested an eleventh-century date and would place the leaf in the vicinity of León. It bears a certain resemblance to manuscripts from the scriptorium at Sahagún, which flourished in the mid-eleventh century to the later half of the century. How and when it reached Lucca is uncertain, but its importance lies in the fact that it is the only known fragment of what was probably a complete manuscript of the *Hispana* in Visigothic script outside Spain.[16] The text is from the *capitulationes* and canons 1–8 of the Council of Merida of A.D. 666.[17]

N.B. Please see additional information in the Addenda.

[15] See p. 305.

[16] Given the fact that only a partial text of the Council of Merida is given, it is possible, of course, that the folio was part of a libellus with the text of the Council of Merida only, if not a fragment of a full manuscript of the *Collectio canonum Hispana.*

[17] See José Vives, *Concilios Visigóticos e Hispano-Romanos,* España Cristiana, Textos 1 (Barcelona-Madrid, 1963), 325–32, based on Gerona, Biblioteca Capitular 4 (olim 13) (s. XI), fols. 244v–251v.

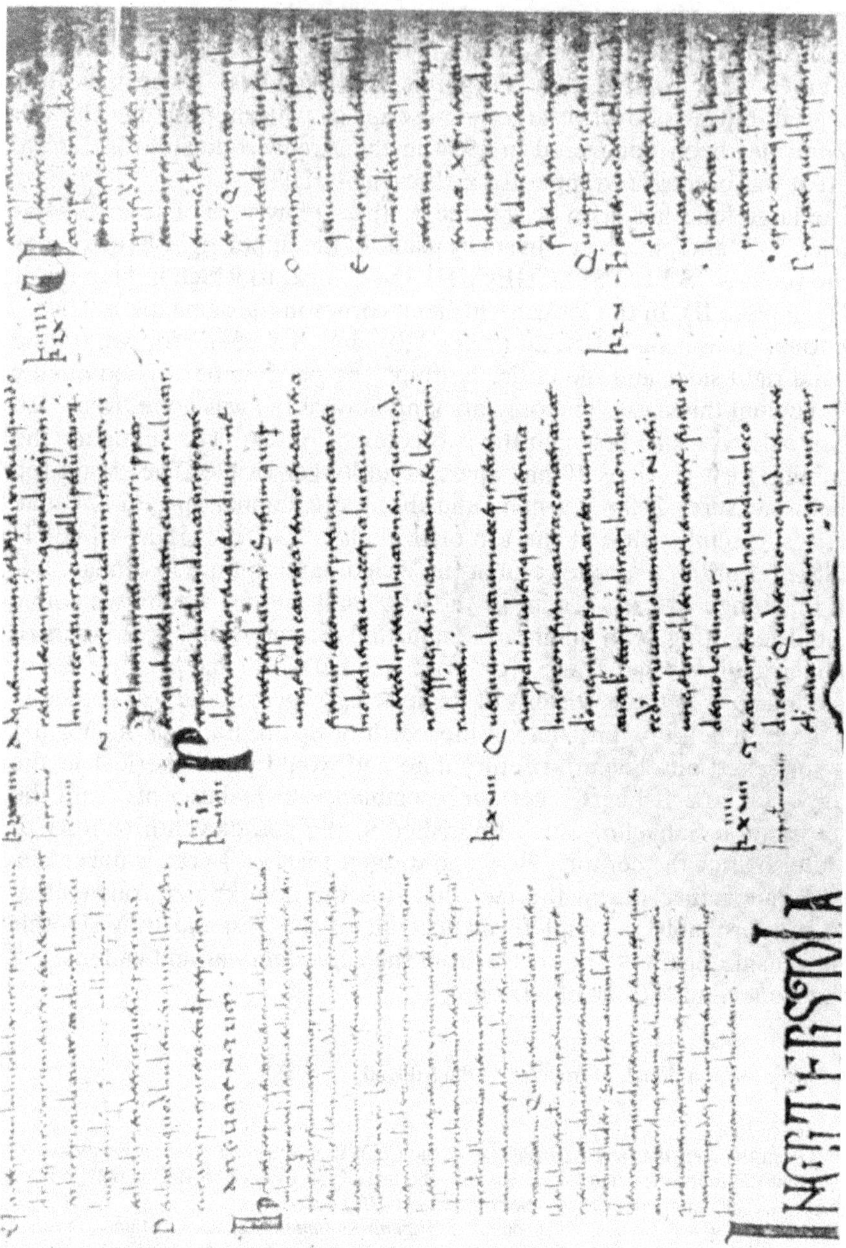

I. Lucca, Archivio di Stato 517. Fragment 1 (bottom recto).

II. Lucca, Archivio di Stato 587 (top recto).

V

A VISIGOTHIC-SCRIPT FOLIO OF A CAROLINGIAN COLLECTION OF CANON LAW

THE use of Visigothic script for canon law collections seems to have been confined almost exclusively to Spanish materials: the *Collectio canonum hispana* in Burgos, Biblioteca Capitular 2 (s. XI), El Escorial, Real Biblioteca de San Lorenzo d.I.1 (994), d.I.2 (976), e.I.12 (s. X–XI), and e.I.13 (s. X–XI), Madrid, Biblioteca Nacional 1872 (s. X/XI) and 10041 (1034), Madrid, Archivo Historico Nacional, Diversos, legajo 14 + Orense, Archivo Capitular 43 (s. X), and Toledo, Biblioteca Capitular 15.17 (1095); a "pre-*Hispana*" compilation in Madrid, Real Academia de la Historia, Aemil. 44 (s. VIII/IX); the *Collectio hispana systematica* in El Escorial, Real Biblioteca de San Lorenzo 1623 (in Arabic with Visigothic notations, 1049), Lyons, Bibliothèque de la Ville 336 (with Visigothic notations, s. IX in.), and Paris, Bibliothèque Nationale lat. 11709 (with Visigothic notations, s. IX); several Spanish councils in León, Archivo de la Catedral 22 (Council of Cordoba in 839, s. IX) and Paris, Bibliothèque Nationale lat. 10876(a) + 10877(b) + Tours, Bibliothèque municipale 615 + New Haven, Yale University, Beinecke Library 481 (II Council of Seville, c. 11, s. IX/X); and Spanish penitentials in London, British Library Add. 30853 (s. X) and Madrid, Biblioteca Nacional 10008 (s. XI). Northern material is known to have come to the Iberian peninsula early and to have been copied in the script; this was the case with material such as the works of the Venerable Bede,[1] but it was rarely the case with canon law material. The major exceptions to this are a penitential ascribed to Pope Gregory I in Cordoba, Archivo de la Catedral n.s. (s. X), and the eleventh-century *Decretum* of Burchard of Worms in Madrid, Biblioteca Nacional Vitr. 5.5 (1105). This is in sharp contrast to the use of another great regional script, the Beneventan, which was used to copy nearly every major canon law collection from the ancient *Collectio Dionysiana* down to Gratian's *Decretum.*[2]

[1] See "Utrecht Fragments in Visigothic Script," pp. 316–17 and 320 above.

[2] See "Gratian's *Decretum* and the *Code* of Justinian in Beneventan Script," pp. 285–87 above.

The folio which is the subject of this note contains a text based on the ancient *Collectio Dionysiana* as modified and widely diffused in Carolingian times and called the *Collectio Dionysio-Hadriana.* Together with another fragment in Visigothic script containing Ecclesiasticus 21:20 through 22:21, it was reported by Millares Carlo in the Archives Nationales in Paris.[3] The canon law folio, AB XIX.1723, is found in a folder from the Departement de l'Aude, labelled in ink as "Tituli canonum Sardicensis concilii N. XXI," with further identification in pencil stating that this was the council of 347 that condemned the Arians and stating, "Le ms. donne la resumé des 17 premieres canons (il y en a eu 21)" which can be found in "Bail, Summa conciliorum omnium I 1659, p. 60 et suiv." and "Labbe et Const. Concilia II 1671, col. 627 et suiv." On the recto side of the folio itself in dark black ink is "Levoir des Censiues de Ribaute Ribaute" and on the verso side is the seal "Archives Departementales Propriété Publique (Aude)" and lists of materials in a modern hand. The folio was used at one time as a wrapper for archival material inasmuch as it is folded in half, and binding holes were made through the fold.

Measuring 294 × 215 (271 × 136) mm., the folio is of medium to poor quality and of medium thickness. Prickmarks (holes) are made from hair to flesh side for twenty-seven lines, 10 mm. apart, for one column of text. Ruling, presumably in drypoint, has disappeared. As to script, titles, which are in Visigothic within the text, are in orange measuring 4 × 4 mm. Initials and capitals, which are in the left-hand column, also in Visigothic, are in orange, measuring 5 × 5 mm. The general text in Visigothic is in brown ink; minims are 2 mm., ascenders 8 mm., and descenders 6 mm. Among the characteristic letters are the *t* in both Visigothic forms, *a,* and *a* with upper tail. The *e* and *t* are frequently joined with subsequent letters. Abbreviations and Nomina Sacra are present. Abbreviations used are the tilde (used in such contractions as "episcopus" [$\widetilde{\textit{eps}}$] or "est" [$\tilde{e}$]), a line with suprascript dot (used as a final *m* in such contractions as "alteram"), a suprascript *s* (used as a *ue* in the contraction for "que," for the *on* or *om* of *con-,* and the final *-us* in a word), a suprascript backward *c* (used as the *ur* in *-tur*), and a line over a word (such as $\overline{\textit{civt}}$ for "civitate" or $\bar{e}$ for "est"). The script is not like the tall elegant script of Escorial d.I.1 or d.I.2, written in the late tenth century in northern Spain. Millares Carlo has, in fact, dated it to the ninth century.[4] Since the script is the smaller, more cramped script often associated with manuscripts from southern Spain in the ninth

[3] The Ecclesiasticus fragment is AB XIX.1730, on which see Agustín Millares Carlo, *Tratado de Paleografía Española, I: Texto,* 3d ed. (Madrid, 1983), 338, no. 272.

[4] Ibid., 338, no. 271.

and tenth centuries, this is possible, but with its tall ascenders it could have been written even in the tenth century and farther north.

If the text itself is compared with the standard editions of the early councils such as those of Labbe and Mansi,[5] with the new edition of the *Collectio canonum hispana,*[6] or with the first recension of the *Collectio Dionysio-Hadriana,*[7] there are clear discrepancies, especially in the division and numbering of canons. Further, material mentioning the Council of Ephesus preceding the Sardican *tituli* is unusual in this position. But if one looks to an abbreviation of the Dionysian collection made most likely in the Carolingian period, the source of the text can be found. This abbreviation, called by canonistic specialists the *Breviarium ad inquaerendas sententias,* is reported in a variety of manuscripts written in the ninth century.[8] Why it was copied in Visigothic is not certain. Carolingian texts were infrequently written in the script in Spain itself,[9] but the script was used by scribes in the Carolingian Spanish March, in the south of France, and occasionally in locations such as Lyons with its concentration of Spanish emigrés.[10] Hence, it is possible that it was written in one of these areas by a scribe trained in Visigothic script. This possibility is further suggested by the fact that the folio came from the Archives Departementales de l'Aube. Whatever the case, the fact that such a Carolingian canon law text was written in Visigothic script is noteworthy in itself.

[5] P. Labbe and G. Cossart, *Sacrosancta concilia ad regiam editionem exacta* . . . 2 (Paris, 1671), cols. 627–28; J. D. Mansi, *Sacrorum conciliorum nova et amplissima collectio,* vol. 3 (Florence and Venice, 1759), cols. 6–38.

[6] See Gonzalo Martínez Díez and Félix Rodrígez, *La colección canónica Hispana,* vol. 3: *Concilios Griegos y Africanos,* Monumenta Hispaniae Sacra, Serie canónica 3 (Madrid, 1982), 119–34.

[7] Adolf Strewe, *Die Canonessammlung des Dionysius Exiguus in der ersten Redaktion,* Arbeiten zur Kirchengeschichte 16 (Berlin and Leipzig, 1931), 19–20, 61–70.

[8] The following manuscripts have been reported to contain the text: Barcelona, Archivo de la Corona de Aragón, Ripoll 105 (s. XIII); Berlin, Staatsbibliothek zu Berlin, Phill. 1744 (s. X); Hamburg, Staats- und Universitätsbibliothek, Cod. 26 in scrinio (s. IX in.; southern Burgundy); Paris, Bibliothèque Nationale lat. 1452 (s. $IX^{4/4}$ or s. IX–X; Rhône area), 3844 (s. IX ca. 2/4–med.; Loire area), 11710 (olim Sangerm. 367) (a. 805; Burgundy), and 12446 (olim Sangerm. Harl. 391) (s. $IX^{1-2/4}$; perhaps central France); Vatican City, Biblioteca Apostolica Vaticana Reg. lat. 1021 (s. $IX^{1/4}$; St-Amand); Vienna, Österreichische Nationalbibliothek 524 (s. IX; Salzburg) and 737 (s. IX; Salzburg); and two unidentified manuscripts once in Ripoll (catalogue of 1649, items 3 and 24).

[9] See Manuel C. Díaz y Díaz, "La circulation des manuscrits dans la Péninsule Ibérique du VIIIe au XIe siècle," *Cahiers de Civilisation Médiévale* 12 (1969): 232–41, 388, and items in "Note additionnelle" of the reprint in his *Vie chrétienne et culture dans l'Espagne du VIIe au Xe siècles* (Aldershot, 1992), XII.

[10] See "Visigothic-Script Remains of a Pandect Bible and the *Collectio canonum hispana* in Lucca," p. 310 above.

Since the *Breviarium* has never been edited, the portion found in our Visigothic folio is transcribed here. Orthography has been maintained. Words and letters in pointed brackets < > have been supplied from the text of the *Breviarium* in Paris, Bibliothèque Nationale lat. 1452, fol. 7r–v.

[recto] . . . necnon et in ephesninas [*sic*] cum sinodo praeful<g>ere recte et inmaculate et in ipsa constitutione per dei gratiam de patre et filio et sancto spiritu plenitudin<em> docet et domini inhumanation<em> fideliter accipientibus repraesentat et ut sancta et universalis synodus alteram fidem nulli licere proferre aut conscribere aut docere aliter et si aliqui ausi fuerint conponere fidem alteram episcopi aut clerici, alieni a clericatu monachi aut laici anathematixuri [*sic*].

TITULI CANONUM SARDICENSIS CONCILII N. XXI.

In primo capitulo de episcopis etiam laica communione privandisque [*sic*] civitates mutaverunt.
Et in ii. capitulo de eisdem episcopis ut si per ambitionem sedem mutaverint nec in exitu<m> communionem saltim laicam consequentur.
Et in iii. capitulo, <ut> in<ter> discordes episcopos conprovintiales antes<tites> audiant. quod si invitatus [*sic*] <dampnatus> appellaverit romanum pontificem ad observandum quod ipse censuerit et ut episcopus de sua provintia ad aliam <non> transeat nisi forte invitatus fuerit.
In IIII. capitulo ut nullus accusati sedem usurpet episcopi nec si proclama<veri>t sibi agendum negotium in urbe roma in eius cathedra ordinetur antequam suo iudicio fuerit terminata.
In v. vero capitulo quando quis debeat a vicinis provintie episcopos [*sic*] ordinari si necessitas evenerit.
In vi. capitulo de non ordinandis episcopis per vicos et modicas civitates et pro ea ratione non invitare episcopum ex alia provintia.
In vii. capitulo ergo de provintiali sinodo retractanda per vicarios idem [*sic*] missi episcopi urbis romae si ipse decreverit.
// verso // Et in viii. capitulo quando et in quibus causis episcopi ad comitatum <ire debeant>.
In viiii. vero capitulo de laic [*sic*] <diaconis> ad comitatum dirigendis cum consilio episcoporum provintialium maxime metropolitano.
Et in x. capitulo quod ad comitatum pro pupillis et viduis ac necessitatem pat<i>entibus sit eundum.
In xi. vero capitulo ut qui in canali sunt episcopi euntes ad comitatum sollicite discutiant progrediente episcopo inquirant transitum eius et videat causas agnoscat quo tendat ne propter disideria et ambitiones comitatus fiat.
Et in xii. capitulo de his qui ignorant quid sit in sinodo constitutum ne subito adhuc aliqui nescientes quid decretum sit in sinodo prevaricationem admittant.

In xiii. ergo capitulo de laicis non temere faciendis episcopis si forte dives aut scolasticus non prius ordinetur quam per singulos gradus si dignus fuerit ascendat utique prolixum tempus probari qua fide sit qua modestia et cetera et si dignus fuerit probatus divino sacerdotio inlustretur.

Et in xiiii. capitulo quamdiu episcopus in aliena civitate <re>moretur non pro ambitione nullomodo in aliena civitate moretur quia perniciosum est. Meminere debemus superiori concilio fratres nostros constituisse si quis laicus in sua civitate tres septimanas commoratur conventum non celebrasse a communione privari quantomagis episcopos nec licet nec decet.

In xv. autem capitulo ne liceat <episcopo a> sua et ta [*sic*] <ecclesia> plus tribus ebdomadibus abe<esse>.

Et in xvi. capitulo de clericis a communione submotos [*sic*] balus [*sic*] non recipiendis ep<iscopis>.

In xvii. autem capitulo de excomunicates apud vicinos episcopos audiendis forte episcopus si iracundus aut aspere cito commobetur providendum est.

VI

UTRECHT FRAGMENTS IN VISIGOTHIC SCRIPT*

THE Rijksmuseum of the Catherijneconvent in Utrecht is renowned for its collection of religious objects and art in the Netherlands from earliest times to the present. In an outstanding exhibition of the manuscripts of the museum in 1993, two fragments written in Visigothic script were displayed. In the catalogue of the exhibition these were described as coming from printed volumes of the *Opera praeclarissima* of Alphonsus Thostatus, 1528–30, published in Venice by Petrus Liechtenstein, which came to the Rijksmuseum from the O. L. Vrouwe van de Allerheiligste en St. Dominicusparochie of Haarlem in 1955–60(?).[1] The script itself is said to have been written possibly in northern Spain in the twelfth century and the text to be from a version of Genesis 46:14. In fact, the text of the two fragments displayed is from Numbers 26:21–45, and the volumes from which the two fragments came contain not only the two described in the catalogue but thirty-two fragments and offsets almost all of which contain Visigothic script of the twelfth century.

Given the relatively small number of all extant items in Visigothic script —less than four hundred are listed in the standard catalogue by Millares Carlo[2]—and given the fact that these fragments and offsets in Utrecht were written after the late eleventh century, when writing of Visigothic script was prohibited in Spain,[3] they are of more than ordinary interest. Moreover, because they were used as supports for volumes published in Venice they are yet another piece of evidence for the presence in northeastern Italy of manuscripts written in Visigothic script. It is understandable why manuscripts such as the renowned seventh-century *Orationale* of Verona traveled to Italy in the eighth century as Christians in Spain fled the Iberian peninsula with their books in face of the Muslim

* I am very grateful to Dr. W. C. M. Wüstefeld, Librarian of the Rijksmuseum, for her kindness while I examined the fragments and for permission to reproduce portions of them in this article.

[1] W. C. M. Wüstefeld, *Middeleeuwse Boeken van Het Catharijneconvent* (Utrecht, 1993), 22.

[2] See Roger E. Reynolds, "Baptismal Rite and Paschal Vigil in Transition in Medieval Spain: A New Text in Visigothic Script," *Mediaeval Studies* 55 (1993): 260 and n. 11.

[3] Ibid., 263.

onslaught.[4] But it is not so clear why and when manuscripts such as the recently described late eleventh-century baptismal fragment[5] or the Utrecht fragments found their way to Venice.

The Utrecht fragments and offsets all come from the covers and bindings of a set of five volumes of the *Opera praeclarissima* of Thostatus. The majority are or were attached to the binding of the spines. Each spine is divided into "compartments," as they are called in Utrecht, that is, sections separated by the binding thongs (single at the top and bottom and the others double; see plate I). The fragments were pasted around these compartments and on to the covers of the volumes. Each volume has six compartments, except Vol. 4, which has five. It appears that almost all of the compartments were covered by fragments in Visigothic script, although in several cases all traces have disappeared. In one case, in Vol. 5, a fragment can be seen pasted on to the original pastedown on the cover, over which another pastedown has been placed. As will be seen, these fragments and offsets appear to have come from at least three different manuscripts or parts of a heterogeneous manuscript.

The five volumes of Thostatus now bear the shelfmarks BMH Sp p i 8, I–V, and it is from this designation that the fragments which have been given marks derive. Five fragments have been detached from Vol. 1 by the Librarian of the Rijksmuseum and placed in a small translucent envelope with the designations Sp 8 I^{va}, 8 I^{vb}, BMH Sp 8 I^{R}c, Sp 8 I^{v}d, and Sp 8 I^{v}e, the letters ^{a}, ^{b}, c, d, and e corresponding to the compartments on Vol. 1 from which they were taken. The two fragments exhibited in 1993 were detached from Vol. 5 in May 1991 and are now kept in a second translucent envelope. The remainder of the fragments and offsets remain, as of October 1994, on or in the volumes.

For ease of citation here, the fragments and offsets will be given numbers corresponding to their place in the volumes in much the same fashion as those now detached and assigned numbers by the Librarian. Hence, for example, the offset in the second compartment of Vol. 1, that is, between the second and third binding thongs, is designated as Sp 1 b; the loose fragment in Vol. 1, Sp 1 x (x denoting extra to the compartmental fragments or offsets); and the pastedown fragment on the cover of Vol. 5, Sp 5 x.

The following table presents an overview of the fragments and offsets as they are presently attached to or appear in the five volumes. [ ] = no text

4 On this manuscript, see Agustín Millares Carlo, *Tratado de Paleografía Española, I: Texto,* 3d ed. (Madrid, 1983), 342, no. 345; and Klaus Gamber, *Codices liturgici latini antiquiores* (Fribourg/S, 1968), no. 330.

5 See Reynolds, "Baptismal Rite," 257–72.

visible in compartment itself. < > = fragment taken from compartment now in a translucent envelope (env 1 or env 2).

Vol. 1: BMH Sp p i 8 I	Vol. 2: BMH Sp p i 8 II	Vol. 3: BMH Sp p i 8 III	Vol. 4: BMH Sp p i 8 IV	Vol. 5: BMH Sp p i 8 V
[Sp 1 a] <Sp env 1 a>	Sp 2 a offset	[Sp 3 a]	Sp 4 a offset	[Sp 5 a]
Sp 1 b offset <Sp env 1 b>	Sp 2 b offset	Sp 3 b offset	Sp 4 b fragm.	Sp 5 b offset
[Sp 1 c] <Sp env 1 c>	Sp 2 c offset	Sp 3 c offset	Sp 4 c fragm.	Sp 5 c offset
Sp 1 d offset <Sp env 1 d>	[Sp 2 d]	Sp 3 d offset	Sp 4 d fragm.	Sp 5 d offset <Sp env 2 a>
Sp 1 e fragm. <Sp env 1 d>	Sp 2 e fragm.	Sp 3 e fragm.	[Sp 4 e]	Sp 5 e offset <Sp env 2 b>
Sp 1 f fragm.	Sp 2 f offset	[Sp 3 f]	no com- partment	[Sp 5 f]

Vol. 1. The fragments and offsets from this volume are described as follows: first, those now in the translucent envelope, and second, those still on the volume.

Envelope fragments:

—**Sp env 1 a** (labelled as Sp 8 I^{va}): a fragment measuring 26 × 43 mm. with no writing, lines ruled with drypoint measuring 8 mm. apart.
—**Sp env 1 b** (labelled as 8 I^{vb}): a fragment measuring 42 × 23 mm., with seven lines of text on the hair side visible in brown ink and five on the flesh side in orange. Lines in drypoint measure 6 mm. apart. Letter measurements: minims 2.5 mm., ascenders 5.5 mm., and descenders 5.5 mm. The texts on the two sides of the manuscript have not been identified.
—**Sp env 1 c** (labelled as BMH Sp 8 I^{R}c): a fragment measuring 44 × 33 mm. There are prick marks and a drypoint rule for a marginal line from hair side to flesh side. There is no writing.
—**Sp env 1 d** (labelled as Sp 8 I^{v}d): a fragment measuring 45 × 21 mm. with seven lines, 6 mm. apart, written in brown ink. Letter measurements: minims 2.5 mm., ascenders 5.5 mm., and descenders 5. The text is from Leo I, *Trac-*

tatus septem et nonaginta 92, ed. A. Chavasse, CCL 138A (Turnhout, 1973), 568–69, lines 15–19 (flesh side) and p. 570, lines 46–51 (hair side).
—**Sp env 1 e** (labelled as Sp 8 i^{v}e): a fragment measuring 28 × 42 mm., with three lines of text barely visible on flesh and hair sides in brown ink. There is a margin of 20 mm. and 22 mm. of text. Lines are 8 mm. apart. Letter measurements: minims 3 mm., ascenders 5 mm., and descenders 4/5 mm. According to the Librarian at Utrecht, this fragment was pasted on to the full fragment (Sp 1 e) in this compartment as it was folded on to the cover of the manuscript. The texts on the two sides of the fragment have not been identified.

Spine fragments and offsets:

—There is no evidence of a fragment or offset in the top compartment of the spine of this volume or what would have been **Sp 1 a**.
—**Sp 1 b**: an offset measuring ca. 43 × 60 mm. Six lines of text measuring 6 mm. apart are visible in orange and black ink. Visible letter measurements: minims 2 mm. and ascenders 4 mm. The text of the visible letters has not been identified.
—There is no evidence of a fragment or offset in the third compartment of the spine of this volume or what would have been **Sp 1 c**.
—**Sp 1 d**: an offset measuring ca. 45 × 60 mm. Six lines of text measuring 6/8 mm. apart are visible in brown ink. Letter measurements: minims 2 mm., ascenders 5 mm., and descenders 5 mm. The text has not been identified.
—**Sp 1 e**: a partially darkened fragment measuring 123 × 36 mm., bearing signature labels I and 8. Sixteen lines of text measuring 8/9 mm. apart are visible in brown ink. There are two vertical marginal lines measuring 8 mm. apart. Ruling is from hair side to flesh side. Letter measurements: minims 3 mm., ascenders 4 mm., and descenders 4 mm. The text on both sides of the fragment, written in the same hand as that of Sp env 1 e, has not been identified.
—**Sp 1 f**: a partially darkened fragment measuring 40 × 122 mm. still sewed on to the spine and turned on to the covers of the volume. Seven and eight lines measuring 8 mm. apart and written in brown ink are visible on the hair side and flesh side respectively, the hair side facing out of the spine. Letter measurements: minims 2 mm., ascenders 6 mm., and descenders 5 mm. The text on the hair side is from the Venerable Bede, *In Lucae evangelium expositio* 3, ed. D. Hurst, CCL 120 (Turnhout, 1960), 208–9, lines 1672–77 (cf. Jerome, *Commentariorum in Mattheum libri IV* 3, ed. D. Hurst and M. Adriaen, CCL 77 [Turnhout, 1969], 152, lines 371–76); and on the flesh side from the same *expositio,* CCL 120:208, lines 1640–43 (cf. Venerable Bede, *In Marci evangelium expositio* 3, ed. D. Hurst, CCL 120:547, lines 207–9).
—**Sp 1 x**: a fragment loose in the flyleaves of the volume measuring 32 × 42 mm. Eight lines measuring 6 mm. apart are visible in brown and orange ink.

Visible letter measurements: mimims 2 mm. and ascenders 4 mm. The barely visible text has not been identified.

Vol. 2.

—**Sp 2 a**: an offset measuring ca. 36 × 65 mm. Four lines measuring 6 mm. apart are visible in brown and orange ink. Visible letter measurements: minims 2 mm. The text has not been identified.
—**Sp 2 b**: an offset measuring ca. 45 × 65 mm. Four lines measuring 7/8 mm. apart are visible in brown ink. The text is illegible.
—**Sp 2 c**: an offset measuring ca. 50 × 65 mm. Eight lines measuring 7 mm. apart are visible in brown ink. Letter measurements: minims 2 mm., ascenders 5 mm., and descenders 5 mm. The text is from the Venerable Bede, *In Marci evangelium expositio* 3, CCL 120:590–91, lines 1914–18.
—There was a pastedown in what would have been **Sp 2 d**, but it has disappeared and no writing is now visible in the compartment.
—**Sp 2 e**: a fragment bound to the spine measuring ca. 46 × 110 mm. and bearing the signature labels II and 8. Eight lines of text measuring 6 mm. apart are written in brown and orange ink. There is a marginal line ruled in drypoint from hair side to flesh side of a folio that was likely in two columns. Letter measurements: minims 2 mm., ascenders 5 mm., and descenders 5 mm. The text on the hair and flesh sides is from the Venerable Bede, *In Marci evangelium expositio* 3, CCL 120:590, lines 1880–89 and 1903–8.
—**Sp 2 f**: an offset measuring ca. 33 × 65 mm. Four or five lines in brown and orange ink are barely visible.

Vol. 3.

—There is no evidence of a fragment or offset on what would have been **Sp 3 a**.
—**Sp 3 b**: an offset measuring ca. 35 × 54 mm. Five lines measuring 6 mm. apart are written in brown ink. Visible letter measurements: minims 2 mm. and ascenders 4 mm. The text has not been identified.
—**Sp 3 c**: an offset measuring ca. 48 × 50 mm. Seven lines measuring 6 mm. apart are written in brown and orange ink. Visible letter measurements: minims 2 mm. and descenders 6 mm. The text has not been identifed.
—**Sp 3 d**: an offset measuring ca. 47 × 53 mm. Six lines measuring 7 mm. apart written in brown ink are barely visible.
—**Sp 3 e**: a fragment measuring 45 × 53 mm. bearing the signature label 8.3. Seven lines measuring 7 mm. apart are written in brown ink. Visible letter measurements: minims 2 mm. The text, almost illegible, has not been identified.
—There is no evidence of a fragment or offset on what would have been **Sp 3 f**.

Vol. 4.

—**Sp 4 a**: an offset measuring ca. 28 × 50 mm. Four lines measuring 6 mm. apart are written in brown ink. Letter measurements: minims 2 mm. The text, almost illegible, has not been identified.
—**Sp 4 b**: a fragment measuring 120 × 57 mm., bearing number 118 in brown ink. The text is written in two columns with an intercolumnar margin of 16 mm. Four lines measuring 7 mm. apart are written in brown and orange ink. Letter measurements: minims 2 mm., ascenders 5 mm., and descenders 5 mm. The text on the hair side and flesh side has not been identified.
—**Sp 4 c**: a darkened fragment measuring 53 × 50 mm. Nine lines measuring 6 mm. apart are written in brown ink. Letter measurements: minims 2 mm., ascenders 5 mm., and descenders 5 mm. The texts on the hair side and flesh side have not been identified.
—**Sp 4 d**: a fragment measuring 53 × 50 mm., bearing the signature labels IV and 8. Five lines measuring 6 mm. apart are written in brown ink. The text would have been in the upper left hand corner of either the folio or a column inasmuch as there is a margin on the top and to the left hand side. Letter measurements: minims 2 mm., ascenders 5 mm., and descenders 5 mm. The text, largely covered by the signature labels, has not been identified.
—There is no evidence of a fragment or offset in the compartment that would have been **Sp 4 e** of this volume with only five compartments.

Vol. 5.

Envelope fragments without current labels:

—**Sp env 2 a**. The fragment, shown in the exhibition catalogue in the compartment Sp 5 c of the spine, was detached from the book in May 1991, and is, as of October 1994, kept in a translucent envelope. The fragment itself measures 84 × 43 mm. Twelve lines measuring 9 mm. apart are written in a dark brown ink. Letter measurements: minims 2.5 mm., ascenders 5/7 mm., and descenders 5/7 mm. The text on the flesh side is from Numbers 26:42–45 (see plate II.2), and the text on the hair side is from Numbers 26:25–29.
—**Sp env 2 b**. The fragment has been detached from the book in May 1991 and is, as of October 1994, kept in a translucent envelope. The fragment measures 101 × 45 mm. and on the hair side bears the signature labels V and 8. Nine lines of text measuring 9 mm. apart are written in dark brown ink and would have been at the top of the folio or column inasmuch as there is a blank margin above. Letter measurements: minims: 2.5 mm., ascenders 5/7 mm., and ascenders 5/7 mm. The text on the flesh side is from Numbers 26:38–42 (see plate II.1), and the text on the hair side is from Numbers 26:21–25.

Spine fragments and offsets:

—There is no evidence of a fragment or offset in the compartment that would have been **Sp 5 a**.
—**Sp 5 b**: an offset measuring ca. 40 × 50 mm. Five lines measuring 9 mm. apart are written in brown ink. There is a margin for the text. Visible letter measurements: minims 2.5 mm. and ascenders 6 mm. The text, almost illegible, has not been identified.
—**Sp 5 c**. On a blank paper front flyleaf in the volume there are 4 lines of an offset for this compartment. On the back paper flyleaf an offset with the number LXIII is visible. In the compartment itself is an offset measuring ca. 40 × 50 mm. Five lines measuring 9 mm. apart are written in brown ink. Letter measurements: minims 2 mm., ascenders 5 mm., and descenders 6 mm. The text in all three offsets, almost illegible, has not been identified.
—**Sp 5 d**. An offset of the fragment Sp env 2 a is visible on the spine of the volume. There is also an offset of this fragment on a blank paper front flyleaf.
—**Sp 5 e**. On a blank paper front flyleaf there is an offset of the fragment Sp env 2 b, which was originally Sp 5 e.
—There is no evidence of a fragment or offset in Visigothic script in the lowest compartment of the spine, or what would have been **Sp 5 f**, although a blank piece of parchment is still sewn in as a support.
—**Sp 5 x**: a narrow fragment measuring 72 × 5 mm. pasted on to the original pastedown of the front cover of the volume and overlaid by another later pastedown. Nine lines measuring 8 mm. apart are written in brown and orange ink. Letter measurements: minims 2 mm., ascenders 4 mm., and descenders 4 mm. Only one letter on each line is extant. The text has not been identified.

As for the writing of the fragments and offsets, the script is generally vertical and typical of Visigothic manuscripts written in nothern Spain in the twelfth century. Letter forms, ligatures, and abbreviations are also typical for manuscripts of this type. In several fragments there are hyphens in words at line ends and ticks above syllables to be accented.

It appears that at least three manuscripts or three parts of a heterogeneous manuscript were used as supports for the five volumes: MS 1 would have contained the items Sp 1 d and f; Sp 2 c and e; Sp 4 b, c, and d; and Sp env 1 b, c, and d. MS 2 would have contained Sp 1 e and Sp env 1 e. MS 3 would have contained Sp 5 d and e. The offsets, with the exceptions of Sp 1 d and Sp 2 c, are not clear enough to allow them to be assigned to individual manuscripts.

The texts in the manuscripts have all been checked against the CETEDOC program of the *Corpus Christianorum* series and the Vulgate. The variety of texts in MS 1 is puzzling in that they are from Bede's commentaries on Mark and or possibly Luke (one fragment even having a text on the flesh and hair sides from these commentaries), possibly Jerome's commentary on Matthew, and Leo I's *Tractatus septem et nonaginta.* Perhaps all of these texts were in a homily or florilegium of some type, but this is only speculation. The presence of Bede's commentaries is further confirmation of the observation of Manuel C. Díaz y Díaz that the works of Bede early travelled to Spain to be copied in Visigothic script.[6]

[6] See Manuel C. Díaz y Díaz, "La circulation des manuscrits dans la Péninsule Ibérique du VIIIe au XIe siècle," *Cahiers de Civilisation Médiévale* 12 (1969): 237; reprinted in his *Vie chrétienne et culture dans l'Espagne du VIIe au Xe siècles* (Aldershot, 1992), XII.

I. Utrecht, Rijksmuseum of the Catharijneconvent BMH Sp p i 8, I–V
(reverse view of spines).

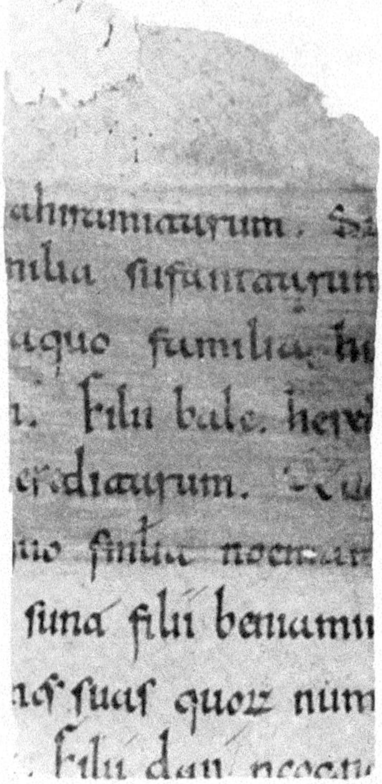

1

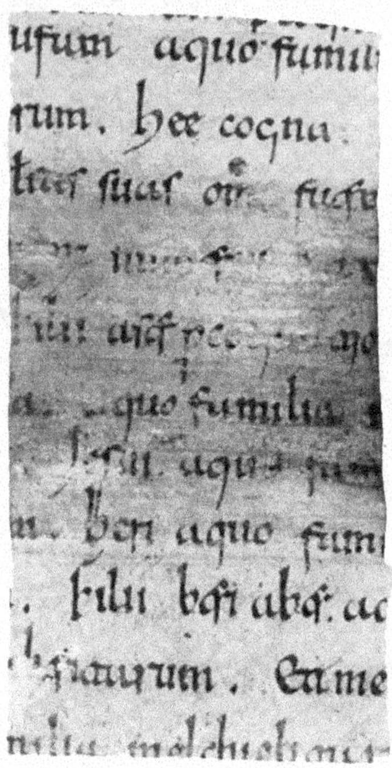

2

II. Utrecht, Rijksmuseum of the Catharijneconvent.
1. Sp env 2 b (flesh side). 2. Sp env 2 a (flesh side).

VII

AN EARLY RULE FOR CANONS REGULAR FROM SANTA MARIA DE L'ESTANY (NEW YORK, HISPANIC SOCIETY OF AMERICA, MS HC 380/819)*

The foundation of a house of canons regular following the Rule of St. Augustine at Santa Maria de l'Estany in 1080/81 by bishop Berenguer Seniofed from Lluça was one of the first or perhaps the first such foundation on the Iberian peninsula.[1] It is not that a church was not there earlier and that clerics in Catalonia did not live the life of canons under a rule. Perhaps as early as A.D. 990 there existed a small church dedicated to Santa Maria in the valley of Estany not far west of Vic;[2] and canons in other churches in Catalonia are reported to have lived the *vita regularis canonica* by the first quarter of the eleventh century.[3] Moreover, there existed copies of the *Regula Augustini* for canons in churches such as Vic.[4] But documents related to Santa Maria de l'Estany are the earliest to mention specifically that the canons there followed the *Regula Augustini*.[5] The impetus for such a life there most likely originated with

* Portions of this article were completed with the support of a grant by the Social Sciences and Humanities Research Council of Canada for the programme *Monumenta liturgica beneventana*. I am most grateful for assistance from Professor Miquel-S. Gros, who not only urged me to publish the texts, but also kindly provided me with a number of offprints and photocopies of materials rare in North America. The Hispanic Society of America has generously given its permission to study and edit the text in this article.

1. A. Pladevall and J. Vigué, *El Monestir romànic de Santa Maria de l'Estany* (Barcelona, 1978) 23.
2. Ibid., p. 21.
3. See the comment of Anscaro Mundó in D. Misonné, «La legislation canoniale de Saint-Ruf d'Avignon à ses origins. Règle de Saint Augustin et Coutumier,» *Annales du Midi* 75 (1963) 488.
4. Ibid., p. 288. Ch. Dereine, «Coutumiers et ordinaires de chanoines réguliers,» *Scriptorium*, 5 (1951), 109, item 12, notes that Estany was founded in 1120; and P. H. Freedman, *The diocese of Vic: Tradition and Regeneration in Medieval Catalonia* (New Brunswick, N.J., 1983), says it was first described as an Augustinian house in 1096.
5. Pladevall and Vigué, *El Monestir romànic de Santa Maria de l'Estany*, p. 25.

the Avignon house of St. Ruf, founded in A.D. 1039. Indeed, in A.D. 1084 the abbot of St. Ruf had attempted to establish a filial at Santa Maria de Besalú, but because of opposition there failed, and it was only after 1112 that such a community was established.[6]

It is widely recognized that the *Regula Augustini* was diffused through southern France and the Iberian peninsula largely through the influence of the canons regular at St. Ruf in Avignon. It is often stated that all of the bishops of Catalonia during the heyday of St. Ruf were 'Ruffians',[7] and that its rule had its greatest diffusion between 1080 and 1120, the period of the great Avignonese leaders, Arbert, Lietbert, and Oléguer[8] (who as abbot of St. Ruf was made bishop of Barcelona and archbishop of Tarragona).[9] The earliest customary or use of St. Ruf has been edited together with a redaction of Lietbert by Dom Daniel Misonné,[10] the former from an early eleventh-century codex, Paris, BN lat. 1877, and the later from a twelfth-century codex, Paris, BN lat. 1233.[11] Further, there is an edition of a customary of St. Ruf adapted to the cathedral of Maguelone by Carrier from a fourteenth-century codex, Avignon, Bibliothèque municipal, 716.[12] The widespread influence of the customaries of St. Ruf throughout Europe can be found in manuscripts from as far north as Trondheim in Norway[13] to as far south as Coimbra,[14] and from as far west as England to Marbach in the east.[15] But little notice has been given to another early manuscript attributing a customary to a church and convent of St. Ruf from the Catalan house of canons regular at Santa Maria d'l'Estany.

The existence of this manuscript with its rules was noted as far back as 1806 by Jaime Villanueva, who described it in his *Viage Literario a las Iglesias de España:*

6. Ibid., p. 25.
7. See, e.g., A. Carrier, *Coutumier du XI siècle de l'ordre de saint-Ruf (Chanoines réguliers de Saint-Augustin) en usage à la cathédrale de Maguelone. Études et documents sur l'ordre de St-Ruf* 8 (Sherbrooke, 1950) 20.
8. Ibid., p. 26.
9. See L. J. McCrank, «The Foundation of the Confraternity of Tarragona by Archbishop Oleguer Bonestruga, 1126-1129,» *Viator* 9 (1978) 157-177.
10. Misonné, «La legislation canoniale ,» pp. 479-486.
11. Lilli Gjerløw has produced a preliminary draft of this for publication, on which see P.-M. Gy, «L'influence des chanoines de Lucques sur la liturgie du Latran,» *Revue des sciences religieuses* 58 (1984) 537-552, reprinted in P.-M. Gy, *La liturgie dans l'histoire* (Paris, 1990) 127-139, esp. 129.
12. Carrier, *Coutumier du XI siècle du l'ordre des saint-Ruf*, pp. 53-107. For the date of the manuscript see Misonné, art. cit., p. 473, n. 10.
13. *Ordo Nidrosiensis ecclesiae*, ed. L. Gjerløw, *Libri liturgici provinciae Nidrosiensis medii aevi* 2 (Oslo, 1968) 105-108. She and Père Gy, «L'influence des chanoines de Lucques sur la liturgie du Latran,» p. 129, propose that the influence of St-Ruf came by way of England, but it must be remembered that before he became pope Adrian IV, Nicholas Breakespear was abbot of St. Ruf and later was sent to Trondheim to reform the clerics there.
14. We eagerly await the study of Agostinho Frias of the Faculdade de Letras do Porto, Portugal, on the *Liber ordinis colimbriensis*, using manuscripts from Coimbra.
15. J. Siegwart, *Die Consuetudines des Augustiner-Chorherrenstiftes Marbach im Elsass (12. Jahrhundert). Spicilegium Friburgense* 10 (Fribourg/S, 1965) 57-60.

> ... un vol. en 4.º vit. MS. del siglo XI ó principios del XII que contiene: I. *Incipit capitulatio super canon habitum in civitate Trecas temporibus Ludovici imperatoris à Iohanne papa romano, atque episcopis LV.* Son 78 capítulos: I. *de fide Sancte Trinitatis, qualiter à presbiteris tenenda sit et populis predicanda.* El último 78: *de his qui alienum vendiderint corpus, vel suum.* = II. *Consolatio beati Isidori episcopi Spalensis ad universos sacerdotes post lapsum penitentes.* Princip.: *Domino vero (vere) sancto, meritisquae beato Masoni episcopo, Isidorus. Veniente ad nos famulo vestro viro religioso Nicetio &c.* = III. Varios fragmentos del Concilio Niceno y otros antiguos. = IV. *Incipit prologus in vita preclarissimi confessoris Xpi Hylarii Pictaviensis episcopi. Domino patri, et meritis beatissimo patri Pascentio papae, Fortunatus.* = *Religiosi pectoris studio sollicitante commonitus,* ò *papa beatissime....* Sigue la vida. = V. *Epistola S. Hylarii ad Abram filiam.* = VI. Himno en elogio de S. Hilario, de poca entidad. = VII. Fragmentos de consueta antigua de este monasterio (Estany).[16]

The last of these texts is a customary at Estany, but Villanueva did not mention that it is said in the manuscript to be the use of St. Ruf. In 1951 the great specialist on the canons regular, Ch. Dereine noted the existence of the Estany manuscript from Villanueva's description, but he had not seen or used the manuscript itself.[17] That this was the case is not surprising. Sometime after Villanueva's description, the manuscript had left Estany and had come into the hands of the Leipzig antiquariat Karl W. Hiersemann,[18] from whom the Hispanic Society of America acquired it and assigned it the shelfmark HC 380/819. Its presence there came to the attention of the author of this article through his colleague, J. N. Hillgarth, who had learned of its existence from Antonio García y García, who had seen it briefly in New York City. Having been granted permission to publish the contents of the manuscript by the Hispanic Society of America, the present author edited a number of texts in the manuscript deriving ultimately from southern Italy, citing in passing the *ordo canonicorum* at the conclusion of the manuscript.[19] In that article mention was made of the catalogue of manuscripts in the library of the Hispanic Society of America by Charles B. Faulhaber,[20] who had based his description of several of the texts in the manuscript on information supplied by the present author, and who noted the presence of an «Order of St. Rufus?»[21] Clearly the manuscript, written by four scribes

16. Tom. VII, *Viage a la iglesia de Vique, año 1806* (Valencia, 1821) 235 f.
17. Dereine, «Coutumiers et ordinaires de chanoines réguliers,» p. 109, item 12.
18. Karl W. Hiersemann, *Bibliotheca Iberica: Being a Choice Collection of Scarce and Valuable Books and Manuscripts on Spain and Portugal* (Leipzig, 1910?) 185.
19. R. E. Reynolds, «South Italian *Liturgica* and *Canonistica* in Catalonia (New York, Hispanic Society of America MS. HC 380/819),» *Mediaeval Studies* 48 (1987) 481; reprinted in R. E. Reynolds, *Law and Liturgy in the Latin Church, 5th-12th Centuries* (Aldershot, 1994) XV.481.
20. C. B. Faulhaber, *Medieval Manuscripts in the Library of the Hispanic Society of America: Religious, Legal, Scientific, Historical, and Literary Manuscripts* 2 vols. (New York, 1983) I, 1.8 f., 19 f., 23 f., 38 f., 79, 87, 119-121, 131-134, 138-141, and II, pls. 1 and 2.
21. Ibid., I.119, item 117.

in the late eleventh or early twelfth century, is a composite canonical-liturgical codex for use by canons regular. The first item is a text of the Council of Troyes (878) edited shortly before Faulhaber's catalogue appeared by Hubert Mordek and Gerhard Schmitz, but without the benefit of the Hispanic Society witness.[22] The index to the full text of the council is separated by a short florilegium of canonistic texts designated as «Canonum collectio I» by Faulhaber.[23] Following the text of the Council of Troyes is another longer canonistic florilegium designated by Faulhaber as «Canonum collectio II.»[24] Following this canonistic florilegium is a group of texts on Hilary of Poitiers – lives, letters, and verse. That such a group of Hiliarian texts should be found in this manuscript is not surprising given the special place of Hilary at Vic and the surrounding territory.[25] There then follows the group of texts most of which derive from southern Italian models. Several of these would have been of special interest to the canons at Estany. The text explaining the meaning of Septuagesima fits well with the texts later in the customary dealing with Quadragesima. The Pseudo-Damasus-Pseudo-Hieronymian correspondence explaining the time at which Mass should be said finds resonance in the directions later on the place of Mass during the liturgical day of the canons regular. The same is true with the three canons on Mass practice from the south Italian canonical *Collection in Five Books.* The one surprising text in this group is the preface from the *Regula canonicorum* of Chrodegang of Metz. It has been pointed out by Anscaro Mundó that the *Regula Augustini* is rarely combined in manuscripts with Chrodegang's regulations for canons.[26] Rather, the most com-

22. H. Mordek and G. Schmitz, «Papst Johannes VIII. und das Konzil von Troyes (878),» in *Geschichtsschreibung und geistiges Leben im Mittelalter: Festschrift für Heinz Löwe zum 65. Geburtstag.* eds. K. Hauck and H. Mordek (Cologne-Vienna, 1978), pp. 179-225. The manuscript is also noted by Peter Brommer, *Capitula episcoporum* I, *Monumenta Germaniae historica. Leges, Capitula episcoporum* 1 (Munich, 1984) 86, who curiously places the *Schriftheimat* in England.
23. Faulhaber, *Medieval Manuscripts in the Library of the Hispanic Society of America,* pp. 130 f. Faulhaber's description of these texts has been improved upon by H. Mordek, , «Von der Alten in die Neue Welt ... Eine spanische Rechtshandschrift des Frühmittelalters in Amerika,» in *In Iure Veritas: Studies in Canon Law in Memory of Schafer Williams,* eds. S. B. Bowman and B. E. Cody (Cincinnati, 1991) 172, n. 21. On the Isidorian text see R. E. Reynolds «The Isidorian *Epistula ad Massonam* on Lapsed Clerics: Notes on the Earliest Manuscripts and Textual Transmission,» *Grundlagen des Rechts: Festschrift für Peter Landau,* eds. R. Helmholz, P. Mikat, J. Müller, and M. Stolleis (Paderborn, 2000), 77-92. Citing Faulhaber, p. 139, R. Meens, *Het tripartite boeteboek: Overlevering en betekenis van vroegmiddeleeuwse biechtvoorschriften (met editie en vertaling van vier tripartita). Middeleeuwse studies en bronnen 41* (Hilversum, 1994) 510 states that the manuscript contains the penitential *Excarpsus Cummeani.*
24. Faulhaber, *Medieval Manuscripts in the Library of the Hispanic Society of America,* pp. 131-134. Faulhaber's description of these texts has been improved upon by Mordek,, «Von der Alten in die Neue Welt,» p. 171, n. 15.
25. See Freedman, *The diocese of Vic,* p. 5, for the location southeast of Vic called Sant Hilari Sacalm; and M. S. Gros, «El *Liber consuetudinum vicensis ecclesie* del Canonge Andreu Salmúnia –, Museu Episcopal, MS. 134 (LXXXIV),» *Miscel·lània Litúrgica Catalana* 7 (1996) 182.
26. Misonné, art. cit., p. 488.

mon combination in manuscripts is that of the *Regula Augustini* with the *Institutio canonicorum* of the Council of Aachen (816).[27] Following this preface of Chrodegang is an *Ordo Romanus* with directions for the saying of private prayers and texts for the divine office and Mass. Particularly noteworthy is the Mass *pro defunctis* and the reference to the deacon and subdeacon, often mentioned later in the customary. An Ordinal of Christ follows in the so-called Hibernian-Chronological form found in manuscripts throughout Europe, including southern France and Catalonia.[28] It is interesting that Ordinals of Christ with their lists of clerical orders were at times included in customaries for canons regular, as can be seen in the *Ordo officiorum* of the Lateran canons[29] or the

27. Ibid., p. 488. For manuscripts of the *Institutio canonicorum* see R. E. Reynolds, «The 'Isidorian' *Epistula ad Leudefredum:* An Early Medieval Epitome of the Clerical Duties,» *Mediaeval Studies* 41 (1979) 254, n. 3, reprinted in R. E. Reynolds, *Clerical Orders in the Early Middle Ages: Duties and Ordination* (Aldershot, 1999) III.254, n. 3; and H. Mordek, *Bibliotheca capitularium regum Francorum manuscripta. Überlieferung und Traditionszusammenhang der fränkischen Herrschererlasse. Monumenta Germaniae Historica, Hilfsmitttel* 15 (Munich, 1995) 1045-1056.

28. This is the manuscript mentioned in the proceedings of a Symposium on the 900th Anniversary of the Reception of the Roman Rite in Leon-Castile, 1080-1980: Columbia University, The Hispanic Society of America, Fordham University, New York as being in a private collection (inasmuch as permission to publish had not been given by the Hispanic Society of America), on which see R. E. Reynolds, «The Ordination Rite in Medieval Spain: Hispanic, Roman, and Hybrid,» *Santiago, Saint-Denis, and Saint Peter: The Reception of the Roman Liturgy in Leon-Castile in 1080*, ed. B. F. Reilly (New York, 1985) 150, n. 34; reprinted in *Clerical Orders in the Middle Ages*, XIII.150, n. 34. From the ninth century and beyond the following manuscripts contain this text, sometimes with slight variants: Paris, BN lat. 614A (s.IX-X, southern France), fol. 186r-v; 2175 (s.IX), fol. 124r-v; 10612 (s.IX), fol. 120r-v; Cologne, Dombibliothek XV (s. IX), fols. 93v-94r; LXXXV (s.IX), fol. 118r; New York, Columbia University Plimpton 58 (s.IX2/3, southern France with Spanish symptoms); Munich, Bayerische Staatsbibliothek Clm. 14532 (s IXex., northeast France/Lotharingia), fols. 92v-93r; Clm. 22053 (s. IX1/4, Regensburg?), fol. 40av-40br; Karlsruhe, Landesbibliothek Aug. CXII (s. IX), fol. 48r; Albi , Bibliothèque Rochgude 43 (s.IX4/4, southern France), fol. 16v; Barcelona, Biblioteca Universitaria 228 (s. X, southern France/northern Italy? or Catalonia?), fol. 136v; Florence, Biblioteca Riccardiana 256 (s. X/XI), fol. 126v; Paris, BN lat. 1207 (s. XI), fol. 106r; Cava, Archivio della Badia della SS. Trinitá 3 (s. XI, southern Italy), fol. 334r; Rome, Biblioteca Vallicelliana Tom XVIII (s. XI, southern Italy), fol. 149v; Vat. Lat. 1349 (s. XI, southern Italy), fol. 4v; Vat. Lat. 1339 (s. XI, Rieti?), fol. 20r; Vat. Lat. 4317 (s. XI, Farfa), fols 103r-104r; New York, Hispanic Society of America HC 380/819 (s.XIex., Catalonia), fol. 109v; Naples, Biblioteca Nazionale XII A 28, (s. XI/XII, central Italy), fol. 5r; Vatican, Biblioteca Apostolica Vaticana, Vat. Lat. 4977 (s. XII, central Italy), fol. 37r; Madrid, Biblioteca Nacional lat. 19 (s. XII, southern Italy), fol. 166v; Leipzig, Üniversitätsbibliothek 1642 (s. XII) (text and commentary in H. Weisweiler, *Das Schrifttum der Schule Anselms von Laon und Wilhelms von Champeaux in deutschen Bibliotheken, [Beiträge zur Geschichte der Philosophie und Theologie des Mittelalters* 33.1-2] Münster/W, 1936) 235-238; Douai, Bibliothèque Municipale 357 (s. XIII), fol. 87r; and Paris, BN lat. 7418 (s. XIV) (based on text like the Cava and Madrid manuscripts).

29. *Bernhardi cardinalis et Lateranensis ecclesiae prioris. Ordo Officiorum ecclesiae Lateranensis*, ed. L. Fischer (Munich-Freising, 1916) 36. This Ordinal of Christ is of the «Hiberno-Hispanic Hierarchical» variety, on which see R. E. Reynolds, «Christ as Cleric: The Ordinals of Christ,» in R. E. Reynolds, *Clerics in the Early Middle Ages: Hierarchy and Image* (Aldershot, 1999) II.9, 12. Before this text is the *De distantia graduum/De officiis septem graduum*, on which see R. E. Reynolds, «The *De officiis vii graduum: its Origins and Early Medieval Development,*» *Mediaeval Studies* 34 (1972) 113-151; reprin-

Customary of St. Nicholas of Passau,[30] later to be considered in its relation to our manuscript from Estany. Finally, intruded into this section of the manuscript is a letter of Pope Victor II (1055-57) to bishop Guislabertus of Barcelona (1035-ca.1062) containing various directions for a penitent during the liturgical year, again finding a resonance in texts later in the codex.[31]

Of particular interest regarding the rule and customary followed at Estany are the two concluding texts in the manuscript, both written in a slightly later hand of the late eleventh or early twelfth century that Faulhaber compared to a Vic manuscript of 1056 cited by Millares Carlo.[32] Both texts are continuous in themselves, and their divisions are often denoted with rubrics and highlighting in orange. Occasionally rubrics have been omitted. The second text is virtually run into the first on the same line, probably meaning that they were considered to be an integral pair.

The first text, beginning with the word *Capitula*, consists of a set of rubrics followed by lemmata drawn from the *Regula Augustini* on the subject of each rubric. Clearly the canons of Estany were to follow the *Regula Augustini*, and this list of rubrics and lemmata would have been a useful directory to the subjects dealt with in the *Regula*. It is interesting to note, however, that the complete text of the *Regula Augustini* is not given after each rubric, meaning that for the full text the reader would have had to consult the *Regula* in another manuscript, of which many were being produced in the late eleventh and early twelfth century for the use of canons regular living under the *Regula*.[33] The penultimate text in the rubrics, the *Oratio beati Augustini* from the last section of the *Regula Augustini*, is given in a rather full form, perhaps supplying the authority of the great saint to the list of rubrics and lemmata.

On the same line in the manuscript as the last rubric and lemma of the *Regula Augustini* is a title of particular significance, «Hec que secuntur usu fiunt tam in ecclesia Sancti Ruphi quam domo» for the use of both the church and convent of St. Ruf. The text itself of the cus-

ted in R. E. Reynolds, *Clerical Orders in the Early Middle Ages*, II.esp. 145-47, noting that the verse for the acolyte in this *Ordo* is like that in Montecassino, Archivio dell'Abbazia 451, Rome, Università degli «Studi di Roma,» Biblioteca Alessandrina 173, Vatican, Biblioteca Apostolica Vaticana 631, and Vic, Museu I Biblioteca Episcopal 103 (CXIII). It is interesting, also, that in the *Libellus de diversis ordinibus*, written in defense of the canons regular, there is an unusual Ordinal of Christ, on which see ibid., p. 38.

30. On this text see Reynolds, «Christ as Cleric,» II.45, n. 116.
31. On this text, brought to his attention by the present author, see H. Mordek, «Analecta canonistica I,» *Bulletin of Medieval Canon Law, n.s.* 16 (1986) 11-16; Mordek, «Von der Alten in die Neue Welt,» p. 170, n. 12; and Reynolds, «South Italian *Liturgica* and *Canonistica* in Catalonia,» pp. 494 f.
32. Faulhaber, *Medieval Manuscripts*, p. 239; and A. Millares Carlo, *Tratado de paleografía española* (Madrid, 1983), I.345 f., and II. pl. 104, citing Vic, Museu I Biblioteca Episcopal XXX, fols. 1-5.
33. See Missoné, «La legislation canoniale,» p. 488.

tomary reflects a few of the passages in the primitive *ordo* and Lietbert's redaction of the *Regula sancti Rufi* published by Dom Misonné, but it is clearly of a different type. Unfortunately, the manuscript breaks off in the midst of the famous canon attributed to pope Gregory VII, «In die resurrectionis.» But the text begins with directions for Lent and proceeds through Easter. One wonders whether the text, had it continued, would have proceeded through the complete liturgical year, but in any event, it is unusual that only directions for Lent are given. One wonders, then, if these may be specially selected directions for only part of the liturgical year.

The customary begins with directions for tonsuring before Lent, Ash Wednesday and the imposition of ashes, the first Sunday in Lent, and the following feriae. There is then an extended section on the scrutinies, exorcism, giving of salt to and imposition of hands on catechumens during mid-Lent. Skipping over Palm Sunday and the first three feriae of Holy Week, the customary then goes to *Feria v. in Cena domini*, the *mandatum* for the *pauperes*, Mass, a meal, the *mandatum* for the brethren, the Good Friday liturgy, baptism (probably on Holy Saturday), and finally the canon attributed to Gregory VII.

If one compares this customary for a church of St. Ruf with those edited by Misonné and Carrier, there are several notable differences. The first is the need in the Estany customary to supply canonistic and patristic texts to justify liturgical practices. Especially important are the texts of popes echoing the *Liber pontificalis*, councils such as Braga or Martin of Braga, and the texts drawn from Isidore of Seville, Augustine, and pope Gregory I. Clearly the texts drawn from authorities in the Iberian peninsula would have been appropriate for a Catalan customary. The texts from Augustine would also have been fitting for a community following the *Regula Augustini*. And the popes in the late eleventh and early twelfth century had been enthusiastic promoters of the canons regular movement.[34] Further, many of the texts were available in manuscripts from Catalonia and southern France. For example, several texts in the customary are found in the *Decretum* of Burchard of Worms, manuscripts of which are in Catalonia, especially at Vic.[35] Then there is the canon concluding the manuscript attributed to pope Gregory VII, which was known in Catalonia.[36] But did these texts originate at St. Ruf or Estany or did they derive from other sources?

In comparing the customary of St. Ruf from Estany with those edited by Misonné, one finds a number of the same major concerns that Mi-

34. On this see J. C. Dickinson, *The Origin of the Austin Canons and their Introduction into England* (London, 1950) 49-51.
35. Vic, Museu I Biblioteca Episcopal, fragmenta XV (s.XII); and fragmenta sin. num. (s.XII).
36. See, e.g., Tarragona, Biblioteca Provincial 26 (s.XII), fol. 224r; Barcelona, Archivo de la Corona de Aragón San Cugat 63 (s.XII), unfoliated 4.12; also see Siguënza, Biblioteca del Cabildo, 75 mod. (160) (s.XII-XIII).

sonné emphasized: the offices *pro defunctis* and the BVM, the *mandatum*, liturgical practices at meals, and the connection of a hospice for the poor connected to the abbey.[37] This last concern is interesting because the prior or abbot of Estany was a titular canon in the cathedral of Vic and attached to the hospital for the poor associated with that cathedral.[38] There is no mention in the Estany text, however, of the *trina oratio*, as there was in the primitive *ordo* of St. Ruf, but there is provision for intellectually useful work such as reading and writing in the Estany text, something missing in the primitive *ordo* of St. Ruf.

Another noteworthy aspect of the Estany customary is the number of texts that would come to be visually depicted in the celebrated ornamental capitals gracing the cloister of Estany.[39] It is probable, as will be seen, that the text of the Estany customary was composed before the dedication of the Romanesque church there in 1133, but work on the new edifice had probably been in progress for many years before the dedication, and the subjects of the capitals could have been influenced by the liturgical texts and practices of the community. In the north gallery of the cloister there are capitals depicting the *Cena domini* of Holy Thursday, the *mandatum* emphasizing the figure of St. Peter (a favorite of the canons of St. Ruf[40]), the passion, and a ridiculous figure of the devil (the inimicus of the customary). In the southern gallery of the cloister there is an unusual depiction of a liturgical act, an abbot with an aspergillium, a deacon to his right clad in a dalmatic and stole holding an abbatial baculum, and to the left of the abbot a subdeacon lifting the holy water container. In the Estany text there is a reference to the asperges with *aqua benedicta* (as there is in the primitive *ordo* of St. Ruf[41]), and several references to the deacon and subdeacon.

Another notable feature of the Estany text is that there are references to an *abbas* where one would normally expect the word *prior.* It is true that in the context of the canons regular movement these terms could be interchanged, and that Estany did have abbots and commendatory abbots after 1264. But before this time, the heads of the community were styled as prior – except one, the first prior of the community, Bernat Compar or Bompar, who ruled over the long period 1086 to1122/23.[42] From 1086 to 1111 he was styled as prior, but from 1113 to his death he was styled as abbot. It is precisely in this period that the final part of the Estany manuscript was written.

While most of the script in the codex itself can by styled as Caroline,[43] there is distinct evidence that the last part of the manuscript was

37. Misonné, art. cit., pp. 474 f.
38. Pladevall and Vigué, *El Monestir romànic de Santa Maria de l'Estany*, pp. 30, 49.
39. On these capitals see E. Junyent, «El monasterio del Estany,» *Ausa* 3 (1958-60) 447-461.
40. Carrier, *Coutumier du XI siècle du l'ordre des saint-Ruf*, p. 45.
41. Misonné, art. cit., p. 483, l. 129.
42. Pladevall and J. Vigué, *El Monestir romànic de Santa Maria de l'Estany,* p. 51.
43. Faulhaber, *Medieval Manuscripts*, p. 139.

written by a scribe familiar with Visigothic-script conventions. For example, the script is at times slanted toward the left or is vertical. Then, there is his use of the high-set «s» to stand for «us» or his abbreviation for *nobis/vobis,* the two letters «nb» and «vb» having a slash or a slash + «s» through the «b.» There is a «p,» with a high-set «s» for the word *post,* and there are abbreviations of such words as *diachonus* and *subdiachonus*.[44] Finally, there are such other Hispanic features as the suppression or addition of the letter «h,» «quo» for «co,» «b» for «v,» or «b» for «p.»[45]

Beyond the dating and location of the copying of this manuscript, written probably between 1113-1122/23 by a Catalan scribe familiar with Visigothic-script conventions, there is the problem, noted above, of the source or sources used. Already it has been noted that despite some similarities between the Estany text and those of St. Ruf and Maguelone edited by Misonné and Carrier, the texts are quite different. But there are at least two early customaries for canons regular that have precisely many of the texts found in the Estany customary of St. Ruf. These customaries have been was edited, one long ago by Eusebius Amort from a manuscript now lost but resembling closely Munich, Bayerische Staatsbibliothek Clm. 16401A. This text is an *ordo officorum* for the canons regular at St. Nicholas of Passau.[46] The other customary has more recently edited by Ludwig Fischer as the *Ordo officiorum ecclesiae Lateranensis* from a late twelfth-century codex, Vienna, ÖNB 1482.[47] In a brilliant article on the relationship between these *ordines*, Père P.-M. Gy showed that the original of these related *ordines* was most probably the *ordo* for the canons regular compiled at Lucca in the time of bishop Anselm,[48] who was also responsible for the widely known *Collectio canonum,* which went through at least three recensions.[49] Following the lead of the lamented Norwegian liturgical historian, Lilli Gjerløw, Gy goes on to suggest a dependence on Lucca by St. Ruf and that Lietbert of St. Ruf borrowed elements for his own rule from Lucca.

If one examines the texts printed below of the Estany customary of St. Ruf with the texts published by Amort and Fischer, the connections are clear, suggesting that many, but not all of the texts in the Estany

44. For Visigothic-script conventions see B. Bischoff, *Latin Palaeography: Antiquity and the Middle Ages,* trs. D. Ó Cróinín and D. Ganz, (Cambridge, 1990) 96 f.
45. Cf. J. R. Barriga Planas, *El Sacramentari, Ritual I Pontifical de Roda: Cod. 16 de l'arxiu de la Catedral de Lleida, c. 1000* (Barcelona, 1975) 55 f.
46. E. Amort, *Vetus disciplina canonicorum regularium et saecularium* (Venice, 1747) II.932-1048.
47. For the date of the manuscript (s.XII3/4) and date of the *ordo,* (ca.1139-1145) see Gy, «L'influence des chanoines de Lucques sur la liturgie du Latran,» p. 128.
48. Gy, «L'influence des chanoines de Lucques sur la liturgie du Latran,» pp. 537-552.
49. See P. Landau, «Die Rezension C der Sammlung des Anselm von Lucca,» *Bulletin of Medieval Canon Law n.s.* 16 (1986) pp. 17-54. And on Anselm and his canonistic work in general see K. G. Cushing, *Papacy and Law in the Gregorian Revolution: the Canonistic Work of Anselm of Lucca* (Oxford-New York, 1998).

customary derived ultimately from the Lucchese *ordo* or a close intermediary. It can also be suggested that these texts passed from Lucca to St. Ruf, where they probably underwent some alteration, and from there to Estany, where they also probably underwent more alteration. As Père Gy points out, manuscripts did travel from Lucca to Catalonia, witness a sacramentary-ritual of Lucca taken to Tortosa by Gaufred of St.-Ruf, first bishop of the restored see of Tortosa (1151),[50] and a similar transference could have been made earlier in the case of our Estany customary. If this were the path of transmission, it might explain the presence also of the south Italian texts just before the *Regula Augustini* and the customary of St. Ruf inasmuch as south Italian texts traveled to Lucca, especially through the intermediary of a daughter house of Montecassino there, St. George.[51]

If one compares the texts of the Amort and Fischer editions and the customary of Estany, there are a number of common features. All are concerned to lend authority to liturgical practices by adding papal citations, Hispanic authorities such as the Council of Braga, and texts from Augustine and popes Gregory I and Gregory VII. There are, however, some differences that can be seen in the Estany text beyond the added liturgical directions found in any customary of canons regular. For example, texts from Isidore's *De ecclesiasticis officiis* and *Etymologies* are used, there is a group of biblical citations regarding salt used in the scrutinizes, and, as has been mentioned, the word *prior* in Amort's and Fischer's texts has been changed to *abbas*. All of these variants could have been added at Estany itself, but it is possible that because the texts were commonly known throughout Europe, they could have been introduced at any point as the text passed from Lucca to St. Ruf to Estany. Also, it is noteworthy that although the text from Passau is usually closer to the Estany text, this latter does contain some materials that are in the Lateran but not the Passau text.

In presenting an edition of the Estany rule for canons regular, the orthography of the Hispanic Society of America manuscript has been maintained. Only in cases where words or letters have been omitted < > have been used, and where there are clear anomalies in spelling ( ) have been used. In the manuscript itself the texts are run together, so for ease of use and citation the texts have been broken into paragraphs preceded by numbers in < >.

50. Gy, «L'influence des chanoines de Lucques sur la liturgie du Latran,» p. 130, n. 14.
51. See E. A. Loew, *The Beneventan Script. A History of the South Italian Minuscule*, 2nd ed. prepared and enlarged by V. Brown, *Sussidi Eruditi* 34 (Rome, 1980) I.269, n. 2.

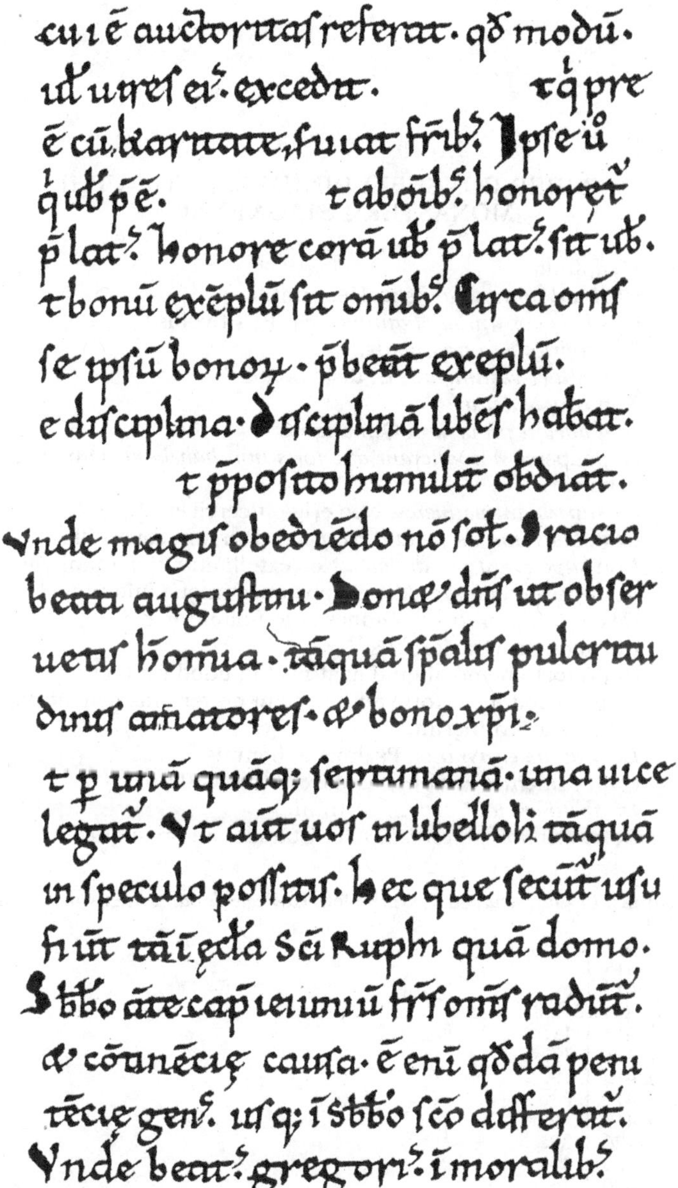

New York, Hispanic Society, ms. HC 380/819, fol. 112ᵛ

<LIBER CONSUETUDINUM SANCTI RUPHI MONASTERII STAGNENSIS>

(fol. 110r) <C>apitula.

<I.>	*Ut simul omnes habitent*. Hec sunt.[1]
II.	*Ut sit eis cor unum et anima una*. Et sit vobis.[2]
III.	*De proprio*. Et non dicatis.[3]
IV.	*De victu et vestimento*. Et distribuatur.[4]
V.	*Non equale detur*.[5]
VI.	*Non abeant proprium*. Qui aliquid.[6]
VII.	*Ut pauperes non querant que foris non habebant*. Qui autem non habebant.[7]
VIII.	*Ne superbiant pauperes*. Nec erigant cervicem.[8]
VIIII.	*Ut nobiles non despiciant pauperes*. Rursum eciam illi.[9]
X.	*Non superbiant pro diviciis*. Nec extollantur si comuni vite.[10]
XI.	*De superbia vitanda*. Alia quippe quecumque iniquitas.[11]
XII.	*De concordia fratrum*. Omnes ergo unanimiter.[12]
XIII.	*De oracione*. Oracionibus.[13]
XIIII.	In oratorio nemo aliquid agat nisi ad quod est factum.[14] Unde et nomen accepit, ut si forte aliqui eciam preter oras constitutas, si eis vacat et orare voluerint.[15]
XV.	*De psalmis et hymnis*. Psalmis et hymnis.[16]
XVI.	*Quid cantetur*. Et nolite cantare.[17] (fol. 110v)
XVII.	*De abstinencia*. Carnem vestram.[18]
XVIII.	*De eo qui non potest ieiunare*. Quando autem aliquis.[19]

1. Augustinus, *Regula tertia*, ed. L. Verheijen, *La Régle de saint Augustin*, I (Paris 1967) p. 417, l. 1.
2. Ibid., p. 417, l. 3.
3. Ibid., p. 418, l. 5.
4. Ibid., p. 418, l. 6.
5. Ibid., cf. p. 418, l. 8.
6. Ibid., p. 418, l. 11.
7. Ibid., p. 418, l. 13.
8. Ibid., p. 419, l. 19.
9. Ibid., p. 419, l. 23.
10. Ibid., p. 419, ll. 26 f.
11. Ibid., p. 420, l. 29.
12. Ibid., p. 420, l. 34.
13. Ibid., p. 420, l. 36.
14. Ibid., p. 420, l. 36.
15. Ibid., p. 420, ll. 37-39.
16. Ibid., p. 421, l. 41.
17. Ibid., p. 421, l. 43.
18. Ibid., p. 421, l. 45.
19. Ibid., p. 421, l. 46.

XVIIII. *Ut assidue legatur dum edunt*. Cum acceditis ad mensam.[20]

XX. *De infirmis*. Qui infirmi sunt ex pristina. [21]

XXI. *Ut nobiles miscericorditer tractentur*. Et si eis qui ue<nerunt>.[22]

XXII. *De egrotantibus*. Sane quemadmodum egrotantes. [23]

XXIII. *Ut post egritudinem redeant ad suum ordinem*. Set cum vires pristinas.[24]

XXIIII. *Ut bonis studeant moribus*. Non sit notabilis.[25]

XXV. *De itinere*. Quando proceditis.[26]

XXVI. *De conversacione*. Cum veneritis quo itis.[27]

XXVII. *De abitu corporis*. Nichil fiat.[28]

XXVIII. *Ut mulieres non concupiscant*. Oculi vestri et si iaciuntur.[29]

XXVIIII. *De pudicicia servanda*. Quando ergo simul estis.[30]

XXX. *De petulancia*. Et si hanc de qua loquor.[31]

XXXI. *Ut duobus vel tribus convincatur testibus*. Si autem et post amonicionem.[32]

XXXII. *<D>e eo qui indicat peccatum alterius*. Nec (fol. 111r) vos iudicetis esse malivolos. [33]

<XXXIII om.>

XXXIIII. *Ut prius preposito vestro ostendatur*. Set antequam aliis.[34]

XXXV. *Qui convictus non emendaverit, de societate proiciatur*. Convictus vero secundum propositi vel eciam presbiter.[35]

XXXVI. *De omnibus similiter peccatis*. Et hoc quod dixi de oculo non figendo.[36]

XXXVII. *De litteris non accipiendis oculte, nec munera, absque licencia*. Qui autem cumque progressus in tantum.[37]

XXXVIII. *Ut vestes in uno habeantur*. Vestes vestras in unum abeant.[38]

XXXVIIII. *<U>t non murmurent de vestibus*. Si autem hic inter vos.[39]

XL. *Ut omnia in comune operentur*. Ita sane ut nullus.[40]

XLI. *De karitate*. Karitas enim de qua scriptum est quod non querit que sua sunt sic intelligitur.[41]

20. Ibid., p. 421, l. 49.
21. Ibid., p. 421, l. 53.
22. Ibid., p. 422, l. 58.
23. Ibid., p. 422, l. 68.
24. Ibid., p. 422, l. 72.
25. Ibid., p. 423, l. 78.
26. Ibid., p. 423, l. 80.
27. Ibid., p. 423, l. 80.
28. Ibid., p. 423, l. 82.
29. Ibid., p. 424, l. 84.
30. Ibid., p. 426, l. 103.
31. Ibid., p. 426, l. 106.
32. Ibid., p. 426, l. 109.
33. Ibid., p. 426, l. 113.
34. Ibid., p. 427, l. 120.
35. Ibid., p. 427, l. 125.
36. Ibid., p. 428, l. 130.
37. Ibid., p. 428, l. 134.
38. Ibid., p. 428, l. 139.
39. Ibid., p. 429, l. 145.
40. Ibid., p. 429, l. 153.
41. Ibid., p. 430, ll. 155 f.

XLII. *Ut quod uni datur inter necessaria deputetur.* Consequens ergo est, ut eciam cum quis suis.[42]

XLIII. *Fur est qui celaverit datum.* Quod si aliquis rem sibi collatam.[43]

XLIIII. *De mensura vestimentorum et lavacionis.* (fol. 111v) Indumenta vestra secundum arbitrium prepositi laventur sive a vobis.[44]

XLV. *De lavacro corporis et medicine.* Lavacrum eciam corpori cuius infirmi.[45]

XLVI. *Ut bini eant aut terni.* Neque eant ad balneas.[46]

XLVII. *Ut non eant quo voluerint.* Et ille qui habet aliquo eundi necessitatem cum quibus prepositus iusserit ire debebit.[47]

XLVIII. *De cura egrotancium.* Egrotancium cura sive post.[48]

XLVIIII. *Ut qui pressunt sine murmure serviant.* Sive autem qui cellario sive qui vestibus.[49]

L. *De codicibus accipiendis.* Codices certa hora.[50]

LI. *Qualiter vestimenta et calciamenta dispensentur fratribus.* Vestimenta vero et calciamenta quam.[51]

LII. *Ut lites cito finiantur.* Lites aut nullas habea<tis>.[52]

LIII. *Ut qui alium ieserit cito satisfaciat.* Quicumque convitio vel maledicto.[53]

LIIII. *Ut qui invicem se ledunt invicem* (fol. 112r) *satisfaciant.* Si autem invicem leserint invicem sibi.[54]

LV. *Ut qui lesus non dimittit sine causa est in monasterio.* Qui autem non vult dimittere fratri, non sperat accipere oracionis effectum.[55] Qui autem nunquam vult petere veniam aut non ex amino petit sine causa est in monasterio eciam si inde non proiciatur.[56]

<LVI> *<U>t dura verba cito emendentur.* Proinde vobis a verbis durioribus parcite.[57]

<LVII> *Ut a subiecto prepositus non petat veniam.* Quando autem necessitas discipline moribus.[58]

<LVIIII> *Qualiter obediant suo proposito.* Preposito tanquam patri obediatur multo magis presbitero qui omnium vestrum curam gerit.[59]

<LX> *<Q>ualiter neglecta corrigantur.* Ut ergo cuncta ista serventur et si quid.[60]

42. Ibid., p. 430, l. 161.
43. Ibid., cf. p. 430, l. 165 apparatus.
44. Ibid., p. 431, l. 166.
45. Ibid., p. 431, l. 169.
46. Ibid., p. 432, l. 179.
47. Ibid., p. 432, ll. 180 f.
48. Ibid., p. 432, l. 182.
49. Ibid., p. 432, l. 186.
50. Ibid., p. 433, l. 188.
51. Ibid., p. 433, l. 190.
52. Ibid., p. 433, l. 193.
53. Ibid., p. 433, l. 196.
54. Ibid., p. 433, l. 198.
55. Ibid., cf. p. 434, l. 203 apparatus.
56. Ibid., p. 434, l. 204.
57. Ibid., p. 434, l. 206.
58. Ibid., p. 434, l. 209.
59. Ibid., p. 435, l. 217.
60. Ibid., p. 435, l. 220.

<LXI> *<U>t quod corrigere prepositus non poterit ad presbiterum referat*. Ad prepositum precipue pertinebit ut ad presbiterum (fol. 112v) cui est auctoritas referat, quod modum vel vires eius excedit.[61]

<LXII.> *<U>t qui preest cum karitate serviat fratribus.* Ipse vero qui vobis preest.[62]

<LXIII> *<U>t ab omnibus honoretur prelatus*. Honore coram vobis prelatus, sit vobis.[63]

<LXIIII> *<U>t bonum exemplum sit omnibus*. Circa omnes seipsum bonorum, prebeant exemplum.[64]

<LXV> *De disciplina*. Disciplinam libens habeat.[65]

<LXVI> *<U>t preposito humiliter obediant*. Unde magis obediendo non sol<um>.[66]

Oracio beati Augustini. Donet dominus ut observetis hec omnia, tamquam spiritalis pulcritudinis amatores et bono Christi.[67]

<LXVII> *<U>t per unamquamque septimanam, una vice legatur*. Ut autem vos in libello hoc tamquam in speculo possitis.[68]

61. Ibid., p. 435, ll. 222-224.
62. Ibid., p. 436, l. 225.
63. Ibid., p. 436, ll. 226 f.
64. Ibid., p. 436, ll. 227 f.
65. Ibid., p. 436, l. 230.
66. Ibid., p. 436, l. 233.
67. Ibid., p. 437, l. 236.
68. Ibid., p. 437, l. 240.

HEC QUE SECUNTUR USU FIUNT TAM IN ECCLESIA SANCTI RUPHI QUAM DOMO

<1> Sabbato ante caput ieiunium fratres omnes raduntur et continenciae causa, est enim quoddam penitenciae genus, usque in sabbbato sancto differatur. Unde beatus Gregorius in Moralibus, (fol. 112v) Tunc surrexit Iob and scidit tunicam suam et tonso capite corruens in terram adoravit.

<2> Mos enim veterum fuit ut quiquis pro specie sui corporis capillos nutriendo servaret, eos tempore afflictionis abscideret, et rursum qui tranquillitatis tempore capillos abscideret eos in ostensione afflictionis nutriret.

<3> Beatus autem Iob qui tranquillitatis tempore capillos servasse ostenditur ad doloris usum caput totondisse memoratur, quatenus cum in cunctis eum rebus manus superna percuteret, eciam sponte illum penitenciae species diversa fuscaret.[1]

<4> <Q>ualiter aut tonderi debeant Anicetus papa Martinus papa constituerunt, ut nullus clericus comam nutriret secundum preceptum apostoli, sed atonso capite superius patentibus auribus et secundum Aaron talarem vestem induere ut sint in habitu ornato.[2]

<5> Unde Ysidorus: Hi qui in divinis cultibus mancipati domino (fol. 113v) consecrantur, quasi Nazorei, id est sancti dei, crine preciso innoventur.[3]

<6> Quod vero detonso capite superius inferius que circuli corona relinquitur, sacerdocium regnumque ecclesie in eis existimo figurari. <T>iara enim apud veteres constituebatur in capite sacerdotum. <H>ec ex bisso confecta rotunda erat quasi spera media et hoc significatur in parte capitis tonsa.

<7> <C>orona autem latitudo aurei est circuli, que regum capita cingit. <U>trumque itaque signum exprimitur in capite clericorum, ut impleatur

1. Sabbato ... fuscaret, Fischer, p. 25. Gregorius Magnus, *Moralia in Iob*, ed. M. Adriaen, *Corpus Christianorum Series Latina* 143 (Turnhout, 1979), Lib. 2, par. 16, p. 78, ll. 45-48.
2. Qualiter ... ornato, Amort, p. 965.
3. Isidorus, *De ecclesiasticis officiis*, ed. C. Lawson, *Corpus Christianorum Series Latina* 113 (Turnhout, 1989), L. 2, cap. 4, p. 55, ll. 7-9).

eciam corporis quadam similitudinem quod scriptum est, Petro apostolo perdocente, Vos estis genus electum regale sacerdocium.[4]

<8> <E>st autem in clericis tonsura signum quoddam quod in corpore figuratur set in animo agitur, scilicet ut hoc (fol. 114r) signo vicia resecantur et criminibus carnis nostre quasi crinibus exuamur atque innovatis sensibus, ut comis rudibus, enitescamus, expoliantes, iuxta apostolum, veterem hominem cum actibus suis et induentes novum qui secundum deum creatus est renovemur in agnicione dei.[5]

<P>RIMA IN CAPITE IEIUNIUM.

<9> Finita prima diei vii. psalmi cum letania dicantur.[6] Cum vero primum inceperint psalmum omnes simul genuflexo in terram, veniam petunt. <P>ost finem autem singulorum, scilicet cum *Gloria* dicitur, similiter faciunt, et et (sic) in matutinis et vesperis, et ad oras, cum primum *Gloria* dicitur, a secunda feria xl. usque ad pascha id ipsum fiat. <Hoc> tamen in dominicis diebus et festivitatibus viiii. leccionum, a vespere usque in vesperam nullomodo faciendum est.

<10> <E>adem die post vi. antequam in coro aliquid incipiatur fratres omnes ibidem in coro discalciantur. <D>einde (fol. 114v) preparatus sacerdos in capa et calciatus cum ministris in albis similiter calciatis coram maiori altari veniens incipitur antiphona in coro, *Exaudi nos domine*. Tunc sacerdos circa altaria fratresque omnes sicut in dominicis diebus ordinate venientes aqua benedicta aspergens dicit postea preces, *Ostende nobis domine, Domine exaudi, Dominus vobiscum, Concede nobis domine*.[7]

<11> Finita oracione, incipit cantor antiphonas huius officii causam satis prenotantes.[8] *Immutemur*.[9] *Iuxta vestibulum*.[10] Cum vero antiphone dicuntur, sacerdos genuflexo coram altari, sibi ipsi prius ac ministris cineres imponit dicens, *O <h>omo*.[11] Deinde versa facie ad corum fratres bini et bini discalciati cum magna cordis contritione coram eo genua flectentes, accipiunt ab eo cineres, recordantes, scilicet, (fol. 115r) per in obedienciam primi hominis, prolatam in se maledictionis sentenciam qua dicitur, quia pulvis es et in pulverem reverteris.[12] Set et repropiciacionis ac pietatis illius clemenciam de quo dicitur, Factus pro nobis maledictum ut nos a maledictione liberaret.[13] Singulis autem dicat, *O homo recognosce quia pulvis es*.[14]

4. Ibid., L. 2, cap. 4, p. 55, ll. 25-33.
5. Ibid., L. 2, cap 4, p. 55, ll. 17-23.
6. vii. ... letania, cf. Fischer, p. 27.
7. Deinde ... domine, Amort, p. 957.
8. Finita ... prenotantes, Amort, p. 957. Cf. Miquel-S. Gros, «El *Liber Consuetudinum Vicensis Ecclesie* del Canonge Andreu Salmúnia – Vic, Museu Episcopal, MS. 134 (LXXXIV) –,» (=Vic) *Miscel·lània Litúrgica Catalana,* 7 (1996) p. 212.173.
9. *Corpus antiphonalium officii*, ed. R.-J. Hesbert (Rome, 1963) (=CAO) 147, Feria iv. Cin. Cf. Vic, p. 212.174.
10. Immutemur ... <h>omo, Amort, p. 957. CAO 147, Feria iv. Cin.
11. CAO 127.2, Pro defunctis.
12. Deinde ... reverteris, Amort, p. 957; Fischer, p. 27..
13. Fischer, p. 27.
14. CAO 127.2, Pro defunctis. Cf. Vic p. 212.174.

<12> <H>is ita gestis sacerdos revertitur in sacrarium, et incipit officium *Misereris omnium domine.*[15] Tuncque ablutis manibus indutus planeta ingreditur ad missam, in qua *Flectamus genua* et *Humiliate* dicitur atque prephacio abetur que ab hac die usque ad cenam domini diebus feriis solummodo dicitur. Set et ministri ab hac die usque ad cenam domini casulis utuntur. Quod Silvester papa constituit ut scilicet pallio linostomo leva diachonorum tegeretur.[16]

<13> Ab hac quoque die *Flectamus genua* dicitur. Hoc autem (fol. 115v) ex concilio aureliani papa cap. xiii. <I>n xl. et in ieiunia iiii. temporum tantummodo ad missarum sollempnia fideles genuaflectere debent. <I>n dominicis econtra diebus vel ceteris festis a vespera usque in vesperum non flectant ienua, set stantes incurvati orent. Nec quisquam uno genu solotenus impresso orare presumant sicut Iudei irridentes dominum in passione eius fecisse leguntur, set utraque genua in terram ponant. Ait enim apostolus, Flecto ienua mea ad patrem domini mei Iesu Christi.[17]

<14> <E>t post inceptum epistula fratres calciantur. <E>t post *Sanctus Sanctus* usque ad pascha diebus feriis tantum ad missam diei in coro prosternuntur, donec *Per omnia secula seculorum* ante *Agnus dei* dicitur.[18]

<15> <In> sequenti prima dominica usque ad cenam domini post missam sacerdos cum ministris in dominicis cantata vi. et in diebus feriis finitis inter se (fol. 116r) vesperis ceteris in coro cantantibus tribus pauperibus in ospitali mandatum faciant. <E>t eundo nudis pedibus in diebus tantumodo feriis cantent hunc psalmum *Verba mea* et compleant cetera solito more.[19]

<16> <P>roxima secunda feria post eandem dominicam ante capitulum cruces quo operiantur et pallia ab altaribus removeantur. Eadem secunda feria et iiii[a] et vi. per totam quadragesimam in claustro silencium custodiatur et in eisdem feriis viiii. lectiones pro defunctis predicto tempore agantur.

<17> Cotidie autem non statim post sextam missa dicatur sed tunc lecciones audiantur. <E>t in diebus quibus oportet loquantur usque ad viiii. et post viiii. cantent missam. <I>n qua nonnisi una oracio dicitur nisi alicuius sancti festivitas ipsa die agatur. Cum vero missa in qua due oraciones (fol. 116v) precedunt et lecciones ii. subsecuntur dicitur prima oracio absque salutacione, secunda solito cum salutacione fit.

<18> <P>ost oracionem vero dominicam incipitur pulsari primum signum ad vesperis usque quo dicitur *Per omnia secula seculorum*. Secundum vero signum post vero iii. *Agnus dei* usque *Dominus vobiscum*. <T>ercium autem cum post [*in marg.* secundum] oracionem super populum incipit *Per*

15. *Antiphonale missarum sextuplex d'après le graduel de Monza et les antiphonaires de Rheinau, du Mont-Blandin, de Compiègne, de Corbie et de Senlis.* (=AMS), ed. R.-J. Hesbert (Rome, 1985) 37a, Fer. iv Cin. Cf. Vic, p. 212.175.
16. cf. L. Duchesne, *Le Liber Pontificalis,* I (Paris, 1886; repr. Paris, 1955) 171. 35
17. <H>is … Christi, Amort, pp. 957 f. cf. Burchardus, *Decretum* 13.3; PL 140.885.
18. <E>t … dicitur, Amort, p. 958.
19. <In> … more, Amort, p. 958.

dominum nostrum Iesum. <Q>uo finito primum quidem vesperes diei, post haec Beate Marie ad hultimum defunctorum dicant. <D>ehinc facto parvo intervallo percusso cimbalo eant cenatum. <Un>de quoque intervallum in aliis ieiuniorum diebus aut post missam cum ante canitur ora viiii. aut post viiii. cum prius canitur missa, semper fit ante cibum.

<19> <C>um vero non ieiunatur sit semper inter missam et vi. <P>ost vi. vero finitam itur in refectorium. <C>um vero missa defuerit fit intervallum tanti pene spacii quanti fuerat inter iii. et vi. missa. <Q>uando cumque (fol. 117r) autem fit intervallum silencium semper custodiatur. <C>um fuerint in claustro fratres aut legant aut scribant aut opus utile quid faciant. <C>um locuntur honeste et moderate et cum nimia cautela non de vanitatibus aut scurrilitatibus set de his que utilitatem conferunt, nec vocum strepitus, alcius perstrepat, tamen in manibus libros semper teneant et numquam in claustro absque eis sint.

<20> Sequenti dominica predictae secunda, videlicet post iiii^{or} tempora de ante cedenti feria iiii. resumit totum officium *Reminiscere.*[20]

<D>E SCRUTINIO QUO TEMPORE VEL QUOCIENS FIAT.

<21> <I>n hac iiii. ebdomada xl. fiunt scrutinia ii. in iii. et vi. feria. In v^{ta} fuint iii. feria ii. et iiii. et vi. <I>n ebdoma maiori ii. feria iiii. et sabbato sancto.

<22> Ex concilio Bracarensi capitula iii. <H>oc omnimodis precipimus et antiqui canones iubent ut ante baptismum xx. dies ad purgacionem (fol. 117v) exorcismi catecumini veniant et in illis diebus iuxta canonum precepta erudiantur et scrutentur.[21]

<23> Ex decretis Celestini pape, Illud etiam quod circa baptizandos in universo mundo sancta ecclesia uniformiter agit, non ociose contemplemur intuitu cum sive parvuli sive iuvenes ad regeneracionis veniunt sacramentum, non prius fontem vite aderant quam exorcismus et exsuflacionibus clericorum spiritus ab eis immundus abigatur ut tunc vere appareat quomodo princebs (sic) huius mundi mittatur foras.[22]

<24> Memorata igitur iiii. feria apud cultores ecclesiae in apertionem aurium dicitur. Eadem die agitur scrutinium quod maximum est inter septem scrutinia. Eadem die tanguntur aures et nares cathecuminorum digitis presbiterorum. Eadem die instituuntur de auctoribus et iniciis iiii. evvangeliorum. Eadem die percipiunt (fol. 118r) simbolum et oracionem dominicam ad reddendum in sabbato sancto. Unde Augustinus in libro De fide et moribus: Baptizandis simbolum tradimus reddendumque reposcimus.[23]

20. Sequenti ... Reminiscere, cf. Fischer, p. 6. AMS 43a, Feria iv Q.T. Quad.
21. Cf. Burchardus, *Decretum* 4.8; PL 140.730.
22. Cf. Burchardus, *Decretum* 4.10; PL 140.730.
23. <D>e scrutinio ... reposcimus, Amort, p. 967. Augustinus, *De fide et operibus*, ed. J. Zycha, *Corpus scriptorum ecclesiasticorum latinorum* 41 (Vienna, 1900) cap. 11, par. 17, pp. 54 f., l. 25.

QUID SIT EXORCIZARE.

<25> Exorcizare grece dicitur, latine autem adiurare vel increpare.[24] Per peccatum enim in primo homine lapsi sumus, et in mortis haereditatem devenimus. Impleti sumus tremoribus et erroribus, merito peccati; cum quo nascimur. Ideo parvuli exsuflantur et exorcizantur, ut pellatur ab eis potestas inimici, que decepit hominem, ut possideret homines. Non ergo dei creatura in infantibus exorcizatur aut exsufflatur, set ille ex quo sunt omnes qui sub peccato nascuntur; est enim princeps peccatorum.[25]

<26> Exorcismus autem sermo est predicationis et adiuracionis contra immundum spiritum. Energuminis sive cathecumenis (fol. 118v) factus per quem ab illis diaboli nequissima vis et inveterata malicia vel violenta incursio expulsa fugetur. Hoc significavit lunaticus ille quem increpavit dominus Iesus et exiit ab illo demonium. Potestas ergo diaboli exorcizatur et exsufflatur in eis ut ei renuncient atque eripi a potestate tenebrarum in regnum domini sui per sacramentum baptismatis transferatur.

QUARE DETUR SAL EXORCIZANDIS.

<27> Sal autem in ministerio chatheminis dandum a patribus, ideo est constitutum ut eius gustu condimentum sapiencie percipiant neque desipiant a sapore Christi, non sint fatui et retro resipiscant sicut uxor Loth que versa est in statuam salis quantinus eius signo condirentur hi qui per fidem mundo et actibus desideriisque renunciant ut affectionis pristine non recordentur neque ad seculi illecebras (fol. 119r) revertantur.[26]

<28> Unde legis mandatum est ut omne sacrificium salis adiectione muniretur condiretur dicente legislatore, Nec aufferes sal federis de sacrificio domini.[27] Propter quod dominus in evangelio ait, Omnis victima sale salietur.[28] Et in alio loco, Habete sal in vobis, et pacem habete inter vos.[29] Apostolus quoque precipit dicens, Sermo vester semper in gratia sale sit conditus.[30]

<29> Unde et vulgo sapientes sulsi et stulti vocantur insulsi.[31] Estimant quidam quod ea apud quosdam gentilium antiquitus erat consuetudo ut qui fidelitatem regibus promittebant salem adiurandum vel consecrandum in presencia eorumdem regum quibus fidem promittebant comederent. Unde in libro Esdre scriptum est quod principes Samaritanorum regi Persarum

24. Cf. Isidorus, *Etymologiarum sive originum libri XX*, ed. W. M. Lindsay (Oxford, 1911) VI.19.55 f.
25. Augustinus, *Sermo de symbolo ad cathecumenum* ed. R. van der Plaeste, *Corpus Christianorum Series Latina* 46 (Turnhout, 1969) cap. 1, p. 186, ll. 39-48.
26. Isidorus, *De ecclesiasticis officiis*, L. 2, c. 21, pp. 96 f., ll. 16-25.
27. Leviticus 1.13.
28. Marcus 9.48.
29. Marcus 9.48.
30. Colossenses 4.6.
31. cf. Hieronymus, *Commentariorum in Hiezechielem libri xiv*, ed. F. Glorie, *Corpus Christianorum Series Latina* 75 (Turnhout, 1964) L. 4, cap. 16, p. 942.

cum de accusacione Iudeorum, scriberent dixerunt, Memores sumus salis quem in palacio comedimus.[32]

QUANDO (fol. 119v) SACERDOS IMPONIT SUPER CATHEMINOS (sic) MANUM.

<30> De hoc officio sanctus Gregorius ait, Sancta quippe ecclesia quotidie spiritualiter facit quod tunc per apostolos corporaliter faciebat. Nam sacerdotes eius cum per exorcismi gratiam manum cathecuminis imponunt et habitare malignos spiritus in eorum mente contradicunt quid aliud faciunt nisi demonia eiciunt?[33]

FERIA V. CENE DOMINI.

<31> Ad oras prosternuntur ad oracionem. Non dicitur *Deus in adiutorium meum intende*, set tantum psalmi suaviter cantantur, nec *Gloria* dicitur, nec capitulum, nec *Kirrieleyson*,[34] nec *Et ne nos*, nec preces, set ad terciam post psalmos incipit unus responsum et dicit versum sine *Gloria*, et repetit *Accipite*,[35] et sic prostrati dicunt *Pater noster*. Et inter se dicunt *Miserere mei deus*,[36] sicque facto spaciolo finitur ora sine oracione.

<32> Ad vi^{am} et ad viiii^{am} eodem ordine (fol. 120r) per singula. Set eadem die ante iii. in mane dicitur missa ad servitores pauperum et ad familiam. Et interim solito more fratres pulsato tintinabulo surgunt, pectuntur et abluuntur et sonato signo ad primam ecclesiam ingressi ad oracionem se prosternunt. Inde surgentes incipiunt psalmos et suaviter cantant. *Gloria patri* non dicitur, nec *Kirrieleyson*, nec preces set prostrati *Pater noster* et *Credo in deum* continuate dicant.

<33> De hinc sicut mos est confessionem dicant et *Miserere mei deus*,[37] et sic facto spaciolo surgunt[38] et capitulum intrant. In quo continuatim annuncietur Kalendarium, legatur lectio de homelia, pronuncientur defuncti, et dicad (sic) sacerdos *Requiescant in pace*, et fratres *Amen*, et recitetur tabula. Postea dicat ebdomadarius *Benedicite* et fratres respondeant *Dominus*, tractates que in capitula tractanda fuerint, exeant (fol. 120v) capitulo nichil dicentes.[39]

<34> Post terciam providentur lecciones[40] et sedilia ante refectorium ubi sedere debeant pauperes honeste adornentur, similiter ante capitulum ubi sedeat conventus, in refectorio quoque operiantur mensae in quibus comedant

32. Esdras I, 4.14.
33. Gregorius Magnus, *Homiliae in evangelia*, ed. R. Étaix, *Corpus Christianorum Series Latina* (Turnhout, 1999) L. 2, hom. 29, cap. 4, p. 248, ll. 86-91.
34. Cf. Vic, p. 221.263.
35. CAO 147, Feria v. in Cena domini.
36. CAO 28, De psalmis.
37. CAO 28, De psalmis.
38. in mane ... surgunt, Amort, p. 972.
39. et capitulum ... dicentes, Amort, p. 973.
40. Post ... lecciones, Amort, p. 973.

pauperes. Interim dum vi. cantatur in collocutorio. a laicis fratribus preparatur aqua calida et frigida et cetera que ad mandatum pertinent. Tot etiam pauperes introducuntur in claustrum quot fuerint seniores et in sedilibus disponuntur.[41]

<35> Finita vi. veniunt fratres per ordinem sedere ante capitulum, alii hinc alii inde et discalciant se. Cum autem cantor antiphonam inceperit *Mandatum novum*[42] et alius huic officio congruas tractim dicendo, fratres sicut sunt in ordine primi, capis depositis et nudis pedibus veniant, et accepto lintea ad instar domini Iesu se precingant et exemplo illius humiliter et devote pedes pauperibus lavant, linteo tergant, capillis etiam sicut illa mulier (fol. 121r) peccatrix texit atque iterum detergunt et osculentur.[43]

<36> Sicque disponatur ut qui simul venerint simul redeant simul in lavatorio manus abluant, simul tergant, simulque sedere veniant. Hic etiam alii succedant[44] qui hoc idem similiter faciant. Post hoc ii. fratribus laicis iniungantur ut aquam ad abluendas pauperum manus deferant, aliique ii. fratres mapulas ad extergendum teneant.

<37> Deinde frater ille qui vestibus preest singulis fratribus tam laicis quam clericis sicut sedent in ordine singuli numos deferat quos illi duo, et duo sicut prius suis pauperibus, genuflexo coram eis osculantes manum offerunt,[45] simulque sedere veniunt. Simulque alii faciant per ordinem. Quo per acto pauperes refectorium introducuntur. Quibus collocatis tintinnabulum. Fratres vero surgentes calciati veniunt ordinate sicut solent ante mensas et deferuntur panes in chofinis a duobus (fol. 121v) fratribus, unus hinc alius illinc, et accepto pane, unusquisque ponit ante suum pauperem. Tunc incipitur *Edent pauperes et saturabuntur.*[46] Duo postea fratres afferunt cibum apptatum et ponunt ante eos. Dehinc pulsato signo ante missam, exeunt per ordinem, remanentibus ii. ministris qui unum deferat et cetera.

DE ORDINE MISSE.

<38> Cum autem cantatur nona preparet se a missa, diachonus in dalmaticam, subdiachonus in tunica.[47] Omnia vero signa productius, solito pulsentur in classicum. Quo finito ligantur corde usque in sabbato sancto. Tunc cantores qui predenti dominica fuerunt, induti capis missam sollempniter incipiunt, que pro presentis sacrificii, recenti institucione devotissime celebretur. In qua iteratur responsum, et cantatur *Credo in unum deum*.

<39> Quod hac die sanctum crisma conficitur, Fabiani (fol. 122r) papa, Quod omni anno in cena domini crisma conficitur, cap. viiii. In illa enim die do-

41. Interim ... disponuntur, Amort, p. 973.
42. Finita ... novum, Amort, p. 973.
43. fratres ... osculentur, Amort, p. 973.
44. Sicque ... succedant, Amort, p. 973.
45. Deinde ... offerunt, cf. Amort, p. 973.
46. Psalmus 21.27.
47. De ordine ... tunica, Amort, p. 973.

minus Iesus postquam cenavit cum discipulis suis et pedes eorum lavit, sicut a sanctis apostolis predecessores nostri acceperunt, nobisque reliquerunt crisma conficere docuit.

<40> Ipsa enim lavacio pedum nostrum significat baptismum quod sancti crismatis unctione perficitur atque confirmatur. Nam sicut ipsius diei sollempnitas per singulos annos est agenda et de anno in annum renovanda et fidelibus tradenda, ita quia novum sacramentum est per singulos annos in iamdicta die innovandum, et vetus est in ecclesia concremandum. Ita a sanctis apostolis et a successoribus eorum accepimus vobisque tenenda mandamus.

<41> Hec sancta Romana et Antiocena ecclesia a tempore apostolorum custodit. Hec et Iherosolimorum et Ephesianorum tenet.[48] Silvester (fol. 122v) papa constituit ab episcopo crisma confici.[49] Quanta sit racio comunicandi hac die. Post *Agnus dei* sacerdos dividat oblatas et qui voluerint comunicent. Congrua siquidem racio postulat ut eo die religiosus quisque a comunione sese minime subtrahat quo videlict sacramentum sui corporis primo Christus instituit, omnique ecclesie quocienscumque id ageret in sui memoriam faciendum mandavit. Hinc est quod in decretis Soteris papa cap. v. sic legitur, In cena domini a quibusdam preceptio eucharistie negligitur. Que quoniam in eadem die ab omnibus fidelibus exceptis his quibus pro gravibus criminibus inibitum est percipienda sit ecclesiasticus usus demonstrat cum eciam penitentes eadem die ad percipiendam corporis et sanguinis domini sacramenta reconcilietur.[50]

<42> Sacerdos autem summat de corpore domini oblatas integras adservandum usque mane die parasceve de quibus communicet. (fol. 123r) Sanguis vero domini ipso die penitus absumatur. Interim dum comunicant dicitur *Agnus dei* et comunio *Dominus Iesus*[51] absque osculo.

<43> Postea incipitur antiphonam *Calicem salutaris*[52] cum psalmis qui suaviter cantentur.[53] Interim sacerdos si volverit sedeat. Post *Magnificat* finita antiphona sequitur oracio ad complendum, et diachonus *Benedicamus domino*. In pluribus autem ecclesiis *Ite missa est* dicitur, quia *Gloria in excelsis deo* dicunt, quod nos non dicimus.

<44> Post hec egressi facto spaciolo sonatur tabula, lotisque manibus refectorium ingressi et in ordine stantes non pulsatur tintinabulum set incipunt *Edent pauperes et saturabuntur,*[54] quod finiatur sine *Gloria* et *Kirrieleyson* et dicitur *Pater noster*. Quo tacite finito dicit sacerdos *Benedic domine dona*

48. Tunc ... tenet, Amort, p. 974; Fischer, p. 48. P. Hinschius, *Decretales Pseudo-Isidorianae et Capitula Angilramni* (Leipzig, 1863; repr. Aalen, 1963) 160 f.
49. cf. L. Duchesne, L., *Le Liber Pontificalis,* I (Paris, 1886; repr. Paris, 1955) 171.35.
50. Quanta ... reconcilietur, Amort, p. 974; Fischer. p. 48. cf. Burchardus, *Decretum*, 5.20; PL 140.756.
51. AMS 77b, Feria v. in Cena domini.
52. CAO 72, Feria v. in Cena domini.
53. Sacerdos ... cantentur, Amort, p. 974; Fischer, p. 48.
54. Psalmus 21.27.

usque *Per omnia secula seculorum*, et fratres *Amen*. Leccio sine benediccione legatur et sine *Tu autem domine* finiatur.

<45> Finito prandio dicant (fol. 123v) *Memoriam fecit* sine *Gloria*. Sicque cantando *Miserere mei deus* pergant ad ecclesiam. Quo finito *Pater noster* tantum sub silencio dicatur et sic egrediantur.

<46> Post haec altaria discooperiantur et usque in sabbato sancto discooperta relinquatur.[55]

DE MANDATO.

<47> Comedentibus servitoribus preparentur omnia ad mandatum seniorum. In capitulo vero ornentur lectricum ubi legendum est evangelium, in refectorio talamus ubi legatur. Postquam vero servitores comederint non differatur sonari tabula ad mandatum. Et cum universi tam clerici quam laici fratres in capitulo convenerint, domnus abbas vel qui vices eius tenuerit lavet omnibus pedes ad exemplum domini. Surgit et ponit vestimenta sua et accepto linteo precingit se, deinde missa aqua in pelvim incipit lavare pedes discipulorum et extergere linteo quo fuerit precinctus. Capillis eciam sicut illa mulier tergit et osculatur.[56] (fol. 124r)

A QUIBUS VERO INCIPIENDUM SIT.

<48> Beatus Augustinus ostendit, Cepit in quid Iesus lavare pedes discipulorum et extergere linteo. Venit ergo ad Simonem Petrum quasi aliquibus iam lavisset et post eos venisset ad primum apostolorum. Set non ita intelligendum est quod post aliquos ad illum venerit set quod ab illo ceperit. Quando ergo pedes apostolorum lavare cepit, venit ad eum a quo cepit, id est ad Petrum.[57] Ab hac vero die usque ad octabas pentecosten mandatum non fiat.[58]

<49> Circa finem mandati pergat diachonus cum ministris in vestiario et duo cerofererii induuntur albis, subdiachonus tunica ad turibulum, diachonus dalmaticam ad textum. Iamque finito mandato cum *Pater noster*, et oracione sine *Kirrieleyson*, et precibus sine *Dominus vobiscum*, procedunt illi de ecclesia. Quibus ingredientibus capitulum assurgit conventus, accedensque diachonus ad (fol. 124v) lectricum, ponit incensum in turibulo. Et postquam apertum incensaverit textum, incipit legere, ceroferariis hinc et unde cum turiferario astantibus.[59] Interim refectorarius preparet luminaria et sedilia et vinum et cetera necessaria opertis tabulis melioribus mapis. Cum autem diachonus dixerit *Surgite eamus*, hinc precedentibus ceroferariis per-

55. Post Magnificat ... relinquatur, Amort, pp. 974 f.
56. De mandato ... osculatur, Amort, p. 976; Fischer, p. 53.
57. Augustinus, *In Iohannis evangelium tractus cxxiv*, *Tractatus lvi*, ed. R. Willems, *Corpus Christianorum Series Latina* 36, (Turnhout, 1954) 467, ll. 11-17.
58. A quibus ... fiat, Fischer, p. 53.
59. Circa ... astantibus, Amort, p. 976; Fischer, p. 53.

gunt ad refectorium. Ubi solito more post mensas residentibus fratribus nemo tamen bibat quo usque duobus fratribus vinum deferentibus domnus abbas legenti innuat ut taceat et ipse dicat, *Potum karitatis benedicat dextera dei patris.* Et cum responsum fuerit *Amen,* fiat potus cum sobrietate.[60]

<50> Finito vero evvangelio, precedentibus ceroferariis ecclesiam intrent et prostrati accepta confessione completorium cantent et interim diachonus cum ministris exutis vestibus potum (fol. 125r) veniant.

<51> Ad completorium *Nunc dimittis servum tuum domine*, sine antiphona finito, prostrati *Pater noster*, et *Credo in deum* tacite dicant et *Miserere mei deus* inter se finant, et *Deus misereatur nostri,* accipientes aquam sine oracione dicant. Interimque se ad oracione prosternant et sic dormitorium petant.[61]

DE FERIA VI. PARASCEVE.

<52> Feria vi. parasceven quicquid de oracione pridie diximus, eodem die totum fiat.[62] Hoc tantum mutato ut pro signo tabula pulsetur[63] et ut ipsa nocte et die nudis pedibus incedant fratres usque ad prandium. Capitulum non tenetur nec tabula recitatur, set idem ipsi in crastinum legant et cantent qui ad matutinas hoc die legerant vel cantaverant.[64]

<53> Ad oras percutitur tabula et sicut pridie diximus, ipse ore dicantur et finiantur. Dum autem nona cantatur induunt se purpura in (fol. 125v) albis sacerdos in stolam et capa purpurea, faciuntque ibidem in vestiario confessionem. Et tunc non accenduntur candele circa altare. Postquam vero sacerdos cum ministris nudis pedibus venerint coram altari, statim subdiachonus accedit ad legendum,[65] pronuncians in lectione nomen prophete sic, *Leccio Oseae prophete.* Qua finita dicitur his cui fuerit iniunctum tractum *Domine audivi.*[66] Interim sacerdos sedeat. Deinde surgens dicit *Oremus.* Et diachonus *Flectamus genua, Levate*, et sacerdos dat oracionem *Deus a quo et Iudas.*[67]

<54> Post oracionem sequitur altera leccio et tractus *Eripe me domine ab homine.*[68] Quo finito pronunciet ita *Passio domini nostri Iesu Christi secundum Iohannem,* et sine responsione incipit legere.[69] Ubi autem dixerit *Partiti sunt vestimenta mea,* duo diachoni ex utraque parte altaris (fol. 126r) preparati statim nudant altare sindone in modum furantis.[70]

60. Cum autem ... sobrietate, Amort, p. 976; Fischer, pp. 53 f.
61. Finito ... petant, Amort, pp. 976 f.; Fischer, p. 54.
62. pridie ... fiat, Amort, p. 975; Fischer, p. 54.
63. Hoc tantum ... pulsetur, Fischer, p. 54.
64. Capitulum ... cantaverant, Amort, p. 976; Fischer, p. 54..
65. Cf. Vic, p. 222.272.
66. AMS 78a, Feria vi. in Parasceve. Cf. Vic, p. 222.272.
67. Oratio in Cena Domini ad Missam. Cf. J. Deshusses, *Le Sacramentaire grégorien: ses principales formes d'après les plus anciens manuscrits,* I, *Spicilegium Friburgense* 16 (Fribourg/S, 1971) 171, nr. 328. Cf. Vic, p. 222.272.
68. AMS 78a, Feria vi. in Parasceve. Cf. Vic, p. 222.272.
69. Ad oras ... legere, Amort, p. 277. Cf. Vic., p. 222.273.
70. Cf. Vic, p. 222.273.

<55> Finita passione incipit sacerdos oraciones.[71] Et cum in omnibus *F<l>ectamus genua* diachonus dixerit, in ea tantum que *Pro perfidis Iudeis* dicitur, non dicad (sic).[72] Nam quia ipso domino Iesu sicut nunc audivimus irridendo genua flectebant in passione, ecclesia tantum sibi illorum ex recenti leccione recitatum exorrescens facinus genua pro ipsis non flectit in oracione.[73]

<56> Post oraciones vero diachonus et subdiachonus de post altare coopertam accipientes crucem, hoc modo omnibus representent. Sint itaque post illos duo preparati fratres depositis capis qui cantent versus, *Popule meus quid feci tibi*?[74] Circa vero finem primi versus, procedant paululum qui deferunt reverentur cum cruce, respondente interim coro vi. *Agios o theos, Sanctus deus, Sanctus fortis*. Quo finito, id est ipsi qui prius cantent versum, *Ego quidem circa illis*, autem (fol. 126v) finem, iterum procedunt paululum, respondente coro eaque supra, rursusque dicitur versus, *Quid ultra debui*, et circa eius finem, procedentes veniunt ante altare.[75]

<57> Finitis vero his que in choro reponderint ipsi qui deferunt crucem subito discooperientes eam crucem, incipiunt antiphonam *Ecce lignum crucis*.[76] Ad quam conversi omnes mox ut crucifixum dominum extensis brachiis ad amplexum nos sue reconciliacionis invitante conspexerint et fons ille reconciliacionis de latere pendentis domini patens in ablucionem peccatoris et mestruate (sic) intuencium oculis ocurrerit, quanto devocionis affectu, erga tantum beneficium incitentur ostendant.

<58> Terre siquidem prostrati quocienscumque antiphona incipitur ad altare, adoret et osculentur ipsam terram.[77] Antiphona vero ad altare incepta tercio, finitur in choro cum psalmo *Beati inmaculati*.[78] Deinde dicitur antiphona *Crucem tuam adoramus*[79] cum psalmo.[80] (fol. 127r)

<59> Cum letaniis iam provectos ampliori munere spiritualium gratiarum perficiendos subvenimus in ordinacione. Cum letaniis moriencium animas comendamus in sanctorum felici societate.

DE OFFICIO BAPTISMATIS.

<60> Postquam venerint ad fontes sic ordinentur stacio circa eos. Stet ille qui crucem portat cum ceroferariis versa facie ad fontes coram sacerdote ad orientem converso. Quod videlicet sacerdos ante se habens fontes a dextris vero diachonum tenentem crisma, a sinistris subdiachonum cum oleo et

71. Cf. Vic, p. 222.274.
72. Finita ... dicad, Amort, p. 977.
73. Nam quia ... oracione, Fischer, p. 55.
74. Post orationes ... tibi, Amort, p. 977; Fischer, p. 55.
75. Circa ... altare, Amort, p. 977; cf. Fischer, p. 55.
76. subito ... crucis, Amort, p. 978; cf. Fischer, p. 56. AMS 78b, Feria vi. in Parasceve.
77. Ad quam ... terram, Amort, p. 978; cf. Fischerf, p. 56..
78. Psalmus 118.
79. AMS 78b, Feria vi. in Parasceve.
80. Antiphona ... psalmo, Amort, pp. 978 f.; cf. Fischer, p. 57.

ab utroque latere fontis cantores letaniam sicut ceperant prosequentes tandem completa letania facto silencio, intrat in consecracionem fontis, sicut in sacramentorio (sic) continetur, conventu hinc et inde in stacionem per ordinem constituto.[81]

<61> De parvulis autem providendem est ut postquam baptizati fuerint, nullum cibum accipiant, nec ablactentur antequam commonicent (sic) sacramento corporis Christi.

<62> Inde Ysidorus in libro Iosue,[82] Postquam sub Iesu Christo (fol. 127v) duce positi per lavacri fluenta transimus ac per fidem spirituali circumcisione signamus, tunc his gradibus pervenientes celebramus pasca, id est immolatum Christum pro mundi salute credimus. Ac deinde credentes statim pane illo dominici corporis pascimur.[83]

Decretum Gregorii pape vii. de officio huius diei in matutinis.

<63> De ordine officii huius diei in matutinis et pentecosten. Gregorius papa vii. in generali sinodo residens dixit, In die ressurrectionis usque in sabbato in albis et in die pentecosten usque in sabbato eius de ebdomade tres psalmos tantum ad nocturnos, tresque lecciones antiquo more cantamus et legimus. Omnis diebus aliis per totum annum si festivitas est viiii. psalmi et viiii. lecciones dicimus. Aliis autem diebus xii. psalmos et iii. lecciones recitamus. In dominicis diebus x. et viii. psalmos excepto die pasche et pentecosten et viiii. lectiones celebramus. Illi autem qui in diebus cotidianis....[84]

81. Postquam ... constituto, Amort, p. 985; Fischer, p. 67.
82. Ysidorus in libro Iosue, cf. Amort, p. 985, Unde Isidorus super Exodum.
83. Isidorus, *Mysticorum expositionis sacramentorum seu quaestiones in vetus testamentum, Expositio in Josue*, c. 6.4; PL 83.373.
84. On this text see A. B. Palacios, «La redacción del c. 'In die resurrectionis' en las colecciones canónicas pregracianas,» *Proceedings of the Ninth International Congress of Medieval Canon Law*, eds. P. Landau and J. Müller, *Monumenta Iuris Canonici, Ser.* D: *Subsidia* 10 (Vatican City, 1997), 923-52; and Ch. Dereine, «Saint-Ruf et ses coutumes aux XIe et XIIe siècles,» *Revue Bénédictine*, 59 (1949) 172.

VIII

Monumenta Liturgica Beneventana
New Directions

The study of manuscripts written in the bold and beautiful script of southern Italy and Dalmatia, the so-called Beneventan script, is an old one. The classic description of the history of the study of these manuscripts is E. A. Lowe's *The Beneventan Script*, published in 1914 by Oxford University Press. Lowe and palaeographical specialists working before him were concerned primarily with the script itself and to a lesser extent with the contents of the manuscripts written in the script. After 1914 Lowe intermittently continued to gather examples of the script - over 625 - which he described briefly in a new Handlist in 1962.[1] While Lowe was interested primarily in the script, other scholars using his study began to work in selected areas on the contents and decorations of the manuscripts. Hesbert, e.g., began work on the musical aspects of the manuscripts,[2] and scholars like Myrtilla Avery studied the illuminations in manuscripts such as the famous Exultet rolls.[3] These studies were largely of a traditional type and depended heavily on Lowe's work for the dating and locating of manuscripts.

New directions in the study of the manuscripts written in Beneventan script began with the reprinting and enlargement of Lowe's classic study. This was undertaken by Lowe's former assistant at the Institute for Advanced Study in Princeton, Virginia Brown, who was charged to do this work by Julian Brown, Augusto Campana, and Guglielmo Cavallo. As she worked Brown came to Toronto and the Pontifical Institute of Mediaeval Studies. There she began to give to me and my seminar students many new items in the script for identification. Why she gave them to us was obvious from their content. Almost all were liturgical, and Lowe and Brown usually identified these only in the most general terms or as 'liturgica'.

1. E. A. LOWE, 'A New List of Beneventan Manuscripts', in *Collectanea vaticana in honorem Anselmi M. Card. Albareda a Bibliotheca Apostolica edita* (Studi e Testi 220). Città del Vaticano, 1962, 211-244.
2. See René-Jean HESBERT, 'La tradition bénéventaine dans la tradition manuscrite,' in *Le Codex 10673 de la Bibliothèque Vaticane. Fonds latin (XIe siècle). Graduel Bénéventain* (Paléographie Musicale 14). Solesmes, 1931, 60-465; and 'L'Antiphonale missarum' de l'ancien rit bénéventain', *Ephemerides Liturgicae* 52 (1938), 28-66, 141-158; 53 (1939), 168-190; 59 (1945), 69-95; 60 (1946), 103-141; 61 (1947), 153-210.
3. On her work see the new volume on the Exultet rotuli by Thomas Forrest KELLY, *The Exultet in Southern Italy*. Oxford, 1996.

With the appearance of the new enlarged *The Beneventan Script* in 1980 a survey was made of the contents of all of the items in the script.[4] To our astonishment, it turned out that over 70% were liturgical. Of all extant Latin manuscripts, it is generally held that the largest proportion is liturgical, representing approximately 10%. Hence, the overwhelming percentage of codices in Beneventan script that are liturgical suggested that the script was par excellence a liturgical one. It is stately, bold, and beautiful, and was 'conservative' or antique. As Gothic type-face has been used in printed liturgical books well into the twentieth century to give an antique and conservative appearance, so Beneventan script was used in the Middle Ages in southern Italy and along the Dalmatian coast primarily for liturgical books to give the same sort of impression to users and readers.

A further development in the early 80s had to do with the dating of items in Beneventan script. One of the new items discovered after 1914 by Lowe himself was a libellus from Caiazzo repaired and then kept in the Vatican Library.[5] Lowe had recognized the text as the office for Corpus Christi, and with his expert eye had dated the script to the twelfth century. When I saw that date I excitedly concluded that this famous liturgical office – the first ever given official status by the papacy in 1264 – could not have been written by its reputedly famous author, St. Thomas Aquinas, as many Thomistic scholars have argued.[6] Hence, after receiving photographs of this item, I asked our two most eminent palaeographers at the Pontifical Institute of Mediaeval Studies for their judgement as to the date of the script. Both said twelfth century, i.e., about a century before the text was supposedly written by Thomas Aquinas and mandated by the papacy. Excitedly as I began to transcribe the text to my surprise I found mentioned the name of Urban IV whose bull *Transiturus* had established the feast in 1264. In other words, a script that had looked to a number of eminent palaeographers as having been written in the twelfth century was actually written at least a century later – that is, it was a conservative script.

At the same time I was working on Beneventan-script texts, I was investigating a number of texts written in the Visigothic script of the Iberian peninsula. Like the Beneventan, Visigothic script was known as a preeminently liturgical one, although far fewer manuscripts of it existed than those in Beneventan. It had been demonstrated not many years back that many of the items in Visigothic script, especially those written in Toledo, that had traditionally been dated to the eleventh century

4. E. A. LOWE, *The Beneventan Script. A History of the South Italian Minuscule*, 2nd ed. prepared and enlarged by Virginia BROWN (Sussidi Eruditi 33, 34). Roma, 1980.

5. Città del Vaticano, Biblioteca Apostolica Vaticana, Ms. Vat. lat. 14733.

6. On this see Ronald John ZAWILLA, *The Biblical Sources of the Historie Corporis Christi attributed to Thomas Aquinas: A Theological Study to Determine their Authenticity* (diss. Toronto, 1985).

were in fact written in the thirteenth. Could it be that many manuscripts in the Beneventan had also been dated too early?

Confirmation of this suspicion was quick in coming from a colleague in the United States studying the musical notation in Beneventan-script codices. Thomas Kelly had discovered that this notation in many manuscripts dated by Lowe to the eleventh and twelfth centuries was actually from the thirteenth century and beyond.[7] Thus, it appeared that all of the palaeographical dating by Lowe had to be rethought.

How could this best be done? For years it has been recognized, although not widely, that liturgical manuscripts are often the easiest of manuscripts to date and locate because of their calendars, specific names, dates, locations mentioned specifically in the texts and liturgical usages peculiar to specific locations and regions. Hence, both Virginia Brown and I, with several students in medieval liturgical studies, began to examine a number of liturgical codices more closely for clues as to their dates and places of origin.

One of the first groups of manuscripts Brown examined consisted of prayer books that Lowe had dated palaeographically to the fourteenth century. In examining those manuscripts with their litanies and prayers for specific names of persons, she discovered that this group of manuscripts had been written in Naples in the late sixteenth century in a convent of conservative Benedictine nuns.[8] This was a further demonstration that Lowe's dates, especially for liturgical manuscripts, were too early and that a careful examination of the texts would lead to more precise locations and origins of the manuscripts.

One further development led to the formation of the program Monumenta Liturgica Beneventana. After the appearance of the revised and enlarged version of Lowe's classic work, the Pontifical Institute of Mediaeval Studies became a magnet for reports by scholars throughout the world regarding the discovery of new items. Individuals, libraries, and auction houses and booksellers such as Sotheby's and Bernard Quaritch deluged the Institute with new information and requests for dating and locations. Further, a large collection of photographic facsimiles was amassed at the Institute. Indeed, since beginning the revision of Lowe's *The Beneventan Script*, over fifteen hundred new items hitherto unknown have been discovered. To study all of this new material – as well as that known to Lowe – the Library of the Pontifical Institute of Mediaeval Studies has been augmented with additional palaeographical, liturgical, historical, art-historical and musical publications.

7. See Thomas Forrest KELLY, *The Beneventan Chant*. Cambridge, 1989.

8. Virginia BROWN, 'The Survival of Beneventan Script: Sixteenth-Century Liturgical Codices from Benedictine Monasteries in Naples', in: *Monastica. Scritti raccolti in memoria del XV centenario della nascita di S. Benedetto (480-1980)*. Montecassino, 1981, vol. 1, 237-355.

The convergence of palaeographical and liturgical studies in terms of codices written in Beneventan script suggested that a more extensive program be undertaken at the Pontifical Institute of Mediaeval Studies. At the time – that is in the early and mid 1980s – there were few models on which to base the program, but it nevertheless went forward under the title Monumenta Liturgica Beneventana, and the Social Sciences and Humanities Research Council of Canada has given generous support ever since.

Early on it was evident that manuscripts in Beneventan script reflect not only an ancient indigenous rite or use called the Beneventan, but also the rites and uses of the nearby see of Rome and those of the conquering Byzantines, Normans, and Angevins throughout the 'Beneventan zone' stretching from southern Italy across to the Dalmatian coast from Istria down into Albania. The monuments of these liturgical rites practiced in the 'Beneventan zone' display an astonishing diversity and reflect the political, social and cultural complexity of the south Adriatic region in the Middle Ages.

The study of the ritual practices of this region within the program of the Monumenta Liturgica Beneventana has had a number of related objectives. First, the microfilm and photographic holdings of appropriate manuscripts have been and are being expanded so that the collection at the Pontifical Institute is now the most extensive in the world, so much so that foreign scholars visit the Institute to consult them and frequently write for information on them. Second, virtually all the liturgical codices in Beneventan script (with the exception of those in war-torn Dalmatia) have been extensively described codicologically and palaeographically and this is included in a computerized database. Third, transcriptions of the liturgical texts in the manuscripts are being entered into a computerized repertory, and this repertory is being and will be used in the fourth objective of the program, critical editions and studies of the various types of liturgical books written in Beneventan script. A fifth objective of the program is to use the edition and study of the liturgical manuscripts in Beneventan script as a means to train graduate students in the various disciplines they must master as medievalists, and to date there have been seven licentiate and doctoral theses at the Pontifical Institute and University of Toronto on Beneventan-script liturgical topics. A sixth objective of the program is to publish our results not only outside the Pontifical Institute but also in current publications series within the Institute. Hence, there has been established a subseries in the Institute's learned journal *Mediaeval Studies* entitled 'Miscellanea Beneventana', and to date twelve numbers of the subseries have appeared. Another subseries in the journal, entitled 'Parerga Beneventana', has just been published in which small discoveries regarding non-Beneventan-script codices made in searches for Beneventan items are reported. Beyond these articles, a series of extensive studies and editions has been initiated with the Publications Department of the Pontifical Institute called *Monumenta Liturgica Beneventana*. A seventh objective of the program is cooperation with projects or programs beyond Toronto engaged in the study of topics involving Beneventan-script liturgical codices. For example, members of the Monumenta Liturgica Beneventana have cooperated with Dom Jean Mallet, O.S.B. and Dom André Thibaut, O.S.B. in the compilation of their monumental catalogue of the Beneventan-script codices in the Biblioteca Capitolare in Benevento[9] and with the Fondation Royaumont in France in the study of the cathedral of Benevento, its music and culture.

All of these objectives will be continued for the foreseeable future. But there are further new directions in which the Monumenta Liturgica Beneventana is moving. One of the most surprising aspects of our work in the past few years has been the large number of hitherto unknown items in Beneventan script that have come to light: no less than 500 in the past four years alone, 300 of which are now described in Virginia Brown's 'Second New List (3)' in 'Miscellanea beneventana'[10] and the other 200 + which will appear in the 1999 issue. Of the new items discovered many have been of extraordinary interest, and the remainder of this paper will be devoted to a description of several of these.

There is first a fragment of an extraordinary liturgical roll Richard Gyug discovered at Montecassino itself.[11] The compactiones in the Archivio dell' Abbadia of Montecassino are folders containing flyleaves, binding strips, and dismembered fragments of other sorts from the codices of the Archive and elsewhere. Although a catalogue of the compactiones has been promised and the folders often searched for new material, this fondo remains without a published guide to its contents. In their present state, therefore, the hundreds of fragments of the compactiones represent the last large collection of unidentified material in the Beneventan script. Thus preserved in Compactiones XVI has been a hitherto unremarked fragment of a liturgical roll in Beneventan script containing the first of the *Orationes sollemnes* for Good Friday. Its interest lies both in its format and in its content: no other roll for Good Friday is reported to have been preserved, nor, apart from my own suggestion several years back, has anyone else guessed that such a roll should exist. As to its content, as we shall see, the formula for the diaconal monition to kneel, say the Pater noster, and rise between the formal invitation to pray and the prayer itself represents the most ancient structure of the rite, preserved elsewhere only among the earliest sources of the liturgy and a handful of later Beneventan manuscripts.

9. See Jean MALLET & André THIBAUT, *Les manuscrits en écriture bénéventaine de la Bibliothèque capitulaire de Bénévent, 1. Manuscrits 1-18*. Paris 1984 (and forthcoming volumes).

10. Virginia BROWN, 'A Second New List of Beneventan Manuscripts (III)', *Mediaeval Studies* 56 (1996), 299-350.

11. For details of this summary of this manuscript see Richard F. GYUG, 'A Fragment of a Liturgical Roll at Montecassino (Compactiones XVI)', *Mediaeval Studies* 52 (1990), 268-277.

Concerning the format, rolls in contrast to codices occupy a small but important niche among the liturgical books of western Europe. Rolls were more prominent in eastern churches, but the Latin churches do not lack instances of liturgical and paraliturgical texts presented on rolls. Conciliar decisions were recorded on rolls, of which at least one copy has survived, and others are portrayed in illustrations such as that in the famous Utrecht Psalter. Paraliturgical drama and music are sometimes written on rolls, an appropriate format for the material required by individual participants in a larger dramatic setting. The form was often used for monastic necrologies and less frequently for vitae.

Several liturgical functions appear in roll-form, beginning with the famous Rotulus of Ravenna containing a series of prayers probably intended for the Vigil of Christmas. Illustrations of the ordination of exorcists indicate that exorcisms to be read by the exorcist were preserved in rolls; a few rotuli containing benedictions performed by bishops have also survived. The canon of the Mass sent by Pope Zacharius in 740-50 to Boniface in Germany is described as a rotulus. And the prayers of ordinations were to be found on rolls according to Hincmar in his letter to Adventius of Metz. In 884 Notker Balbulus describes in the preface to his collection of sequences their composition on rolls before they were codified. The Laudes of Lorsch are testimony to the form used for Christmas and crown wearing, and coronation ordines are also found on rolls. In the tenth-century Pontifical of Egbert a roll is cited for the names of penitents to be read by the archdeacon on Holy Thursday. The litanies of Milan were sung from rotuli according to the twelfth-century description by Beroldus. Rolls, therefore, appear in many ecclesiastical and liturgical functions, especially those with short texts, texts performed by an individual among several coordinated celebrants, and musical texts. Further, the ceremonies in which rolls were used are often moments of the highest significance, public spectacle, and communal importance.

Congruent with such requirements is the most renowned use of the liturgical rotuli, and certainly the most well-attested form: the Exultet rolls of southern Italy. Almost exclusively written in the Beneventan script, and frequently lavish in presentation, illustration and ornament, these rolls contain the text and music of the Exultet sung by the deacon during the Holy Saturday vigil at the blessing of the Paschal candle. Other liturgical rolls have also been preserved from the region, specifically two rolls of the Benedictio fontis to be used on Holy Saturday and an *Ordo officiorum* containing the consecration of the minor and major orders, and now our hitherto-unknown fragment of a Good Friday roll.

While discussions of the rolls of southern Italy have considered them as accommodation to eastern practice or remnants of ancient customs, the solemnity and importance of the ceremonies thus written may be crucial to understanding the form. In Greek rolls, the minister is the defining force, that is, the roll usually contains the text to be sung by the celebrant whereas the other participants used other books. Similarly, Exultet rolls for the deacon were required as separate practical books, just as books of epistles or choir books are specific to particular participants. Such motives certainly define liturgical genres in some instances, and probably play a large part in the production of southern Italian rolls. But the coincidence of the form with some of the most important and conspicuous ceremonies of the liturgy – the lighting of the Exultet candle, baptism, and ordination – suggests that solemnity was also a critical element in the choice to use the roll-form. In this regard, our new fragment containing some of the prayers recited by the principal celebrant (priest or bishop) on Good Friday after the Gospel emphasises the importance of the solemnity in the definition of the form since it expands the number of ceremonies thus presented to include three of the central rituals of Holy Week (the Exultet, baptism, and now Good Friday).

The contents of the fragmentary roll in the Montecassino compactiones are no less remarkable than its format. René Hesbert some years ago described the distinctive practice of the *Orationes sollemnes* among some Beneventan-script manuscripts as having the diaconal monition 'Erigamus nos' rather than the synonymous 'Levate' of the Roman liturgy. Given that the manuscripts with the form 'Erigamus nos' are otherwise the most conservative in preserving the Old Beneventan musical chant, it is likely that the monition is part of a regional and ancient form of the *Orationes sollemnes*.

The indication in our compactiones text to say the *Pater noster* between the commands to kneel and rise is also an unusual feature, although it has been partially erased, perhaps at a later date. The medieval Roman forms of the *Orationes sollemnes* presented modified versions of the universal prayer of the early church that followed the Gospel. Before the development of the medieval corpus, these prayers began with an extended invitation ('Oremus, dilectissimi nobis in primis pro ecclesia sancta' etc.), then a monition to kneel for reflection before rising for the universal prayer itself. Beginning with the prohibitions against kneeling during festive seasons issued by the Council of Nicea in 325, the occasions for such practice diminished: this early form of prayer came to be restricted to a few feasts, including the *Orationes sollemnes* of Good Friday. In the famous Reginensis manuscript of the *Gelasian Sacramentary*, there is a direction to wait a bit 'post paulolum'. For the most part, medieval sources reduce the command to a quick genuflection, 'Flectamus genua-levate'. In some witnesses, the period of kneeling is to end when the celebrant rises from saying his prayer. But what was that prayer? The answer is found in a famous manuscript from Benevento, MS 38, and in our Good Friday fragment: the prayer is the *Pater noster*.

A second discovery by our team in Toronto is fully as unusual as the Good Friday partial roll, this one a fragment containing part of the Greek liturgy of St. John Chrysostom, transliterated into Latin characters in Beneventan script.[12]

The influence of Greek liturgical culture in the areas where Beneventan script was written has long been known and well documented. For example, the renowned Barberini codex, Vatican, Biblioteca Apostolica Vaticana Barb. gr. 336, written in Greek in the late eighth or early ninth century and bearing the earliest surviving text of the Liturgies of St. Basil and John Chrysostom, has long taken pride of place among the scores of liturgical manuscripts from southern Italy. Greek liturgical rolls written in southern Italy, although somewhat rare, are not uncommon, and their influence on Latin liturgical rotuli of the region has often been stressed. The liturgy of the Roman rite, written in Greek in southern Italy, the so-called Liturgy of St. Peter, has been intensively analyzed; and there are multiple studies of the Latin translations by Leo Thuscus and Nicholas of Otranto of the so-called *Missa graecorum* in the late twelfth and early thirteenth centuries.

In his recent important study of the Old Beneventan chant Thomas Kelly has noted numerous instances in which Greek liturgical practice was used in the area where Beneventan script was written, and he has demonstrated that elements of the Greek liturgy were taken into the liturgical rite celebrated in Benevento itself. In some instances the Greek text was transliterated into Latin characters to be used on several of the most significant feasts in the liturgical rite there.

The fragment with our recently discovered Greek liturgical text is now in the Rare Book Room of the Bryn Mawr College Library in Pennsylvania and bears no shelfmark. It first came to the attention of John Mitchell of the University of East Anglia, who generously notified Virginia Brown of its existence.

It is unnecessary here to present extensive codicological and palaeographic details of the fragment. Suffice it to say that it would seem that the surviving bifolium was part of the last quire of a libellus with two or more quires attached because its text falls late in the liturgical rite it represents. Thus, quires before our bifolium would have contained the first and largest part of the liturgical rite, and a bifolium or bifolia bound into our bifolium after fol. 1v would have contained the remainder of the liturgical rite. The blank parts of our bifolium, fol. 2r-v, would have been the outside cover of the last quire of the liturgical libellus.

With the exception of the rubric 'PH<B>ON' (possibly a shortened form of Ekphonos?), a Greek zeta and what resembles the Greek mu, the writing is entirely in Latin characters. The text written in black ink is the transliterated form of the

12. For details of this summary of this manuscript see Roger E. REYNOLDS, 'The Greek Liturgy of St. John Chrysostom in Beneventan Script: An Early Manuscript Fragment', *Mediaeval Studies* 52 (1990), 296-302.

end of the precommunion and beginning of the communion of the Liturgy of St. John Chrysostom. Further, with the exception of the words 'Proschome' and 'Ta agia tis agiis', on fol. 1v, this Greek transliterated text is in an uncalligraphic Beneventan hand. These words and the rubrics for the text in Latin on fol. 1r-v are written in a calligraphic Beneventan hand. It is always risky to date a text on the basis of the few letters in our fragment, but its open character, the lack of a descender on the final *r*, and the *n* and *m* with feet rather than lozenges suggest that the text was written in the late tenth or early eleventh centuries. It is not in Bari-type Beneventan script and therefore was written probably not in Puglia but somewhere else in the lower or central part of southern Italy.

In the examples of transliterated Greek text in Professor Kelly's study, the writing in the manuscripts is in a sure Beneventan hand, probably signifying that there was a long tradition of copying such transliterated texts. In our fragment, however, there appear to be two distinct methods of writing, the calligraphic and uncalligraphic types. The former, the calligraphic, is used for the Latin and a few Greek words on fol. 1v. That one scribe was responsible for both this calligraphic writing and the uncalligraphic sections of the transliterated Greek text is likely if the forms of such letters as *a, c, e,* and *r* are compared. Why the scribe would have used these two types - calligraphic and uncalligraphic - is unclear. It is possible that the scribe was generally accustomed to writing in Latin, and when called upon to transliterate from a Greek text he became unsure and switched into the uncalligraphic style. For example, at times his m's are in proper Beneventan script; at other times they resemble a Greek mu. But if the scribe were uncertain when he came to Greek text, why did he write on fol. 1v in the uncalligraphic script the ***nomina sacra*** 'Isu xps', which he would certainly have known from Latin? Perhaps, the uncalligraphic script is an attempt to imitate the Greek script of his exemplar, but one cannot be certain of this. In any event, all of this suggests that the scribe was not copying from a previously transliterated text but was writing de novo from either 1) a text in Greek, 2) one he knew by heart, or 3) one being dictated to him.

Which was it? There are indications of all three. For a written copy made by a scribe who was acquainted with Greek is the Greek phon, zeta, accents (sometimes misused), and the m's that in some instances resemble the Greek mu. On the other hand, the orthography of the Greek transliterated text may indicate an oral or memory source. Why, for example, would our scribe, if following a written Greek source, change a Greek kappa to a Latin *c* in some places but maintain it in others? Moreover, the sign 7 is used for a Greek accent, for an *iota*, and for *uio, ei*, and *h*. One indication that our scribe was transliterating from a text he knew by heart in Greek but may have had before him a written source or a dictated source appears in the last word of fol. 1r. The scribe originally wrote ***apu*** and then over this wrote ***el***. The former word, ***apu***, comes from one text of the Liturgy of St. John Chrysostom represented in variant manuscripts printed in the classic text by Goar and in such manuscripts as the famous twelfth-century Rossano codex, Vatican, Biblioteca Apostolica Vaticana Vat. gr. 1970, but not in the renowned Barberini text of about the year 800. The text subsequent to the word *apu* emended to *el*, however, is from the Barberini text. This suggests that the scribe recognized the appropriate form found in the Barberini text, but began unthinkingly to write the later variant, probably from memory. In short, the scribe knew both Greek and Latin. He may have been transliterating from a Greek text – hence the uncalligraphic form of the transliteration – but he also was transliterating from what appears to have been dictation or memory. That such might happen in the early Middle Ages has been brilliantly demonstrated by Ann Freeman, who has shown that in the composition of the *Libri Carolini*, Theodulf of Orléans used common Latin Psalter texts but the memory of his native Visigothic liturgical use intruded into the writing of the biblical text.

Because our text appears on such a poor piece of parchment, it might be thought that it is a *probatio pennae*. This is unlikely, however, because of the utilitarian rubrics and because it begins and ends in mid sentences. Thus, it seems to have been part of a more extensive text of the Liturgy of St. John Chrysostom. Our scribe, knowing both Latin and Greek, was thus probably writing the text for a Latin-speaking priest who could not read Greek characters but who had to serve a Greek-speaking community using the Liturgy of St. John Chrysostom. That a Latin-speaking priest might offer the Eucharist according to the Greek rite rather than the Roman or Beneventan might seem extraordinary, until it is remembered that in southern Italy there were frequent liturgical interchanges by Greek and Latin communities, and that prior to the Schism of 1054 between the Greek and Latin churches this probably would not have been considered unusual or uncanonical in southern Italy.

The poor quality of the bifolium and its writing suggest that the libellus to which it belonged was not made for deluxe or continuous usage such as other extant grand Greek manuscripts and rotuli of the Liturgy of St. John Chrysostom or the imposing Latin manuscripts from Benevento with their transliterated Greek elements. We know, for example, of occasional services at Montecassino on a portable altar being celebrated in Latin and Greek in the tower of St. Benedict, and if it were a Greek Mass, there might simply have been a Greek translation of the Latin rite such as is found in later manuscripts. But it is not beyond the realm of possibility that at Montecassino and elsewhere the Greek liturgy celebrated in these occasional joint services might have been that of St. John Chrysostom and that an unprepossessing libellus such as ours might have been used.

Beyond its importance in showing the liturgical interplay between Latins and Greeks in southern Italy, our text is extraordinary for the development of the Greek liturgy itself. As has been noted, the oldest texts of the Liturgies of SS. Basil and John Chrysostom appear in the eighth- or ninth-century Barberini codex in in Greek described by Cardinal Pitra: 'Le plus ancien et le plus beau des nos manu-- scrits liturgiques assurément l'inestimable ***Euchologe*** du viiie siècle, que les princes Barberini ont heureusement conservé dans leur riche bibliothèque'. There are then few witnesses of these liturgies until the thirteenth century, and hence our fragment from the late tenth or early eleventh centuries is precious indeed. If the text is compared with the Liturgies of St. Basil and St. John Chrysostom in the Barberini codex, most of it could, in fact, have derived from either, but the first few words on fol. 1r are found only in the Liturgy of St. John Chrysostom.

Our text is further significant in that it reflects the Liturgy of St. John Chrysostom in transition in southern Italy from what André Jacob calls the Italo-Greek or Calabrese tradition to the Constantinopolitan tradition. The text largely follows the Italo-Greek or Calabrese form, but in several cases variants from later Constantinopolitan witnesses to the Liturgy of St. John Chrysostom appear. The emended 'apu' at the bottom of fol. 1v is an instance of this, as is the 'Eni te to ko' at the bottom of fol. 1r, which appears in variant manuscripts reported by Goar. Also it is interesting that the prayer 'khari tu...' concludes in the tradition of the Liturgy of the Presanctified found both in the Barberini manuscript and in the eleventh-century Liturgy of St. John Chrysostom, but not in the Barberini text of the Liturgy of St. John Chrysostom.

Perhaps the most remarkable discovery made while studying Beneventan-script liturgical fragments is one by Virginia Brown made in the Biblioteca Medicea-Laurenziana in Florence.[13]

Two of the volumes with Beneventan script the Monumenta Liturgica Beneventana team has described codicologically are the famous autographs of the miscellaneous texts or zibaldone of Giovanni Boccaccio. Did Boccaccio write in Beneventan script, one may well ask? No, but he did erase a Beneventan-script text to write over it a number of his works in his early period while he was in Naples with his father from 1327-41. While countless Renaissance scholars have pored over the texts of Boccaccio in these manuscripts, numbered 29.8 and 33.31, in the Laurenziana, the underlying text in Beneventan has never been carefully studied. Yet the underlying text presents a fascinating story involving not only liturgy, but also monastic and religious history and the relationship of the Angevin royal house of Naples to the religious house where the manuscript was made and to the young Boccaccio himself.

The manuscript is part of a graduale that may be the oldest Mass book of Neapolitan origin. To go into the details as to how Boccaccio erased and cut up the parts of this graduale and how they were originally arranged is beyond what can or

13. For details of this summary of this manuscript see Virginia BROWN, 'Boccaccio in Naples: The Beneventan Liturgical Palimpsest of the Laurentian Autographs (MSS. 29.8 and 33.31)', *Italia medioevale e umanistica* 34 (1991), 41-126.

should be said here. Suffice it to say, codicological, palaeographical, textual and musicological features point to a date after the year 1250 and probably at the end of the thirteenth century. Textual evidence also points to a date at the end of the thirteen century and confirms a Neapolitan origin of the book.

Generally, the text of the graduale itself was like that represented in a famous graduale now found in the Biblioteca Capitolare in Benevento, Nr. 34. But the erased text of the Boccaccio manuscripts has a number of special characteristics. First, there are the rubrics, which Boccaccio either could not or did not take the trouble to erase completely. Surprisingly, a number of these rubrics are the same as those in the Franciscan *Ordo missalis* revised in 1243-44 by Haymo of Faversham. This is surprising because they are the only Franciscan rubrics or texts ever found written in the Beneventan script. By this time in southern Italy the use of the Beneventan script had been forbidden by the emperor Frederick II, although in conservative Benedictine monasteries and convents it was continued on, as was noted, into the sixteenth century.

A second unusual feature in the text of the graduale is that one of its rubrics mentions *moniales* – i.e., it was a book made for a convent of nuns. To locate this graduale one would naturally then look for convents of Franciscans in Naples. The earliest convents in Naples were those of S. Lorenzo (given to the Franciscans in 1234 by John, Bishop of Aversa) and S. Maria Palatium (allegedly founded by St. Francis himself). But if the graduale had been made for these convents, one would expect to find a thoroughly Franciscan graduale, both in its rubrics and its texts. But inasmuch as a great deal of the text follows that of MS 34 of the Biblioteca Capitolare in Benevento, our graduale is more in line with older Benedictine practice. This unusual combination of Franciscan and Benedictine rubrics and texts thus suggests another possibility – to wit, that it was compiled for a convent that had been founded as an Benedictine convent but that was being influenced by the rise of the Franciscans.

In fact, in the second half of the thirteenth century the influence of the Franciscans was rapidly increasing in Naples and in the Angevin kingdom. Charles I had given properties to the Franciscans, and Charles II (1285-1309) gave donations to the church and convent of S. Lorenzo, in which his son was eventually buried, and where Boccaccio imagined his first glimpse of Fiametta. The Angevin tie with the Franciscans was literally brought home when Louis, second son of Charles II, joined the order, eventually to become bishop of Toulouse. King Robert the Wise (1309-43), Louis' brother, and Queen Sancia are all known for their ardent patronage of the Franciscans, and indeed the Franciscans played both spiritual and political roles in Robert's court. The king and queen initiated the construction of the church of S. Chiara, where Robert was buried; and Queen Sancia retired to S. Croce, another of her Franciscan foundations, where she lived as 'suor Chiara della Croce' until her death and burial there in 1345.

But to return to our question, in what Neapolitan convent of nuns could our graduale have been made with its mixture of Franciscan an Benedictine elements? In fact, we know of only two convents of nuns where Beneventan script was written, S. Gregorio Armeno and S. Patrizia, but we know only of sixteenth-century codices of the script written for these convents. Nonetheless, in two of the codices from S. Patrizia Franciscan influence is present in that several Franciscan saints are included in the martyrology and there is a text of the Office of the Passion attributed to S. Bonaventure. Despite this Franciscan influence, both S. Gregorio Armeno and S. Patrizia remained adamantly Benedictine until their suppression in the nineteen century.

Another consideration arises in our search for the origins of the graduale. The codex was a large and expensive one to make. Yet sometime between 1327, when Boccaccio came to Naples with his father and 1334, by which time he had written his first texts on the erased folios, the graduale had been discarded by its owners. Had it been at the Benedictine convents of S. Gregorio Armeno or S. Patrizia, the graduale would have served them well for decades beyond this. Hence, a more drastic explanation for the surrender of the graduale is demanded.

Yet this drastic explanation is perhaps the simplest. Could the manuscript have become obsolete because the users needed it no longer? No female monasteries connected with the Angevins failed between 1243, when Haymo's Franciscan *Ordo missalis* was completed, to 1327-34, when Boccaccio acquired the manuscript. But indeed, one convent did become Franciscan, leaving behind its long Benedictine affiliation.

This convent was that of S. Maria Donnaregina. Founded according to tradition in the fifth or sixth century, it early followed the Rule of St. Basil. At the beginning of the ninth century it passed to the Benedictines and remained that way until the first half of the thirteenth century, when, according to another tradition, the nuns at S. Maria Donnaregina abandoned the Benedictine rule for that of S. Chiara. Indeed, in a document of 1236 Pope Gregory IX gave the nuns who wished to do so permission to follow the Rule of the nuns of S. Damiano in Assisi. But this permission did not force all nuns to become Franciscans, only those who wanted it. From the first half of the thirteenth century there is much evidence for a joint Benedictine-Franciscan presence there. Indeed, this fluid situation involving Benedictines and Franciscans in the same convent was not uncommon elsewhere in Italy, as Giorgio Penco has shown.

In 1293 the church and cloister of this joint Benedictine and Franciscan convent of S. Maria Donnaregina was destroyed by an earthquake. The nuns, fortunately, found a generous patron in Queen Mary of Hungary, wife of Charles II of Anjou, who donated large sums of money for the purpose of reconstruction. In contrast to her husband, who supported both Dominicans and Franciscans, Queen Mary was an ardent supporter of only the Franciscans. By the time the new church was finished in 1320, it must have been indisputably Franciscan, thanks to her efforts. In fact, in 1318 at the Queen's request Pope John XXII permitted two nuns to come from another convent in Campania to instruct the young nuns and novices of S. Maria Donnaregina 'ordinis sancte Clare' in singing. Queen Mary died in 1323 and was buried in the church of the convent of S. Maria Donnaregina; in her will she remembered the nuns handsomely, leaving them money for the purchase of land and endowing a chapel with the requisite liturgical furnishings, including missals, graduals, antiphonaries, and so forth.

This monastery is almost the perfect candidate to be the former owner of our graduale in Beneventan script. The evidence suggests that Benedictine and Franciscan nuns lived there together in the second half of the thirteenth century, just as Benedictine and Franciscan elements are found in the text and rubrics of the graduale. There is, moreover, a strong tie with the Angevins that had begun long before Queen Mary's patronage of the convent and her burial there in 1323. This tie is seen in the inclusion of liturgical texts for St. Nicholas of Bari, one of the 'family saints' of the Angevins. The connection of S. Maria Donnaregina with this Angevin dynasty is seemingly documented in 1269 when Charles I imprisoned there two daughters of a nobleman of Aversa. When the church itself was decorated by Tuscan artists in the fourteenth century, among the saints depicted in the Last Judgement fresco was St. Nicholas, who is placed next to the 'family saints', King Louis IX of France and St. Louis, son of Charles II and bishop of Toulouse. Upon the reopening of the new church of S. Maria Donnaregina in 1320, the Franciscan occupants would have had no need of the old hybrid Benedictine-Franciscan graduale, particularly since new books (thoroughly Franciscan with all of Haymo's rubrics) were obtainable through the terms of Queen Mary's will. Finally, Boccaccio, thanks to his father's position, had gained both entree and favour at the Angevin court, and through one of these contacts most likely could have obtained the possession of the now obsolete book, which he dismembered, erased, and onto which he wrote his own texts.

In terms of dating manuscripts new discoveries have been just as exciting as the two oddities just mentioned. For example, two years ago the oldest known example of the script – from the late eighth century – was found by chance in Benevento itself in one of the printed liturgical books there kept apart from the manuscripts.[14] The old printed book had been patched with parchment fragments from the eighth century. Equally interesting in terms of dating have been several new examples of sixteenth-century Beneventan script, and also to our surprise, several examples of

14. For details of this summary of this manuscript see BROWN, 'Second New List', (note 10), 305.

an imitation Beneventan script from the eighteenth century.[15] These were discovered in the past years in Naples in the Biblioteca della Società Napoletana di Storia Patria. The text is a copy of an older twelfth-century codex in Beneventan script now lost. This copy of the liturgical regulations governing the Collegio degli Ebdomadari in the Cathedral of Naples was made in the eighteenth century to support the liturgical prerogatives of the Collegio against the claims of the canons of the cathedral. The scribe attempted to copy the older exemplar, but try as he might, he was unable to follow consistently the rules governing the Beneventan script in its classic form - e.g., the obligatory ei, fi, gi, li, ri, and ti ligatures, or the i longa, the Beneventan abbreviations and punctuation, and other things. Hence, we have here the most recent example of Beneventan script known - although it is imitative in character.

Of all of the new items found, a few were drawn to our attention by scholars, librarians, archivists, and booksellers, but the great majority was found as members of the Monumenta Liturgica Beneventana passed through ecclesiastical archives or consulted incunabula and older printed volumes containing Beneventan-script flyleaves, pastedowns, supports, and the like. That these new items are only now being discovered is perhaps not surprising inasmuch as E. A. Lowe rarely consulted archives for Beneventan-script items[16] and did not systematically search through incunabula and old printed books in those libraries in the 'Beneventan zone' which he visited. Moreover, many archivists and librarians, since they are not palaeographic experts, have been unable to identify Beneventan script in the codices of their own depositories Now, in brief soundings in small ecclesiastical archives and in the incunabula holdings of larger libraries dozens of new examples have turned up As could be predicted from past findings, virtually all of these new items are liturgical. Material in archives takes on special importance because the fragments in Beneventan script often contain notarial entries or are attached to documents that may be helpful in determining origins and provenance. This archival data frequently confirms the tentative conclusions of palaeography. Hence, now and during the next years the holdings of large numbers of local archives and ecclesiastical libraries are being combed systematically for new items.

Beyond this discovery of the Boccaccio palimpsest, members of the Monumenta Liturgica Beneventana team have found many other hitherto

15. For details of this summary of these manuscripts see Virginia BROWN, 'Montevergine 6 and Sixteenth-Century Beneventan Script in Naples', in: G. RAIMONDI & S. PALMIERI (eds.), *Studi di paleografia e diplomatica in memoria di Jole Mazzoleni*. Napoli 1996, 32-42.

16. On archives with known Beneventan script items that Lowe and others have reported see Roger E. REYNOLDS, 'The South Italian *Collection in Five Books* and its Derivatives: Maastricht Excerpta' (Miscellanea Beneventana: Juridica), *Mediaeval Studies* 58 (1996), 273f. n. 2.

unrecognized Beneventan-script palimpsests (even some terscriptus examples), and the texts therein have often proven extremely significant, given their age and the fact that newer texts replaced what may be remnants of a lost rite. New techniques involving ultraviolet lamps, ultraviolet photography, digital scanning, and the identification of virtually obliterated texts using computerized databases of liturgical material has substantially changed the way in which these palimpsests can be studied. (Dom Alban Dold and the Palimpsestinstitut at Beuron, of course, led the way earlier in this century.) The erased texts can be scrutinized adequately only *in situ*, but improvements in ultraviolet photography have made work in Canada on these texts much easier than ever before. The use of digital scanners, with their capacity to modify the appearance of texts, has further assisted in the identification of hitherto unrecognizable texts. With the computerized database of liturgical texts compiled by the investigators and graduate students working for the Monumenta Liturgica Beneventana, the recognition of a few words has led to the identification *in situ* of longer texts hitherto illegible.

One of the exciting byproducts of our computerized descriptions of manuscripts and fragments has been the 'joining' of many *membra disiecta* scattered throughout the world. In the past few years alone more than seventy-five 'reunions' have been made involving 500 fragments.

In North America and sometimes in Europe, people in general and even medievalists will ask us why we are engaged in research as esoteric as the study of Beneventan liturgical manuscripts. There are several reasons, some important on a larger theoretical scale, some important for medieval studies itself. On the practical, economic side, there is another unexpected reason. That is, manuscript collectors, both public and private, have become intensely interested in the rare items we are identifying as they come to booksellers and auctioneers. As this interest increases, so do the prices of the items. But lest this report end on the mundane monetary ramifications of our work, something must be said about its value in larger theoretical terms and to medieval studies in general. Fundamental or basic research such as that of the Monumenta Liturgica Beneventana is often perceived to be without social significance or lacking in theoretical perspectives. But, in fact, fundamental research can and does exist in this larger context. One need only think of Brian Tierney's early obscure research on late medieval conciliar texts, which many scholars and churchmen believe was the impetus for the Second Vatican Council, or modern scholarship on the eucharistic prayer of the second-century Hippolytus of Rome, which has resulted in the revision of the eucharistic rites throughout Christendom, both Catholic and Protestant. Fundamental research like the Monumenta Liturgica Beneventana on liturgical rites does, then, have wider ramifications for both the humanities and social sciences.

The anthropologist Mary Douglas has written that 'ritual is more to society than words are to thought'; hence, at the purely human level ritual responds to and reflects the deepest collective needs of society. But, she continued 'with every new century we become heirs to a longer and more vigorous anti-ritualist tradition ... This is right and good as far as our own religious life is concerned, but let us be aware of importing uncritically a dread of dead formality in ourselves into our judgement of other religions' – and other periods of history, she might have added. In the area of medieval studies, this uncritical 'dread of dead formality in ourselves' has been transformed into an uneasy acknowledgement of the significance of ritual practice and liturgy in the Middle Ages but ignorance of its sources and their meaning. Despite the modern neglect of liturgical history, its centrality in medieval studies is indisputable. Liturgy is a key to a more profound understanding of the medieval past, and its significance in medieval studies is clear in that it touches virtually all areas from such traditional fields as history, literature, music, art, and law to the more functional fields of palaeography, codicology, and chronology.

Beyond its centrality to the wider study of the Middle Ages, a study of the diversity of medieval liturgical practice has implications for our western ecclesiastical culture as well. The liturgies of the Middle Ages have shaped this culture in all subsequent periods. A principal source in the development of modern liturgies is the historical tradition, where the theological significance of practice is determined through examination of the role of liturgy in church and community. For modern churches, the diversity of medieval liturgy is particularly instructive since the power of sacred ritual to express the values and focus the communal identity of a group has long been recognized. The early modern conclusion, rooted in the experience of nationalism, that the communal focus of ritual must be a divisive force, is in fact at odds with the medieval experience of universal ecclesiastical culture expressed in diversity. Modern churches with interests in ecumenism and liturgical reform may look now to this medieval model for social analogies to such questions as the growth of regional liturgies in the African churches or the local focus of the post-Vatican II Roman church. With such issues in mind, the study of medieval regional liturgy – in this case that of the 'Beneventan zone' in the south Adriatic region – is an appropriate means towards the understanding of modern concerns.

The Liturgy of Rome in the Eleventh Century: Past Research and Future Opportunities*

One of the most dramatic events of the eleventh century, the encounter between Gregory VII and Henry IV at Canossa in 1077, was celebrated two decades ago at another conference in a Rocky Mountain location, Ft. Collins, Colorado. One of the papers there, published the following year in the Harvard Theological Review and since reprinted, was entitled "Liturgical Scholarship at the Time of the Investiture Controversy: Past Research and Future Opportunities"[1]. The "liturgical scholarship" described there was actually commentaries on the liturgy, and the paper dealt with three major topics covering commentaries scattered throughout most of Europe from the middle of the eleventh through the second quarter of the twelfth century. The first topic was a report on the status of re-editions of such major liturgical commentaries as the *Micrologus* of Bernold of Constance and the sermons of Ivo of Chartres. The second was an invitation to publish several liturgical commentaries hitherto unedited. The third section of the paper dealt with opportunities for research in practical liturgical documents such as pontificals for light they shed on the origins and sources of well-known liturgical commentaries. The case illustrating this was the liturgical commentary of the so-called Norman Anonymous and his sources in unpublished Anglo-Norman pontifical manuscripts. The present paper deals again with liturgical scholarship – over a broader chronological period, the whole of the eleventh century, over a broader range of subjects, including both liturgical practice and commentary, but restricted to a narrower geographical location, Rome.

In her recently published presidential address at the Catholic Historical Association meeting, Professor Uta-Renate Blumenthal dealt with the pontificate of Gregory VII and touched very briefly on the liturgy of Rome at his time[2]. Her focus, as is common with most historians of the period, was naturally on ecclesio-political conditions and canon law. "Naturally", because the struggles between papacy and empire have fascinated people from that day until this, and because canon law texts and doctrines underlay so much of the combat between pope and secular rulers.

* Research for sections of this article was conducted for the program "Monumenta Liturgica Beneventana" supported by the Social Sciences and Humanities Research Council of Canada.

1 Roger E. REYNOLDS, Liturgical Scholarship at the Time of the Investiture Controversy: Past Research and Future Opportunities, in: Harvard Theological Review 71 (1978), pp. 109–124; reprinted in: ID., Law and Liturgy in the Latin Church, 5th–12th Centuries, London 1994, Nr. XVIII.

2 Uta-Renate BLUMENTHAL, The Papacy and Canon Law in the Eleventh-Century Reform, in: CHR 84 (1998), pp. 201–218.

Oliver Münsch/Thomas Zotz (Hg.), Scientia veritatis. Festschrift für Hubert Mordek zum 65. Geburtstag © Jan Thorbecke Verlag, Ostfildern 2004.

If one looks to the canon law of the day, including papal and conciliar decrees and canon law collections, it is surprising how much canon law dealt with liturgical matters. Pointed reminders of this are the recent studies of the late Reinhard Elze and Arturo Palacios on the decretal *In (A) die resurrectione* of Gregory VII[3] and Professor Robert Somerville's study of the councils of Urban II.[4] The famous *Dictatus papae* in the register of Gregory VII has such liturgically oriented canons as "That his name alone is to be recited in the churches" – a point obviously understood by scribes who erased the names of other bishops mentioned in the Mass canon of earlier liturgical books. If one looks to the canonical collections of the Gregorian reform such the *Collection in 74 Titles*, and the collections of Anselm of Lucca and Deusdedit, one will find a plethora of canons on liturgical subjects. This is probably not unexpected inasmuch as many of the canons were drawn from the Pseudo-Isidorian Decretals, whose liturgical contents Horst Fuhrmann has stressed[5].

The attempt at Romanizing the liturgy of the Church during the second half of the eleventh century has been repeatedly emphasized by historians, especially by Reinhard Elze in his recent study of Gregory VII and the liturgy – the suppression of the Old Spanish rite in the Iberian peninsula, the reputed suppression of the Milanese rite, the attempt to impose Roman liturgical customs on the Armenian church, and so on. Parenthetically, it should be noted that in the last two decades there has been a substantial revision of the view that the liturgy of the church of Rome all but supplanted such rites as the Milanese and Old Spanish. Regarding the former, Professor Richard Gyug and others have shown on the basis of contemporary documents that the reported suppression of the rite in Milan is questionable[6]. And for Spain, it is clear now that while clerics there might profess conformity to the Roman rite, in practice they continued many of the liturgical customs of the Visigothic and Mozarabic past. From marriage rites to clerical ordination, prayers and liturgical rubrics from the past continued to be repeated, as Brian Bethune has shown in his unpublished Toronto doctoral thesis on marriage rites in medieval Spain[7] and as the present writer has shown in papers on ordination rites in Spain[8].

3 Reinhard ELZE, Gregor VII. und die römische Liturgie, in: Studi Gregoriani 13 (1989), pp. 187f.; and Arturo Bernal PALACIOS, La redacción del c. *In die resurrectionis* en las colecciones canónicas pregracianas, in: Proceedings of the Ninth International Congress of Medieval Canon Law, eds. Peter LANDAU and Jörg MÜLLER (MIC, Ser. C: Subsidia 10), Vatican City 1997, pp. 923–952.

4 Robert SOMERVILLE, The Councils of Urban II, vol. 1: Decreta Claromontensia (AHC, Suppl. 1), Amsterdam 1972; and ID. with the collaboration of Stephan KUTTNER, Pope Urban II, the *Collectio Britannica*, and the Council of Melfi (1089), Oxford 1996.

5 Horst FUHRMANN, Einfluss und Verbreitung der pseudoisidorischen Fälschungen von ihrem Auftauchen bis in die neuere Zeit (MGH Schriften 24, 1), Stuttgart 1972, pp. 45f.

6 Richard F. GYUG, The Milanese Liturgy during the Gregorian Reform, in: Scintilla 2 (1985), pp. 29–65; and ID., "Milanese Rite", in: Dictionary of the Middle Ages, ed. Joseph R. STRAYER, New York 1987, vol. 8, pp. 381–384.

7 Brian BETHUNE, The Text of the Christian Rite of Marriage in Medieval Spain, Ph.D. diss. Toronto 1987.

8 The Ordination Rite in Medieval Spain: Hispanic, Roman, and Hybrid, in: Santiago, Saint-Denis, and Saint Peter: The Reception of the Roman Liturgy in Leon-Castile in 1080, ed. Bernard F. REILLY, New York 1985, pp. 131–155; reprinted in: Roger E. REYNOLDS, Clerical Orders in the Early Middle Ages: Duties and

Let us now turn to a survey of research largely in the past two decades on the liturgy of Rome and some opportunities for further research under four categories: liturgical manuscripts, liturgical texts, liturgical practice, and liturgical commentary.

I.

The study of what texts were available in manuscript form in Rome in the eleventh century has been placed on a new foundation with the work of the late Professor Paola Supino Martini on Romanesca script[9]. On the basis of her work we now know what manuscripts still extant were written in Rome in that script. In her study, Professor Supino Martini mentions briefly in two footnotes that there are a number of liturgical manuscripts of the eleventh century written in Romanesca, and she lists seven missals, five psalters, four Gospel books, four sacramentaries, four hymnaries, ten homiliaries, nine passionals, and seven lectionaries[10]. This list, however, contains a majority of books written outside of Rome, especially in Farfa, Subiaco, and San Eutizio presso Norcia. Further, it is somewhat confusing because in her more detailed palaeographical study of manuscripts written in Rome itself, there are a number of liturgical manuscripts not included in her brief list. Professor Supino Martini, a superb palaeographer, was not a specialist in medieval liturgy (neither was the great palaeographer E. A. Lowe[11]), so one gets little sense of what the liturgical landscape in Rome was like on the basis of either her short list of liturgical manuscripts or her longer palaeographical descriptions, which include a number of liturgical items. But on the basis of her study, one can begin to draw an outline of liturgical texts in Rome in the eleventh century far more accurately than has hitherto been done. To the great credit of her study, Professor Supino Martini also excludes as Roman a number of manuscripts often said to have been made in or for the Roman church[12].

From the point of view of the liturgical scholar, one lacuna in Professor Supino Martini's list of liturgical manuscripts is her failure to realize how many more of the manuscripts she treats are actually liturgical in part. This is particularly noticeable in manuscripts containing the ninth-century *Institutio canonicorum* and various martyrologies. It is well known that in the eleventh century there was a resurgence of clerics living under a rule, especially in Rome and promoted by the reforming papacy[13], and

Ordination, Aldershot 1999, Nr. XIII; ID., The Ordination of Clerics in Toledo and Castile after the Reconquista according to the 'Romano-Catalan' Rite, in: Estudios sobre Alfonso VI y la Reconquista de Toledo: Actas del II. Congreso Internacional de Estudios Mozárabes (Instituto de Estudios Visigótico-Mozárabes 4), ed. Ramón GONZÁLVEZ-RUÍZ, Toledo 1990, pp. 47–69.

9 Paola SUPINO MARTINI, Roma e l'area grafica romanesca (secoli X–XII) (Biblioteca di Scrittura e Civiltà 1), Alessandria 1987.

10 Ibid., p. 42 n. 47.

11 On this see my Monumenta Liturgica Beneventana: New Directions, in: Proceedings of the Groningse Codicologendagen 1996, Rijksuniversiteit Groningen, Netherlands, Groningen 1999, pp. 311–327.

12 SUPINO MARTINI, Roma e l'area grafica romanesca (n. 9 above), pp. 309–337.

13 See the yet unpublished paper by Joseph DRYER, The Late Eleventh-Century Lectionary of Santa Cecilia in Trastevere.

early on it was the *Institutio canonicorum* that was used as their *regula*. Indeed, Professor Supino Martini lists four manuscripts of this from Rome written in Romanesca. Historians and canonists have generally considered this text with its many canons to be a canonistic work, in part because it was edited in the "Concilia" series of the "Monumenta Germaniae Historica" under the Council of Aachen of 816, but a careful reading of this text shows how many canons deal with liturgical life. Further, the *Institutio canonicorum*, like the *Regula sancti Benedicti*, was frequently combined in the manuscripts with martyrologies, whose texts have often been investigated by hagiographers and historians, but which have not, according to Richard Pfaff's new study of liturgy in medieval manuscripts[14], been fully appreciated for their liturgical and cultual value. Thus, any study of the liturgy of Rome in the eleventh century would have to take into account the liturgical sections of the *Institutio canonicorum* and the *Regula sancti Benedicti* and the contents of the martyrologies.

The distinction Professor Supino Martini sets out between canonistic and liturgical manuscripts is perhaps justifiable for her manuscripts of such collections as those of Deusdedit, Burchard of Worms, and the south Italian *Collection in Five Books* because all of these collections have been the domain of canonistic scholars in the past[15]. But it should be emphasized that all of these collections are filled with liturgical regulations and even liturgical texts and commentaries[16].

The non-recognition of the liturgical contents in canonistic manuscripts is perhaps most pointed in Professor Supino Martini's study of an immensely important, but little appreciated liturgico-canonical codex of the early eleventh century, Vatican, Biblioteca Apostolica Vaticana, Archivio di San Pietro H 58. Although Professor Supino Martini herself is unwilling to pinpoint exactly the Roman location where it was written (she treats it under San Pietro)[17], palaeographers and scholars such as Professors Bernhard Bischoff and Raymund Kottje have stated that it was written ca. 1000 for or in the Roman church of Sant'Apollinare[18]. This manuscript has in the past been appreciated primarily by hagiographers, who have analyzed and edited its highly interesting martyrology. But it has been 'rediscovered' more recently by canonistic scholars. The present author has written extensively on the canonistic texts in the manuscript drawn from the ancient Irish *Collectio canonum Hibernensis* and other texts that may have been drawn from or that provided the source for the south Italian *Collection in Five Books*[19]. More

14 See Richard W. PFAFF, Liturgical Calendars, Saints, and Services in Medieval England, Aldershot 1998, especially I, IV, and VIII.

15 SUPINO MARTINI, Roma e l'area grafica romanesca (n. 9 above), p. 41.

16 See, e.g., my A South Italian Liturgico-Canonical Mass Commentary, in: Mediaeval Studies 50 (1988), pp. 626–670; reprinted in: ID., Law and Liturgy in the Latin Church (n. 1 above), Nr. XII.

17 SUPINO MARTINI, Roma e l'area grafica romanesca (n. 9 above), pp. 72f.

18 For Bischoff's date see my Unity and Diversity in Carolingian Canon Law Collections: the Case of the *Collectio Hibernensis* and its Derivatives, in: Carolingian Essays: Andrew W. Mellon Lectures in Early Christian Studies, ed. Uta-Renate BLUMENTHAL, Washington, D. C. 1983, p. 135 n. 220, reprinted in: REYNOLDS, Law and Liturgy in the Latin Church (n. 1 above), Nr. IV.

19 Excerpta from the *Collectio Hibernensis* in three Vatican manuscripts, in: BMCL, N. S. 5 (1975), pp. 4–9, reprinted in: REYNOLDS, Law and Liturgy in the Latin Church (n. 1 above), Nr. V; ID., South and Central

recently Raymund Kottje has studied the ninth-century penitential texts of Halitgar in the manuscript[20], and his student, Ludger Körntgen, has identified and published from this manuscript what is most likely the oldest penitential of the Roman church.[21] But besides its canonistic and hagiographical texts, the manuscript is replete with liturgical texts yet to be identified and published. Indeed, Dom Salmon two decades ago wrote a brief article on the manuscript styling it as a *Liber officialis*, or a book given to priests on their ordination containing the liturgical and canonistic texts necessary to fulfill their office[22]. The manuscript takes on special importance when its early eleventh-century date is recognized. That is, the manuscript reflects at least some of the texts that were known and used by Roman priests before the reforms of the middle and second half of the eleventh century.

In later sections of this paper the contents of this manuscript will be described more fully, but there is a palaeographic peculiarity in it, as well as in many others noted by Professor Supino Martini, that points to the influence in Rome of texts originating farther south on the Italian peninsula. That is, many of these manuscripts written in Romanesca, including our manuscript from the Archivio di San Pietro, have Beneventan-script influence, such as distinctive interrogation marks[23] and the like or have Beneventan-script additions and entries. Indeed, it was long ago noted by hagiographers that the martyrology of the *Liber officialis* is related to those of Benevento[24].

The fact that there are traces of Beneventan-script influence in this manuscript leads one to a further conclusion, one dealt with at length by Professor Supino Martini. That is, there were manuscripts in Rome in the eleventh century that were not in Romanesca (or that were in Romanesca written outside of Rome) that migrated to Rome and were used there. For example, it is likely that one of the most famous manuscripts of the *Pontificale Romanum XII saeculi* (= *PR* 12), Vatican, Biblioteca Apostolica Vaticana, Barb. Lat. 631, written in the classic Beneventan script of Montecassino was used in Rome by Pope Victor III, who before his consecration as pope was Abbot Desiderius of Montecassino and promoter of the creation of some of the most beauti-

Italian Canonical Collections of the Tenth and Eleventh Centuries (non-Gregorian), in: Studies in Medieval Canon Law, eds. Wilfried HARTMANN and Kenneth PENNINGTON, Washington, D. C., in press since 1993.

20 Raymund KOTTJE, Die Bussbücher Halitgars von Cambrai und des Hrabanus Maurus: ihre Überlieferung und ihre Quellen (BGQM 8), Berlin – New York 1980, p. 65, who dates the manuscript to s. XI/XII, and locates it to Sant'Apollinare(?).

21 Ludger KÖRNTGEN, Ein italienisches Bussbuch und seine fränkischen Quellen. Das anonyme Paenitentiale der Handschrift Vatikan, Arch. S. Pietro H 58, in: Aus Archiven und Bibliotheken. Festschrift für Raymund Kottje zum 65. Geburtstag, ed. Hubert MORDEK (FBMG 3), Frankfurt/Main etc. 1992, pp. 189–197.

22 Pierre SALMON, Un *Libellus officialis* du XIe siècle, in: Revue Bénédictine 87 (1977), pp. 257–288; ID., Un témoin de la vie chrétienne dans une église de Rome au XIe siècle: le *Liber officialis* de la basilique des Saints-Apôtres, in: RSCI 33 (1979), pp. 65–73.

23 See my South Italian Mass Commentary (n. 16 above), p. 642.

24 Henri QUENTIN, Les martyrologes historiques du moyen âge. Étude sur la formation du martyrologe romain, Paris 1908, pp. 39–42.

ful books written in Beneventan script[25]. Further, it is beyond question that books in Romanesca copied at such monasteries as Farfa made their way to Rome to be used in its dependencies there. In short, the liturgical landscape of Rome in the eleventh century must be written on the basis not only of manuscripts in Romanesca, but in other scripts used or imported there.

II.

Turning to the liturgical contents of manuscript used in Rome in the eleventh century, many have been edited or described either long ago or in the last two decades. Representative of the former would be the contents of the *Pontificale Romanum XII saeculi,* edited so well by Michel Andrieu[26]. The same is true for the contents of the *Pontificale Romano-Germanicum* (= *PRG*), edited by Andrieu's successor Cyrille Vogel and Reinhard Elze[27], although there are no manuscripts of undoubted Roman origin extant[28]. Regarding these two pontificals, recent research has modified the traditional views of their origin and use in Rome. The present author, for example, has called into question the view by Andrieu and Vogel, and often repeated by others, that the *PRG*, compiled in Mainz in the tenth century, had reached Rome by the 960s and was used in the ordinations of popes there[29]. This has even more recently been supported by the work of John Gibaut on the clerical interstices, who has shown that ordinations like those represented in the *PRG* were probably being made as early as the late eighth century in the Lateran itself[30]. In other words, one cannot use the ordinations in Rome in the 960s to date manuscripts of the *PRG* to that decade, as has been done. It is

25 On this manuscript, see Richard F. GYUG, The Pontificals of Monte Cassino, in: L'età dell'abbate Desiderio. Atti del IV Convegno di studi sul medioevo meridionale, Montecassino e Cassino 4–8 ottobre 1987, ed. Faustino AVAGLIANO and Oronzo PECERE (Miscellañea Cassinese 67), Montecassino 1992, pp. 413–439.

26 Michel ANDRIEU, Le Pontifical romain au moyen âge. 1. Le Pontifical romain du XIIe siècle (Studi e Testi 86), Vatican City 1938.

27 Cyrille VOGEL and Reinhard ELZE, Le Pontifical romano-germanique du Xe siècle (Studi e Testi 226), Vatican City 1963.

28 Despite its clear Roman connections, the codex Rome, Università degli Studi di Roma, Biblioteca Alessandrina 173 is often judged to have been copied simply in Italy. Such is the case in Die Konzilsordines des Früh- und Hochmittelalters, ed. Herbert SCHNEIDER (MGH Ordines de Celebrando Concilio), Hannover 1996, pp. 300, 416. It seems significant that Supino Martini, who taught at the La Sapienza in Rome, did not consider this manuscript in the library of her own University. Indeed, in a letter to Professor Uta-Renate Blumenthal of 18 January 1999, Supino Martini says, "la scrittura conferma che fu scritto a Salzburg", citing Andrieu as authority, and referring to an article in: Il Bibliotecario. Rivista semestrale di studi bibliografici, N. S. 8 (1991), pp. 89–91, which speaks of the model for the manuscript as originating in Salzburg.

29 Roger E. REYNOLDS, The Ritual of Clerical Ordination of the Sacramentarium Gelasianum saec. viii: Early Evidence from Southern Italy, in: Rituels: Mélanges offerts au Père Gy O. P., eds. Paul DECLERCK and Eric PALAZZO, Paris 1990, pp. 437–445; and the expanded version of this in: ID., Clerical Orders in the Early Middle Ages: Duties and Ordination, Aldershot 1999, Nr. XII. Eric PALAZZO, L'Évêque et son image: l'illustration du pontifical au moyen âge, Turnhout 1999, p. 44 n. 121, cites this article, but without providing any evidence says: "L'analyse paléographique du manuscrit fait pencher en faveur du Xe siècle".

30 John St. H. GIBAUT, The Clerical Cursus of Constantine of Nepi: Two Accounts, in: Ecclesia Orans 12 (1995), pp. 195–205.

more likely that the *PRG* reached Rome in the eleventh, not the tenth century. Turning to the *PR* 12, Richard Gyug has made the exciting discovery that the pontifical of Abbot Desiderius noted above was based on the famous Montecassino manuscript of the *PRG*, Montecassino, Archivio dell'Abbazia 451, whose marginal notes (unseen by Vogel and Elze) reflect the contents of the Desiderian pontifical[31].

The contents of another type of liturgical manuscript used in Rome in the eleventh century, the graduale, were scrutinized a decade ago in the study and partial facsimile by Max Lütolf of the famous Old Roman chant book used at Santa Cecilia in Trastevere[32]. Further study on what Michel Huglo has called this singular and mysterious type of chant in this and other manuscripts[33] was the focus of a conference sponsored by the Fondation Royaumont not long ago, whose proceedings one hopes will soon see the light of day.

In various older articles and manuscript descriptions of missals, sacramentaries, psalters, Gospel books, hymnaries, homiliaries, passionals, and lectionaries made in Rome, their contents have been in part described. Since the descriptions of the contents of many of these books often depend on much earlier texts that have been edited, it could be argued that the contents should not be edited as they stand in the Roman manuscripts themselves. But inasmuch as liturgical books are rarely exact copies – they are living books made for particular circumstances and liturgical tastes and necessities – ideally one should have editions and critical studies of the texts as they stand in the Roman liturgical manuscripts of the eleventh century to form an exact picture of liturgical life there in that century.

Returning to our early-eleventh-century *Liber officialis* of Archivio di San Pietro H 58, one could certainly form a better picture of what liturgical *ordines* existed in Rome or were being used by Roman priests by editing and studying the liturgical texts therein. Besides the martyrology with its Beneventan influence, which has been edited[34] together with the unusual poetic *Carmen alpha* attributed to Sedulius[35], there are *ordines* (sometimes multiple) for penitential discipline, benediction of holy water, litanies, funerals, visitation of the sick, consecration of a cemetery, making of a catechumen, veiling of a virgin, marriage Mass, Palm Sunday Mass, an *Ordo missae*, and various passions and homilies[36].

31 See n. 25 above.

32 Max LÜTOLF, Das Graduale von Santa Cecilia in Trastevere (Cod. Bodmer 74), 2 vols., Cologny 1987.

33 Michel HUGLO, Le Chant 'vieux-romain,' manuscrits et témoins indirects, in: Sacris Erudiri 6 (1954), pp. 96–124.

34 See Henri QUENTIN, Les martyrologes (n. 24 above), pp. 39–42; and Hippolyte DELEHAYE, Martyrologium e codice basilicae Vaticanae nunc primum editum, in: Analecta Bollandiana 49 (1931), pp. 51–97.

35 Bernhard BISCHOFF, Eine karolingische *Vita pastorialis*: Sedulius, *Carmen alpha*, in: DA 37 (1981), pp. 559–575, using this manuscript and Pistoia, Biblioteca Capitolare, MS 102 (130, olim IX), saec. IX ex. (IX/X).

36 For the contents see SALMON, Un *Libellus officialis* du XIe siècle (n. 22 above), p. 259.

The veneration of saints in Rome, especially the Lateran and St. Peter's was the subject of the excellent study of Pierre Jounel published twenty years ago[37]. Among the eleventh-century documents from Rome that he used to illustrate the growth of the cult of saints in the city were a lectionary-homiliary, passional, martyrologies-obituaries, Gospel book-sacramentaries, epistolary, antiphonaries, and ritual-collectar[38]. Several of Jounel's dates and localizations of the manuscripts have since been challenged by Professor Supino Martini, but the general outlines of his findings remain secure and interesting. In the veneration of the saints in eleventh-century Rome, Jounel concludes that 126 feasts were added to sanctorales of the ninth century. Given the growing influence of Frankish and German liturgical texts, one would expect that most of the saints would be from the North. Jounel shows, however, that more came from elsewhere in Italy and from the Orient than from northern Europe[39].

One of the martyrologies that Jounel used was our early eleventh-century *Liber officialis*, Archivio di San Pietro H 58, as edited by the Bollandists. But there is a group of martyrologies from eleventh-century Rome that he did not use. They have long been known and partially studied and edited, but in light of advances in the study of Romanesca and Beneventan scripts these might profitably be compared and analyzed. Among these martyrologies are those attached especially to the *Institutio canonicorum* and *Regula sancti Benedicti* in Vatican, Biblioteca Apostolica Vaticana, Vat. Lat. 4885 and Barb. Lat. 646, and to the *Institutio canonicorum* in Vat. Lat. 1351, Vat. Ottob. Lat. 38, and London, British Library, Add. 14801[40]. Not only do these martyrologies list names of saints, but they also have additions of names of clerics and others who died in the eleventh century, thereby making them forms of necrologies or obituaries furnishing information on the liturgical and clerical structure of the Roman church in the eleventh century.

III.

It is widely recognized that even though a liturgical manuscript was written in or found its way into a particular location, it was not necessarily used there and reflects actual liturgical practice. Such might be the case with some of the manuscripts with their contents described thus far. But when additional texts are inserted into manuscripts or marginal entries made, especially liturgical entries, one can assume that the manuscript was used in a particular location. Moreover, corroborating the evidence provided by these additions are external descriptions of liturgical practice in a particular location. Fortunately, for the eleventh century we have such evidence, especially

37 Pierre JOUNEL, Le culte des saints dans les basiliques du Latran et du Vatican au douzième siècle (Collection de l'École française de Rome 26), Rome 1977.

38 Ibid., pp. 50f.

39 Ibid., p. 146.

40 On these manuscripts see my South Italian Liturgica and Canonistica in Catalonia (New York, Hispanic Society of America MS. HC 380/819), in: Mediaeval Studies 49 (1987), p. 491; reprinted in: REYNOLDS, Law and Liturgy in the Latin Church (n. 1 above), Nr XV.

in the *Micrologus de ecclesiasticis observationibus* written by the pro-Gregorian reformer, Bernold of Constance[41]. In his commentary Bernold strongly defends liturgical traditions in Rome, attributes many to individual popes, and contrasts them with customs north of the Alps (Germanic customs).

Reinhard Elze and others have pointed out that well into the second half of the eleventh century a series of northern popes did introduce northern liturgical customs and books[42]. But with Gregory VII and his successors there was a new emphasis on ancient Roman customs[43] and an insistence that other churches conform to these. Perhaps best known among these was Gregory VII's insistence that the Roman dates for the ember days be followed, not those of the Gallican and Frankish churches[44]. Almost as well known, especially now with the study of Arturo Palacios, is Gregory VII's decree *In die resurrectionis* with regulations regarding the number of psalms and lessons to be used at various times of the year[45].

Beyond these two well-known Gregorian regulations are other significant liturgical developments under Gregory's reign, such as clarification of the number of signs to be said over the eucharistic species and vessels; a synodical decree calling for Mass offerings of the faithful; the institution of new antiphons at matins of Sexagesima; the commemoration of saintly popes throughout the Church; and a ritual of papal coronation including the ceremonial burning of the tuft of oakum[46]. Elze has noted that a number of liturgical specialists, including Theodor Klauser, have judged these to be minor liturgical changes[47], but coupled with the insistence by Gregory that they and other Roman customs be followed by all churches, they take on major significance as signs of his promulgation of the rite in Rome as normative for the universal Church.

One other change in the second half of the eleventh century studied by the author of this article touched the liturgy of clerical ordination, canon law, and sacramental theology. This was the elevation of the clerical grade of subdeacon to a sacred or major order. While Bernold of Constance and at least one of the ordination rites of the *Ordines romani* appear to have considered this grade as one of the minor orders, from the time of Leo IX and beyond, the subdeacon came to be considered as a sacred or major order because he handled the eucharistic species and hence was obliged to the celibacy

41 PL 151, cols. 973–1022. According to Daniel Scott TAYLOR, Bernold of Constance, Canonist and Liturgist of the Gregorian Reform: An Analysis of the Sources in the *Micrologus de ecclesiasticis observationibus*, Ph.D. diss., Toronto 1994, pp. 356–358, there are no less than fourteen published editions of the *Micrologus*.

42 ELZE, Gregor VII. und die römische Liturgie (n. 3 above), pp. 180f.

43 Daniel S. TAYLOR, An Early Liturgical Compilation of Bernold of Constance? A Comparative Analysis of Codex Stuttgart, Württembergische Landesbibliothek HB VI 107 and Bernold's *Micrologus*, in: Sacris Erudiri 37 (1997), p. 178, emphasizes that Gregory VII disliked the *Pontificale Romano-Germanicum*.

44 On this see Daniel S. TAYLOR, Der *Micrologus* Bernolds von Konstanz und der Codex Stuttgart, Württembergische Landesbibliothek, HB VI 114, in: DA 52 (1996), pp. 171–179; and ID., An Early Liturgical Compilation (n. 43 above), p. 172.

45 PALACIOS, La redacción del c. *In die resurrectionis* (n. 3 above), pp. 923–952.

46 Reinhard ELZE, *Sic transit gloria mundi*, in: DA 34 (1978), p. 18.

47 ELZE, Gregor VII. und die römische Liturgie (n. 3 above), p. 179.

demanded of the higher orders of deacon, presbyter, and bishop[48]. Related to this change and reflected in liturgical rites of ordination in the second half of the eleventh century was the requirement that for an ordinand to move to a higher order, he must have been previously ordained to the order directly below it. Hence, in the ordination rites of the second half of the eleventh century, one ordained to the priesthood was asked if he had been ordained to the diaconate and how long he had served in that order[49]. A similar practice also came into effect with the offices of archdeacon and archpresbyter, whereby one had to be ordained to the 'underlying' order; that is, an archdeacon was to be ordained as a deacon, and an archpresbyter as a presbyter[50].

IV.

We turn finally to liturgical scholarship or liturgical commentaries in Rome in the eleventh century. The church in Rome has always been noted more for its liturgical practice and liturgical legislation than for reflective scholarship on the meaning of liturgy. Thus one would not expect to find much original scholarship of this sort in Rome in the eleventh century. While this may be true, Rome was not without knowledge of such scholarship. Not only were northern liturgical commentaries known there but also ones composed in southern and central Italy itself. One of the most interesting and entertaining of these latter was edited and studied a decade ago by the present author. It is a commentary on the celebration of the Mass[51]. The origins of the tract, a pseudonymous exchange of letters between Pope Damasus and St. Jerome on the hour of the Mass said to have been legislated in the First Council of Nicea, perhaps were north of the Alps inasmuch as our first manuscript evidence is from a Rhaetian-script manuscript of the late eighth century. This original text was quickly taken to central and southern Italy by the tenth century and is represented in many manuscripts copied there. As time passed the original text was expanded into ten more recensions, several of which were extensive numerological commentaries on liturgical practices in the Mass. The longest of these recensions is found in codices from southern Italy, many written in Beneventan script. The Vulgate form of this text is found as a canon in the south Italian *Collection in Five Books* and its many derivatives. But a slightly abbreviated form also appears in our Roman *Liber officialis* of Archivio di San Pietro H 58. Since this manuscript likely predates the compilation of the *Collection in Five Books*, it is virtually certain that the slightly longer Vulgate version of the commentary was in circulation in Rome at least by the late tenth century.

48 See my The Subdiaconate as a Sacred and Superior Order + Addendum The Subdeacon's Symbols of Status + Table, in: Roger E. REYNOLDS, Clerics in the Early Middle Ages: Hierarchy and Image, Aldershot 1999, Nr. IV.

49 See my Patristic 'Presbyterianism' in the Early Medieval Theology of Sacred Orders, in: Mediaeval Studies 45 (1983), p. 341; reprinted in: REYNOLDS, Clerics in the Early Middle Ages (n. 48 above), Nr. V.

50 Ibid., p. 341.

51 See my A South Italian Liturgico-Canonical Mass Commentary (n. 16 above), pp. 626–670.

This *Liber officialis* also provides evidence that all or parts of several of the most noted liturgical commentaries of the Carolingian era were available in Rome. Among the liturgical texts in the manuscript there is one section of explanations of liturgical practices. These begin with a portion from Rabanus Maurus's *De institutione clericorum*, notable for the unusual form it takes[52]. It is to be hoped that on the basis of the new edition of the *De institutione clericorum* by Detlev Zimpel, one will be able to elucidate what tradition or version was being used for this text[53]. After the Rabanus text there are snippets from the *De exordiis et incrementis* of Walafrid Strabo, again in unusual forms and abbreviations[54]. Unfortunately, the new edition of Walafrid's text by Alice Harting-Correa does not consider these texts as they appear in the Roman manuscript[55]. Following the snippets from Walafrid's commentary in the *Liber officialis* are snippets from the most popular early medieval commentary until that of Bernold of Constance, the *Liber officialis* of Amalarius of Metz[56].

This paper began by looking briefly at liturgical scholarship at the time of the Investiture Controversy in that article presented two decades ago and by mentioning Bernold's *Micrologus*. A number of the commentaries mentioned in that article have since been edited[57], but perhaps the most exciting scholarship on liturgical commentaries of the eleventh century since then is now underway by Daniel Taylor. Bernold's *Micrologus* with its liturgical and canonistic sources has been the subject of his recent doctoral thesis at Toronto[58], and Taylor is continuing that work with the much-desired critical edition of the commentary begun long ago by Vincent Kennedy of the Pontifical Institute of Mediaeval Studies[59]. In his thesis Taylor deals with past editions of the work, describes the forty-five surviving manuscripts of the tract (none copied in Rome)[60], and examines closely 203 sources, liturgical and canonistic, cited by Bernold. Taylor's study of these sources has been especially fruitful because insofar as possible he has returned to the surviving manuscripts that Bernold used at Constance. For example, Taylor has recently published in the "Deutsches Archiv" a solution based on a Constance manuscript now in Stuttgart to one of the most vexing references in the *Micro-*

52 See my Excerpta from the *Collectio Hibernensis* (n. 19 above), p. 4.

53 Hrabanus Maurus, *De institutione clericorum libri tres*. Studien und Edition, ed. Detlev ZIMPEL (FBMG 7), Frankfurt/Main etc. 1996.

54 See my Excerpta from the *Collectio Hibernensis* (n. 19 above), pp. 4f.

55 Alice L. HARTING-CORREA, Walahfrid Strabo's *Libellus de exordiis et incrementis quarundam in observationibus ecclesiasticis rerum*. A Translation and Liturgical Commentary (Mittellateinische Studien und Texte 19), Leiden – New York – London 1996; and see my review in: The Journal of Medieval Latin (in press).

56 See my Excerpta from the *Collectio Hibernensis* (n. 19 above), pp. 4f.

57 E.g., *Liber Quare*, ed. Georg Polycarp GÖTZ (CC, Cont. Med. 60), Turnhout 1983; and Ronald John ZAWILLA, The *Sententia Ivonis Carnotensis episcopi De divinis officiis*. The 'Norman School' and Liturgical Scholarship: Study and Edition, in: Mediaeval Studies 49 (1987), pp. 124–151.

58 TAYLOR, Bernold of Constance (n. 41 above).

59 Sadly, all of the research notes and collations of Kennedy were lost or destroyed long ago, and Taylor had to begin anew on the project, depending only on the photographs of a few manuscripts sent to Kennedy by Dom Mohlberg and stored in the Library of the Pontifical Institute of Mediaeval Studies.

60 See now Daniel S. TAYLOR, A New Inventory of Manuscripts of the *Micrologus de ecclesiasticis observationibus* of Bernold of Constance, in: Scriptorium 52 (1998), pp. 162–191.

logus to a decision of a council of Mainz or Seligenstadt regarding the ember days[61]. Also Taylor has recently shown in "Sacris Erudiri" how the liturgical *ordines* of another Constance codex were probably ordered by Bernold himself and later used and modified in his *Micrologus*[62].

While Taylor's identification of the liturgical and canonistic texts cited by Bernold is especially thorough and precious (and will be included in his critical edition and study of the text), perhaps for our purposes his insights about the place of the *Micrologus* in the promulgation of the liturgy of the church of Rome, Bernold's methodology, and the role of the *Micrologus* in the Romanization of the western Church are most important. It is worth concluding this paper on the liturgy of Rome in the eleventh century by summarizing Taylor's own eloquent conclusions[63].

Taylor himself emphasizes that although the bulk of his thesis is an identification of sources, it is not so much a history of liturgy as an examination of liturgy in history, assessing the role of ritual in transmitting and forming ideas in an era when ritual played an important role in the definition and designation of ecclesio-political power. When it is viewed in the context of eleventh-century controversies concerning the nature and source of sacramental authority, with its concomitant ramifications for the ecclesio-political order, Bernold's text takes on a new importance. It is a witness to the renewed interest in the maintenance of the integrity of the sacraments and the hierocratic order based on Roman supremacy.

Like many of Bernold's other texts (many published in the "Libelli de lite" of the "Monumenta Germaniae Historica") the *Micrologus* can be read not only as a commentary on select decrees of Gregory VII, but also as a commentary on the application of the pope's general policies on liturgy. Taylor makes the interesting observation that the polemical treatises of the Gregorian epoch about which volumes have been written by historians circulated in far fewer copies than the *Micrologus*. The substantial number of surviving manuscripts of the *Micrologus* with its spirit of the Gregorian reform is evidence of its importance.

Bernold's interpretation of the legislation concerning the commemoration of the Roman pontiffs demonstrates, according to Taylor, how the Gregorian program in liturgical matters might have played a larger role in the history of the Church than historians have heretofore admitted. Just as individual churches have their patron saints and confessors, Bernold says, the universal Church has the Roman pontiffs, who are better considered fathers than mere patrons. Gregory's enactment has at times been recognized as a significant, singular event in the reform period. But this example can serve to demonstrate the lasting effect of the papal program beyond the eleventh century in the way that such a policy influenced the practitioners of the liturgy. It is a clear indication of how liturgical matters, often overlooked as a force upon the histori-

61 See n. 44 above.

62 See n. 43 above.

63 I am most grateful to Dr. Taylor for his permission to quote extensively from the conclusion to his thesis, pp. 335–339.

cal process, helped shape the perspectives of its members. One might well question whether or not the dramatic moments during the Investiture crisis, so often repeated by historians, really had a greater impact upon the subsequent development of papal *auctoritas* and the Romanism of the western Church than the perennial recitation by the clergy of the West of the Office, replete with reminders of Roman pontiffs of the past. Bernold is a witness to the many facets of the reform program; he evidently recognized the effect that liturgical centralization would have upon the clergy and people of the Church.

During the eleventh century the very struggle for definition and clarification to questions of authority and order inspired an examination of ancient texts[64]. The analysis of the major issues that characterized the eleventh century was largely a matter of interpreting sources, particularly those of the Church Fathers, Innocent I, Gregory I, the early councils, and contemporary synods. All of this contributed greatly to the emerging science of canon law. These same principles were operative in the area of liturgical scholarship: the sacred liturgy, the sacramental center of the cult, was not to be an exception to this activity. The liturgical polemic, with its canonistic underpinning, proved to be a forum in which authorities were cited and tested: disconcordant canons were dismissed after they were ranked in accordance with a hierarchy of texts, or they were reconciled on the principle of harmony and non-contradiction. That such an effort was part of a conscious liturgical program is borne out not only in the policies of Gregory VII, but especially in his tireless advocate, Bernold of Constance, in whom one sees the wielding of canon law cast in the service of the propagation of the Roman liturgy.

Vincent Kennedy of the Pontifical Institute of Medieval Studies, to whom we owe a debt for his preliminary work on the *Micrologus*, wrote that Bernold's aim was "reform" and "a return to the Roman way in the liturgy"[65]. Although Bernold makes repeated appeals to the Roman sources of the past, his treatise is novel in several respects. When Bernold had finished writing the *Micrologus*, he had produced a text that was replete with the spirit of *Romanitas*, manifest not just because a plethora of ancient Roman *fontes* had been cited, but because it envisioned a new Roman *ordo*, a critical method of textual analysis, and an ecclesiological order under the auspices of Rome.

64 On this see my The Law of the Church in the Central Middle Ages: Its Creation, Collection, and Interpretation, in: The Contentious Triangle: Church, State, and University. A Festschrift in Honor of Professor George Huntston Williams, eds. Rodney L. PETERSEN and Calvin PATER, Kirksville 1999, pp. 112–115; and Robert SOMERVILLE and Bruce C. BRASINGTON, Prefaces to the Canon Law Books in Latin Christianity: Selected Translations. 500–1245, New Haven 1998, pp. 106f.; and my review in: The American Journal of Legal History 42 (1998), pp. 299–301.

65 Vincent Lorne KENNEDY, For a New Edition of the *Micrologus* of Bernold of Constance, in: Mélanges en l'honneur de Monseigneur Michel Andrieu (Revue des sciences religieuses, Vol. hors série 1), Strasbourg 1956, p. 230.

X

A HOMILY IN BENEVENTAN SCRIPT ON THE SACRED ORDERS, CANONICAL HOURS, AND CLERICAL VESTMENTS

(VAT. BORGHESE 86)*

During the past decade Father Boyle has been honored in several volumes of articles and essays, where his many roles and achievements have been described[1]. Among the most significant of these are his role as a priest in sacred orders, his membership in the Order of Preachers, his involvement in teaching and using palaeographical skills, and his leadership of the Vatican Library. Less well-known but equally important has been his constant and generous support of various exhibitions, projects, and programs of research ranging from frequent displays of materials from the Vatican Library to programs of research, such as the « Monumenta Liturgica Beneventana » at Toronto's Pontifical Institute with its study of liturgical manuscripts written in the Beneventan script. It is appropriate, therefore, that this article on a sermon on sacred orders from the Vatican Library written in Beneventan script should be included in a volume honoring Father Boyle.

* Research for this article was conducted for the program « Monumenta Liturgical Beneventana » supported by the Social Sciences and Humanities Research Council of Canada.

[1] See, e.g., *Rome : Tradition, Innovation and Renewal. A Canadian International Art History Conference 8-13 June 1987, Rome, in honour of Richard Krautheimer on the occasion of his 90th birthday and Leonard Boyle O.P. Prefect of the Biblioteca Apostolica Vaticana*, eds. C.M. Brown, J. Osborne and W.C. Kirwin, Victoria, B.C., 1991 ; and *A Distinct Voice. Medieval Studies in Honor of Leonard E. Boyle, O.P.*, eds. J. Brown and W.P. Stoneman, Notre Dame, Ind., 1997.

From patristic times throughout the Middle Ages it was expected that in the ceremony of clerical ordination an allocution, admonition, exhortation, sermon, or homily of some type would be given by the bishop or his delegate to the ordinands or to those witnessing the ordination. This address might deal with such matters as the origins of the particular grade or grades into which the candidates were passing, biblical justifications for the grades, qualifications of the ordinand, his life after ordination, the duties incumbent on the ordinand, and so forth. Evidence for such allocutions in the liturgical practice of the western Church is early found in the *Statuta ecclesiae antiqua*, whose late fifth-century rubrics were used in ordination rites down to the twentieth century. In the rite for the doorkeeper, for example, the archdeacon gives the admonition : « Ostiarius ... postquam ab archidiacono instructus fuerit qualiter in domo dei debeat conversari ... »[2]. For the lector's ordination the witnesses are addressed by the bishop : « ... faciat de illo verbum episcopus ad plebem, indicans eius [lectoris] fidem ac vitam atque ingenium »[3]. And in the rubric for the acolyte's ordination it is also directed that the bishop give an admonition : « Acolitus cum ordinatur ab episcopo quidem doceatur qualiter se in officio suo agere debeat ... »[4].

Over the course of the Middle Ages a variety of texts was chosen for these addresses. In the early Middle Ages segments from the genuine works of Isidore, the *Origines*[5] and *De ecclesiasticis officiis*[6], were perhaps used. Slightly later, a text attributed to Isidore entitled *De distantia graduum* or *De officiis septem graduum* was read either before the ordination rites of all the grades or as verses before the ordination into single grades[7]. This text appears to have had its first witness in the

[2] *C. 97. Concilia Galliae A. 314 - A. 506*, ed. C. MUNIER, Turnhout, 1963, p. 183 (*Corpus Christianorum Series Latina* 148).

[3] *C. 96, ibid*, p. 183.

[4] *C. 94, ibid.*, p. 182.

[5] *Isidori hispalensis episcopi Etymologiarum sive Originum Libri XX*, ed. W.M. LINDSAY, 2, Oxford, 1911.

[6] *Sancti Isidori episcopi hispalensis De ecclesiasticis officiis*, ed. C.M. LAWSON, Turnhout, 1989 (*Corpus Christianorum Series Latina*, 113).

[7] On this text see R.E. REYNOLDS, « The *De officiis vii graduum* : its Origins and Early Medieval Development », in *Mediaeval Studies*, 34 (1972), pp. 113-151.

Irish *Collectio canonum hibernensis,* but it quickly made its way into the ordination ceremony proper of Roman and non-Roman pontificals. To this text in the ordination allocution there might be added a recension of an Ordinal of Christ, texts again popular in Irish circles, especially in their canon law collections, in which the various ecclesiastical grades were justified by some deed or word of Christ[8]. By the tenth and eleventh centuries other texts were read as ordination allocutions. Portions of the Pseudo-Alcuinian *Liber de divinis officiis,* composed in the late ninth or early tenth centuries, quickly made their way into pontifical ceremonies of ordination[9]. Further, the seventh- or eighth-century Pseudo-Isidorian *Epistula ad Leudefredum,* also first found in canon law collections, was added to ordination ceremonies in pontifical manuscripts[10].

By the late eleventh and early twelfth centuries new ordination allocutions and sermons, usually heavily dependent on the older texts, were being composed and placed in pontifical manuscripts, where an ordaining bishop might turn to them easily. Of these sermons, one entitled « Quia christianam militiam », attributed to the canonist-bishop of Chartres, Ivo (*Sermo II*)[11], and related texts attributed to Hugh of St. Victor, seem clearly to have been the most popular[12]. In fact, by the fifteenth century there is a direction in a sumptuous pontifical manuscript commissioned by Johannes Barotius, bishop of Bergamo (1449-1465), patriarch of Venice, and grand-nephew of Pope Eugenius IV, that says a bishop on the completion of an ordination Mass might take those clerics

The verses are sometimes en bloc before all the rites, but is very probable that even in this case individual verses were used for each grade.

8 On these texts see R.E. Reynolds, *The Ordinals of Christ from their Origins to the Twelfth Century,* ed. H. Fuhrmann, Berlin – New York, 1978 (*Beiträge zur Geschichte und Quellenkunde des Mittelalters,* 7).

9 See R.E. Reynolds, « Marginalia on a Tenth-Century Text on the Ecclesiastical Officers », in *Law, Church, and Society : Essays in Honor of Stephan Kuttner,* eds. K. Pennington and R. Somerville, Philadelphia, 1977, pp. 115-129.

10 On this text see R.E. Reynolds, « The 'Isidorian' *Epistula ad Leudefredum :* An Early Medieval Epitome of the Clerical Duties », in *Mediaeval Studies,* 41 (1979), pp. 252-330.

11 On this sermon see R.E. Reynolds, « Ivonian Opuscula on the Ecclesiastical Officers », in *Mélanges Gérard Fransen, Studia Gratiana,* 20 (1976), pp. 309-322.

12 See R.E. Reynolds, *Ordinals of Christ, op. cit.,* p. 150.

he has ordained into the sacristy and there read to them as they kneel the sermon « Quia christianam militiam »[13].

Beyond the Ivonian sermon and its Hugonian variants, there are other ordination sermons of the late eleventh and early twelfth centuries that have come to light. Among these are a sermon attributed in some manuscripts to Ivo but taken almost entirely from the canonical *Institutio canonicorum* of 816/17[14], an unpublished series of sermons in Reims[15], and admonitions in a group of Anglo-Norman pontificals[16]. Further, there is an interesting sermon in one of the best-known codices of the *Pontificale Romanum XII saeculi,* Vatican, BAV Vat. lat. 7818, based almost entirely on extracts from the south-Italian canonical *Collectio in V Libris,* which, like the pontifical, may have originated in Chieti or the vicinity[17].

The sermon on sacred orders from the manuscript, Vatican, BAV Borghes. 86, that is the subject of this article is, unlike the south-Italian ordination allocution in Vat. lat. 7818, found not in a pontifical but in a series of sermons. Virginia Brown, in her article in this collection on another sermon in the Borghese manuscript, has dated the Beneventan-script portions of the codex to the early thirteenth century and places their origin in the city of Benevento or the vicinity. Further, she has described in detail the various sequences of sermons in the manuscript. Our sermon on sacred orders is the third in the first series of nine sermons in Beneventan script (fols. 74v-102r), the first two of which begin with an antiphon or responsory for Advent. Hence, our sermon would have been appropriate for ordinations held after the rogation days of Advent. While the beginnings of the other sermons are more typical of medieval sermons, where a pericope or other introductory text is given, ours begins after the first five words with a snippet drawn from the prologue to Rupert of Deutz's *Liber de diviniis officiis*. This might

13 Vatican, BAV Vat. lat. 1145, fols. 20-24r ; on which manuscript see M. ANDRIEU, *Le Pontifical romain au moyen-âge, tome III. Le Pontifical de Guillaume Durand,* Vatican, 1940, pp. 220 f (*Studi e Testi,* 86).

14 See R.E. REYNOLDS, « Ivonian Opuscula », *art. cit.*

15 In a future study I shall be dealing with these sermons.

16 R.E. REYNOLDS, *Ordinals of Christ,* p. 136.

17 See R.E. REYNOLDS, « A South Italian Ordination Allocution », in *Mediaeval Studies,* 47 (1985), pp. 438-444.

indicate that it was not necessarily a sermon originally, but the conclusion, « qui cum Patre », suggests that at least in our manuscript it was so considered. Also, the fact that the *Visio sancti Pauli,* (fols. 165v-166v) studied by Virginia Brown could be cast in a homiletic setting shows that a non-homiletic text could be used as a sermon. Further, almost all ordination sermons to the thirteenth century were built up of snippets of texts that in their origins were not homiletic.

The fact that the sermon deals with three subjects -- the sacred orders, the liturgical hours of the day, and clerical vestments -- may seem puzzling at first. Perhaps there were originally three shorter sermons that were united in our manuscript, perhaps the compiler was unorganized as a preacher, or perhaps the introduction to the sermon was lost. Nonetheless, there is a certain connection in the topics, inasmuch as clerics do observe the canonical hours and do wear liturgical vestments. Moreover, there is some effort to connect the three topics. The section on sacred orders is connected to that on the hours by a reference to the psalmist (although not the clerical psalmist of the ecclesiastical hierarchy)[18], and the section on the hours is connected to that on vestments by citations based on the *Liber pontificalis*, presenting liturgical decisions of two popes. Moreover, it was not unusual for ordination sermons to contain related but separate topics. Ivo's *Sermones II* and *III*, almost always written together in the manuscripts, are on orders and vestments. In the manuscripts of Cambrai, Tours, and Paris there are two short ordination sermons placed back to back on the orders, vestments, and liturgical celebration[19]. And in many liturgical commentaries these same topics are treated, often together[20].

The sources used by the compiler to build his sermon were widely known in Europe by the late twelfth and early thirteenth centuries, although, unlike those used in the Chieti pontifical sermon on orders,

[18] On the clerical psalmist as added to a text on the bishop, see R.E. Reynolds, *Ordinals of Christ*, p. 155.

[19] See R.E. Reynolds, « Ivonian Opuscula », *art. cit.*, pp. 317-322.

[20] For a list of these commentaries see R.E. Reynolds, « Guillaume Durand parmi les théologiens médiévaux de la liturgie », in *Guillaume Durand, Évêque de Mende (v. 1230-1296) : Canoniste, liturgiste et homme politique, Actes de la Table Ronde du C.N.R.S., Mende 24-27 mai 1990*, ed. P.-M. Gy, Paris, 1992, pp. 164-167.

they are of northern origin, perhaps brought to south Italy by the Normans either in pure forms or as parts of florilegia. As can be seen in the apparatus fontium following the text below, the sections on orders and vestments are drawn largely from the *De sacramentis* of Hugh of St. Victor. The section on the hours is based largely on the *Liber de divinis officiis* of Rupert of Deutz. There are, however, reflections of other texts, some dating back centuries before the twelfth century. Several texts are based ultimately on the *Liber officialis* of Amalarius of Metz, and one even reflects the tract *De septem ordinibus* at times attributed to the Venerable Bede. In treating individual topics the compiler usually follows the text of his source, but at times he abbreviates or combines texts from his sources.

Because there is no mention of an author and because the sermon is largely a mosaic of earlier texts, its authorship is unknown. There are, however, indications in the text itself that the sermon could very well have been compiled for archiepiscopal Benevento itself rather than for nearby episcopal sees. When the compiler comes to his description of the episcopal grade, he does not follow his model in Hugh of St. Victor's *De sacramentis,* « Episcopi vero successores sunt apostolorum », but states, « Episcopi vero aut archiepiscopi successores sunt apostolorum ». He then adds a sentence regarding the pope, « Dominus papa vicarius est Christi ». Later, modifying Hugh's text, he describes the honor of archiepiscopal pallium with its purple crosses « propter apostolicam vicem », and then returning to Hugh's text mentions that both bishops and cardinal presbyters may wear liturgical sandals. All of these texts correspond well with the situation at Benevento in the late twelfth and early thirteenth century. Its prelate was the important cardinal presbyter, Archbishop Rogerius (1179-1221), born of a noble Norman family and one-time monk of Montecassino, who was responsible for the new great bronze doors of the cathedral depicting the archbishop in a tiara and impressive pallium[21]. The city

[21] On these doors and the depiction of the tiara see B. Schimmelpfennig, « Die Tiara des Erzbischofs von Benevent », in *Ex ipsis rerum Documentis. Beiträge zur Mediävistik, Festschrift für Harald Zimmermann zum 65. Geburtstag*, eds. K. Herbers, H.H. Kortüm, and C. Servatius, Sigmaringen, 1991, pp. 363-371 ; and « Ein Bischof dem Papste gleich ? An den Insignien und Vorrechten des Erzbischofs von Benevent », in *Aus Archiven und Bibliotheken : Studien zum Recht*

itself, governed by a papal rector, was under the temporal jurisdiction of the pope who more than any of his predecessors stressed his position as *vicarius Christi*, Innocent III (1198-1216)[22]. Finally, the fact that the sermon is based largely on northern European models is also reflected in a pontifical manuscript in Beneventan script containing many Norman and northern European texts, including ordination texts, that may have been ordered by Rogerius, Rome, Biblioteca Casanatense 614[23]. In his study of the bronze doors of Archbishop Rogerius, Bernhard Schimmelpfennig notes an interesting observation by Reinhard Elze that in the scene depicting a bishop's consecration the book held by one of the clerics to the right may be the Casanatense pontifical from which the ordination rite is read[24]. This may be correct, but in light of our sermon on sacred orders, it can also be suggested that the volume may be a manuscript such as our Borghese codex in which a sermon for ordinations is found.

In presenting the text of the sermon below individual topics have been divided into paragraphs for convenient reading. The orthography of the manuscript is maintained, but modern capitalization and punctuation is used. Syntax and spelling in codices written in Beneventan script present examples of seemingly strange but normal medieval usage[25] and our sermon is no exception. Further, there are a number of scribal slips and errors that arose from a misunderstanding of the script of the text copied. There is, for example, « Pretera » for « Plectra » (l. 8), « finis » for « funis » (l. 9), « pontifes » for « pontifex » (l. 30), « ad duobis » for « a duobis » (l. 76), « sanguine » for « sanguinee » (l. 79),

und zur Kirchengeschichte des Mittelalters : Festschrift für Raymund Kottje zum 65. Geburtstag, ed. H. Mordek, Bern – Frankfurt/M – Las Vegas, 1991, pp. 391-411 (*Freiburger Beiträge zur mittelalterlichen Geschichte*, 3).

22 B. Schimmelpfennig, *The Papacy*, trs. J. Sievert, New York, 1992, p. 181.

23 On this manuscript and the texts within it see R.E. Reynolds, « Les cérémonies liturgiques de la cathédrale de Bénévent », in *Musique et rituels dans les cathédrales européennes (IXe-XVIIe siècles) : La cathédrale de Bénevént*, eds. T. Kelly and M. Pérès (*Atelier de Recherche et d'Interprétation des Musiques Médiévales*, Royaumont, France) (in press).

24 B. Schimmelpfennig, « Die Tiara », *art. cit.*, p. 364, n. 11.

25 On this see R. Jacobsson, « Short Reflexions on Beneventan Easter Sequence Texts », in *La Sequenza Medievale, Atti del Convegno Internazionale Milano 7-8 aprile 1984*, ed. A. Ziino, Lucca, 1992, pp. 129 f.

« justa » for « juxta » (l. 81), « pulchitudinem » for « pulchritudinem » (l. 91), « In » for « Inde » (l. 112), « nescibus » for « nexibus » (l. 113), « vitare » for « visitare » (l. 122), « destrum » for dextrum » (l. 111), « negligentiiis » for « negligentiis » (l. 145), and so forth. But since our text is found in a single manuscript and the unusual features may perhaps be used in future to identify related texts, it is maintained here.

(fol. 79v) <Q>ue in ecclesia fiunt et in divinis aguntur officiis, altissimarum signa sunt rerum et maxima continent celestium sacramenta secretorum ; ad quorum excellentiam contemplandam non nisi eruditus quisquam aspirare idoneus est[1].

In veteri siquidem testamento tube argentee a domino precepte sunt fieri quibus multitudo populi convocari debuissent. Ad similitudinem harum tubarum campane in ecclesia facte sunt ut per eas signum detur quando debeant in unum convenire fideles. Que quidem campane ora predicantium significant. Pretera ferrea quibus interius tunduntur ut sonum emittant lingue sunt eorumdem. Finis autem mensura vite est et conversa(fol. 80r)tionis modus qui in scriptura proponitur. Finis manu tenetur quando scriptura opere impletur. Finem sursum sequitur qui ductum scripture sacre ad bona elevatur. Finem deorsum trahit qui eadem ducente quantum in malis pressus iaceat agnoscit[2].

Dato signo clerici festine conveniunt. Dicuntur autem clerici ad cleros, quod est sors. Inde clerici quasi sortiti quia de sorte sunt domini vel quia domini partem habent, pro eo quod Mathias ab apostolis in ministerium dei primus sorte electus est.[3] Primum signaculum clerici est corona, cui capitis summitas desuper in modum spere nudatur ut per hoc datur intelligi quia ad regiam in Christo potestatem assumitur, et quia inter ipsum et deum deinceps velamen esse non debet ut revelata facie et mente pura domini sui gloriam contempletur. Summum capitis summum est mentis. Denudatio capitis illuminationem mentis significat[4]. Clericus quippe secretorum dei non ignarus esse debet quoniam ad populum eius est nuntius cuius capilli tondentur ne eum ab audiendo et intelligendo verba dei terrenorum occupatio, que per capillos significantur inpediat[5].

Clericorum autem septem sunt gradus. Primus est hostiarium, secundus lectorum, tertius exorcistarum, quartus acolitarum, quintus subdiaconorum, sextus diaconorum, septimus presbiterorum. Hic gradus dispares habet in eodem ordine dignitates. Nam super simpliciter sacerdotes sunt episcopi. Super episcopos archiepiscopi ; (fol. 80v) supra quos sunt patriarche qui etiam dicuntur primates. Supra quos omnes est summus pontifes quem papam, id est patrem patrum consuetudo ecclesiastica nominavit[6].

Ad officium ostiarii pertinent claves ecclesie ut claudat et aperiat horis competentibus templum dei et omnia que sunt intus extraque custodiat, fideles recipiat, excomunicatos et infideles excipiat[7].

Lectores potestatem habent in ecclesia propheticas lectiones coram populo recitandi[8].

Exorciste postestatem habent imponendi manus super inerguminum sive baptizatum sive cathecuminum ut inmundos spiritus de corporibus obsessis eieciat[9].

Acoliti grece, latine ceroferarii dicuntur quia cereos deferunt accensos dum legitur evangelium vel dum offertur sacrificium[10].

Subdiaconi levitis subserviuntur et vasa corporis et sanguinis Christi diaconibus ad altare domini offerunt et iterum referunt[11].

Diaconi interpretantur ministri nam ipsi hostias super altare ponunt et mensam domini componunt et altari consistunt sacerdotibus ministrantes[12].

Presbiteri interpretantur seniores. Debent enim seniores esse in populo non tantum etate corporis quantum prudentiam morum et maturitate bone conversationis. Presbiteri successores sunt et vicarii septuaginta discipulorum qui precedebant Christum in omnem civitatem et locum quo ipse erat venturus[13].

Episcopi vero et archiepiscopi successores (fol. 81r) sunt apostolorum[14]. Dominus papa vicarius est Christi. Ceterum sicut dicit psalmista, Media nocte surgebam ad confitendum tibi, congregati in ecclesia clerici[15].

Septem oras domino concinunt : matutinas, primam, tertiam, sextam, nonam, vesperas, et completorium[16].

Matutinas in nocte canimus quia dominus noster media nocte est de virgine natus et confractis portis inferni a mortuis resurrexit[17], et Petrum quia ter negaverat gallicantus redarguit[18]. Media nocte nichilominus venturus asseritur ad similitudinem Egiptiii temporis quando pascha celebratum est et exterminator angelus super domos Isrhaellitarum pertransivit[19]. Quia vero primum querendum est regnum dei et cetera addicuntur nobis et in lege iubet dominus omne sibi primitium offerri[20].

Ideo prima hora diei creatori nostro laudes referre debemus ante omnem curam corporis, qua scilicet hora dominus noster illusus atque alapis cesus et adhuc obprobriis saturandus Pilato propter nos ligatus astitit[21].

Hora tertia domino laudes referimus quoniam hac hora Christus pro nobis spinis coronatus est et linguis Iudeorum crucifixus clamantibus Pilato, Crucifige, crucifige eum. Et eadem hora spiritus sanctus super apostolos in linguis igneis descendit[22].

Hora sexta dominum collaudamus quia ea hora Christus dominus propter nos in cruce exaltatus est ut ad se traheret universa et corporalibus tenebris (fol. 81v) super terram irruentibus ad illuminationem gentium lumen verum transivit[23].

Nona quoque iure domino laudem clamamus quando clamans dominus Iesus voce magna emisit spiritum ; latrone in paradisum admisso et resisso velo legis et prophetarum cepimus gloriam domini revelata facie contemplari[24].

Vespertine itidem laudis officium domino solvimus quia in vespera Christus dominus sepelitur et resurgens ad duobus discipulis in habitu peregrini cognoscitur in fractione panis[25].

Completorium etiam ideo decantamus quia hora completorii egresso Iuda Christus pavere ac tedere cepit et prolixius oravit, de cuius corpore sanguine gutte fluxerunt[26].

Sane quia iusta Marci evangelium hora tertia dominus noster crucifixus asseritur[27], ideo Telesphorus papa constituit missam debere hora tertia celebrari[28], et Stephanus papa statuit ut sacerdotes et levite in cotidiano usu sacris vestibus non utantur nisi in ecclesia[29].

Sunt autem hec sacerdotalia vestimenta, scilicet amictus, alba, cingulum, stola, manipulus, tunica, dalmatica, casula, et preteria pallium et sandalia. Hee quidem vestes innuunt qualem oporteat esse domini sacerdotem.

Amictus enim munditia bonorum operum sacerdotum designat sub quibus oportet unum quemque ordinari ad magisterium populi dei (fol. 82r) ut ex his cordis eius et fidei sinceritas comprobetur.

Alba que camisa dicitur lineum est indumentum et strictum et significat castitatem et corporis castigationem. Hec enim vestis manus hac brachia debet astringere sacerdotis ne quid nisi utile faciat pecctus, ne quid innane cogitet ventrem ne delicias ultra modum appetendo gulosus existat, subiecta ventris membra ne lasciviendo totam sacerdotalis habitus pulchitudinem ipsa corrumpant, genua ne ab orationis instantia torpeant, tibias et pedes ne ad malum currant. Induitur ergo sacerdos linea stricta ut et corpus ab iniquis operibus et a pravis mente cogitationibus compescat[30].

Cingulum quo utitur ne ipsa vestis diffluat et gressum inpediat mentis designat custodia que necessaria est ne castitas per albam significata fiat remissa et vento elationis et frigore iniquitatis patefacta cursum bonorum inpediat et ad ultimum sordibus concupiscentie polluta vilescat et superbientes ad ruinam impellat[31].

Quia vero mentibus bene compositis et divino cultui mancipatis aliquotiens negligentia subrepit, necesse est ut ad eam detergendam adhibeatur diligentia, qua sepius ab oculis velut lacrima emundetur, propter quod in sinistra manu quedam apponitur mappula[32], que nobis innuit in temporali vita tedium (fol. 82v) nos pati superflue cogitationis, quod aliquotiens pervenit ex conscientia peccatorum[33].

Stola que alio nomine orarium vocatur que collo sacerdotis imponitur ut eum iugum domini assumpsisse significet, que a collo per anteriora descendens destrum latus ornat et sinistrum, docet ipsum per arma iustitie a dextris et a sinistris, id est in prosperis et in adversis debere esse munitum. In est quod stola cum zona albe quibusdam nescibus colligatur quia virtutes virtutibus sociantur atque aliquo temptationis moveantur inpulsu[34].

Tunica quam subter casulam habet pontifex significat rationem sublimium non patere omnibus sed maioribus atque perfectis[35]. Et quia est interior vestis designat virtutes anime que non sunt cognite multis, quas semper debet habere perfectus[36].

Dalmatica a Silvestro papa inventa religionem sanctam et immaculatam designat et proximorum curam propter sui latitudinem. Habet autem dalmatica duas coccineas lineas retro et ante quia vetus testamentum et novum rutilat dilectione dei et proximi. Inmaculatum esse ad deum pertinet, vitare fratres ad proximum. Fimbrie que procedunt de dalmatica verba sunt predicatoris, cuius religio sancta est et immaculata[37].

Cunctis postremo vestibus casula superponitur que caritatem significat. De qua enumeratis virtutum ornamentis (fol. 83r) Apostolus ait, Super omnia autem hec caritatem habentes quod est vinculum perfectionis[38].

Archiepiscopo pallii honor propter apostolicam vicem decernitur quod significat torquem auream quam solebant legitime certantes accipere. Circuli autem quo humeri constringuntur timor et disciplina domini intelligitur, quo se et subditos sibi regere debeat. Per duas vero lineas ex utraque parte, id est ante et retro a summo deorsum pendentes, predicatio utriusque testamenti vel dilectio dei et proximi fuguratur[39]. Purpureo crucis eiusdem vestimenti signaculo demonstrat se de passione redemptoris pia mente sentire[40].

Utuntur autem episcopi et cardinales presbiteri sandalis que calciamenta sunt predicatorum. Habent autem hec desubtus soleam integram ne pes terram contingat. Desuper vero constat ex corio per loca perforato quia gressus predicatoris et subtus muniti esse debet ne terrenis polluantur et desuper aperti ut ad celestia cognoscenda revelentur. Quod autem locis quibusdam aperiuntur, hoc significat quod evangelica predicatio nec omnibus revelari debet nec ab omnibus abscondi. Illic quippe sandalia aperiuntur ubi misteria regni dei cognoscuntur. Prius autem quam sandalia in pedibus assumant, induuntur caligis bissinis vel lineis usque ad genua protensis et ibidem constrictis per quod significatur quod rectos gressus (fol. 83v) debent facere pedibus suis et genua debilia, id est negligentiiis resoluta robarare, et sic ad predicandum evangelium festinare[41].

Utuntur pontifices baculis, anulis, cirotecis, et mitra. Baculus per rectitudinem sui iustitiam significat prelatorum qua subiectos regere debent. Qui iccirco subtus acumen habet ut rebelles per increpationem pungat. Desuper recurvus est ut per consolationem mites trahat. Anulus sacramentum fidei significat quo sponsa Christi ecclesia subarrata est, cuius custodes et pedagogi sunt episcopi, et prelati pro signo ferentes hoc in testimonium illi[42].

Manus eius significant opera quia manibus operantur. Debent manus cirotecis abscondi, id est pro invisibilibus scilicet spiritualibus non carnalibus opera debemus[43].

Mitra que capiti pontificis super inponitur quinque sensuum qui in capite sedem habent regnum significat. Minister ergo bene vitam suam regens caput suum scilicet Christum ornat[44]. Sic igitur sacerdos domini corporaliter et spiritualiter decoratus digne satis et competenter accedere potest ad interpellandum pro populo et exorandum dominum nostrum Iesum Christum, qui cum Patre.

APPARATUS FONTIUM

ABBREVIATIONS

ALO = *Liber officialis, Amalarii episcopi Opera liturgica omnia* 2, ed. J.M. HANSSENS, Vatican, 1948 (*Studi e Testi*, 139).

HDS = HUGH OF ST. VICTOR, *De sacramentis*, PL 176, c. 183-618.

IDEO = *Sancti Isidori episcopi hispalensis De ecclesiasticis officiis*, ed. C.M. LAWSON, Turnhout, 1989 (*Corpus Christianorum Series Latina*, 113).

LQ = *Liber Quare*, ed. G.P. GÖTZ, Turnhout, 1983 (*Corpus Christianorum Continuatio Mediaevalis*, 60).

RLDO = *Ruperti tuitiensis Liber de divinis officiis*, ed. H. HAAKE, (Turnhout, 1977 *Corpus Christianorum Continuatio Mediaevalis*, 7).

[1]ll. 1-4 : RLDO, prol. p. 5. [2]ll. 5-13 : HDS II.9.6 ; col. 474. [3]ll. 14-17 : cf. IDEO II.1, p. 53. [4]ll. 17-21 : HDS II.3.1 ; col. 421. [5]ll. 22-24 : HDS II.3.2 ; col. 421. [6]ll. 25-31 : HDS II.3.5 ; col. 423. [7]ll. 32-34 : HDS II.3.6 ; cols. 423 f. [8]ll. 35-36 : HDS II.3.7 ; col. 424. [9]ll. 37-39 : HDS II.3.8 ; col. 424. [10]ll. 40-41 : HDS II.3.9 ; col. 425. [11]ll. 42-43 : HDS II.3.10 ; col. 426. [12]ll. 44-45 : cf. HDS II.3.11 ; col. 427. [13]ll. 46-49 : HDS II.3.12 ; col. 428. [14]l. 50 : cf. HDS II.3.12 ; col. 428. [15]ll. 51-52 : cf. RLDO I.8 ; p. 9. [16]ll. 53-54 : RLDO I.9 ; p. 9. [17]ll. 55-56 : RLDO I.9 ; p. 9. [18]ll. 56-57 : RLDO I.6 ; pp. 8 f. [19]ll. 57-59 : RLDO I.8 ; p. 9. [20]ll. 59-61 : RLDO I.2 ; p. 7. [21]ll. 62-64 : RLDO I.2, p. 7. [22]ll. 65-68 : cf. RLDO I.3 ; p. 7. [23]ll. 69-71 : cf. RLDO I.4 ; p. 8. [24]ll. 72-74 : RLDO I.5 ; p. 8. [25]ll. 75-77 : RLDO I.6 ; p. 8. [26]ll. 78-80 : RLDO I.7 ; p. 9. [27]ll. 81-82 : cf., e.g., *Pascasii Radberti Expositio in Matheo Libri XII (IX-XII)*, ed. Paulus, B. (*Corpus Christianorum Continuatio Mediaevalis* 56B ; Turnhout, 1984) 1375 f. [28]l. 82 : cf. LQ Append. II, Add. 49 ; p. 193. [29]ll. 83-84 : cf. LQ Quest. 242 ; p. 97. [30]ll. 91-98 : ALO II.18.3 ; pp. 240 f. [31]ll. 97-101 : cf. Ps.-Bede, *De septem ordinibus*, PL 94.554. [32]ll. 104-107 : HDS II.4.12 ; col. 437. [33]ll. 107-108 : ALO II.24.2 ; p. 250. [34]ll. 109-114 : HDS II.4.10 ; col. 437. [35]ll. 115-116 : RLDO I.23 ; p. 19. [36]ll. 116-118 : ALO II.22.1 ; p. 247. [37]ll. 119-124 : ALO II.21.1f ; pp. 243 f. [38]ll. 125-127 : HDS II.14.11 ; col. 437. [39]ll. 128-133 : HDS II.4.16 ; col. 438. [40]ll. 133-134 : cf. *Rabani Mauri De institutione clericorum libri tres*, ed. A. Knoepfler (Munich, 1900) I. 23 ; p. 40 ; and see PL 159.67 f., n. 11. [41]ll. 135-145 : HDS II.4.14 ; col. 438. [42]ll. 146-151 : HDS II.4.15 ; col. 438. [43]ll. 152-154 : cf. Honorius « of Autun », *Gemma animae* I.215 ; PL 172.609. [44]ll. 155-157 : HDS II.4.8 ; col. 436.

CORPUS CHRISTI IN AGNONE*

CORPUS Christi and its liturgical office have played a major role in the formation of the programme entitled *Monumenta Liturgica Beneventana* at the Pontifical Institute of Mediaeval Studies in Toronto.[1] First, it was a *libellus* containing the office of Corpus Christi written in Beneventan script and coming from Caiazzo, which E. A. Lowe had dated to the twelfth century[2] (a century before Thomas Aquinas has supposedly composed the office[3]), that in part has caused a reassessment of Lowe's dates for all the manuscripts he had considered. When photographs of this *libellus,* found as part of the miscellaneous codex, Vatican, Biblioteca Apostolica Vaticana Vat. lat. 14733, were sent to the Pontifical Institute in the late 1970s it was found by this author that Pope Urban IV, whose bull *Transiturus*[4] established the feast in 1264, was mentioned in the fifth lection of the first nocturn of Matins. Hence, the date of the *libellus* had to be pushed up to the late thirteenth or early fourteenth century. Indeed, it was soon discovered that many of Lowe's dates for manuscripts in his classic work, *The Beneventan Script: A History of the South Italian Minuscule* (Oxford, 1914), were too early, largely because he believed at that time that the script ceased to be written by the fourteenth century without realizing that it was used into the late sixteenth century and even persisted into the eighteenth in an imitation Beneventan script.[5]

* Research for this article was conducted with a Research Grant from the Social Sciences and Humanities Research Council of Canada.

1 For a brief history of the programme, see R. E. Reynolds, "*Monumenta Liturgica Beneventana* — New Directions," in *Sources for the History of Medieval Books and Libraries,* ed. J. Hermans (Groningen, forthcoming).

2 E. A. Lowe, "A New List of Beneventan Manuscripts," in *Collectanea vaticana in honorem Anselmi M. Card. Albareda a Bibliotheca Apostolica edita,* vol. 2, Studi e Testi 220 (Vatican City, 1962), 211–44, esp. 218.

3 See J. A. Weisheipl, *Friar Thomas d'Aquino: His Life, Thought, and Work* (New York, 1974), 176–84, 400.

4 On the bull, see E. Franceschini, "Origine e stile della bolla 'Transiturus,' " *Aevum* 39 (1965): 218–43; and T. Bertamini, "La bolla 'Transiturus' di papa Urbano IV e l'ufficio del 'Corpus Domini' secondo il codice di S. Lorenzo di Bognanco," *Aevum* 42 (1968): 29–58.

5 See V. Brown, "The Survival of Beneventan Script: Sixteenth-Century Liturgical Codices from Benedictine Monasteries in Naples," in *Monastica* 1: *Scritti raccolti in memoria del XV centenario della nascita di S. Benedetto (480–1980)* (Montecassino, 1981), 237–355,

Stimulated by work on this *libellus* with the office of Corpus Christi, Ronald J. Zawilla completed a doctoral thesis in Toronto showing that although the so-called "first" Roman office of Corpus Christi, *Sapientia aedificavit sibi domum*,[6] could have been written by the Dominicans Hugh of St.-Cher or St. Thomas, the "second" office, *Sacerdos in aeternum*, promulgated in the papal bull *Transiturus* could only have been written by St. Thomas.[7] This was demonstrated by an examination of the uses of the scriptural passages found in the office and in the works of many authors from the eleventh through the thirteenth century, including St. Thomas.[8] The Caiazzo *libellus* in Beneventan script now in the Vatican Library, probably written in the late thirteenth or early fourteen century in southern Italy, was one of several *libelli* containing the office, some of which, Père Gy suggested, were sent out by Pope Urban IV together with a copy of the bull of promulgation.[9] While full manuscripts containing the office among other liturgical pieces have a text as good as or even better than the *libelli* thus far reported, the *libelli* as manuscript artifacts are striking reminders of the way in which the office was originally dispersed.[10] In a sense, they are like the rare *Exultet* rolls, whose format is a reminder of the way in which the *Exultet* was sung in southern Italy in the Middle Ages.[11]

Another *libellus* containing largely the Mass chants from the office of Corpus Christi has recently come to light in the Biblioteca Emidiana in the small mountain town of Agnone in the *regione* of Molise. Like the Vatican *libellus* that stimulated the formation of the *Monumenta Liturgica Beneventana*, this *libellus* was written in the Beneventan script of the late thirteenth or early fourteenth century and seems also to have come from Caiazzo.[12] That a manuscript from Caiazzo is now in the distant town of Agnone is not necessarily surprising inasmuch as a tenth-century bifolium of Bede's *In Marci evangelium expositio*

"Montevergine 6 and Sixteenth-Century Beneventan Script in Naples," in *Studi di paleografia e diplomatica in memoria di Jole Mazzoleni*, ed. G. Raimondi and S. Palmieri (Naples, 1996), and "Beneventan Fragments in the Biblioteca della Società Napoletana di Storia Patria," *Archivio storico per le province napoletane* 113 (1995): 32–50 and plates 14–16.

[6] Ed. C. Lambot, "L'office de la Fête-Dieu: Aperçus nouveaux sur ses origines," *Revue Bénédictine* 54 (1942): 97–123.

[7] For editions of this office, see *S. Thomae Aquinatis . . . Opera omnia* 15 (Parma, 1864), 233–38; and *D. Thomae Aquinatis . . . Opera omnia* 17 (Rome, 1570), 40–43.

[8] R. J. Zawilla, "The *Historiae Corpus Christi* Attributed to Thomas Aquinas: A Theological Study of Their Biblical Sources" (Ph.D. diss., Toronto, 1985).

[9] See P.-M. Gy, "L'office du Corpus Christi et S. Thomas d'Aquin: État d'une recherche," *Revue des sciences philosophiques et théologiques* 64 (1980): 501.

[10] On liturgical *libelli* and their characteristics, see M. Huglo, *Les livres de chant liturgique*, Typologie des sources du moyen âge occidental 52 (Turnhout, 1988), 64–75, esp. 70 on *libelli* for the office of Corpus Christi.

[11] See T. F. Kelly, *The Exultet in Southern Italy* (Oxford, 1996).

[12] V. Brown has kindly suggested this date and provenance to me.

now at Agnone reported in the second edition of *The Beneventan Script* has recently been shown by Virginia Brown to have been part of a Caiazzo manuscript now in the Vatican, Vat. lat. 14730.[13]

The new *libellus* with parts of the office of Corpus Christi was found in 1997 as members of the équipe of the *Monumenta Liturgica Beneventana* were searching at Agnone for further unreported fragments written in Beneventan script. Among those discovered at the Archivio della Parrocchia di S. Antonio Abate were a thirteenth-century folio with a missal and a bifolium of the same century with an antiphonale.[14] The Archivio Storico has a thirteenth-century bifolium containing *Vitae sanctorum.*[15] At the Biblioteca Emidiana there was a rich harvest of Beneventana: a bifolium of a twelfth-century graduale, flyleaves of a fifteenth-century series of *Orationes ad crucem,* a bifolium of a twelfth-century graduale, a bifolium of what is probably a missal, strips from the outer edge of a leaf with what is probably a sacramentary of the twelfth century, two heavily damaged strips from the lower part of a leaf containing an unidentified text in Bari-type Beneventan script of the early twelfth century, and four strips containing an unidentified text written in Beneventan script of the twelfth century.[16] Several of these were of more than ordinary interest, such as the fragment in a script similar to the Bari type of Beneventan script, but the most surprising discovery was the *libellus* with texts from the office of Corpus Christi, which with its musical notation had attracted the attention of the priest-librarian-music composer-choir director, don Giovanni Fangio.[17]

The *libellus* consists of five leaves (two bifolia and one folio), each measuring 368×251 mm. (251×181 mm.).[18] The damaged and worn folios are spotted with a purple mould found on many leaves of manuscripts from Caiazzo, including the *libellus* with the office of Corpus Christi in the Vatican, Vat. lat. 14733. Pricking with slits (probably nine, although some are no longer visible because of damage to the bifolia) was made on the flesh side of the parchment, and ruling was done in drypoint. There is a single vertical bounding line on each side of the one column of text and music. The bifolia are arranged with

13 V. Brown, "A Second New List of Beneventan Manuscripts (III)," *Mediaeval Studies* 56 (1994): 341.

14 Don Remo Quaranta kindly allowed us to search through the archive.

15 This fragment was discovered by Luigi Misischia and shown to Virginia Brown on 6 July 1998.

16 All of these items will be described in more detail by V. Brown in "A Second New List of Beneventan Manuscripts (IV)" (forthcoming).

17 Don Giovanni's cordial reception and generous assistance in the Biblioteca Emidiana were most touching and are gratefully acknowledged.

18 While it is possible that what now appears to be a *libellus* was part of a larger manuscript or had a few other quires bound to it (see n. 24 below), our specimen as it stands fits all the criteria for a liturgical *libellus* detailed by Père Gy in Huglo, *Les livres*, 64–65.

flesh side on fol. 1r. The writing is in a brown ink with rubrics in red. Distance between the seven lines of text is 45 mm. Minims measure 4 mm. and ascenders and descenders 8 mm. Among the distinctive features of the script are a final *r* that does not descend below the line (usual for a musical text), an *m* abbreviation with a larger right shoulder sweeping downward, and an abbreviation for *-us* consisting of a semicolon resembling a sideward *m* sweeping downward. In the Agnone *libellus* there are seven lines of musical text written on supports consisting of one red line with clef-marks f, c, and b, and two or three drypoint lines. There are custos marks at the end of each line of music. On a small piece of paper kept with the *libellus* the manuscript is described as an "innario" of the thirteenth century in "Scrittura gotica corale con notazione neumatica lombarda"; "Carte 6." There is also a letter of 26 May 1955 from the Soprintendenza alle Biblioteche per l'Abruzzo e il Molise regarding the restoration of the manuscript.

The final folio of the *libellus* is blank on the recto side and has on its verso side, upside down, in non-Beneventan script with square musical notation, the Vespers antiphon "Sacerdos in eternum Christus dominus secundum ordinem Melchisedech panem et vinum obtulit" and the psalm "Dixit dominus."[19] The majority of the remaining text of the Agnone *libellus* beginning on the first folio is in Beneventan script and is completely notated. It begins with the Office antiphon "O sacrum convivium" followed by a notation for the "Magnificat" and a rubric "Ad missam."[20] Thereafter is the Mass introit "Cibavit eos" with psalm, the gradual "Oculi omnium," "Alleluia," and the response "Caro mea."[21] Following this, over the "Lauda Syon" is the rubric "Sequentia," written once in a non-Beneventan hand and once in a later Beneventan hand; and the "Lauda Syon" is followed by the offertory "Sacerdotes incensum domini" and the communion "Quotiescumque manducabitis."[22] After the "Alleluia" of this communion a later non-Beneventan hand has written brief rubrics for celebrating the octave of the liturgy of the feast of Corpus Christi.

The individual texts in the Agnone manuscript are those expected for the feast of Corpus Christi, but the *libellus* takes on special interest when it is compared with *libelli* of the same office in Vat. lat. 14733. This manuscript, noted earlier, came from Caiazzo and was lodged permanently in the Vatican Library after its restoration in exchange for two great urns still kept in Caiazzo. The manuscript as a whole contains a number of pieces, some in Beneventan, some in other hands. There are actually two *libelli* in the manu-

[19] See *S. Thomae Aquinatis . . . Opera omnia* 15:233.

[20] Ibid., 236–37.

[21] Ibid., 237.

[22] Ibid., 237–38.

script with texts and music for the office of Corpus Christi. The first occupies fols. 56–65 of the manuscript and is described in the second edition of *The Beneventan Script* as a breviarium.[23] It consists of five parchment bifolia measuring 318×215 mm. with a written space of 231×164 mm. The parchment folios, now restored, are worn, damaged, and darkened. They are spotted with the same purple mould as found on the Agnone *libellus*. There are nine pricking slits seen at the extreme edge of the leaves, which are now 3–5 mm. from the edge of the folio, with ruling on the flesh side in drypoint. Single vertical bounding lines enclosing the single column of text are now 22 and 183 mm. from the edge of the page. The lower margin is 59 mm. There are 32 lines of text written 8 mm. apart. For the musical supports there is one red line with three drypoint lines. The red lines, bearing the clef marks c and f, are 27–37 mm. apart. The script of the text has the following measurements: minims 3 mm., ascenders 4.5 mm., and descenders 5 mm. The five bifolia, sewn with modern binding holes in the restored manuscript, are arranged so that the hair side is outside. The text is written in brown ink with rubrics in red with brown or red infilling.

The text of the Caiazzo *libellus* in Beneventan script, unlike that in the Agnone *libellus*, is for the full office and mass of Corpus Christi, including music and lections. In some instances the musical texts are those found in the Agnone *libellus*, such as the "O sacrum convivium," "Cibavit eos," "Sacerdotes incensum domini," and "Quotiescumque manducabitis," but they are in a different order.[24] Also, the Caiazzo *libellus* lacks the sequence "Lauda Syon." The musical notation matches that in the Agnone *libellus*. At times, such as in the "Pange lingua," there is notation for only the first few lines, suggesting that the full text for the musical sections would have been sung by a choir from a fully noted *libellus* or manuscript.

Evidence for the existence of *libelli* to be used in this way is found not only in the Agnone manuscript but also in the second *libellus* in the Vatican manuscript, fols. 84–95, written in a non-Beneventan hand of the fourteenth century. This fully notated *libellus* is remarkably similar to the Agnone *libellus* in its codicological features. Its size, 339×235 mm., is larger than the Agnone *libellus*, which was trimmed, but its written space, 255×181 mm., is close to the Agnone manuscript. Like the Agnone *libellus*, the Vatican *libellus* has stains of purple mould and is written in one column of seven notated lines in brown ink with red rubrics. The musical supports are a single red line with clef marks f,

[23] E. A. Lowe, *The Beneventan Script: A History of the South Italian Minuscule*, 2d edition prepared and enlarged by V. Brown, 2 vols. (Rome, 1980), 2:158.

[24] "Sacerdotes incensum domini" (fol. 56r); "Quotiescumque manducabitis" (fol. 56r); "O sacrum convivium" (fol. 64r); and "Cibavit eos" (fol. 65r).

c, b, together with three additional lines in drypoint or ink. There are custos marks at line ends.

The text of the Vatican *libellus* begins with "Sacerdos in eternum" (fol. 84r) and is followed by the Office chants. From "O sacrum convivium" (fol. 91r) through to "Quotiescumque manducabitis" the Vatican and Agnone *libelli* are virtually identical in their text, sequence, and musical notation.[25] The similarity of the individual texts and music chosen to be copied and especially the codicological features suggests that the two *libelli* were made in the same or nearby scriptoria, where both Beneventan and non-Beneventan scripts were used.

That both scripts could be written in the same place is not surprising. In his discussion of scripts written in southern Italy E. A. Lowe contended that from the eighth through the twelfth centuries the ordinary script was Beneventan and that others were foreign importations.[26] That contention has of late been substantially modified. Caterina Tristano showed in 1979 that southern Italy might be divided into various sectors in which Beneventan and Caroline scripts were used.[27] A few years later it was shown that manuscripts like the canon law codex, Rome, Biblioteca Vallicelliana Tom. XVIII, were written in Caroline by a scribe who on occasion lapsed into Beneventan.[28] More recently in a masterful article Francis Newton has considered the larger issue of one scriptorium where two scripts, the Beneventan and Caroline, were used.[29] Newton has suggested that for display books ("libri nobilissimi") Beneventan was the script of choice. For more notable common books (Newton's "libri notabiliores"), such as those containing patristic texts and some classical and contemporary texts, most were written entirely in Beneventan and some entirely in Caroline. For less common books (Newton's "libri viliores"), such as those containing school texts, canon law, logic, medicine, and grammar, either Beneventan or Caroline could be used entirely in a manuscript or a mixture of the two. Since our *libelli* with the office of Corpus Christi date to the late thirteenth and fourteenth centuries they do not fit exactly into Newton's schema. They are clearly not "libri nobilissimi" in that they lack lavish decoration. Rather, given their size and

[25] The facts that the Vatican *libellus* has more of the Office chants than the Agnone *libellus* and that "O sacrum convivium" begins a new folio in both *libelli* suggest that the Agnone *libellus* may at one time have had a quire before it with the same Office chants as the Vatican *libellus*.

[26] Lowe, *The Beneventan Script*, 2d ed., 1:90.

[27] C. Tristano, "Scrittura beneventana e scrittura carolina in manoscritti dell'Italia meridionale," *Scrittura e civiltà* 3 (1979): 89–150.

[28] See R. E. Reynolds, "Odilo and the *Treuga Dei* in Southern Italy: A Beneventan Manuscript Fragment," *Mediaeval Studies* 46 (1984): 454 n. 25.

[29] F. Newton, "One Scriptorium, Two Scripts: Beneventan, Caroline, and the Problem of Marston MS 112," in *Beinecke Studies in Early Manuscripts*, ed. R. G. Babcock, Supplement to *The Yale University Library Gazette* 66 (1991): 118–33.

liturgical significance they fit more properly into Newton's "libri notabiliores," which he suggests might be written entirely in either Beneventan or other scripts.

It is not certain that the *libelli* were in fact written in Caiazzo itself or travelled there from another place. Further, it is not certain why a church or monastery would need or want two texts for Corpus Christi in two different scripts. Perhaps one of the *libelli* was written for another place. Perhaps, Beneventan was used to signify the dignity and importance of this newly composed feast. Perhaps two different scripts were used for two groups of choristers, one more at home with Beneventan script than the other. Or perhaps as the Beneventan item went out of style, it was replaced by a *libellus* in a different hand. But whatever the reason, the *libelli* from Agnone and Caiazzo remain interesting witnesses to the early spread of the office of Corpus Christi in southern Italy, that region in which St. Thomas of Aquino was born and spent significant parts of his life.

XII

Canonistica Beneventana

It was in Munich nearly ninety years ago that the topic of this article had its genesis. A young North American student, *E. A. Loew*, came to study with the eminent palaeographer, *Ludwig Traube*. For a doctoral dissertation *Traube* suggested to *Loew* that he travel to southern Italy to work on the transmission of ancient authors at Montecassino. This was the beginning of *Loew's* lifelong fascination with manuscripts written in a bold and beautiful script known in his day as Lombardic and rechristened by him as Beneventan for the duchy in which many of the codices were written. After completing his thesis on the four oldest calendars of Montecassino,[1] *Loew* set to work on his magisterial palaeographical study, *The Beneventan Script*, which appeared in 1914[2]. Included in this volume was a handlist of some 600 items written in the script. Since then the number of items found has increased by over a thousand.[3]

Loew himself was preeminently a classicist. Thus, his main interest lay in those manuscripts bearing the works of classical antiquity, and he paid little attention to the precise contents of many other types of books written in the Beneventan script, giving the impression that the primary importance of Beneventan script lay in its transmission of classical texts. A recent census of all items in the script shows, however, that an astonishing seventy per cent of all items are liturgical, thus making Beneventan script a liturgical one par excellence.[4] Not unlike Gothic type used until recently in liturgical printed books, Beneventan script appears to have been used to lend beauty, dignity, and an air of antiquity to liturgical texts. In fact, this 'air of antiquity' misled

---

1 *Die ältesten Kalendarien aus Monte Cassino*, Munich 1908 (Quellen und Untersuchungen zur lateinischen Philologie des Mittelalters, 3,3).

2 *The Beneventan Script. A History of the South Italian Minuscule*, Oxford 1914.

3 See the items listed in E. A. Loew, *The Beneventan Script. A History of the South Italian Minuscule*, 2nd edit. prepared and enlarged by Virginia Brown, Rome 1980, 2 (Sussidi eruditi 34); Virginia Brown, *A Second New List of Beneventan Manuscripts (II)*, Mediaeval Studies 50 (1988), 584-625; and another 'new list' by Virginia Brown forthcoming in *Mediaeval Studies*.

4 See the comment by Virginia Brown in *Beneventan Script*, London 1990, 5 (*Bookhands of the Middle Ages Part IV*).

Loew at times to date some hands as much as two to three centuries too early. On the basis of these discoveries regarding the numbers and dates of the codices, a major programme is now being carried out by scholars based in Toronto to describe, study, and redate all items written in the script.[5] Although this programme concentrates on the liturgical manuscripts - often easy to date and locate because of names, dates, and locations mentioned in them - canonistic manuscripts written in the script have also been of keen interest, not only for their dates and origins, but also for their distribution, contents, and relationship to related canonistic codices not written in the script.

At the last International Congress of Medieval Canon Law in San Diego one of the major collections of canon law written in what can be called the 'Beneventan zone' - the region defined by the use of the script, Dalmatia and Italy between Rome and Calabria - was described.[6] In the present paper several general observations will be made about all the canonical collections written in Beneventan script, concluding with a report of one of the more interesting recent discoveries of a canonistic fragment written in the script and its relation to monastic practice in the Beneventan zone.

To facilitate discussion of Beneventan-script canon law collections there are four appendices at the conclusion of this paper. The first is a list of all of the canonical items written in the script arranged broadly according to the century in which they were written. The dates are approximate and generally follow those assigned them by *Loew*. In using this list, three points must be remembered. First, several of the codices listed here are not written wholly in Beneventan script. It is sometimes the case that a collection is written partly in Carolingian or Romanesca script and partly in Beneventan. The reasons for this are many. At the simplest level, a scribe might be capable of writing in both scripts and would change from one to the other as he wrote, witness the famous codex, Rome, Biblioteca Vallicelliana, Tom. XVIII.[7] In other codices, it appears that a scribe who wrote in Carolingian script might be temporarily replaced by one who wrote in Beneventan script, witness, Rome,

---

5 See Roger E. Reynolds, *Monumenta Liturgica Beneventana*, in: M. Dimnik, P. Pobst, C. Hilken, and L. Denesiuk (Edd.), *Jubilee 1989: Pontifical Institute of Mediaeval Studies: Foundation 1929 - Papal Charter 1939*, Toronto 1989, 61.

6 Roger E. Reynolds, *The South-Italian Canon Law Collection in Five Books and its Derivatives: New Evidence on its Origins, Diffusion, and Use*, Mediaeval Studies 52 (1990), 278-95.

7 Roger E. Reynolds, *Odilo and the Treuga Dei in Southern Italy: A Beneventan Manuscript Fragment*, Mediaeval Studies 46 (1984), 454, n. 25.

Biblioteca Vallicelliana, F 54, Part III, fol. 219.[8] Then, there are other instances in which the writing of separate quires was assigned to one scribe writing Carolingian script and to another writing in Beneventan, and when the quires were joined, there was an unusual juxtaposition of Carolingian and Beneventan scripts, witness again Rome, Biblioteca Vallicelliana, F 54, Part I, in Carolingian script, and Part II, carrying on a sentence of the *Epistula ad Leudefredum* of Part I in Beneventan script.[9] Sometimes it may have been the case that a portion of a codex written in Carolingian script had to be replaced, and therefore portions of the text were replaced by a scribe writing in Beneventan script. Finally, there are cases in which a Beneventan scribe added material to an older codex written in Carolingian script. For example, the codex, Vatican, BAV, lat. 1347, containing the *Collectiones Cresconii* and *Dacheriana* and the *Quadripartitus*, was written in Reims in the third quarter of the ninth century, but by the early eleventh century it had travelled to southern Italy, where it was augmented by a Beneventan scribe[10] and then was perhaps used as a model for another codex with like texts written completely in Beneventan script, Montecassino 541.[11]

Second, it must be stressed that in the first appendix a single codex might contain more than one collection. Montecassino 541, just mentioned, is an example of this. Further, as this same codex illustrates, the collections themselves were often augmented with additional canonistic texts in Beneventan script.[12]

Third, included in the first appendix are several codices that do not contain 'recognized' collections, but a mélange of canon law texts, at times mixed through other non-canonical material. Among these codices are Montecassino 384 and 216.

It should be stressed, further, that there is a dispute about the date and script of the 'earliest' canonistic codex in Beneventan script, Vatican, BAV, Reg. lat. 1997. According to some palaeographers the script is of the late

8 Loew-Brown, *The Beneventan Script* (see note 3), 2. 130.

9 Roger E. Reynolds, *The 'Isidorian' Epistula ad Leudefredum: An Early Medieval Epitome of the Clerical Duties*, Mediaeval Studies 41 (1979), 298.

10 Franz Kerff, *Der Quadripartitus: Ein Handbuch der karolingischen Kirchenreform: Überlieferung, Quellen und Rezeption*, Sigmaringen 1982, 27-30 (Quellen und Forschungen zum Recht im Mittelalter 1).

11 Ibid., 18-20.

12 See especially 140-143.

eighth century and is 'proto-Beneventan,'and according to others it is mid-ninth century and is 'old Italian.'[13]

Finally, in the first appendix there are items that are not collections of canon law in the proper sense of the word and also fragments that may or may not come from formal collections. Among the former is Vatican, Archivio, 1, the famous Register of John VIII,[14] and among the latter is the tiny fragment from Goslar containing a text of the *Second Epistle of Clement* in an unusual recension related to a similar text in the Beneventan-script miscellany, London, BL, Addit. 16413.[15]

The second appendix is based on the first and lists the manuscripts according to the collections and canonistic material they contain.

The third appendix contains a list of canonistic manuscripts written in another regional or national script, the Visigothic; and the fourth appendix lists codices written in Visigothic script according to the collections they contain. These third and fourth appendices will be used to compare canonistic activity in two zones with regional hands written during approximately the same chronological period.

Turning to the canonical codices in Beneventan script, one is first struck by the relatively small number that has survived, only thirty-four out of the total 1600 items written in the script. Many reasons can be suggested for this small number. It may be that it is simply happenstance that so few have survived. Why, then, have nearly fifty times that number survived in all, especially liturgical items that were discarded as rites changed or when they were used beyond repair? It can be answered that because Beneventan script was preeminently a liturgical one, more of these have survived.

There are other good reasons, however, for the small number of canonistic items in Beneventan script. First, if one looks at the dates of the surviving items, it is striking that there is only one codex written in the thirteenth century, a manuscript of Burchard's *Decretum.*[16] Second, it is noteworthy that except for fragments from Gratian's *De consecratione* imbedded in St. Tho-

---

13 See Roger E. Reynolds, *The Ritual of Clerical Ordination of the Sacramentarium Gelasianum saec. viii: Early Evidence from Southern Italy*, in: P. De Clerck and E. Palazzo (Edd.), *Rituels: Mélanges offerts au Père Gy O.P.*, Paris 1990, 440 f.

14 Loew-Brown, *The Beneventan Script (see note 3)*, 2. 142.

15 Roger E. Reynolds, *A South Italian Liturgico-Canonical Mass Commentary*, Mediaeval Studies 50 (1988), 633, n. 21.

16 Vatican, BAV, lat. 4981.

mas's Office of Corpus Christi,[17] there are no canonistic texts copied that were compiled beyond the *Collection in Seventy-Four Titles.* These two facts are puzzling because Beneventan script was used to copy many non-canonistic texts even into the late sixteenth century.[18] Moreover, some of these non-canonistic texts were not ancient ones antedating Gratian but texts written long after Gratian's time. In short, canonistic texts written in the Beneventan script are few in number and all pre-Gratian.

A combination of factors probably explains this dearth of canon law items in Beneventan script. First, it is significant that many of these items are monastic in origin. On occasion it has been claimed that monks were inhibited from studying canon law.[19] The codices written in monastic centres put this claim in doubt. Nonetheless, beyond the time of Gratian, the professional study of canon law was not primarily a monastic enterprise. Rather, it had gone to the universities and urban centres. As *Loew* and his successors have often emphasized, the Beneventan script was written primarily in monasteries, and thus it is perhaps not surprising that the only two canonistic codices in Beneventan script from beyond Gratian's time contain texts antedating him, Montecassino 216, written in the late twelfth century with texts antedating Gratian, and Vatican, BAV, lat. 4981, with Burchard's *Decretum.*

Beyond the fact that Beneventan script was chiefly monastic and that canonistic collections from the time of Gratian and after were preeminently non-monastic, university texts, there are other reasons for the small number of canonistic items in Beneventan script. As beginners in calligraphy or palaeographical study will attest, Beneventan script is slow to write and difficult to read, until one becomes accustomed to its peculiarities. From the mid-twelfth century on, professors and students in such university centres as Bologna, hailing as they did from throughout Europe, would find a regional monastic script like the Beneventan difficult to use and read. Further, it was

---

17 For a late thirteenth-century *libellus* written in Beneventan script with these fragments, see Vatican, BAV, lat. 14733; and on the dating of this manuscript see Reynolds, *The South-Italian Canon Law Collection in Five Books*, 282, n. 25.

18 Virginia Brown, *The Survival of Beneventan Script: Sixteenth-Century Liturgical Codices from Benedictine Monasteries in Naples*, in: *Monastica. Scritti raccolti in memoria del XV centenario della nascita di S. Benedetto (480-1980)*, Monte Cassino 1982, 1.237-355 (Miscellanea cassinese 44).

19 On this question and Pseudo-Isidore at Cluny, see Horst Fuhrmann, *Einfluß und Verbreitung der pseudo-isidorischen Fälschungen von ihrem Auftauchen bis in die neuere Zeit*, Stuttgart, 1974, 757-68 (MGH Schriften 24,3).

not a script that would find favour in legal chanceries, where more universally-accepted scripts would be preferred. In fact, in the Constitutions of Melfi in 1231, the Emperor Frederick II forbade the use of Beneventan script for legal documents.[20] In a sense, this was an official suppression of the script much like that of the Visigothic script in Spain at the Council of Leon in 1090. According to one report this regional script of the Iberian peninsula, also beautiful but difficult to read, was prohibited for liturgical books, and according to another report, it was prohibited for all books.[21] Here, it is instructive to see in the third appendix that there are only two extant canon law codices written in Visigothic script beyond 1090, one, a codex of the *Collectio hispana* copied in Mozarabic Toledo in 1095, and the other, a Burchard manuscript copied in 1105.

Despite the facts that there are few surviving canon law collections in Beneventan script and that they are all pre-Gratian collections, it is nonetheless surprising to find the wide range of major early medieval canon law collections represented in these manuscripts. There are, of course, several major transalpine collections and even Italian collections that are not represented among Beneventan-script items: the *Libri duo* of Regino from north of the Alps, and the *Collectio Anselmo dedicata,* Anselm of Lucca, or Deusdedit from the Italian peninsula. It is astonishing, however, that not only are there represented such indigenous collections as the *Dionysiana, Collection in Five Books* and the *Seventy-Four Titles,* but that such transalpine collections as the *Vetus Gallica, Hibernensis, Dacheriana,* Pseudo-Isidore and Burchard are represented in as many as three manuscripts.

In this respect it is instructive to compare in appendix four the canon law collections written in another contemporary regional hand, the Visigothic. Nearly all the collections written in that script are the *Hispana* or *Hispana*-related collections. The area in which Visigothic script was written was, of course, more isolated from the rest of Europe than was the Beneventan zone. This zone was host to waves of settlers, invaders, and inhabitants from both east and west: Lombards, Byzantines, Carolingians, Ottonian and Salian Germans, and finally the Normans and Angevines, and all of these brought their canon law texts with them, many of which were copied in Beneventan

---

[20] Loew, *The Beneventan Script (see note 2),* 45 n.1.

[21] See Antonio García y García, *Reforma gregoriana e idea de la 'Militia sancti Petri' en los reinos ibéricos, Studi Gregoriani 13,* Roma 1989, 259 f, who deals with the issue as to whether the prohibition extended only to liturgical books or to all books.

script. This is probably one of the reasons for the relative wealth of collections represented in the Beneventan script. Reflecting Carolingian influence are the manuscripts of the *Dacheriana;* reflecting Byzantine influence are manuscripts of the *Collection in Five Books* and its derivatives with eastern texts unknown elsewhere in the west; reflecting Germanic influence are the *Decretum* of Burchard and texts of Henry II in the *Collection in Five Books;*[22] and reflecting Norman influence is the Montecassino codex of the *Pseudo-Isidorian Decretals* containing texts such as the *Epistula ad Leudefredum* in a Norman recension.[23]

Given the wide range of canonical collections represented in Beneventan-script codices, is it possible to say that there was a single dominant regional collection for the Beneventan zone in the same way that the *Hispana* was the chief regional collection for the Visigothic-script zone? In the Beneventan zone the answer is not as clear-cut as it is for the Visigothic script zone, where three of the seven collections are *Hispana*-related and twelve of the nineteen manuscripts are *Hispana*-related. In the Beneventan zone there are twenty-one collections represented in the thirty-four items in the script. But within these twenty-one items there is a clear preponderance of those related to the *Collectio hibernensis,* not only the *Hibernensis* itself, but also the *Collection in Nine Books,* and the *Collection in Five Books* and its many derivatives; that is, three of the twenty-one collections are related to the *Hibernensis,* but of these, twelve of the total thirty-four manuscripts contain these *Hibernensis*-related texts. Thus, in terms of a regional favourite in the Beneventan zone, it appears that the *Hibernensis*-related collections with their mixture of canonistic, patristic, biblical, liturgical, and monastic texts were dominant - at least for scribes writing Beneventan script.

Four years ago at the International Congress of Medieval Canon Law in San Diego, it was suggested that the *Collection in Five Books* and its derivatives - twenty-five codices of which are in both Beneventan script and other scripts - could be counted as a monastic collection or a collection containing a variety of texts beyond the usual papal and episcopal decrees and conciliar canons found in most major collections.[24] Thus, it is perhaps not surprising

---

22 Reynolds, *The South-Italian Canon Law Collection in Five Books (see note 6)*, 289; and Myron Wojtowytsch, *Die Kanones Heinrici regis. Bemerkungen zur römischen Synode vom Februar 1014*, in: H. Mordek (Hg.), *Papsttum, Kirche und Recht im Mittelalter*. FS Horst Fuhrmann zum 65. Geburtstag, Tübingen 1991, 155-68.

23 Reynolds, *The 'Isidorian' Epistula ad Leudefredum (see note 9)*, 288 f.

24 Reynolds, *The South-Italian Canon Law Collection in Five Books* (see note 6), 292-95.

that Beneventan script, a preeminently monastic script, would be used heavily for such 'monastic' collections.

But how then does one explain the seeming anomaly that there are three codices of Burchard's *Decretum* and four of the *Collection in Seventy-Four Titles* with their heavy concentrations of papal and conciliar canons? Regarding Burchard's *Decretum,* the answer probably lies in the fact that it was a traditional, balanced systematic collection that continued to be useful especially for its penitential texts in L. XIX, the *Corrector sive Medicus*. Indeed, it was shown four years ago at San Diego that many of the derivatives of the *Collection in Five Books* had large admixtures from L. XIX of Burchard's *Decretum*.[25] Regarding the *Collection in Seventy-Four Titles*, the relatively large number of manuscripts in Beneventan script probably can be explained by the close relations in the late eleventh and early twelfth centuries between the papacy and the area south of Rome, especially Montecassino, where the Beneventan script was written. It has recently been emphasized that many of the Roman cardinals of the reform period were from the Beneventan zone and that two popes of the period had been abbots of Montecassino, Victor III and Gelasius II.[26] Under the former, the Abbot Desiderius, Beneventan script reached its classical apogee,[27] and the Roman church itself both liturgically and artistically was heavily influenced by Montecassino and the Beneventan zone.[28] Hence, it is not surprising that the premier canonical collection of the reform period, the *Collection in Seventy-Four Titles,* should be copied in Beneventan script, monastic as it might have been.

It has been stated that the *Collection in Five Books* and its derivatives can be seen as monastic collections. But there is another collection with monastic canons that surprisingly made its way into the Beneventan zone and was copied in the script. This was the major Merovingian systematic collection, the *Collectio vetus gallica,* and *Hubert Mordek* has shown that the youngest

---

25 Ibid., 287.

26 See Richard F. Gyug, *The Pontificals of Monte Cassino*, in: *L'etá dell'Abate Desiderio. Atti del IV Convegno di studi sul medioevo meridionale, Montecassino e Cassino 4-8 ottobre 1987, Miscellanea cassinese,* Montecassino 1992; and *Rome and the Benedictines during the Gregorian Reform*, in: *Monasticism and Mendicant Life in the Middle Ages: Proceedings of the Medieval Studies Conference, Toronto, 22 February 1992,* Toronto (both forthcoming).

27 Loew, *The Beneventan Script (see note 2),* pls. III and IV.

28 See Gyug, *Pontificals (see note 26)*; and Hélène Toubert, *Rome et le Mont-Cassin: Nouvelles remarques sur les fresques de l'église inférieure de Saint-Clément de Rome,* Dumbarton Oaks Papers 30 (1976), 2-33.

copy of that collection is in Beneventan script, made for the Cassinese dependency of San Nicola di Cicogna, located only a few kilometres down the mountain from the abbey.[29] Strangely, however, this manuscript of the *Collectio vetus gallica*, Montecassino 372, lacks many of the monastic canons of the collection that would have been of use or interest to the monks there.[30] But a recent discovery of extracts from the monastic canons of the *Collectio vetus gallica* now shows that even into the twelfth century it was of use and interest to religious communities in the Beneventan zone.[31] These extracts are found in a chapter book of the monastery of San Pietro intra muros of Benevento, now Benevento, Biblioteca Capitolare, 37. Inserted between texts that would have been read during the chapter, a necrology and the *Regula Benedicti*, there are seven canons from the *Collectio vetus gallica*. Unexpectedly, in several instances the text has been altered so as to make it applicable to nuns, which were at San Pietro intro muros. But this is perhaps not so surprising because the monastic oath of profession written immediately after the texts from the *Collectio vetus gallica* is directed to an abbess.

The conservative Benedictine nuns of Benevento reading the monastic texts in chapter from the ancient Merovingian *Collectio vetus gallica* is an appropriate place to make a concluding remark regarding *canonistica beneventana*. The Beneventan script, like Visigothic script, was a conservative one, beautiful but difficult to read, and used primarily to copy liturgical texts. It is perhaps surprising that any canon law collections at all were written in the Beneventan script, except, of course, where scribes could write only in this script. But the conservative mentality underlying the use of the script may help explain in part why collections, especially such older ones as the Merovingian *Collectio vetus gallica* or the Carolingian *Dacheriana* or *Pseudo-Isidorian Decretals,* should have been copied in the script in the eleventh century. Simply put, the monastic scribes who copied these older collections were often preservers of texts and very conscious of their role as the guardians of antique culture, both secular and ecclesiastical. The Beneventan script in which the canonical codices were copied was thus considered the most

29 Hubert Mordek, *Kirchenrecht und Reform im Frankenreich: Die Collectio Vetus Gallica, die älteste systematische Kanonessammlung des fränkischen Gallien: Studien und Edition* Berlin-New York 1975, 280 f. (Beiträge zur Geschichte und Quellenkunde des Mittelalters 1).

30 Ibid., 325 f.

31 For a study of this excerptum see Roger E. Reynolds, *A Beneventan Monastic Excerptum from the Collectio Vetus Gallica*, Revue Bénédictine 102 (1992), 298-308.

appropriate and beautiful format for this enterprise of conserving the ancient law of the Church.

Postscript: After this paper was presented in Munich, members of the Toronto Beneventan Project discovered pastedown fragments of the *Decretum* of Gratian in the manuscript, Monte Vergine, Biblioteca dell'Abbazia, Perg. 6518, dating to the late twelfth or early thirteenth century. While this discovery is certain proof that the *Decretum* was copied in Beneventan script, it remains clear that the script was used virtually exclusively to copy pre-Gratian collections.

APPENDIX I

Canon Law Collections in Beneventan Script by Century

Eighth/ninth century

Vaticano, BAV, Reg. lat. 1997, *Collection of Chieti* (s.VIII/IX)

Tenth century

Montecassino, Archivio della Badia, 384, miscellaneous *canones* (s.X^{in})
Montecassino, Archivio della Badia, 439, *canones* and parts of the *Collectio canonum hibernensis* (s.X)
Montecassino, Archivio della Badia, 554, *Collectio Dacheriana, Penitentiale in II libris* (s.X)
Roma, Bibl. Cas., Nr. 641, papal canons (s.X)
Vaticano, BAV, lat. 5845, *Collectio Dionysiana* (915-34)

Eleventh century

El Escorial, Bibl. Cor., Z.III.19, *Collection in 74 Titles* and extract of *Collection in 5 Books* (s.XI^{ex})
Firenze, BN Cour., Nr. 604, *Decretum Gelasianum* (s.XI^{in})
Goslar, StA, s.n., fragment of the *Epistula Clementis secunda* (s.XI)
London, BL, Add. Nr. 16413, miscellaneous *canones*, the *Capitula iudiciorum,* and fragments of other penitentials (s.XI^{in})
Montecassino, Archivio della Badia, 1, *Decretales Pseudo-Isidorianae* (s.XI)
Montecassino, Archivio della Badia, 45, *Decretum Burchardi* (s.XI)
Montecassino, Archivio della Badia, 125, *Collection in 5 Books* (s.XI^{med})
Montecassino, Archivio della Badia, 297, *Collectio canonum hibernensis* (s.XI^{in})
Montecassino, Archivio della Badia, 372, *Collectio vetus gallica* and *Penitentiale Casinense* (s.XI^{in})
Montecassino, Archivio della Badia, 541, *Collectio Cresconii, Collectio Dacheriana, Quadripartitus, Breviatio canonum* (s.XI)
Rieti, Arch. Capit., s.n., derivative of the *Collection in 5 Books* (s.XI)
Roma, Bibl. Vall., T. 18, *Collectio Cresconii, Collection in 72 Chapters, Collectio canonum hibernensis, Collectio De episcoporum transmigratione,* and *Collection in 448 Chapters* (s.XI)
Roma, Bibl. Vall., B 66, glosses on canons of councils (s.XI^{ex})
Roma, Bibl. Vall., F 2, derivative of the *Collection in 5 Books* (s.XI$^{2/2}$)

Roma, Bibl. Vall., F 8, derivative of the *Collection in 5 Books* (s.$XI^{2/2}$)
Vaticano, Arch. Seg. Vat., Reg. Vat. 1, Register of Pope John VIII (s.XI^{ex})
Vaticano, BAV lat. 1347, *Collectio Cresconii, Collectio Dacheriana, Quadripartitus* (s.$IX^{3/4}$ [Rheims], s.XI [Beneventan])
Vaticano, BAV, lat. 1349, *Collection in 9 Books* (s.XI)
Vaticano, BAV, lat. 4939, *Collectio canonum beneventana* (s.$XI^{1/2}$)
Vaticano, BAV, lat. 14731, *Decretum Burchardi* (s.XI^{ex})

Twelfth century

Benevento, Bibl. Capit., 37, excerpts of *Collectio vetus gallica* (s.XII)
El Escorial, Bibl. Cor., L.III.19, *Collection in 74 Titles* (s.XII)
Madrid, BN, Nr. 373, derivative of the *Collection in 5 Books* (s.XII)
Montecassino, Archivio della Badia, 216, *Canonum epitome* (s.XII^{ex})
Montecassino, Archivio della Badia, 220, papal letters (s.XII)

Monte Cassino, Archivio della Badia, 522, *Collection in 74 Titles, Collectio Dionysio-Hadriana*, and extract of *Collection in 5 Books* (s.XII)
Roma, Bibl. Vall., F 54, *Collection in 74 Titles*, derivative of the *Collection in 5 Books* (s.XII)

Thirteenth century

Vaticano, BAV, lat. 4981, *Decretum Burchardi* (s.XIII)
There are also miscellaneous canons found in such Beneventan manuscripts as the Caiazzo *libellus* of the office of Corpus Christi (on which see Roger E. Reynolds, *The South-Italian Canon Law Collection in Five Books and its Derivatives: New Evidence on its Origins, Diffusion, and Use*, Mediaeval Studies 52 (1990) 282, n. 25) or the Pontifical of Kotor (on which see Roger E. Reynolds, *The 'Isidorian' Epistula ad Leudefredum: an Early Medieval Epitome of the Clerical Duties*, Mediaeval Studies 41 (1979) 310 f.).

Total items: 34

Total items by century:

s.VIII/IX: 1; s.X: 5; s.XI: 20; s.XII: 7; s.XIII: 1

APPENDIX II

Canon Law Collections in Beneventan Script

[] = Manuscript contains more than one collection

Collectio Dionysiana/derivatives

Vaticano, BAV, lat. 5845, *Collectio Dionysiana* (915-34)
Montecassino, Archivio della Badia, 522, *Collectio Dionysio-Hadriana* (s.XII)

Breviatio canonum

Montecassino, Archivio della Badia, 541, *Breviatio canonum* (s.XI)

Collectio Cresconii

[Montecassino, Archivio della Badia, 541, *Collectio Cresconii* (s.XI)]
Roma, Bibl. Vall., T. 18, *Collectio Cresconii* (s.XI)
Vaticano, BAV, lat. 1347, *Collectio Cresconii* (s.IX$^{3/4}$ [Rheims], s.XI [Beneventan])

Collection of Chieti

Vaticano, BAV, Reg. lat. 1997, *Collection of Chieti* (s.VIII/IX)

Collectio vetus gallica/related

Montecassino, Archivio della Badia, 372, *Collectio vetus gallica* (s.XI^{in})
Benevento, Bibl. Capit., 37, excerpts of *Collectio vetus gallica* (s.XII)

Collectio hibernensis/related

Montecassino, Archivio della Badia, 439, *canones* and parts of the *Collectio canonum hibernensis* (s.X)
Montecassino, Archivio della Badia, 297, *Collectio canonum hibernensis* (s.XI^{in})
[Roma, Bibl. Vall., T. 18, *Collectio canonum hibernensis* (s.XI)]

Collectio Dacheriana

Montecassino, Archivio della Badia, 554, *Collectio Dacheriana* (s.X)
[Montecassino, Archivio della Badia, 541, *Collectio Dacheriana* (s.XI)]
[Vaticano, BAV, lat. 1347, *Collectio Dacheriana* (s.IX$^{3/4}$ [Rheims], s.XI [Beneventan])]

Decretales pseudo-isidorianae

Montecassino, Archivio della Badia, 1, *Decretales Pseudo-Isidorianae* (s.XI)

Penitentials

London, BL, Add. Nr. 16413, *Capitula iudiciorum* and fragments of other penitentials (s.XI^{in})
[Montecassino, Archivio della Badia, 372, *Penitentiale Casinense* (s.XI^{in})]
[Montecassino, Archivio della Badia, 541, *Quadripartitus* (s.XI)]
[Montecassino, Archivio della Badia, 554, *Penitentiale in II libris* (s.X)
[Vaticano, BAV, lat. 1347, *Quadripartitus* (s.IX$^{3/4}$ [Rheims], s.XI [Beneventan])]

Collection in 72 chapters

[Roma, Bibl. Vall., T. 18, *Collection in 72 Chapters* (s.XI)]

Collectio de episcoporum transmigratione

[Roma, Bibl. Vall., T. 18, *Collectio De episcoporum transmigratione* (s.XI)]

Collection in 448 chapters

[Roma, Bibl. Vall., T. 18, *Collection in 448 Chapters* (s.XI)]

Collection in 9 books

Vaticano, BAV, lat. 1349, *Collection in 9 Books* (s.XI)

Decretum Burchardi

Montecassino, Archivio della Badia, 45, *Decretum Burchardi* (s.XI)

Vaticano, BAV, lat. 14731, *Decretum Burchardi* (s.XI^{ex})
Vaticano, BAV, lat. 4981, *Decretum Burchardi* (s.XIII)

Collection in 5 books

Montecassino, Archivio della Badia, 125, *Collection in 5 Books* (s.XI^{med})

Derivatives of Collection in 5 books

El Escorial, Bibl. Cor., Z.III.19, extract of *Collection in 5 Books* (s.XI^{ex})
[Montecassino, Archivio della Badia, 522, extract of *Collection in 5 Books* (s.XII)]
Rieti, Arch. Cap., s.n., derivative of the *Collection in 5 Books* (s.XI)
Roma, Bibl. Vall., F 2, derivative of the *Collection in 5 Books* (s.XI$^{2/2}$)
Roma, Bibl. Vall., F 8, derivative of the *Collection in 5 Books* (s.XI$^{2/2}$)
Roma, Bibl. Vall., F 54, derivative of the *Collection in 5 Books* (s.XII)
Madrid, BN, Nr. 373, derivative of the *Collection in 5 Books* (s.XII)

Collectio canonum beneventana

Vaticano, BAV, lat. 4939, *Collectio canonum beneventana* (s.XI$^{1/2}$)

Collection in 74 Titles

[El Escorial, Bibl. Cor., Z.III.19, *Collection in 74 Titles* (s.XI^{ex})]
El Escorial, Bibl. Cor., L.III.19, *Collection in 74 Titles* (s.XII)
[Roma, Bibl. Vall., F 54, *Collection in 74 Titles* (s.XII)]
[Montecassino, Archivio della Badia, 522, *Collection in 74 Titles* (s.XII)]

Papal canons

Roma, Bibl. Cas., Nr. 641, papal canons (s.X)
Firenze, BN Cour., Nr. 604, *Decretum Gelasianum* (s.XI^{in})
Goslar, StA, s.n., fragment of the *Epistula Clementis secunda* (s.XI)
Vaticano, Archivio Segreto Vaticano, Registri Vaticani, 1, Register of Pope John VIII (s.XI^{ex})
Montecassino, Archivio della Badia, 220, papal letters (s.XII)

Conciliar canons

Roma, Bibl. Vall., B 66, glosses on canons of councils (s.XI^{ex})

36

Miscellaneous canons

Montecassino, Archivio della Badia, 384, miscellaneous *canones* (s.X^{in})
[London, BL, Add. Nr. 16413 (miscellaneous *canones);* (s.XI^{in})]
Montecassino, Archivio della Badia, 216, *Canonum epitome* (s.XII^{ex})

Total items: 34

Total collections: 21

Total items for each collection:

Coll. Dionysiana/derivatives: 2
Breviatio canonum: 1
Coll. Cresconii: 3
Coll. of Chieti: 1
Coll. vetus gallica/related: 2
Coll. hibernensis/related: 3
Coll. Dacheriana: 3
Decretales pseudo-isidorianae: 1
Penitentials: 5
Coll. in 72 chapters: 1
Coll. de episcoporum transmigratione: 1
Coll. in 448 chapters: 1
Coll. in 9 books: 1
Decretum Burchardi: 3
Coll. in 5 books: 1
Derivatives of Coll. in 5 books: 7
Coll. canonum beneventana: 1
Coll. in 74 Titles: 4
Papal canons: 5
Conciliar canons: 1
Miscellaneous canons: 3

APPENDIX III

Canon Law Manuscripts in Visigothic Script by Century

[If date is at the turn of century, the earlier century is used, but the actual date is given]

Eighth century

Madrid, Acad. Hist., Aemil. 44 (F.218), *Proto-Hispana Collection of Canons* (s.VIII/IX)

Ninth century

Leon, Arch. Cat., 22, *Acts of the Council of Cordoba in 839* (s.IX)
Lyons, BM, 336 (269), *Collectio hispana systematica* (with Visigothic notations) (s.IX^{in})
Paris, BN, lat. 10876 (a) et 10877 (b) + Tours, BM, 615 + New Haven, Yale, Bein. Libr., 481, *II Council of Seville, c. 11* (s.IX/X)
Paris, BN, lat. 11709, *Collectio hispana systematica* (with Visigothic notations) (s.IX^{in})
Paris, Arch. N., AB XIX.1723, *Collectionis canonum epitome of Dionysius Exiguus* (?) (s.IX)

Tenth century

Cord., Arch. Cat., 123, Alvarus Paulus, *Iudicium penitentie excerpta canonum a beato Gregorio papa romensis edita* (s.X)
El Escorial, Bibl. Cor., d.I.1, *Collectio hispana* (994)
El Escorial, Bibl. Cor., d.I.2, *Collectio hispana* (976)
El Escorial, Bibl. Cor., e.I.12, *Collectio hispana* (s.X-XI)
El Escorial, Bibl. Cor., e.I.13, *Collectio hispana* (s.X-XI)
London, BL, Add. Nr. 30853, *Penitentiale ecclesiasticum (Silos)* (s.X)
Madrid, BN, 1872 (P. 21 y Vitr. 14.4), *Collectio hispana* (s.X/XI)
Madrid, Arch. Hist. N., Diversos, legajo 14 + Orense Archivo Capitular, 43, *Collectio hispana* (s.X)

Eleventh century

El Escorial, Bibl. Cor., 1623, *Collectio hispana systematica* (in Arabic with Visigothic notations) (1049)
Madrid, BN, 10008 (Hh.3 y Toledano 15.9), *Penitentiale* (s.XI)
Madrid, BN, 10041 (Toledano 15.16), *Collectio hispana* (1034)
Toledo, Bibl. Capit., 15.17, *Collectio hispana* (1095)

Twelfth century

Madrid, BN, Vitr. 5.5 (6367; R.216), *Decretum Burchardi* (1105)

Total items: 19

Total items by century:

s.VIII: 1; s.IX: 5; s.X: 8; s.XI: 4; s.XII: 1

APPENDIX IV

Canon Law Collections in Visigothic Script

Collectio Dionysiana/related

Paris, Arch. N., AB XIX.1723, *Collectionis canonum epitome of Dionysius Exiguus (?)* (s.IX)

Proto-hispanic collection of canons

Madrid, Acad. Hist., Aemil. 44 (F.218), *Proto-Hispana Collection of Canons* (s.VIII/IX)

Collectio hispana

El Escorial, Bibl. Cor., d.I.1, *Collectio hispana* (994)
El Escorial, Bibl. Cor., d.I.2, *Collectio hispana* (976)
El Escorial, Bibl. Cor., e.I.12, *Collectio hispana* (s.X-XI)
El Escorial, Bibl. Cor., e.I.13, *Collectio hispana* (s.X-XI)
Madrid, BN, 1872 (P. 21 et Vitr. 14.4), *Collectio hispana* (s.X/XI)
Madrid, Arch. Hist. N., Diversos, legajo 14 + Orense Archivo Capitular, 43, *Collectio hispana* (s.X)
Madrid, BN, 10041 (Toledano 15.16), *Collectio hispana* (1034)
Toledo, Bibl. Capit., 15.17, *Collectio hispana* (1095)

Collectio hispana systematica

Lyons, BM, 336 (269), *Collectio hispana systematica* (with Visigothic notations) (s.IX^{in})
Paris, BN, lat. 11709, *Collectio hispana systematica* (with Visigothic notations) (s.IX^{in})
El Escorial, Bibl. Cor., 1623, *Collectio hispana sytematica* (in Arabic with Visigothic notations) (1049)

Penitentials

Cord., Arch. Cat., 123, Alvarus Paulus, *Iudicium penitentie excerpta canonum a beato Gregorio papa romensis edita* (s.X)
London, BL, Add. Nr. 30853, *Penitentiale ecclesiasticum (Silos)* (s.X)
Madrid, BN, 10008 (Hh.3 y Toledano 15.9), *Penitentiale* (s.XI)

Decretum Burchardi

Madrid, BN, Vitr. 5.5 (6367; R.216), *Decretum Burchardi* (1105)

Conciliar canons

Leon, Arch. Cat., 22, *Acts of the Council of Cordoba in 839* (s.IX)
Paris, BN, lat. 10876 (a) et 10877 (b) + Tours, BM, 615 + New Haven, Yale, Bein. Libr., 481, *II Council of Seville, c. 11* (s.IX/X)

Total items: 19

Total collections: 7

Total items for each collection:

Collectio Dionysiana/related: 1
Proto-hispanic collection of canons: 1
Collectio hispana: 8
Collectio hispana systematica: 3
Penitentials: 3
Decretum Burchardi: 1
Conciliar canons: 2

XIII

The Transmission of the *Hibernensis* in Italy: Tenth to the Twelfth Century[1]

In 1982 the late, lamented Maurice Sheehy published an article entitled, 'The *Collectio canonum hibernensis* a Celtic phenomenon'.[2] In it Sheehy correctly emphasised the 'Irishness' or 'Celticity' of the *Hibernensis* and its originality and importance as a canonical collection in terms of its organisation and completeness. Despite these virtues of the *Hibernensis* Sheehy seemed to minimise its influence in medieval canon law as a whole. To support this he noted—not quite accurately—that Paul Fournier had suggested the history of the *Hibernensis* stopped with Burchard and that the *Hibernensis* made little impression on the jurisprudence of the church as represented in the *Decretum* of Gratian and the classical canon law.[3] Further, he cited the study of Charles Munier on the use of patristic sources used in pre-Gratian collections to support this contention.[4] Unfortunately, Munier's study (actually his thesis), while valuable and suggestive, was flawed not only with respect to the *Hibernensis*, but also with respect to later collections and does not really support

1. Portions of the research for this article were conducted for the program *Monumenta Liturgica Beneventana* supported by the Social Sciences and Humanities Research Council of Canada.

2. M. P. Sheehy, 'The *Collectio canonum hibernensis*—a Celtic phenomenon', H. Löwe (ed), *Die Iren und Europa im früheren Mittelalter* (2 vols, Stuttgart 1982) 525–35.

3. ibid. 525.

4. Ch. Munier, *Les sources patristiques du droit de l'Église du viii*^{e} *au xiii*^{e} *siècle* (Mulhouse 1957).

Sheehy's contention.[5] Sheehy acknowledged that the *Hibernensis* took on something of an afterlife, that is a post-Burchardian afterlife, especially in many Italian collections of the eleventh century and beyond, but he argued that the compilers of these collections had no comprehension of the Celtic origins of the collection. They sometimes changed Gildas to Gelasius and Patrick to Pelagius and even glossed a text to read 'Hibernia est provincia in Gallia que vulgo Alverniae vocatur'.

Even Paul Fournier in his classic articles of 1899 and 1915 on the *Hibernensis* and its influence spoke about the 'old-fashioned' or anachronistic nature of several of the south Italian collections that he dated to the tenth century, implying it was material from the *Hibernensis* that made them old-fashioned.[6] That is, they contained much material that was particular to the *Hibernensis*, such as multiple patristic and biblical texts, not found in collections after the ninth century that emphasised papal and conciliar decrees or those types of decrees and canons that became normative from the twelfth-century and beyond.

To argue that because the *Hibernensis* played little role in the 'scientific' canonistic jurisprudence represented in Gratian and classical canon law does not mean, however, that it played little role in medieval canon law. Few military historians would say that swords have played no role in military history because they were replaced later by dynamite and gunpowder as more lethal weapons. Moreover, simply because the Italian compilers of canonical collections from the tenth century on had, understandably, not appreciated as fully as we do the 'Irishness' of the collection does not mean that the collection played an 'ephemeral' role in Italy, especially south and central Italy, in the eleventh and twelfth centuries. Anyone who has worked his way through these multiple collections knows the enormous role that the *Hibernensis* played in them.

Sheehy also claimed that any influence the *Hibernensis* might have had was brushed aside in the wake of the papal reforms of the eleventh century and the new codifications of law that accompanied them.[7] Perhaps Sheehy did not appreciate that the scribes who copied these reform collections, especially the *Collection in 74 titles,*

5. Munier's faulty calculation of the influence of the patristic Fathers even in the *Hibernensis* can be seen in the number of citations in the A (shorter) recension (Munier's count, op. cit. 30 is given in brackets): Jerome 209 [168], Augustine 115 [94], Isidore 77 [65], Gregory I 69 [54], Origen 52 [43], Patrick 25, Gregory Nazianzus 17 [11], Vitae Patrum 17 [19], Eusebius/Rufinus 16 [9], Gildas 13, Clementine *Recognitiones* 8, Ambrose 6 [3], Cassian 4 [4], Basil 3 [3], Gennadius 3 [3], Faustus 3, Pelagius 2 [1], Dionysius 2, Theophilus 1, Johannes 1, Suplicius 1 [1], Orosius 1 [1], Eucherius 1 [1], Lactantius 1. Total 646 [479]. On the number of texts of Basil of Caesarea in the A and B recension of the *Hibernensis* and their diffusion in later canonical collections see my 'Basil and the early medieval Latin canonical collections', P. J. Fedwick (ed), *Basil of Caesarea: christian, humanist, ascetic: a sixteen-hundredth anniversary symposium* (Toronto 1981) 513–32.

6. Paul Fournier, 'De l'influence de la collection irlandaise sur la formation des collections canoniques', *Revue historique de droit français et étranger 4eme sér* 23 (1899) 27–78 and 'Un groupe de recueils canoniques italiens des Xᵉ et XIᵉ siècles', *Mémoires de l'Académie des Inscriptions et Belles-Lettres* 40 (1915) 99.

7. Sheehy, art. cit. 526.

often appended canons from the *Hibernensis* to them and that canons from the *Collection of 74 Titles* were included in these so-called old-fashioned collections.[8] If Sheehy's minimisation of the influence of the *Hibernensis* beyond Burchard is questionable, it is the more so for the pre-Burchardian period. I have already showed that in the late eighth and ninth centuries alone at least seven collections were heavily dependent on the *Hibernensis*.[9]

And in my forthcoming chapters on the *Hibernensis* and its influence in the multi-volume *Studies in medieval and early modern canon law,* edited by W. Hartmann and K. Pennington (in press lamentably since 1993), it is shown that there are five additional collections from Carolingian times alone,[10] and that beyond the very late ninth to the early eleventh century the *Hibernensis* influenced no less than nine additional northern European collections.[11] Beyond this, the chapter on matrimony from the *Hibernensis*, book 46, appears in at least twenty-four early medieval manuscripts,[12] and isolated excerpta in another eighteen.[13] But nowhere was the influence

8. On this see my 'The South-Italian canon law collection in five books and its derivatives: new evidence on its origins, diffusion, and use', *Mediaeval Studies* 52 (1990) 278–79.

9. 'Unity and diversity in Carolingian canon law collections: the case of the *Collectio hibernensis* and its derivatives', U.-R. Blumenthal (ed), *Carolingian essays: Andrew W. Mellon lectures in Early Christian studies* (Washington DC 1983) 108–14.

10. The *Collectio Sangermanensis* and its extracts found in Paris, Bibliothèque nationale lat. 12444 (olim Sangerman. 938) (s.VIII–IX; probably Fleury, provenance Corbie); Albi, Bibliothèque municipale 38bis (s. IX ca. med; southern France); Cologne, Erzbischöfliche Diözesan- und Dombibliothek 117 (olim Darmst. 2116) (s. IX ca. med; France); London, British Library Harley 3034 (s. X); Munich, Bayerische Staatsbibliothek Clm. 14508 (s. IX 3/4; northern France; early in St Emmeram in Regensburg).

11. These include the Acts of the Council of Tribur (895), the *Libri duo de synodalibus causis* of Regino of Prüm, the *Collection of Verona, Biblioteca Capitolare LXIII,* the *Decretum* of Burchard of Worms, the *Collection in twelve parts,* the *Excerptiones Egberti,* the *Collection of Salzburg, St. Peter a. IX 32*, the *Collection of Arras,* and the *Collectin of Turin (BNU E V 44).*

12. Avranches, Bibliothèque municipale 146 (s. XII, Rheims region); Bamberg, Staatliche Bibliothek Can. 9 (olim P.I.9) (s. XII 2/3, Freising, and s. XI in., southern Germany), 127 (olim B.V.24) (s. XII); Florence, Biblioteca Medicea Laurenziana XX.48; Freiburg i. Breisgau, Üniversitatsbibliothek 8 (s. IX 2/2, Bodensee); London, BL Cotton Cleopatra C.VIII (s. XII); Montecassino, Archivio della Badia 1 (s. XI, southern Italy); Montpellier, Bibliothèque Interuniversitaire, Section Médecine H. 137 (s. XI, France); Munich, Bayerische Staatsbibliothek Clm. 6241 (s. X, Freising), 6242 (s. IX 1/3, Freising), 6245 (s. IX/X, Freising); Palermo, Archivio della Cattedrale 14 (s. XII, France); Paris, Bibliothèque nationale, lat. 1557 (s. IX 3/4, Laon); 3839 (s. IX 2/2, France), 3839A (s. XI 2/2, Angers), 3852 (s. XI-XII, perhaps Angers); Rouen, Bibliothèque municipale, E.27 (olim 702) (s. XI, Angers); Vatican, Biblioteca Apostolica Vaticana lat. 3791 (s. XI ex, northern France), Pal. lat. 973 (s. IX 2/2, northeastern France), Reg. lat. 407 (s. IX med., vic. St. Gall), Reg. lat. 421 (s. IX 2–3, St. Gall); Vienna, ÖNB 424 (s. IX 2/4, Salzburg), 1370 (s. IX 1/4, Mondsee), and 2198 (s. X 1/2–med., southern Germany). It has also been shown by Fournier that the *Capitula Theodori* or the *Penitential of Pseudo-Theodore* contains snippets from the same book, 46.

13. Excerpta and fragments from the *Hibernensis* can also be found in the following manuscripts: Barcelona, Archivo de la Corona de Aragon Ripoll 105 (s. XIII); Bern, Burgerbibliothek 89+A 26 (s. IX in., Alsace?); Montecassino, Archivio della Badia 439 (s. X, southern Italy);

of the *Hibernensis* more striking than in collections compiled in southern and central Italy from the tenth to the twelfth centuries, and it is these which are the focus of this paper.

Several preliminary questions must be raised. It is well known that the *Hibernensis,* wherever it was compiled—either in Ireland itself or elsewhere by compilers influenced by Irish law and customs—was early spread widely north of the Alps by Irish wanderers and in Irish ecclesiastical and monastic establishments. But how was it transmitted to Italy? In northern Italy the Irish presence at Bobbio is well known. And as Michel Huglo has demonstrated, Breton musical notation was rather common in Pavia[14] not far from Bobbio, perhaps explaining why the B version of the *Hibernensis* found in the Breton manuscript, Oxford, Hatton 42, might have been in northern Italy. South of this, we find a bishop of Fiesole in the mid-ninth century, Donatus, and it has been speculated that he was Irish.[15] In the middle of the ninth century abbot Conuuioion from the Breton monastery of Redon journeyed to Rome to consult pope Leo IV on a canonistic matter, simony, and it is possible that he had in his baggage a copy of the B version of the *Hibernensis.*[16] And finally, in the south of Italy the Anglo-Saxon pilgrim and future bishop of Eichstätt, St Willibald, spent nearly a decade at Montecassino from 730 to 740, and it is again possible that the *Hibernensis*, so well represented in texts from that monastery, came with or to Willibald when he was there[17]—although, as David Dumville has pointed out, there is no evidence for the circulation of the *Hibernensis* in England in the eighth century.[18]

Looking to manuscript evidence, if the Copenhagen manuscript, Kongelige bibliotek, Ny Kgl. Saml. 58 8° is from northern Italy, as Bernhard Bischoff thought, rather than southern France, as Lowe thought,[19] our earliest manuscript evidence for the *Hibernensis*—or a florilegium on which it perhaps drew—is from northern Italy.[20]

Munich, Bayerische Staatsbibliothek Clm. 6433 (s. VIII, Freising); 14468 (c.821, St Emmeram); Münster, Staatsarchiv MSC VII.5201 (s. X 2/2, Corvey); New Haven, Yale University, Beinecke Library 413 (c.875, Rheims); Padua, Biblioteca Antoniana 27 (post–880); Paris, BN lat. 4281A (s. XII, prov. a monastery of Beaupré); Salzburg, a lost manuscript described by Bernhard Bischoff; Vatican, Biblioteca Apostolica Vaticana Vat. lat. 4162 (s. XII), Vat. lat. 5748 (s. IX–X, northern Italy), Archivio di San Pietro H 58 (c.1000, Rome); Ottob. lat. 6 (s. X, Nonantola), Pal. lat. 577 (s. VIII/IX, Germany with Insular symptoms); Vesoul, Bibliothèque municipale 73 (s. X ex.); Vienna, ÖNB 2232 (s. X in., southern Germany); and Wolfenbüttel, Herzog-August-Bibliothek 579 Helmst. (s. IX 2/4, Salzburg).

14. Michel Huglo, 'Le domaine de la notation bretonne', *Acta Musicologica* 35 (1963) 71–73.

15. Ludwig Bieler, *Ireland: harbinger of the middle ages* (London 1963) 120.

16. See Caroline Brett (ed), *The monks of Redon: Gesta sanctorum Rotonensium and Vita Conuuoionis* (Woodbridge 1989) 3, 66, 174–83.

17. See Mariano Dell'Omo, *I Fiori e'frutti santi: S. Benedetto, la regola, la santità nelle testimonianze dei manoscritti cassinesi* (Montecassino 1998) 40, 62, 75–76.

18. David Dumville, 'Ireland, Brittany, and England: transmission and use of the *Collectio canonum hibernensis*', C. Laurent & H. Davis (ed), *Irlande et Bretagne: vingt siècles d'histoire: actes du Colloque de Rennes (29–31 mars 1993)* (Rennes 1994) 91.

19. CLA 10 (Oxford 1963) 1568.

20. See, however, Rob Meens's contribution to this volume, above 1–19.

And it is interesting that the canons there often are in the B tradition of the *Hibernensis*.[21] Beyond this, there is ninth- and tenth-century manuscript evidence for the presence of the *Hibernensis* in the north of Italy: first, in the late ninth or early tenth century manuscript from Padova, Biblioteca Antoniana 27 (s. X, post a. 880; Verona); second, in fragment in a late ninth or early tenth-century manuscript from northern Italy containing the *Concordia Cresconii,* Vatican, Biblioteca Apostolica Vaticana, Vat. lat. 5748 (s. IX–X or Xin; upper Italy); third in the collection of Verona, Biblioteca Capitolare LXIII [61] (s.X med–2/2; probably upper Italy, Verona?); fourth, in the eleventh or twelfth-century codex of the *Hibernensis* written in northern Italy, now Livorno, Biblioteca Labronica, sine num. (olim 10) (s. XI–XII; probably northern Italy), which Mordek classified as a B manuscript, but Sheehy in his Alpha category; and fifth, in the eleventh-century manuscript, Milano, Biblioteca Ambrosiana M 79 sup. (s. XI, northern Italy), which has the Hiberno-Hispanic Hierarchical Ordinal of Christ appearing in the *Hibernensis*, 8:1.[22]

According to many canon law specialists, the *Hibernensis* had reached southern and central Italy by the tenth century as evidenced in the famous manuscript of the B version of the *Hibernensis*, Rome, Biblioteca Vallicelliana T. XVIII (or as Maassen tragically stated, MS A.18[23]—a mistake that has misled dozens of scholars and cost them fortunes in misordered microfilm since his time).[24] To use this codex as evidence to show that the *Hibernensis* had come to central and southern Italy in the tenth century is faulty, however, since this dating is based on the internal evidence of the texts in that manuscript and not on more solid palaeograhical evidence. In fact, the manuscript was copied by at least three hands, all of which could write in both

21. On this manuscript see my forthcoming 'The Isidorian *Epistula ad Massonam* on lapsed clerics: notes on the earliest manuscripts and textual transmission', R. Helmholz, M. Stolleis, & J. Müller (ed), *Festschrift für Peter Landau.* The canons paralleling the *Hibernensis* in the B tradition found in the south Italian manuscript, Rome, Biblioteca Vallicelliana T. XVIII are: 17 [=15 in A]:8 (Augustine), 8 (Jerome) (Vallicelliana, f 72v); 15:1 (Origen), :2c (unidentified ecclesiastical decree, said in the *Hibernensis*, Form A, to be a 'Sinodus Romana'), :2b (Augustine); 17:8 (Gregory) (Vallicelliana, f 72v); 15:3c (Gregory), :3d (Gregory); 47:5b (Jerome); 12(=11 in A):1 (Origen) (Vallicelliana, f 67r); 11:1b (Patrick), :1a (Jerome), :2 (Augustine), :4a (Apoc. 2.5), :3 (unidentified synod, said in the *Hibernensis,* Form A, to be a 'Synodus Hibernensis'); the Isidorian *Epistula ad Massonem*; 15:6a (Jerome), :6b (Jerome), :6c (Jerome); 13:8 (Jerome and Augustine, said to be Jerome alone in the *Hibernensis*, Form A); 47:13b (Augustine); and 48 (= 47 in A):8. (Nicea, said to be Arles in the *Hibernensis,* Form B) (Vallicelliana, f 123v); 47:22 (Vallicelliana, f 125v attributed to an unidentified synod); 47:22 (Vallicelliana, f 125v attributed to a 'Synodus Hibernensis'); 45:4b, :4a, :4c, :4d; 45:5.

22. On which see my *The ordinals of Christ from their origins to the twelfth century*, Beiträge zur Geschichte und Quellenkunde des Mittelalters 7 (Berlin & New York 1978) 95.

23. Friedrich Maassen, *Geschichte der Quellen und der Literatur des canonischen Rechts* (Graz 1870, repr. 1956) 806, dating the manuscript to the tenth century.

24. In fact, even recently some scholars place the origin of the codex in the north of Italy and date it to the tenth century: see, for example, Luned Mair Davies, 'Isidorian texts and the *Hibernensis*', *Peritia* 11 (1997) 216, for an origin in Ravenna. For a tenth-century date in central Italy, see Rob Meens, *Het tripartite boeteboek: Overlevering en betekenis van vroegmiddeleeuwse biechtvoorschriften (met editie en vertaling van vier tripartita)* (Hilversum 1994) 253.

Carolingian and Beneventan scripts (often slipping from one to the other even in mid-word), and the Beneventan script has been dated not to the tenth but to the eleventh century.[25] In other words, the *Hibernensis* copied in that manuscript does not demonstrate that the collection was in southern-central Italy by the tenth century Another piece of evidence used to demonstrate that the *Hibernensis* had arrived in these regions by the tenth century was its heavy use in the canonical *Collection in nine books* of Vat. lat. 1349. But here again, the palaeographical judgement by specialists in the Beneventan script in which it is copied shows that the codex itself was written in the eleventh, not the tenth century.[26] So, is there any palaeographical evidence that the *Hibernensis* was present in southern and central Italy in the tenth century? Indeed, there is.

From central Italy there is a tenth-century MS from Nonantola, Vatican, Biblioteca Apostolica Vaticana Ottob. lat. 6.[27] This miscellaneous manuscript has as its first section an abbreviation of the *Hibernensis* under the title *Excerpta SS patribus et conciliis*. After two long sections from the middle and final books of the *Hibernensis*, there are canons from the first books on the ecclesiastical hierarchy from bishop down through subdeacon, and these are followed by extracts from books running to book 43 of the *Hibernensis*. The compiler is at least in part dependent on the B recension of the *Hibernensis*, but he has included additions from the works of the Fathers to supplement the *Hibernensis*.

Evidence for the presence of the *Hibernensis* in southern Italy in the tenth century comes in the tenth-century codex Montecassino, Archivio della Badia 439, written in Beneventan script. Beginning on p 129 there are snippets from book 39 of the *Hibernensis* on monks. Although the snippets do not always follow the order of the *Hibernensis*, it is clear that they derive from the B version of the collection.

Much more substantial southern Italian evidence for the *Hibernensis* comes in a very important *Liber officialis* written in Rome c.1000, Vatican, Biblioteca Apostolica Vaticana, Arch. San Pietro H 58.[28] This codex, reflecting a Beneventan script exemplar, has a variety of penitentials and excerpta from earlier collections. But most important are canons from or related to the *Hibernensis*. Canons from books 1 through 10 are found distributed throughout much of the second half of the manuscript. They are in the B redaction of the *Hibernensis* found in the *Collection of Vallicelliana T. XVIII*.

25. For the Beneventan hands and an eleventh-century date, see E. A. Loew, *The Beneventan script: a history of the south Italian minuscule*, 2nd enlarged edition prepared by Virginia Brown, Sussidi eruditi 33–34 (2 vols, Rome 1980), ii 131; and my 'Odilo and the *treuga Dei* in southern Italy: a Beneventan manuscript fragment', *Mediaeval Studies* 46 (1984) 454 n 25 and literature therein.

26. See Loew-Brown, ii 145.

27. See my 'Excerpta from the *Collectio hibernensis* in three Vatican manuscripts', *Bull Mediev Canon Law* NS 5 (1975) 2–3.

28. On this important manuscript see my *Law and liturgy in the Latin church, 5th–12th centuries* (Aldershot 1994), II 528, IV 135, V 4-9, XII 667, XIV 281, XV 485, 487, 490.

Close in date to this manuscript from the Archivio di S. Pietro is another from Montecassino, Archivio della Badia 297 (s. XI in; southern Italy). Again, extracts but quite substantial ones from the *Hibernensis*, are given, and they are, so Sheehy has said, in his Beta or B redaction of the *Hibernensis.*

We come now to the manuscript of the *Hibernensis* in its B redaction, which with Hatton 42 has always taken pride of place among manuscripts of the *Hibernensis,* Rome, Biblioteca Vallicelliana T. XVIII, one of the most celebrated of early medieval canonistic manuscripts because of the wealth of material in it. Its rich contents have on several occasions been described in detail—by Fournier and in the modern catalogue of the Tomi in the Biblioteca Vallicelliana[29]—and for limited sections, such as the early sections of the manuscript by Raymund Kottje[30] and the central sections by Jean Pozzi.[31] Even in the late nineteenth century it was recognised that the codex, although written largely in a Carolingian or Romanesca hand, also contained sections in Beneventan script, a fact E. A. Lowe overlooked in his study of 1914 of that script of south Italy but later noted in his new hand-list of Beneventan-script codices.[32] As has been noted, numerous entries in Beneventan hands noted since Lowe's description now demonstrate that at least three scribes who copied the codex could change from one script to the other without difficulty. Moreover, the Beneventan script is now dated to the eleventh century.

Unlike the *Collection of San Pietro H 58*, which had only blocks of canonistic materials from known collections, the *Collection of Vallicelliana T. XVIII* contains a number of complete collections together with excerpta from other collections filling the chinks. Among the best-known collections in the manuscript are the *Concordia Cresconii, Collection in 72 chapters,* our *Hibernensis,* the small collection known by its incipit as *Incipit de episcoporum transmigratione,* and a large farraginous collection of 448 texts (although thirty of these are missing at the end of the now mutilated manuscript).

The exact relationship of the B redaction of the *Hibernensis* in the Vallicelliana manuscript to the A, A/B, and C redactions will be clarified in the new edition of the *Hibernensis*. But there are several aspects of the text in the Vallicelliana codex that relate it to other texts and reforming currents in the Italian church of the eleventh century. First, Fournier pointed out that the incipit of the *Collectio canonum Hiber-*

29. Anna Maria Giorgetti Vichi & Sergio Mottironi (ed), *Catalogo dei manoscritti della Biblioteca Vallicelliana*, 1, Indici e cataloghi, NS 7 (Rome 1961) 243–52.

30. Raymund Kottje, *Die Bussbücher Halitgars von Cambrai und des Hrabanus Maurus: ihre Überlieferung und ihre Quellen,* Beiträge zur Geschichte und Quellenkunde des Mittelalters 8 (Berlin & New York 1980) 56–57, who opts for a tenth-century date and places the codex in central Italy in the vicinity of Rome.

31. G. Pozzi, 'Le manuscrit tomus XVIIIus de la Vallicelliana et le libelle "De episcoporum transmigratione et quod non temere iudicentur regule quadraginta quattuor"', *Apollinaris* 31 (1958) 313–50.

32. *The Beneventan script: a history of south Italian minuscule* (Oxford 1914), and 'A new list of Beneventan manuscripts', in *Collectanea vaticana in honorem Anselmi M. Card. Albareda a Bibliotheca apostolica edita*, Studi e Testi 220 (Vatican City 1962) 233.

nensis in the Vallicelliana manuscript is 'Incipit gratissima canonum collatio', and that Peter Damian called one of his treatises the *Liber gratissimus*, in which he used a text little known in the West but found in the Vallicelliana manuscript of the *Canones apostolorum*. Just as interesting, however, the *capitulationes* of the *Collectio canonum Hibernensis* and book 1 in the Vallicelliana codex are prefaced by a number of chapters from Isidore's *Etymologies* defining synods, epitomising the decisions of the first four ecumenical councils, and c. 20 of the Council of Antioch. These texts are similar to ones used by the compiler of the *Collection of San Pietro H 58* on f 135r–v to preface canons drawn from book 1 of the *Hibernensis*.

A final extract from the *Hibernensis* can be found in a manuscript copied as late as the twelfth century, Vatican, Biblioteca Apostolica Vaticana, Vat. lat. 4162.[33] This manuscript is made up of a miscellany of texts, and inserted into it are three folios with descriptions of the higher ecclesiastical orders from the first several books of the *Hibernensis*.

The B redaction of the *Hibernensis*, as found in the Vallicelliana manuscript and other central and southern Italian collections, came to play a major role in the formation of a host of south and central Italian collections in the eleventh and twelfth centuries. In Fournier's magisterial articles of 1899 and 1915 on the *Hibernensis* and Italian collections this influence was traced in some thirteen collections, and these can be seen in Appendix I of this paper (36–37) listed by the suprascript F: the *Collection in nine books;* the *Collection in five books*; the *Collection of Naples XII.A.28*; in a manuscript of the *Collection in 74 titles* (Casan. 2010); in the Collections of Vallicelliana E 62, F 2, F 8, and F 92; in the *Collection of Montecassino 216;* in the collections of Vat. lat. 4977; Vat lat. 8487 (the so-called *Collection of Farfa); the Collection of Florence Ricc 300*; and the *Collection of Veroli* (Vallicelliana B 32). But many more have been found since his examples, as will be seen. Let us look first at two major early south Italian eleventh-century collections, the *Collection in nine books* and the *Collection in five books*.

There is first the renowned *Collection in nine books*, organised into specific books, although contents in each book can be somewhat disorganised. There is only one manuscript of the *Collection in nine books*, Vatican, Biblioteca Apostolica Vaticana, Vat. lat. 1349. This codex, one of substantial proportions, was written in Beneventan script in the eleventh century, although there have been claims by non-specialists in the script that it was written as early as the ninth century. The script itself is not of the Bari or Dalmatian type of Beneventan script, nor does it have characteristics of the type written in the Abruzzi. Therefore, the codex was presumably copied in the area where 'classical' Beneventan script was written, that is, the area south of Rome reaching down to the southern boundaries of the Campania. The manuscript, prominent in the Latin fondo of the Vatican Library, has often been described, and the preface to the collection and the *capitulationes* of each book published by Mai[34]

33. On this manuscript see my 'Excerpta', 3–4.
34. A. Mai, *Spicilegium Romanum* 6 (Rome 1841) 396–47.

and later entered into PL 138, 397–442. Also, some of the penitential material was edited by Schmitz.[35]

The plan of the collection is not unlike other systematic collections going back the *Hibernensis*. After a title and general description of the contents of each book, book 1 begins with an introduction to the clerical grades taken from the works of Isidore, the south-Italian redaction of the Hibernian Chronological *Ordinal of Christ* found in the *Collection of Vallicelliana T. XVIII* and the *De distantia graduum* drawn from the *Hibernensis*. It should be emphasised here that although the former text resembles that in the *Hibernensis*, it is different, but that the latter text, the *De distantia graduum*, does come from the *Hibernensis*.[36]

Book 6 of the *Collection in nine books* bears a title similar to the *Hibernensis* in the *Collection of Vallicelliana T. XVIII*, 'De gratissima canonum collatione', and is followed by the preface to the *Collectio canonum Hibernensis* and a list of *capitulationes* obviously based on selected sections of the later books of the *Hibernensis*. The canons in this and the following book are divided into sections, clearly based on the *Collectio canonum Hibernensis*, and over each section there is added a 'divisional rubric' beginning with the word 'Incipit': for example, 'Incipit de locis sanctis …'. As will be seen, these 'divisional rubrics' came to play an important role in the later *Collection in five books*.

Book 7 deals with homicide, matrimony, oaths, fasting, eleemosynary activity, and prayer. Again, the *Hibernensis* is used together with divisional rubrics, such as 'Incipit de ratione matrimonii …', prefacing canons based on the *Collectio canonum hibernensis*, book 46.

Although the canons in the *Collection in nine books* all date to the tenth century or before, its most famous south Italian derivative, the *Collection in five books* can be dated to at least the early eleventh century because of its canons attributed to the Ottonian emperor St Henry II. The collection is an enormous one, and this probably explains why there are only three fairly complete and huge manuscripts of it still extant. The books deal particularly with the ecclesiastical hierarchy, monks and women religious, the sacraments, penance, and matrimonial and sexual questions. The sources are very similar to those found in the codex *Rome, Biblioteca Vallicelliana T. XVIII* and in the *Collection in nine books*. But for our purposes, it is the many canons from the *Hibernensis* which are important. As might be expected, they follow the B redaction of the *Hibernensis*. Unlike the *Collection in nine books*, where canons from the *Hibernensis* are concentrated in only a few books, canons from the *Hibernensis* are found in every book of the *Collection in five books* and are drawn from the entirety of the B redaction of the *Hibernensis*. For Fournier the surest sign of the significance of the *Collection in five books* in the history of canon law was its influence on later collections; and he was able to list over a dozen, each in a single

35. H. J. Schmitz, *Die Bußbücher und die Bußdisciplin der Kirche* (2 vols, Mainz 1883, Düsseldorf 1898; repr. Graz 1958), ii 209–13.

36. As respects this text, Sheehy, 'The *Collectio*', 526, claimed that it antedated the *Hibernensis*, but he gave no evidence in support of this, and I have found none in my own study of the text.

codex. He might also have added that one of the surest signs of the continuing importance of the *Hibernensis* in the eleventh and twelfth centuries was its incorporation into the derivatives of the *Collection in five books*. Fournier's conclusions as to the significance of the *Collection in five books* have been confirmed over the years as more derivatives and excerpta have been discovered and reported. The variety of derivatives and excerpta is wide indeed, and they may be classified according to several broad categories, although individual derivatives may fall within several categories. First, there are what may be styled as an abbreviated type of derivatives, and there are three sub-forms of this type; one in which the basic sequence of canons in the *Collection in five books* is followed, another where the canons are spread over more than five books and are at times arranged according to the divisional rubrics of the *Collection in five books* itself, and the third, where shorter extracts from the *Collection in five books* basically follow the arrangement there. Second, there are derivative collections of a farraginous type in which the canons of the *Collection in five books* are thrown together helter-skelter or combined with canons from other collections in little or no discernible order. Third, there are those collections in which material from the *Collection in five books* is combined with material from Burchard's *Decretum*, especially the penitential *Corrector*. A fourth type of derivative consists of canons from the *Collection in five books* combined or attached to canons or collections of the Gregorian reform, especially the *Collection in 74 titles*. Finally, there are derivative collections where canons from the *Collection in five books* are associated with liturgical material, either formulaic or expositional or both.

ABBREVIATED COLLECTIONS

Probably the 'purest' type of abbreviation of the *Collection in five books* is found in a small handbook in Naples, Biblioteca Nazionale Vittorio Emanuele II, XII.A.28, written in a mid-eleventh-century Italian hand. The collection is divided into five books and within each are the divisional rubrics of the *Collection in five books* with a severely reduced number of canons. But within these canons is a substantial number from the *Hibernensis*. A similar small handbook can be found in Madrid, Biblioteca Nacional 373 written in both Carolingian and Beneventan hands in the late eleventh or early twelfth century. The manuscript now is in a mutilated state and contains only four books, but it may have had a fifth. Like the Naples manuscript the order of canons follows that of the *Collection in five books*, and although the number of canons is reduced, canons from the *Hibernensis* are still present. Yet a third example of this type of abbreviation can be found in another mutilated manuscript written in an eleventh-century Beneventan hand, Rieti, Archivio Capitolare 5. The canons, including many from the *Hibernensis*, are drawn largely from books 3 through 5 of the *Collection in five books* and follow the arrangement there.

There are two abbreviations of the *Collection in five books* in which there are more than five books inasmuch as the divisional rubrics of the *Collection in five books* are used as titles. The first of these abbreviations is a small handbook of Florence, Biblioteca Riccardiana 300, written in an early twelfth-century central Italian hand. There are seventeen so-called books in the collection, including multiple canons from the *Hibernensis.* The second abbreviation of the *Collection in five books* divided according to divisional rubrics is in an important but virtually unknown codex in Rome, Biblioteca Angelica 1447, a palimpsest manuscript written in a central Italian hand of the late eleventh or early twelfth century. How many books the collection originally had is uncertain because the manuscript is mutilated at beginning and end, but still extant are thirteen books. Again, canons from the *Hibernensis* can be found in abundance. This collection is especially interesting in two ways. First, some of the canons from the *Collection in five books* are set in variant and fuller forms than in the *Collection in five books* itself, suggesting that the *Collectio angelica* may be based on a collection antedating our currently known versions of the *Collection in five books.* Second, the collection ends with canons drawn from the reforming collection, the *Collection in 74 titles.*

There are two manuscripts containing very brief abridgements of parts of the *Collection in five books* and both contain canons from the *Hibernensis.* The first is Rome, Biblioteca Vallicelliana B 63, a miscellaneous manuscript written in an eleventh-century Italian hand and belonging at one time to the Benedictine monastery of Sant'Eutizio presso Norcia, the home of one of the extant manuscripts of the *Collection in five books.* The second is a double bifolium now in Maastricht, Rijksarchief Cat. nr. 196 [18.A] written in an Italian Romanesca hand of the second half of the eleventh century.[37] Both of these manuscripts have extracts from the *lection in five books*, including *Hibernensis* canons, arranged generally in an order following the *Collection in five books.*

FARRAGINOUS COLLECTIONS

The first of the two farraginous collections containing canons from the *Collection in five books* and *Hibernensis* is found in a miscellaneous manuscript, Rome, Biblioteca Vallicelliana T. XXI, written in Romanesca script of the late eleventh century and almost certainly originating at Sant'Eutizio presso Norcia.[38] It draws especially on canons from book 4 of the *Collection in five books*, and hence is heavily penitential in nature. The *Collection of Veroli,* now in Rome, Biblioteca Vallicelliana B 32, written in Beneventan script between c.1059 and c.1070, contains not only its famous Roman and Lombard law canons, but also a farrago of canons from the *Collection in five books* and *Hibernensis*, especially from books 1, 3, and 5 of the *Collection in five books*

37. On this manuscript see my 'The South Italian *Collection in five books* and its derivatives: Maastricht Excerpta', *Miscellanea Beneventana: Juridica, Mediaeval Studies* 58 (1996) 273–84.

38. On this manuscript see my 'The South-Italian *Collection in five books* and its derivatives: the *collection of Vallicelliana Tome XXI',* S. Chodorow (ed), *Proceedings of the Eighth International Congress of Medieval Canon Law: San Diego, University of California at La Jolla, 21–27 August 1988,* Monumenta Iuris Canonici, Ser. C, Subsidia 9 (Vatican 1991) 77–92.

DERIVATIVES OF THE *COLLECTION IN FIVE BOOKS* COMBINED WITH BURCHARD'S *DECRETUM*

One of the most interesting groups of derivatives of the *Collection in five books* containing canons from the *Hibernensis* is formed by the combination of canons from the *Collection in five books* and the *Decretum* of Burchard of Worms, especially book 19, the penitential *Corrector sive medicus.* The *Collection in five books* and the *Corrector,* particularly, seem to have had a mutual affinity not merely because they were both penitential in character, but also because they were complementary, that is, the *Collection in five books* had early Greek patristic material as well as a wide range of conciliar, synodal and other authoritative texts, while the *Corrector* gave an explicit list of sins together with a clear statement of penalties. There are no less than eight of these collections of combinations of Burchard and the *Collection in five books*.

The first is now in Toledo, Archivio Capitular 22–32.[39] Of the 376 canons, 232 come from the *Collection in five books*. The lack of any canons from book I of the *Collection in five books* indicates that the compiler was little interested in the ecclesiastical hierarchy and matters of ecclesiastical administration. But the heavy use of canons from books 4 and 5 of the *Collection in five books*, including canons from the *Hibernensis*, shows that the compiler was more interested in penitential material and sexual matters.

Heavily penitential in nature is another collection written in an eleventh-century Italian hand over a lower Beneventan-script palimpsest, Rome, Biblioteca Vallicelliana F 2. Like the *Collectio Toletana*, this collection is heavily penitential, again demonstrating the complementarity of the penitential sections of the *Collection in five books* and Burchard's *Corrector.* Yet another manuscript from the Biblioteca Vallicelliana, F 8, written in part in Beneventan script contains a mixture of the *Collection in five books*, including canons from the *Hibernensis* and the *Decretum* of Burchard. There are texts drawn directly from the *Hibernensis* that are not found in the *Collection in five books*, as well as canons from the *Hibernensis* drawn from the *Collection in five books*. A third manuscript from the Biblioteca Vallicelliana, F 92, written at Sant'Eutizio presso Norcia in the second half of the eleventh century, contains canons from Burchard and the *Collection in five books*, especially from books 3 and 5. Among these are canons from the *Hibernensis.*

The *Collection of Santa Croce*, now found in Florence, Biblioteca Medicea Laurenziana [Santa Croce], 4.4, was written in central Italy in the eleventh century. Penitential canons from the *Collection in five books,* including some from the *Hibernensis,* are combined with canons from Burchard, strangely not from the *Corrector*, but from books 1 and 2. A similar farraginous collection is found in Vatican, Biblioteca Apostolica Vaticana Vat. lat. 4977. The canons from the *Collection in five books,* including *Hibernensis* canons, are drawn largely from books 1 and 2 of the

39. This collection has been edited by John Douglas Adamson, The *Collectio Toletana:* an eleventh-century Italian collection of canon law (Lic. diss. Toronto 1987).

Collection in five books, and hence deal largely with administrative, not penitential matters.

The collection of the famous *Register of Farfa,* now Vatican, Biblioteca Apostolica Vaticana Vat. lat. 8487, has two books whose canons are heavily dependent on the *Collection in five books.* All of the five books have been used, and hence canons from many parts of the *Hibernensis*.

A final collection with a mixture of canons from the *Collection in five books* and Burchard's *Decretum* is found in the youngest canonistic manuscript written in Beneventan script, Montecassino, Archivio della Badia 216. The codex was written in the late twelfth century and for the complexity of its codicological structure and palaeographical features it is one of the most unusual canonistic codices in the script. In fact, it is a terscriptus codex. The first part of the collection consists largely of excerpts drawn from the *Collection in five books,* books 4 and 5, including *Hibernensis* canons, but penitential material from the *Corrector* of Burchard is introduced, together with canons from the reforming *Collection in 74 titles*.

EXTRACTS FROM THE *COLLECTION IN FIVE BOOKS* AND THE *COLLECTION IN 74 TITLES*

It is perhaps surprising that Beneventan-script codices, which were the primary vehicle for the *Collection in five books* and its derivatives, should also be a vehicle for one of the earliest and most popular collections of the Gregorian reform period, the *Collection in 74 titles*. Four of the codices of this collection are written in Beneventan script of the late eleventh and early twelfth centuries, and a fifth, Rome, Biblioteca Casanatense 2010, was written either in Rome or Farfa and contained large numbers of texts from southern Italy found in codices written in Beneventan script, including those in Vallicelliana T. XVIII. Because scholars have generally concentrated their attention on the important reforming collection itself in these manuscripts, they have usually overlooked the fact that attached to the text of the *Collection in 74 titles* are canons from the *Collection in five books*, including those from the *Hibernensis*. Three of the manuscripts in the Beneventan script contain texts from the *Collection in five books*: Montecassino, Archivio della Badia 522 (s. XII, southern Italy), El Escorial, Real Biblioteca de San Lorenzo, Z.III.19 (s. XI ex; southern Italy), and Rome, Biblioteca Vallicelliana F 54 (s. XI/XII; southern Italy), the latter two with texts from the *Hibernensis*. The fourth manuscript of the *Collection in 74 titles* with *Collection in five books* addenda is the Casanatense codex. Already it has been noted that several derivative collections of the *Collection in five books* have canons added from the *Collection in 74 titles*.

DERIVATIVES OF THE *COLLECTION IN FIVE BOOKS* AND LITURGICAL TEXTS

That the *Collection in five books* was not only a canon law collection but a vast florilegium of patristic texts has often been noted by scholars. But its place as a liturgical florilegium has been insufficiently appreciated. In several instances liturgical canons and expositions only tangentially disciplinary were used in the collection, witness the frequent use of such texts from the *Hibernensis* as the 'De distantia graduum' and *Ordinals of Christ*. Hence, in several types of liturgical texts based on the *Collection in five books* we find canons from the *Hibernensis*. One of the most interesting of these is in an early twelfth-century Roman Pontifical from Chieti written in part in Beneventan script, now Vatican, Biblioteca Apostolica Vaticana Vat. lat 7818.[40] It is very likely that an early copy of the *Collection in five books* was in this city on the Adriatic before being transmitted to Montecassino, where the earliest manuscript was written, and hence it is not surprising to find that part of it was used to compile a sermon to be used by a bishop during ordination. In the pontifical sermon texts from the *Collection in five books*, all ultimately drawn from the *Hibernensis*, were cobbled together to make an allocution to ordinands concerning the origins of their grades and their liturgical duties.

In a Missal-Ritual of Rome, Biblioteca Vallicelliana E 62, written in the late eleventh or early twelfth century in central Italy, a section on penance has been appropriately added, the texts being drawn largely from books 3 and 4 of the *Collection in five books*, and one of the texts on oaths in this section comes from the *Hibernensis*.

Having all too briefly surveyed these southern and central Italian collections into which canons from the *Hibernensis* were inserted, largely by way of the *Collection in five books*, several more general comments are in order.

First, why were these canons from the ancient or, as Sheehy and Fournier put it, old-fashioned Irish *Hibernensis* used? The answer probably lies in a assumption underlying these collections differing from that underlying most other eleventh and twelfth-century collections. That is, the compilers of our collections, like the early Celtic christian compilers, saw that canon law regulations should not be confined to the decrees of popes and synods alone, but might also be found in the writings of the Fathers and in Scripture itself. As Richard Sharpe put it in his 1984 paper on Gildas and the *Hibernensis*, 'Penitential writing and the collections of ancient authorities as distinct from *concilia* and *decreta*, are perhaps the most notable contribution of the Celtic churches to the ecclesiastical practice of Europe'.[41] One of the wealthiest sources of these ancient authorities—and a canon law source at that—was the *Hibernensis*. Hence the *Hibernensis* was mined for its treasure-trove of these texts. As one peruses an unidentified canonical manuscript, one of the surest indicia pointing to a southern or central Italian origin is the presence of these patristic and biblical texts. In a sense, this is not unlike the presence of the tell-tale 'hera' indicating canons drawn from Mordek's *Collectio vetus gallica*.[42]

40. On this manuscript see my 'A South Italian ordination allocution', *Mediaeval Studies* 47 (1985) 438–44.

41. Richard Sharpe, 'Gildas as a father of the church', M. Lapidge & D. Dumville (ed), *Gildas: new approaches*, Studies in Celtic History 5 (Woodbridge 1984) 201.

42. Hubert Mordek, *Kirchenrecht und Reform im Frankenreich: die Collectio Vetus Gallica, die*

A second comment. What types of canons from the *Hibernensis* were most frequently used in the southern and central Italian collections? This depends on the type of collection it is. There could be all-purpose collections, penitential collections, monastic collections, and so forth, and depending on the purpose to which it was to be put, the types of canons drawn from the *Hibernensis* would vary. For general, all-purpose collections canons from the *Hibernensis,* books 1–9, were often used to describe and regulate clerics and their conduct. For monastic collections a few of the canons on monks, book 39, from the *Hibernensis* might be used. And for penitentially-oriented collections, canons from throughout the *Hibernensis* might be used, especially in conjunction with canons from Burchard's *Corrector.*

A third observation. How many canons were actually drawn from the *Hibernensis* in these collections? Of course, this depends on the size of the collection itself. But some idea of the wealth of canons taken from the *Hibernensis* can be had by looking at three representative collections based on the *Collection in five books* and therefore the *Hibernensis*: one from the early eleventh century, a second from the late eleventh century, and one from the late twelfth century.[43] There do exist editions or partial editions of the early eleventh-century *Collection in five books* (the first three books by Fornasari),[44] the late eleventh-century *Collectio Toletana*,[45] and the late twelfth century *Collectio Casinensis*.[46] In the first three books of the *Collection in five books* there are more than 330 canons drawn from the *Hibernensis*,[47] and a preliminary implicit edition of the latter two books indicates a similar proportion—that is there are likely over 500 canons drawn from the *Hibernensis* or almost a third of all the canons found in the *Hibernensis*. The late eleventh-century *Collectio Toletana* contains 376 canons *in toto,* and thirty-one of these or about 9% derive from the *Hibernensis.* And finally, the *Collectio Casinensis,* copied almost fifty years after the appearance of Gratian's *Decretum*, contains 378 canons, of which 178 or 47% are drawn from the *Collection in five books*. Strangely, however, only sixteen or 5% come ultimately from the *Hibernensis*. Since the *Decretum* of Burchard, which itself has fifty-eight canons from the *Hibernensis*, is the other major source of the *Col-*

älteste systematische Kanonessammlung des fränkischen Gallien: Studien und Edition, Beiträge zur Geschichte und Quellenkunde des Mittelalters 1 (Berlin & New York 1975).

43. Several of my students and I in Toronto are currently working on and publishing implicit editions of all of these collections, and with the appearance of these the exact number of canons drawn from the *Hibernensis* either directly or through the *Collection in five books* will be clarified.

44. Mario Fornasari, *Collectio canonum in v libris (lib. i–iii)*, CCCM 6 (Turnhout 1970); on which see Gérard Fransen, 'Principes d'édition des collections canoniques', *Revue d'histoire ecclésiastique* 66 (1971) 125–36; Hubert Mordek, 'Anzeigen', *Z Savigny-Stift Rechtsgesch Kan Abt* 60 (1974) 477–78.

45. Above n 39.

46. See my forthcoming *The Collectio canonum Casinensis duodecim saeculi (codex terscriptus: a derivative of the South-Italian collection in five books: incipit-explicit edition with an introductory study,* Monumenta Liturgica Beneventana, Texts and Studies (Toronto 2001).

47. See Appendix II below, 38–50.

lectio Casinensis, one might expect some of the canons from the *Hibernensis* to have come through Burchard. But there is only one.

To conclude. During the seventh and eighth centuries three great 'national' canonical collections were compiled: the *Collectio canonum hispana* for Spain, the *Collectio vetus gallica* for Frankish territories, and the *Hibernensis* for Ireland or wherever Celtic christians could be found. Perhaps unexpectedly, all three survived into the eleventh and twelfth centuries in some form or another. The *Hispana*, as an enormous historically arranged collection, was copied repeatedly in manuscripts in Spain even into the nineteenth century.[48] It was *the* national collection there even beyond the time of Gratian. The *Vetus gallica*, Hubert Mordek has shown, was copied into the eleventh century in a full form in southern Italy and, as I have shown recently, even in an excerpted form into the twelfth in Benevento itself.[49] Given the long life and influence of these two ancient national collections, one would expect the same for the *Hibernensis*, and as we have seen, this expectation is clearly fulfilled, especially in southern and central Italy from the tenth through the twelfth centuries. In a recent article in the Munich Proceedings of the Ninth International Congress of Medieval Canon Law, it was shown that in this region there were twenty-two collections copied in Beneventan script alone.[50] The largest proportion of these collections in terms of surviving manuscripts is related to the *Hibernensis* in some way, making the *Hibernensis*, as it were, not only the national Irish collection but also the 'national' or at least 'regional' collection where the Beneventan script was written.

48. For a list of these manuscripts see Gonzalo Martínez Díez, *La colección canonica Hispana* 1, Monumenta Hispaniae Sacra, Serie Canónica i (Madrid 1966) 11–13, 104–46. To be added to these are Florence, Biblioteca Medicea Laurenziana Ashburnham 1554 (s. XII1/2) [excerpts]; Florence, Biblioteca Riccardiana 258 (s. XII) [excerpts]; Oxford, Bodleian Library Holkham misc. 19 (s. XII in; Tuscany, perhaps Pistoia); Paris, Bibliothèque nationale lat. 4280 (s. XII) [excerpts]; and the fragment described in my 'Visigothic-script remains of a Pandect bible and the *Collectio canonum hispana* in Lucca', *Miscellanea Beneventana: Parerga Beneventana, Mediaeval Studies* 58 (1996) 305–31.

49. 'A Beneventan monastic excerptum from the *Collectio Vetus Gallica*', *Revue Bénédictine* 102 (1992) 298–308.

50. See my 'Canonistica Beneventana', Peter Landau & Jörg Müller (ed), *Proceedings of the ninth international congress of medieval canon law, Munich, 13–18 Juli 1992,* Monumenta Iuris Canonici, ser. C, Subsidia (Vatican 1997) 21–40.

APPENDIX I
Transmission of the *Collectio canonum hibernensis* in Italy from the tenth to the twelfth century:

Manuscripts (F=noted by Fournier; B=Beneventan Script)

A. NORTHERN ITALIAN

1. København, Kongelige Bibliotek, Ny Kgl. Saml., 58 8°. (s. VIII 1/2; southern France [Lowe], northern Italy [Bischoff]) [excerpt? of CCH, Form B]
2. Padova, Biblioteca Antoniana, 27 (s. X, post a. 880; Verona) [excerpt of CCH]
3. Vaticano, Città del, Biblioteca Apostolica Vaticana, Vat. lat. 5748 (s. IX–X or X in; upper Italy) [excerpt of CCH] F
4. Verona, Biblioteca Capitolare, LXIII [61] (s. X med–2/2; probably upper Italy, Verona?) [excerpt of CCH] F
5. Livorno, Biblioteca Labronica, sine num. (olim 10) (s. XI–XII; probably northern Italy) [CCH, Form B?]
6. Milano, Biblioteca Ambrosiana, M 79 sup. (s. XI, northern Italy) [excerpt of CCH]

B. CENTRAL AND SOUTHERN ITALIAN

1. Vaticano, Città del, Biblioteca Apostolica Vaticana, Ottob. lat. 6 (s. X; Nonantola) [excerpt of CCH]
2. Montecassino, Archivio della Badia, 439 (s. X; southern Italy) [excerpt of CCH] B
3. Vaticano, Città del, Biblioteca Apostolica Vaticana, Arch. San Pietro H.58 (s. XI in; Rome) [excerpt of CCH]
4. Montecassino, Archivio della Badia, 297 (s. XI in; southern Italy) [excerpt of CCH] B
5. Roma, Biblioteca Vallicelliana, T. XVIII (s. XI; southern Italy) [CCH, Form B] F, B
6. Vaticano, Città del, Biblioteca Apostolica Vaticana, Vat. lat. 4162 (s. XII) [excerpt of *CCH*]

C. SOUTH AND CENTRAL ITALIAN CANONICAL COLLECTIONS CONTAINING THE *HIBERNENSIS*

1. *Collection in nine books*

Vaticano, Città del, Biblioteca Apostolica Vaticana, Vat. lat. 1349 (s. XI med; southern Italy) F, B

2. *Collection in five books*

Montecassino, Archivio della Badia, 125 (s. XI med; Montecassino) F, B

Roma, Biblioteca Vallicelliana, B 11 (s. XI, before 1087); Sant'Eutizio in Val Castoriana, near Nursia) F

Roma, Biblioteca Vallicelliana R 32 (f 50) (s. XI 3/4, middle Italy) [fragment?]

Vaticano, Città del, Biblioteca Apostolica Vaticana, Vat. lat. 1339 (s. XI med; Italy, provenance Santa Maria, Narni) F

3. *Collection of Naples*
Napoli, Biblioteca Nazionale Vittorio Emanuele II, XII.A.28 (s. XI; central-southern Italy) F
4. *Collectio Matritensis*
Madrid, Biblioteca Nacional, 373 (s. XI/XII, southern Italy) F, B
5. *Collection of Rieti*
Rieti, Archivio Capitolare, 5 (s. XI, southern Italy) B
6. *Collectio Riccardiana*
Firenze, Biblioteca Riccardiana, 300 (saec. XII 1/4; central Italy) F
7. *Collectio Angelica*
Roma, Biblioteca Angelica, 1447 (s. XI ex; central Italy)
8. *Collection of Vallicelliana B 63*
Roma, Biblioteca Vallicelliana, B 63 (s. XI; Sant'Eutizio in Val Castoriana, near Nursia)
9. *Collection of Maastricht*
Maastricht, Rijksarchief Limburg, Cat. nr 196 [18.A] (olim 167.I.27) (s. XI; central Italy)
10. *Collection of Vallicelliana T. XXI*
Roma, Biblioteca Vallicelliana, T. XXI (s. XI ex; Sant'Eutizio in Val Castoriana, near Nursia)
11. *Collectio Verulae*
Roma, Biblioteca Vallicelliana, B 32 (s. XI ex; Veroli) F, B
12. *Collectio Toletana*
Toledo, Archivo y Biblioteca del Capitular, 22–32 (s. XI; central Italy)
13. *Collection of Vallicelliana F 2*
Roma, Biblioteca Vallicelliana, F 2 (s. XI 2; southern Italy) F, B
14. *Collection of Vallicelliana F 8*
Roma, Biblioteca Vallicelliana, F 8 (s. XI 2; southern Italy) F, B
15. *Collection of Vallicelliana F 92*
Roma, Biblioteca Vallicelliana, F 92 (s. XI 2/2; Sant'Eutizo in Val Castoriana, near Nursia) F
16. *Collectio Sanctae Crucis*
Firenze, Biblioteca Medicea Laurenziana, [Santa Croce] 4.4 (s. XI; central Italy) F
17. *Collection of Vat. lat. 4977*
Vaticano, Città del, Biblioteca Apostolica Vaticana, Vat. lat. 4977 (saec. X–XII; central Italy) F
18. *Collectio Farfensis*
Vaticano, Città del, Biblioteca Apostolica Vaticana, Vat. lat. 8487 (s. XI ex–XII in; Farfa) F
19. *Collectio canonum Casinensis (Codex terscriptus)*
Montecassino, Archivio della Badia, 216 (s. XII ex; southern Italy) F, B
20. *Collectio 74 titulorum*
Roma, Biblioteca Casanatense, 2010 [olim B.V.17] (s. XI ex; possibly Farfa or Rome) F
El Escorial, Real Biblioteca de San Lorenzo, Z.III.19 (s. XI ex; southern Italy) B
Roma, Biblioteca Vallicelliana, F 54 (s. XI/XII; southern Italy) F, B

APPENDIX II

CANONS FROM THE *HIBERNENSIS* IN THE *COLLECTION IN FIVE BOOKS*, BOOKS 1–3

(F=Fornasari's edition; H=Wasserschleben's edition; V=Vallicelliana T. XVIII; 1349=*Collection in nine books*)

Aaron, primus in lege, sacerdotale nomen accepit. [F.I.4; H I.3; V 59v]

Abbas remissum non retineat monachum suum ad districtiora se tendentem. [F II.112; H 39:6]

Adam duos filios genuit, primo unum electum habuit et alterum reprobum. [F III.297.1; H 40:14c]

Adolescentulae, sic uiuite, nihil scientes praeter domum parentum.[F II.197; H 45:16]

Alexander quidam confessionis titulo satis clarus Hierosolymitanae ecclesiae subrogatur episcopus cum superesset adhuc Narcissus, qui prius ibi functus est pontificatus officio. [F I.159.1; H 1:17a]

Ammonendi sunt subditi ne praepositorum suorum uitam temere iudicent. [F III.158; H 37:5; 1349 II.121]

Ammoneo uos pariter ut nullus ex uobis caragios et diuinos et sortilogos requirat. [F III.330.1; H 64:1]

Ananias et Saphira retrahentes quae Domino dederunt morte multantur. [F III.133.1; H 17:3a; 1349 III.72]

Animae defunctorum quattuor modis soluuntur: oblationibus presbyterorum, praece sanctorum, karorum helymosinis, ieiunio cognatorum. [F III.319.2; H 15:1;1349 III.97]

Apud grecos yppodiacones id est subministri dicuntur, eo quod oboediunt diaconibus, et officiis laeuitarum. [F.I.13; H 4:1; V 64R]

Arca Noe et tabernaculum et templum bonos et malos continebat. [F III.297.3; H XL.14 a et c]

Auferte malum ex uobis ipsis; audet aliquis uestrum negotium habens iudicare apud iniquos, et non apud sanctos? [F I.224.1; H 21:26a]

Boni pastoris est pecus tondere non deglomerare. [F I.233.3; H 25:16c]

Castigo corpus meum et in seruituti subicio, ne forte aliis praedicans ipse reprobus efficiar. [F III.156.2; H 38:4f]

Causa ruinae populi, sacerdotes mali. [F I.193.2; H 2:17b]

Certum est perfectos rusticitate esse quam scientia peccatores. [F III.169.2; H 38:11a; 1349 II.139]

Christus quaerit de imagine mundi, alia est imago Dei et alia imago mundi; imaginem caesaris non habet Christus, quia imago Dei est, qui ait: regnum meum non est de hoc mundo. [F I.237.4; H 25:10e]

Christus antequam pateretur, triduo non comedit in Hierusalem, sed ibat ad Bethaniam. [F III.293.1; H 40:2a; 1349 VI.49]]

Clerici qui seruiunt Christi ecclesiae primum uocabulum suum ex nominis distinctione creditur esse prolatum. [F I.24; V 65R]

Clericus non [necessarie] pro emendo aliquid in nundinis uel in foro deambulat, ab officio suo degradetur. [F III.244.2; H 10e]

Clericus qui causam suam siue iusta siue iniusta ad iudicium alterius fidei iudicis prouocat, excommunicetur. [F.I.224.3; H 21:26c]

Clericus professionem suam etiam habitu et incessu probet et ideo nec uestibus nec calceamentis decorem quaerat. [F III.197; H 10a]

Columba si uiderit aliam auem trahere cibum, a nido eius non mouet pennam neque ungulam neque rostrum, neque cracitat; sic ecclesia Dei, quae uera columba est, rapta non repetat. [F III.138.1; H 42:4e]

Comae Hierusolimitarum tonsuram fore, cuius tonsurae origo in lege a nazareis coepit. [F III.202; H 52:2; 1349 VI.43]

Comparemus si placet illis doctam ignorantiam et nostram indoctam scientiam. [F III.168; H 38:12; 1349 II.138]

Cum audisset autem Symon quia per impositionem manus apostolorum daretur Spiritus sanctus, optulit ei pecuniam dicens: date et mihi hanc potestatem ut cuiuscumque imposuero manus accipiat Spiritum sanctum.[F I.49.1; H 2:13b]

Cum bene facimus laudem Domini acquirimus, quae laus non uitanda a bonis. [F III.141.5; H 42:12f]

Cum Dominus aliquando dicit: nolite iudicare et non iudicabimini, non utique iudicii homini prohibuit facultatem, sed differentiam iudicii nosse nos docet, ut sciamus quid iudicemus. [F I.220.3; H 21:11b]

Cum huiusmodi homine nec cibum quidem sumere. [F III.292.1; H 40:1b]

Cum peccauerit ecclesia a malis reprobatur. [F III.141.4; H 42:12e]

De corporibus hominum intra basilicas sanctorum nullatenus sepeliendis nisi probatissimi fuerint. [F III.309.1; H 18:8]

De oblationibus eorum continent tegimen tantum et alimentum, ce+tera iniquorum reprobat altissimus. [F III.300.4; H 2:23;1349 III.15]

Decet hominem huiusmodi mansuetum esse, non elatum, non superbum. [F III.126.5; H 37:10f; 1349; II.119]

Decet principi ecclesiae nihil proprium scire, sed omnia sub manu ministri colligere uel habere, nudos uestire, egenos sumere seniores honorare, omnibus ministrare, exemplo Christi dicentis: non uenit Filius hominis ministrari sed ministrare. [F III.123; H 37:13; 1349 II.113]

Definimus monachos fugientes malos principes suscipi ab alia ecclesia ut sciatur causa. [F II.113.1; H 39:7]

Deo se amicum denegat qui eius inimico placet. [F III.292.2; H 40:2a;1349 VI.49]

Deus uos constituit sacerdotes et potestatem uobis dedit de nobis quoque iudicandi, et ideo nos a uobis recte iudicamur uos, non potestis ab hominibus iudicari propter quod Filius Dei in uos expectat iudicium. [F III.177; H 1:16a; 1349 II.161]

Diacones graues esse oportet, pudicos, non bilingues, non turpia lucra sectantes, habentes ministerium fidei in conscientia pura. [F.I.12; H 3:4; V 64R]

Diaconorum ordo a Leui tribu accepit exordium. [F.I.11; H 3:2]

Diaconus greco nomine, quod latine sonat, interpretatur minister, eo quod altario et gradui sacerdotali ministret. [F I.9; H 3:1]

Dignum est ut ab eis terrena stipendia consequamur quibus praemia patriae coelestis offerimus. [F III.130.1; H 38:1b; 1349 II.128]

Docta rusticitas tantum sancta collegit exemplo et opere, indocta uero scientia tantum peccatrix destruit exemplo, non implens opere quod docet ore. [F III.169.3; H 38:11b]

Doctor docens et non implens similis est uerberanti aerem sonans sonum et non dans uirtutem. [F III.156.3; H 38.4g]

Dominus dicit: Pectus et armum dextrum tuli a filiis Israel iure perpetuo et sacerdotum erit. [F III.131.3; H 2:11c; 1349 III.11]

Dona iniquorum quae reprobantur a Deo, reprobantur a sanctis. [F III.300.2; H 2:22b]

Duo uel tres termini circa locum sanctum debent fieri. [F III.152; H 44:5]

Duos filios artificis legimus quorum pater ad artificium iuit. [F III.104; H 17:11]

Ebron ciuitas quattuor uirorum qui in ea sepulti sunt, tres patriarchae in spelunca duplici cum tribus uxoribus suis id est Abraham cum Sara, Isaac et Rebecca, Iacob et Lia praeter ipsum Adam et Euam uxorem suam. [F III.307.1; H 18:1a;1349 III.65]

Ecclesia grece, latine conuocatio pro eo quod omnes ad se uocet. [F III.137.1; H 42:1; 1349 VI.1]

Ego quos amo arguo et castigo. [F III.142.4; H 42:13e]

Eorum qui pauperes praemunt, dona a sacerdotibus refutentur. [F III.300.3; H 2:22c]

Episcopo decet iudicare et interpretare et consecrare et consummare et ordinare et offerre et baptizare. [F. I.3; H 8:2]

Episcopum ordinare successorem in exitu uitae consensu synodi et regionis illius sententia, ne irritum fiat.[F I.156.3; H 1:18b]

Episcopus, aut presbyter aut diaconus nequaquam seculares curas assumat, sin aliter deiciatur. [F III.247; H 2:27]

Episcopus nomen grecum in usum conuertens, et latine superspeculator siue superintendens dicitur. [F. I.5; H I1a]

Ergo liberi sunt filii ecclesiae in omni regno. [F I.237.1; H 25:10a]

Et ei qui uult te cum in iudicio contendere et tunicam tuam tollere, dimitte ei et pallium. [F III.138.3; H 42:4h]

Etenim doctor debet considerare quid loquatur et cui loquatur et quando loquatur. [F III.161; H 38:18a; 1349 II.143]

Exiit edictum a caesare Augusto, ut censum profiterentur omnes per orbem terrae. [F I.236.4; H 25:9f]

Fac in uita quod post mortem possis redimi. [F III.321.2; H 15:8b]

Flores inter spinas oriuntur; rosa quae redolet crescit cum spina quae pungit. [F III.297.4; H 40:14b]

Fugiunt oues uocem pastoris quem non cognoscunt et deserta petunt: ita mali principis ouilia uitanda sunt et deserta uita petenda. [F II.114.2; H 39:12b]

Fures et latrones et raptores de ecclesia eiciendi sunt. [F III.134.2; H 42:3c]

Gregorius ait de sepultura sororis Benedicti, quae sepulta est in sepulcro quod sibi ipse parauerat: ut quorum mens una semper in Domino fuerat, eorum quoque corpora non sepultura separarentur. [F III.308.1; H 18:9; 1349 III.90]

Haec ipsa pro minimo suscipientes. [F III.130.2; H 38:1b; 1349 II.128]

Helymosina non est neganda pro mortuis aut enim peccata redimit aut poenam releuat aut remissionem in futuro praestat aut consolationem quampiam uiuorum. [F III.320; H 15:6a]

Hi sunt modi excommunicationis hominis mali: a celebratione missarum, a communicatione mensae, a cohabitatione, a colloquio pacifico, a benedictione, a comitatu et muneribus. [F III.291.2; H 40:1d]

Hic gradus ab Esdra sumpsit initium, qui in templo Salomonis iussit dispositores esse, quos actores templi memorat Esdras, eos quos nunc ecclesia Dei exorcistas nominat, id est orationibus deseruientes. [F I.19; H 6:1; V 64V]

Hii quorum manus plenae sunt sanguine, non accedant ad altare meum. [F I.42.1; H 37:24a]

Honorandus in quantum homo, inhonorandus in quantum contrarius. [F III.163.3; H 38:6d]

Hostia pro peccato et delicto sacerdotum erit iure perpetuo, ita erit quod datur ecclesiae Dei. [F III.110.2; H 16:14b]

Huic, consecratus, datur baculus ut eius iudicio subditam plebem uel regat uel corrigat uel infirmitates infirmorum sustineat. [F I.33.1; H 1:6a; V 60R]

Huius praepositi principes Helias et Heliseus discipulus eius fuerunt et alii prophetarum qui remoti ab urbibus iuxta fluenta Iordanis habitabant. [F II.108; H 39:2; 1349 IV.2]

Huius sermo debet esse purus et apertus, plenus grauitatis honestate, plenus suauitatis gratia, tractans de ministerio legis, de doctrina fidei, de uirtute continentiae, de disciplina iustitiae, cuius prae ceteris speciale est officium scripturam legere, percurrere canones, exempla sanctorum imitari, ieiuniis et uigiliis et orationibus intentus esse, pacem habere, curam pauperum agere, uestire nudos, suscipere peregrinos, captiuos redimere, uiduas ac pupillos tueri, cuius diuersorium cunctorum debet esse receptaculum. [F I.28; V I.8a; V 60R]

Illos uero monachos quorum abbatem de mensa sanctorum propter infamiam non arcemus si non debemus illo nolente facile suscipere quanto magis fugientes a sanctis abbatibus et in nullo alio modo suspectis nisi cum praesumptione et superbia. [F II.115.1; H 39:7]

In commentario Ionae ubi dicitur: cecidit sors super Ionam. [F III.326.2; H 26:3b]

In eadem domo manete edentes et bibentes quae apud illos sunt. [F III.130.3; H 38:1a; 1349 II.128]

In euangelio ad Dominum haec quaestio refertur, si licet caesari tributum dari an non. [F I.236.1; H 25:9a]

In monte in quo lex data est posuit Dominus terminum inter se et Moysen, inter Moysen et Ihesum, inter Ihesum et seniores, inter seniores et populum. [F III.148.6; H 44:6a]

In nouo hii denique inter sanctum et iniquum discernentes, eos tamen in ecclesia recipiunt, qui sunt fideles. [F I.21; H 7.2; V 64V]

In porta tabernaculi iudicabat Moyses, ut conuocaret multitudinem populi et seniorum Israelis ad ostium tabernaculi. [F I.216; H 21:4; 1349 VI.77]

In quibus dimissa peccata non fiunt sacris locis post mortem adiuuari non possunt. [F III.310.6; H 18:8f]

In quantum bestia est, tantum ad nocendum nutritur. [F III.343.3; H 53:2b]

In rusticitate sancta cauendum est ne aut minuat aut augeat. [F III.166.1; H 38:8; 1349 II.135]

In sorte non est electio sed Dei uoluntas. [F III.325; H 26:2a–c;1349 VI.170]

In toto orbe terrarum instituta sunt regna caelorum. [F III.173; H 42:8; 1349 VI.27]

Indigni sunt huiusmodi qui etiam de minimis iudicent. [F I.224.2; H 21:26a]
Intelligendum est liberos esse filios ecclesiae, id est non esse uectigales, multo ergo liberiores esse debent a quolibet in regno filii regis ipsius, sub quo sunt omnia terrena. [F I.237.2; H 25:10b]
Inter humana diuina que seruitia hoc interest, quod humana coacta sunt, diuina uoluntaria. [F III.143.2; H 42:16]
Ioseph uectigal redidit regi, Deo timorem. [F I.236.3; H 25:9d]
Is qui tantam dignitatem acceperit rex, tantum timorem habere debet. [F I.234.3; H 25:6b]
Isti oblationes in templo Domini suscipiunt a populis; isti uasa corporis et sanguinis Christi diaconibus ad altarium offerre praecipitur. [F.I.14; H 4:2; V 64R]
Itaque omnes qui in ecclesiastici ministerii gradibus ordinati sunt, generaliter clerici nominantur. [F I.25; V 65V]
Iudas Scarioth de gradu suo cecidit et iterum non inuenit. [F II.93.3; H 11:2b]
Iustitia uero iusti regis haec est: nemini iniuste iudicare, aduenis et pupillis et uiduis defensorem esse, furta prohibere, adulteria punire, impudicos et histriones non nutrire, iniquos non exaltare, impios de terra perdere, homicidas et paricidas et periurantes uiuere non sinere, senes et sapientes et sobrios consiliarios habere, magorum et phitonum et augurum superstitionibus non intendere, patriam fortiter et iuste contra aduersarios defendere, et per omnia in Deo confidere. [F I.234.1; H 25:4a]
Lectores sunt qui uerbum Dei praedicant, quibus dicitur: clama ne cesses, et cetera. [F I.16; H 5:1; V 64V]
Lupus uitandus, pastor bonus adeundus. [F II.114.1; H 39:12a]
Melior est docta sapientia non minus erudiens, quam sancta rusticitas. [F III.165.2; H 38:7b]
Melius est pro ueritate supplicium quam pro adulatione beneficium. [F I.221.2; H 21:11c & 21:13b]
Misericordia et ueritas custodire legem et roboratur clementia thronus eius. [F I.234.2; H 25:4c]
Monachi procreantes filios in carcere retrudantur, tantum facinus continua lamentatione deflentes ut eis ad mortem solius misericordiae intuitu communionis possit gratia indulgeri. [F II.171; H 39:14; 1349 IV.11]
Monachum suscipite qui ueniunt ad uos de loco uiliori ad perfectiorem quorum abbas ita degenerauit ab opere Dei ut mereatur ad mensam sanctorum non recipi et fornicationis crimine non suspicionis sed malitiae uidentes onerare. [F II.113.2; H 39:7]
Moyses consensu coram multitudine filiorum Israel ordinauit Aaron. [F I.157.1; H 37:20]
Moyses de se ait: erat Moyses uir mitissimus coram Deo. [F III.126.3; H 37:10c; 1349 II.119]
Mulieres in ecclesia taceant. [F III.238; H 45:19; 1349 VII.144]
Mundari se prius oportet et sic alios mundare. [F III.156.1; H 38:4a; 1349 II.130]
Ne enutrieris immanem bestiam, in quantum enim proderit tibi tantum proximis nocet. [F III.343.2; H 53:2d]
Ne nomen Christi blasphemetur per nos. [F III.141.2; H 42:12c]

Necesse sit illos restaurare honori qui per poenitentiam reconciliationem meruerunt diuinae pietatis. [F.II.103; H 11:5]

Neminem fraudaui, bouem et ouem alicuius non rapui, nichil per uim abstuli. [F I.233.2; H 25:16b]

Neminem laesi, asinum alicuius non tetigi. [F I.233.1; H 25:16a]

Neminem contempsi et humilis fui ad uniuersos. [F III.126.2; H 37:10a; 1349 II.119]

Nichil boni gerentes malo estis intenti. [F III.142.6; H 42:13g]

Nolite tangere sancta non solum interiora sed etiam exteriora. [F III.148.3; H 44:7e]

Non autem in clericis signum tonsurae tantum in corpore, sed in anima intus agitur. [F III.204; H 52:4; 1349 VI.45]

Non declinabis ad partem aliquam a ueritate. [F I.219.3; H 21:10d]

Non est enim potestas nisi a Deo data, itaque qui resistit potestati, Dei ordinationi resistit.[F I.239.1; H 24:4b]

Non est hoc nostrae disciplinae ut conuertatur quis inuitus. [F III.143.1; H 42:16a]

Non grauis fui populo huic, neque per uim quicquam tuli. [F III.126.4; H 37:10b; 1349 II.119]

Non gressu pedum sed morum quaerendus est Deus. [F III.172.2; H 43:8c; 1349 VI.27]

Non oportet iudices ecclesiae habere timorem humanum sed timorem Dei, quia timor Dei principium sapientiae est. [F I.223.1; H 21:12; 1349 VI.86]

Non potest caput dicere pedibus: non estis mihi necessarii, sed multo magis quae uidentur membra corporis inferiora necessaria sunt. [F III.346; H 37:36]

Non te fallor, quia quod tibi post mortem, non proficit non suadeo; dico namque ut in uita emendes et meritu redimas et orationibus aut helymosinis. [F III.321.4; H 15:8c]

Nonus abusionis gradus est: rex iniquus qui cum malorum sectator esse uult. [F I.235; H 25:3]

Nulli dantes offensionem ut non uituperetur ministerium nostrum ab illis qui foris sunt. [F III.141.1; H 42:12b; 1349 VI.8]

Nullus ex uobis obseruet qua die ex domo exeat et qua die de itinere reuertatur, quia omnes dies Deus fecit aequales, ut factus est dies primus et secundus et dies tertius et reliqua. [F III.334.2; H 64:8]

O homo, noli quaerere post mortem, nisi prius in uita quaesieris. [F III.321.3; cf. H 15:8]

Omne quod dabatur Aaron in hostio tabernaculi ponebat manus suas super caput hostiae et nemo poterat commouere. [F III.110.1; H 16:14a]

Omnes sanctorum locorum termini consecrati debent habere signa circa se ut plebilium signo separentur. [F III.151;. H 44:3]

Omnia quae in macello uenient manducate nichil interrogantes propter conscientiam, quia Domini est terra et plenitudo eius. [F III.293.2; H 40:11a–40:11b;1349 VI.54]

Omnia quae praeceperis nobis faciemus et quocumque miseris ibimus. [F III.128.2; H 37:6]

Omnibus potestatibus sublimioribus subditi estote. [F III.349.2; H 24:4b]

Omnis igitur qui stipem templi et his quae offeruntur ad usus ecclesiae habent et alias res quibus suas expleant uoluptates, similes sunt scribarum redimentium mendacium et Saluatoris sanguinem.[F III.109; H 16:16; 1349 III.83]

Omnis iudex tribus indiget, hoc est dignitate loci, testificatione bonorum, sobrietate morum.[F I.217.2; H 21:5b]

Omnis mundialis etiam si sapiens sit, non iudicet iudicia ecclesiae. [F I.224.4; H 21:26b]
Omnis ordinatio a Deo, opera maligna a diabolo. [F I.232.2; H 25:15b]
Omnis quicumque bestiam habet, stringat eam; si bos cornupeta uirum aut feminam occiderit, bos lapidibus obruetur et non comedentur carnes eius, dominus autem bouis innocens erit. [F III.342.2; H 53:2a–53:3;1349 VI.217]
Omnis qui dolum facit, reatum doli effusi sanguinis suscipit. [F III.339.2; H 59:4b; 1349 VI.224]
Omnis qui ducit alienos, si affectum animi complere non possit, reatum omnium sumpsit. [F III.340; H 59:4a;1349 VI.224]
Oportet eum qui uult principari ante subiectum esse, et eum qui uult haereditari, prius pium esse, et eum qui uult docere, dudum discipulum esse. [F I.32.1; H 38:7]
Ostiarii sunt qui in ueteri testamento ianitores templi uocabantur, qui erant portis Hierusalem, quique, ordinati per uices suas, omnia interiora templi uel exteriora custodiebant. [F I.20; H 7:1; V 64V]
Otiosus sermo est qui sine utilitate audientis loquendo profertur. [F III.242.2; H 64:3b]
Otiosus sermo est qui uel ratione uel pace caret. [F III.242.3; H 66:3c]
Otiosus sermo est quo in hoc saeculo siue in futuro bonum non acquiritur. [F III.242.1; H 64:3a; 1349 VI.250]
Peccantes coram omnibus arguet. [F III.142.1; H 42:13a]
Petrum quinque ex causis tonsuram accepisse. [F III.203; H 52:3; 1349 VI.44]
Philippus apostolus et quattuor filiae eius apud Hierapolim in uno sepulcro sepulti sunt. [F III.308.2; H 18:2c; 1349 III.88]
Polluistis templum Domini, ideo super uos mala uestra reddam. [F III.148.2; H 44:7d]
Populus terrae oboediat Deo et principi nec contradicat illi. [F III.127.1; H 37:6]
Porro uox lectoris simplex erit et clara, ad omne pronuntiationis genus comoda, plena suco uiribus agrestis, rusticum effugiens sonum, non multum humilis, nec addens sublimis, non fracta nec tenera, nichil que femininum sonans.[F I.18; H 5:4; V 64V]
Post quinque episcopos qui ex circumcisione post Iacobum Hierosolymitanae ciuitatis praefuerit, primus Marcus eiusdem cathedrae eligitur episcopus. [F I.166; H 1:19]
Presbyter grece nominatur, quod latine senior dicitur. [F. I.6; H 2:1]
Presbyterorum ordo principium sumpsit a filiis Aaron. [F.I.7; H 2:2]
Primitiae omnis populi Israelis erant sacerdotum et decimae et plura de primogenitis. [F III.131.1; H 2:11a; 1349 III.11]
Princeps debet seruus esse et minister, quia gradus ministrationis accipit. [F III.122; H 37:11b]
Princeps ecclesiae debet esse humilis. [F III.126.1; H 37:10e; 1349 II.119]
Princeps priuatam domum non habeat, sed quasi hospes esse debet, ut Christus ait: Filius hominis non habet ubi declinet caput. [F III.124; H 37:12]
Progenies uiperarum, quis demonstrabit uobis fugere ab ira uentura? [F III.142.5; H 42:13f]
Prouidentes bonum non solum coram Deo sed etiam coram hominibus. [F III.141.3; H 42:12d]
Psalmistarum auctores Dauid siue Asaph extiterunt. [F.I.23; H 9:2; V 65R]
Qua fronte oblationes Dei accipimus, cum mandata eius non seruemus, et reliqua similia. [F III.136.2; H 17:37]

Quaedam femina sanctimonialis in ecclesia sepulta est iuxta altare, pars eius una igni consumpta uisa est, pars altera intacta permansit inferior, quia ipsa mulier uirgo fuit, tamen stultiloquium non uitauit. [F III.310.2; H 18:8b]

Quanto cultu loca sancta honoranda sunt, uiuis enim custodia, mortuis refugium, malis confugientibus defensio. [F III.150.1; H 44:10a]

Quarto et quinto pro sola interni iudicii intentione subiectorum causam pontifex discutere debet, ut nichil ei humanitatis admisceat qui diuina positus uice dispensat, ne correctionis studium priuatus dolor exasperet ne tranquillitatem iudicii aut latens inuidia mulceat aut praeceps ira perturbet .[F I.222.2; H 21:14]

Quattuor genera ordinationis sunt. [F I.29; H 37:2]

Quattuor modis offert ecclesia pro animabus defunctorum. [F III.319.3; H 15:2b]

Quattuor modis iudicium humanum peruertitur: timore, cupiditate, odio, amore. [F I.221.1; H 21:13a; 1349 VI.87]

Quattuor modis offert ecclesia pro animabus defunctorum. [F III.319.3; H 15:2a;1349 III.98]

Quattuor genera monachorum dicuntur. [F II.109.2; H 39:3c]

Qui bene docet et male uiuit, uidetur uelut cereus aliis bonam exponit lucem praestare, se uero malis suis consumere atque extinguere. [F III.162.2; H 38:5f]

Qui contendunt terrena, oblationibus priuandi sunt. [F III.136.4; H 42:10d]

Qui contumaciter monachus uagari per quaelibet loca, aut aliquid habere proprium praesumpserit omnia quae acquisierit abbati deferantur secundum monasterii regulam, ipse uero tamquam fugax sub custodia reuocetur uel constringatur sicut sancta regula docet. [F II.117; H 39:8]

Qui fastus superbiae domino suo contradixerit a communione fratrum et ab ecclesia est abiciendus. [F III.128.4; H 37:17]

Qui gradu peccat debet excommunicari quia dignitas huius nominis tantum potest redimere animam suam post poenitentiam ad priorem enim gradum uenire est difficile an non. [F II.93.2; H 11:2b]

Qui huiusmodi probetur ad agendum, iste erit in doctrina et libris imbutus, sensuum ac uerborum scientia ornatus, ita ut distinctionem sententiarum intelligat, ubi firmatur iunctura, ubi adhuc pendat oratio, ubi sententia extrema claudatur, hoc est discernens genus pronuntiationis et his similia. [F I.17; H 5:3; V 64V]

Qui murmurat uerba blasphemiae contra principem bonum odio uel inuidia, poeniteat cum pane et aqua VII diebus ad exemplum Mariae contra Moysen. [F III.128.5; H 37:27]

Qui non oboedierit principi morte moriatur. [F III.128.1; H 37:8]

Qui praebet ducatum barbaris, XIIII annos poeniteat. [F III.341; H 59:2;1349 VI.225]

Qui scit fratrem suum peccare peccatum non ad mortem postulet pro eo et dabit ei Deus uitam. [F III.321.10; H 15:8d]

Qui sine abbatum suorum licentia discurrunt, in nullo monasterio suscipiantur, et qui susceperit ambo excommunicandi sunt. [F II.115.2; H 39:10]

Qui sub gradu cecidit post poenitentiam contentus fiat baptizare communionem infirmis dare et altario ministrare. [F II.94; H 11:2]

Qui supradictis malis, id est caragiis et diuinis et aruspicibus et philacteriis et aliis quibuslibet auguriis crediderit, etsi ieiunet, etsi oret, etsi largas helymosinas faciat et corpus suum in omni afflictione cruciauerit, nihil ei prodiderit quamdiu in illa obseruantia sit. [F III.330.2; H 64:2]

Quia non oportet seruum Dei cautum esse, non oportet iudices ecclesiae Dei tam ueloces esse in iudicio ut nesciant quid prouerbii fiant, quia dictum est: noli iudex esse cito. [F I.223.2; H 21:12]

Quia sunt multi praepositi qui cupiditate pecuniae magis se exercent quam animae. [F III.314.3; H 2:13c]

Quicumque contristauerit doctorem ueritatis peccat in Christum. [F III.159; H 38:17; 1349 II.141]

Quicumque dignitatem gradus diuini non custodit contentus fiat animam suam saluare, reuerti enim in eum gradum nescio an non, Deus scit.[F II.93.1; H 11:1a; 1349 II.268]

Quicumque hoc donum studet donatione mercari, non officium sed nomen attendit, sacerdos non esse decreuit.[F I.48.3; H 2:13a]

Quicumque loca sacra polluerit duplicia persoluet. [F III.148.1; H 44:7c]

Quicumque noluerit occidere proximum suum, ne enutriat bestiam. [F III.343.1; H 53:2c]

Quicumque peccauerit in locis sanctis, dignus est morte.[F III.148.5; H 44:7b]

Quicumque sub gradu cecidit sine gradu consurgat. [F II.93.4; H 11:2b]

Quicumque uenerit contra decretum principis ab ecclesia abiciatur. [F III.128.3; H 37:6; 1349 II.122]

Quid faciemus si auguria ipsa uera nuntiant? De hac re scriptura nos contestatur et admonet dicens: etiam si uera dixerint uobis nolite credere eis. [F III.334.1; H 64:6]

Quid per baculum nisi pastoralis cura? baculus enim sustinet, erigit, custodit. [F. I.33.2; H 1:6b]

Quid uobis uidetur commutare gubernatoris nostri sententiam? Si enim illi Deus maiora credidit, cur minima non credimus? [F I.157.5; H 1:17c]

Quidam defensor alicuius ecclesiae, uir mundialibus actibus implicatus humatus in ecclesia Syri martiris, nocte media cum tumultu ab ecclesia tractus est alligatis pedibus et in alio loco positus est. [F III.310.4; H 18:8d]

Quidam in ecclesia beati Ianuarii humatus est a coniuge et quadam nocte clamauit dicens: ardeo, ardeo. [F III.310.5; H 18:8e]

Quidam paruam messem enutriens bestiae deuorauerunt; et orauit ad Dominum ut suas bestias prohiberet et prohibuit. [F III.343.4; H 53:2e–f]

Quidam patricius locum sepeliendi in ecclesia praetio redemit, inde mortuus sepultus est in eo. [F III.310.3; H 18:8c]

Quod iustum est iudicate, siue ciuis sit ille, siue peregrinus, ut non sit ulla distantia personarum; ita paruum audientes ut magnum, quia Dei iudicium est. [F I.219.1; H 21:10a]

Quod si doctor haerrauerit in quo emendabitur? ITEM. [F III.163.2; H 38:6b]

Quodcumque potest manus tua facere, instanter operare. [F III.321.1; H 15:8a;1349 III.102]

Quomodo impleuit Christus septem gradus ecclesiae: primum gradum lectoris, [F. I.2; H 8:1]

Quos coniunxit unum coniugium, coniungat unum sepulcrum quia una caro est. [F III.307.2; H 18:1c]

Quos peccata grauia non deprimunt, possunt quidem mortui sepeliri in ecclesia quia eorum proximi ad sacra loca uenientes pro eis sepultis preces Domino fundunt. [F III.310.1; H 18:8a;1349 III.94]

Reddite omnibus debita, cui tributum tributum, cui uectigal uectigal, cui honorem honorem, cui timorem timorem. [F I.236.2; H 25:9c & 33:1c]

Regula canonica Romana statuit possessiones quas unusquisque ecclesiae proprio arbitrio dedit uel reliquit quibuslibet titulis atque contractibus uel quibuslibet argumentis, non patimur ab ecclesia alienari, nisi necessitas suaserit largiri melioribus aut certe peregrinis religionis intuitu. [F III.136.1 H 17:8; 1349 III.76]

Reliquias sanctorum nemo potest polluere, quorum uisione Dei animae satiatae, mundialia obliuioni tradunt. [F III.150.2; H 44:9b]

Sacerdos non quaerat praetium ministrationis, quia gratis accepit gratis det. [F I.174; H 2:21]

Saepe cum quaerimus mutare locum, conamur secretum uitae remotioris eligere, uidelicet ignorantes, quia si desit spiritus, locus non adiuuat. [F III.172.1; H 43:7; 1349 VI.26]

Sancta quippe rusticitas sola sibi prodest et quantum aedificat ex uitae merito ecclesiam Christi, tantum nocet si contradicentibus non resistat. [F III.165.1; H 38:7a; 1349 II.134]

Sanctimoniales qualibet uita eorum et mores probatae, sint ante annum aetatis suae duodecimum non uelentur. [F II.143; H 44:11]

Serui, subditi estote omni ordinationi humanae propter Deum, siue regi, quasi praecellenti, siue ducibus, tamquam ab eo missis ad uindictam malefactorum, laudem uero bonorum. [F III.349.1; H 24:4a; 1349 VI.144]

Serui, oboedite dominis uestris carnalibus cum timore et tremore sicut Christo. [F III.347.1; H 24:2a; 1349 VI.143]

Serui estote subditi dominis uestris non tantum bonis sed etiam discolis. [F III.347.2; H 24:2b]

Seruus oboediuit Abraham et sermonem eius non mutauit. [F III.129; H 37:16a; 1349 II.124]

Sex genera monachorum sunt, quorum tria optima, reliqua uero deteriora atque omnimodis euitanda. [F II.109.1; H 39:3a]

Si doctor herrauerit et in suo sensu firmatus fuerit, nisi per auctoritatem regiam aut episcopalem nemo potest emendare. [F III.170.2; H 38:15b]

Si enim grandis sit laicus et necesse sit ut episcopus fiat, biennio lector siue exorcista stet, quinquennio subdiaconus, post decimum quintum annum presbyter siue episcopus subrogetur. [F I.88; H 1:11]

Si episcopo animas nostras et colla submittimus, quanto magis gubernandam ecclesiam successorem ordinare. [F I.157.4; H 1:17d]

Si paradysus excommunicatum Adam eiecit, quanto magis ecclesia Dei. [F III.292.4; H 40:2b]

Si pater reticuerit uotum filiae, uoti reus tenebitur.[F III.105; H 17:12]

Si peccata tua non nocent, cur peccatis alienis communicas? [F III.292.3; H 40:3b]

Si quis dona Dei retraxerit sine poenitentia hominum, quanto magis dona hominum fieri sine poenitentia. [F III.134.4; H 17:3g]

Si quis ecclesiae coniunctus fuerit, in ea sepeliatur. [F III.308.3; H 18:3a]

Si quis ecclesiam Dei nudauerit anathema sit. [F III.134.1; H 17:3a]

Si quis excommunicatus fuerit, solus ex eadem hora orationem faciat nec offerre liceat ei nec eius helymosinae in ecclesia recipiantur, donec se faciat emendatum. [F III.291.3; H 40:9; 1349 VI.58]

Si quis perdiderit aliquid et dixerit: Dominus dedit, Dominus abstulit, pro ista placita sententia Deo aut coronam accipiet si est iustus, aut indulgentiam peccatorum si peccator. [F III.138.4 H 42:4g]

Si quis sua uoluntate discesserit, notetur coram testibus et relinquatur Deo. [F III.143.3; H 42:16c]

Si quis subtrahit hostias catholicas oblatas, excommunicetur. [F III.134.3; H 17:3d; 1349 III.72]

Si quis uenit ad uos et sanam doctrinam non defert, nolite recipere eum in domo nec aue ei dixeritis. [F III. 298; H 40:4;1349 VI.52]

Si quis uiolauerit templum Dei disperdet illum Deus. [F III.148.4; H 44:7a]

Si quis uir siue mulier ecclesiam habet, in ea sepeliatur, siue in sepulcro paterno. [F III.307.5; H 18:4a]

Si quis uiuus firmauerit super mortuo, accedat uiuens et firmet sermonem mortui et heres reddet quod firmauit uiuus. [F III.323.1; H 16:10b;1349 III.103]

Si rusticus herrauerit in quantum rusticus, tantum facilius corrigitur. [F III.170.1; H 38:15a; 1349 II.140]

Si sal euanuerit in quo salietur? ad nichilum utile est nisi ut mittatur foras et conculcetur pedibus. [F III.163.1; H 38:6a; 1349 II.133]

Sicut ouis tunicam suam dimittit tondenti se neque aperit os, sic ecclesia raptori et tollenti tunicam suam debet dimittere. [F III.138.2; H 42:4f]

Sollicite praecauendum est ne quis pastorem quaerens, lupum inueniat. [F I.48.1; H 37:28]

Sors inter dubia aut inter duo aequalia aut inter duo catholica mitti debet. [F III.327; H 26:5;1349 VI.173]

Sors inter dubia mittitur; et inde dicitur sors quia de sursum est et a Deo temperatur. [F III.324.1; H 26:1a;1349 VI.189]

Sors non aliud mali est, sed res in dubitatione humana diuinam nobis indicans uoluntatem. [F III.324.2; H 26:1b]

Sortes non semper mittendae sunt, quia aliquando fallunt. [F III.326.1; H 27:9a;1349 VI.171]

Stulti, aliquando sapite. [F III.142.3; H 42:13d]

Stultitia, si sui rusticitate contenta esset, minus aliquid haberet malitiae. [F III.167.2; H 38:9b]

Subdiaconi inueniuntur in Esdra et appellantur ibi nathynei, id est mundi in humilitate, Deo seruientes. [F I.15; H 4:4; V 64V]

Sunt praeterea quinque causae quibus commutantur iudices: primo ministri mali, secundo elatio, tertio ira, quarto priuatus dolor. [F I. 222.1; H 21:14; 1349 VI.88]

Sunt septem quae omni regi conueniunt: I, deum timere, II, ueritatem iudicare, III, humilem in bonos, IIII, saeuum in malos, V, pauperes alere, VI, ecclesias adiuuare, VII, inter propinquos et alienos similis esse. [F I.232.1; H 25:15a]

Super cathedram Moysi sederunt scribae et pharisaei, quodcumque dixerint uobis facite secundum opera eorum ne faciatis. [F III.162.1; H 38:5a; 1349 II.132]

Superbus angelus de caelo eiectus est. [F III.164; H 37:34–35; 1349 II.118]

Surgentes iuuenes sepelierunt uirum et reuertentes inuenerunt uxorem eius mortuam et extulerunt eam ad uirum suum. [F III.307.4; H 18:1e]

Timeat unusquisque uestrum principem suum. [F III.127.2; H 37:6]

Timeo quod uideo canes affectare officium pastorale, maxime cum nichil in semetipsis pastoralis praeparauerint disciplinae. [F.III.314; H 27:4a]

Timeo quod uideo canes affectare officium pastorale, maxime cum nichil in semetipsis pastoralis praeparauerint disciplinae, sed laniare tantum didicerint, quia facilius semper sciunt perdere quam conseruare. [F I.31.2; H 27:4a]

Tonsurae ecclesiarum usus a nazareis ce+pit qui in crine seruato post uitae magnam continentiam caput radebant et capillos in ignem mittebant ut deuotionem Domini consecrarent. [F III.199; H 52:1]

Tres tantum ecclesia custodit et nutrit: theoricam, actualem, poenitentem, ultra nec ecclesia sumit nec custodit. [F III.137.2; H 42:1; 1349 VI.2XXVII.13]

Tria ecclesia debet custodire: dona iniquorum non recipere, quae reprobat Altissimus; aliena non rapere, praetium sanguinis innocentis non accipere. [F III.137.3; H 42:2; 1349 VI.3]

Tria in ordinationibus necessaria sunt: consensus bonorum, testimonium multorum, electio principis. [F I.157.3; H 37:20d]

Tribus indiget iudex: sedes, iudicium, sobrietatem sensus, consensus plurimorum. [F I.217.1; H 21:5a; 1349 VI.78]

Tribus modis excommunicare decreuit, hoc est: a pace, a mensa, a missa. [F III.291.1; H 40:1c;1349 VI.48]

Tribus modis iudicibus iudicandum est: natura, hoc est indagatione rerum, et similitudine praecedentium, et ex uerbis scripturae. [F I.218; H 21:6a]

Tunc sancta rusticitas bene utitur et cum sub regimine monasterii et abbatis uerbis scripturae doceatur. [F III.166.2; H 38:10; 1349 II.136]

Vae pastoribus Israhelis, qui pascebant semetipsos, nec greges custodiebant, nec pascebant lac a gregibus bibebant et lanis operiebantur, et quod crassum erat occidebant, gregem autem meum non pascebant, dicit Dominus. [F I.31.5; H 37:4b]

Vae uobis qui sapientes estis ad faciendum malum. [F III.169.1; H 38:14]

Vae uobis, principes Israelis [F.I.31.3; H. 37:4a]

Vae uobis, scribae et farisei. [F III.142.2; H 42:13b]

Valde boni non egent remedium post mortem, quia se ipsos in uita sua liberauerunt. [F III.319.5; H 15:2c]

Variis speciebus constructum est tabernaculum, partim speciosis, partim uilibus; per quod demonstratur alios sanctos alios esse peccatores in ecclesia. [F III.297.2; H 40:14d]

Ve! sacerdotibus qui comedunt peccata populi mei; hoc est siue eorum sumentes uictimas et non orantes pro eis, siue comedentes hostias et non corripientes malos. [F I.193.1; H 2:17a]

Verba oris insipientis grata et labia sapientis praecipitabunt eum. [F III.167.1; H 38:9; 1349 II.137]

Verum etiam senior, cum pontificali ministerio sufficere non posset, Alexandrum, qui dum esset etiam episcopus alterius loci, diuina dispensatione, in adiutorium Narcissi senis euidentissimis rationibus euocauit. [F I .159.2; H 1:17b]

Victimam pro peccato comedunt ipsi et omne uotum in Israel, et omnia libamenta ex omnibus quae offeruntur sacerdotum et primitiua ciborum. [F III.131.2; H 2:11b; 1349 III.11]

Vides quia sacra loca non liberant, sed culpa temeritatis accusat. [F III.310.7; H 18:8g]

Vidua electa est si fuerit operis boni testimonium habens, si filios educauit, si hospitalis, etc. [F II.155.3; H 45:7c]

Viduae adulescentulae quae corpore debiles sunt de sumptu ecclesiae sustententur. [F II.155.6; H 45:8]

Viduae quae ex stipendio ecclesiae sustentantur ita assiduae in Dei opere esse debent quae meritis et orationibus suis ecclesiam adiuuent. [F II.155.7; H 45:7e]

Vir siue mulier in quibus pithonicus uel diuinationis spiritus fuerit, morte moriatur: lapidibus obruent eos, sanguis eorum sit super eos. [F III.329; H 44:3]

Virginitas ecclesiae pulchritudo, ornamentum religionis, sanctimoniae caput, flos pudicitiae, uitae ingressus, sobrietatis custos, innocentiae auctrix, amica iustitiae, eradicatrix uitiorum, libidinum uictrix. [F II.122; H 45:1; 1349 IV.75]

Vnaquaeque mulier sequatur uirum suum siue in uita siue in morte. [F III.307.3; H 18:1d]

Vt ea quae illata sunt uel fuerint ecclesiis uel titulis, nullus exinde subtrahere praesumat.[F III.113; H 27:8]

Vt episcopus gubernationem uiduarum ac peregrinorum non per seipsum, sed per archipresbyterum aut per archidiaconum regat. [F III.86; H 1:10g]

Vt episcopus non longe ab ecclesia, tantum propter susceptionem pauperum, hospitiolum habeat. [F III.72.1; H 1:10a]

Vt in peregrinatione mittantur et ibi ministrare sub manu abbatis. [F II.95; H 11:3]

Vt mihi uidetur effundens sanguinem et praebens ducatum barbaris simili condicione punietur. [F III; H 59:1a; 1349 VI.292]

Vt quod testficauerint uiui super mortuo, ab haeredibus detur, ne in peccatum fiat mortuo. [F III.323.2; H 16:10c]

Vt sacerdos non accipiat munera iniquorum quorum conscientiam non nouerit. [F III.300.1; H 2:22a; 1349 II.14]

A MONASTIC FLORILEGIUM FROM THE *COLLECTIO CANONUM HIBERNENSIS* AT MONTECASSINO[1]

In two classic articles of 1899 and 1915 Paul Fournier stressed the importance of canons from the *Collectio canonum hibernensis* (hereafter CCH) in the south Italian *Collection in Five Books* (hereafter Coll 5L) and its derivatives.[2] These canons derive from the form of the CCH called the B recension, a recension known in southern Italy in the early Middle Ages.[3] With the publication in 1970 of Mario Fornasari's edition of the first three books of the Coll 5L,[4] it is now clear that more than 330 canons in those books alone are drawn from the CCH either directly or through previous or nearly contemporary collections.[5] It has even been maintained — perhaps excessively — that in southern Italy

1. Research for this article was conducted for the program Monumenta Liturgica Beneventana supported by the Social Sciences and Humanities Research Council of Canada. I am grateful for the help of Don Faustino Avagliano, O.S.B., who kindly gave permission to publish material from the Montecassino manuscripts cited in this article, and for the support of the George William Cottrell Jr. Membership in the School of Historical Studies at the Institute for Advanced Study, Princeton.

2. 'De l'influence de la collection irlandaise sur la formation des collections canoniques,' *Nouvelle revue historique de droit français et étranger* 23 (1899) 27-78; repr. in *Mélanges de droit canonique*, ed. T. Kölzer (Aalen, 1983) 2.93-144; and 'Un groupe de recueils canoniques italiens des xe et xie siècles,' *Mémoires de l'Institut National de France de l'Académie des Inscriptions et Belles-Lettres* 40 (Paris, 1916) pp. 95-213; repr. in *Mélanges de droit canonique*, 2.213-331.

3. On the different recensions see my 'The *Collectio canonum hibernensis* and its Influence in the Early Middle Ages,' *The History of Western Canon Law to 1000*, eds. W. Hartmann and K. Pennington (*History of Western Canon Law*: Washington, D. C., in press since 1993).

4. M. Fornasari, *Collectio Canonum in V libris (Lib. i-iii)* (*Corpus Christianorum, Continuatio mediaevalis* 6; Turnhout, 1970).

5. Among these collections might be the *Collection in Nine Books* in Vatican, *Biblioteca Apostolica Vaticana*, Vat. lat. 1349 (saec. xi^{med}; southern Italy) which appears to have been a source of the Coll 5L or the extracts from the CCH in Vatican, *Biblioteca Apostolica Vaticana*, Archivio San Pietro H 58 (1000, Rome), with its Beneventan-script symptoms, on which see my 'Excerpta from the Collectio hibernensis in three Vatican manuscripts,' *Bulletin of Medieval Canon Law*, NS 5 (1975) 4-9. For a list of these canons from Books I-III of the Coll 5L, see my 'The Transmission of the Hibernensis in Italy: Tenth to the Twelfth Century,' *Peritia: Journal of the Medieval Academy of Ireland* 14 (2000) 38-50.

of the late tenth and early eleventh century the CCH was *the* 'national' or at least 'regional' collection, not unlike the *Collectio Vetus Gallica* was for Merovingian times or the *Collectio Hispana* for Spain.[6]

It has generally been said that there remain three manuscripts of the CCH in southern Italy : ROME, *Biblioteca Vallicelliana* Tom. XVIII, MONTECASSINO, *Archivio dell'Abbazia* 297, and MONTECASSINO, *Archivio dell'Abbazia* 439.[7] Pride of place among them has always gone to the south Italian manuscript, ROME, *Biblioteca Vallicelliana* Tom. XVIII, written in the eleventh century in both Romanesca and Beneventan scripts.[8] Like an earlier ninth-century Breton manuscript, OXFORD, *Bodleian Library*, Hatton 42,[9] the Vallicelliana manuscript contains the longer text of the B recension of the CCH. A partial manuscript of the same form is found in an eleventh-century codex in Beneventan script at MONTECASSINO, *Archivio dell'Abbazia* 297.[10] It is probable that this manuscript at one time contained substantially more or even the complete text of the CCH. At the beginning of the CCH, there is a list of sixty-eight books, corresponding to the list in the Vallicelliana manuscript, but the text of the CCH itself breaks off after a quire on p. 248 (*De elimosina*). This break was noted even in the Middle Ages, since a medieval scribe has entered the word 'actenus' in the table of contents on p. 206 next to the book entitled *De elimosina*. Where the missing folios went is unknown. At present, the manuscript is in rather poor condition with folios and quires either loose or about to fall out of the binding. It is interesting to compare the texts of the CCH in the Vallicelliana and Montecassino manuscripts. Often the scribe of the former misunderstood the text from which he was copying and made mistakes of spelling and grammar as well as haplography. Since the scribe wrote in a Romanesca hand heavily influenced by the Beneventan script — even slipping into Beneventan script at times — one wonders what type of exemplar he was using. Perhaps it was one writ-

6. See my 'The Transmission of the Hibernensis in Italy', 35.

7. Ibid., pp. 25-27.

8. See my 'Odilo and the treuga Dei in southern Italy : a Beneventan manuscript fragment,' *Mediaeval Studies* 46 (1984) 454, n. 25.

9. OXFORD, *Bodleian Library*, Hatton 42 (saec. IX$^{1 \text{ and med}}$: BISCHOFF; saec. IX^{2} : Bieler; saec. IX-X : KER; Brittany, later at Worcester).

10. On this manuscript see E. A. LOEW, *The Beneventan Script. A History of the South Italian Minuscule*, 2nd edit. prepared and enlarged by Virginia BROWN, (*Sussidi eruditi* 34 : Rome 1980) [hereafter TBS] 2.80 f. Parts of the manuscript, especially the *De temporum ratione* of Bede (pp. 138-203), the CCH (pp. 204-248), and the *Breviarium* of Festus (pp. 249-264) were probably written at Montecassino since the flesh-side folios have rubbing of the writing characteristic of eleventh-century codices written at the abbey.

ten in a northern script such as an Insular or Merovingian model that the scribe had difficulty in reading. The scribe of the Montecassino codex written entirely in Beneventan script, on the other hand, presents a superior text.

The third codex said to have texts of the CCH is another manuscript at Montecassino, *Archivio dell'Abbazia* 439. The texts cited as having been drawn from the CCH are on pp. 256-260 (= fols. 129v-131v)[11] and deal with monks and monastic discipline, a subject appropriate for a manuscript kept in the monastery of Montecassino. While this may be appropriate, the manuscript itself was almost certainly not written there. In his description of the manuscript Don Mauro Inguanez, following Ambrogio Amelli and E. A. Loew,[12] opted for an Apulian origin of the manuscript and correctly noted that pp. 212, 251, 257-60 are copied in the form of Beneventan script known as the Bari type written in Apulia.[13] Beyond this script there are other indications that point to origins in northern Apulia, and more specifically the area of Siponto. On pp. 244-248 there are a number of letters extracted from the *Registrum* of Gregory I to individuals in Siponto.[14] There is also a letter on pp. 222-27 by the grammarian Petrus to Eusebius of Siponto, and one on pp. 249-51 by the grammarian Guiselgardus to Eusebius of Siponto.[15] On p. 135 there is a text mentioning Monte Gargano and nearby Siponto :

> Cum plures nostri latini grecique auctores aiunt Diomedem ad Italiam delatum a dauno officio exceptum, in Apulia iuxta Garganum montem oppidum condidisse quod patrio nomine Argosippon nominavit eaque urbs corrupto nomine Argiripa...

On p. 176 there is a formula mentioning ships and maritime matters, perhaps appropriate to Siponto.[16] And finally on p. 284 there is an

---

11. The manuscript, as well as having the page numbers in pencil by Don Mauro Inguanez, has another set(s) of foliation/paginated numbers in ink that are by no means consistent.

12. A. Amelli, *Spicilegium Casinense, complectens Analecta Sacra et Profana e Codd. Casinensibus aliarumque bibliothecarum collecta atque edita cura et studio monachorum S. Benedicti archicoenobii Montis Casini.* I (Montecassino, 1888) lxxxvi; and TBS 1.330.

13. M. Inguanez, *Codicum Casinensium Manuscriptorum Catalogus* III.1 (Montecassino, 1940) 55.

14. Four Epistolae to Felix of Siponto (*Registrum* I.51; III.41; III.42; IV.17; *Corpus Christianorum Series Latina* [hereafter CCSL] 140.64 f., 186 f., 235 f.), and one to Vitalianus of Siponto (*Registrum* VIII. 8; CCSL 140A.525 f.)

15. *Spicilegium Casinense* I.386-393, 394 f.

16. *Spicilegium Casinense* I.365 (formula IX).

Oratio Eugenii episcopi : ... followed by what Amelli called 'Versus Petri seu Guiselgardi Grammatici' beginning with the words : *Suscipe Eusebi Siponti clara lucerna* ...[17] The influence of Byzantium along the Apulian coast is also suggested by the list of Roman and Byzantine emperors[18] and the name of a scribe in Greek letters, 'Ego Madelbertos.'[19]

The manuscript, which was written by numerous hands and is palimpsested at some points,[20] is variously dated from the early tenth to early eleventh century, although the later tenth century is more accurate for most of the hands.[21] At what time the manuscript came to Montecassino is not clear, although a modern hand at the beginning of the manuscript notes that it is 'Theobaldian'.[22] While the date of the writing largely predates Theobald, it is conceivable that the manuscript was one that Theobald brought from San Liberatore to Montecassino when he became abbot.[23]

Our Montecassino manuscript from Apulia is a small-sized (212 x 135 mm.) vast vademecum of useful texts, most of which are described in the catalogue of Inguanez.[24] They include several glossaria, formulae, a text

17. Ibid., I. 406 f. Amelli points out that this *oratio* is found in the *Opera Alcuini,* PL 101.1397. See *Opuscula. S. Eugenii,* PL 87.359. Seven verses are in the *Carmina dubia* of Bede, PL 94.638.

18. pp. 273-76.

19. p. 269, on which see TBS 1.330.

20. E.g., pp. 141, 196, 197, 254, 255, 256, 257, 258, 259, 277, 292. There is also a small support gutter in a Beneventan hand of the eleventh century around pp. 1 and 16 containing Daniel 4 : 22, 29; 5 : 7-8, on which see V. Brown, 'A Second New List of Beneventan Manuscripts (III),' *Miscellanea beneventana VIII, Mediaeval Studies* 56 (1994) 346 f. This support gutter, as well as many others in the manuscripts of Montecassino come from a Bible, whose major portions are found in Montecassino, Archivio dell'Abbazia Compactiones I, that is the subject of a forthcoming study by Virginia Brown. These support gutters are the remnants of flyleaves now in the Compactiones at Montecassino that were left when the larger 'recycled' folios were removed as flyleaves and the manuscripts they were used to support were rebound.

21. See TBS, 2.86. On the flyleaf of the manuscript is a note 'saec. x (E.A.L.)'. Virginia Brown would also date most of the hands to the later tenth century and would locate the them to northern Apulia.

22. A pastedown on the flyleaf notes : 'Codex Sign. numo 439, alias 557 in octavo membranaceus characteribus Longobardis seculi xi. tempore Theobaldi Abbatis Casinensis. Memoratur in Codice 28, pag. 585.' Codex 28 contains Augustine's *De civitate Dei* and was written in the time of Theobald.

23. See TBS, 1.80 f. on the codices Theobald brought with him, although the list of manuscripts does not seem to contain the contents of MS 439. It is interesting that on the early modern parchment binding of the manuscript one can make out the number 1023 twice in faint hands, and one wonders if that might be related to the date of Theobald's coming to Montecassino and hence led someone to think of a 'Theobaldian' origin for the codex.

24. The manuscript at one time contained even more texts since the first quire of the manuscript is numbered as IIII. Despite its great multiplicity of texts the manuscript is described on its spine simply as 'Vocabularium Rabbani de vestibus sacerdotalibus et alia,' (a reference to the abbreviated text on pp. 201 f. on vestments from

on orthography, homilies of Gregory I and snippets from his *Dialogues*, a text on the eight tones, *sententiae morales*, snippets from the *Vitas patrum,* a list of Roman and Byzantine emperors from Augustus to Justinianus minor, the *Martyrologium Erchemperti,* and various prayers.

Especially notable are the many canonical texts scattered throughout the manuscript : the *Exemplum Fidei Nicenae* with the creed of the I Council of Nicea and the canons of that council;[25] the Isidorian *Epistula ad Massonam* on lapsed clerics,[26] a capitulary of Theodosius of Oria to his presbyters with ten canons;[27] the letter cited earlier from

---

Rabanus Maurus, *De institutione clericorum,* I. 14-22 : on which see D. ZIMPEL, *Hrabanus Maurus. De institutione clericorum libri tres. Studien und Edition* (*Freiburger Beiträge zur mittelalterlichen Geschichte* 7; Frankfurt am Main, Berlin, Bern, New York, Paris, Vienna, 1996) pp. 309-15 ff; and on p. 3 as 'Rabbanus diuarii vocabulis'. The manuscript has been the subject of many recent studies, including J. BOE, 'Hymns and Poems at Mass in Eleventh-Century Southern Italy (Others than Sequences)' in *Trasmissione e recezione delle forme di cultura musicale. III. Free Papers.* (Turin, 1990) 520 n. 39, 540 f.; G. BRAGA, 'Eugenio Vulgario' in *Dizionario biografico degli italiani* 43 (Rome, 1993) 506; N. CILENTO, *Pluralismo ed Unità del Medioevo Cassinese (Secoli IX-XII)*, ed. F. AVAGLIANO (Montecassino, 1998) 205, 233; M. DELL'OMO, 'La Regola vissuta : consuetudini monastiche e cultura spirituale a Montecassino tra alto e basso medioevo' in *I Fiori e' Frutti santi. S. Benedetto, la Regola, la santità nelle testimonianze dei manoscritti cassinesi* (Milan, 1998) 52; M. FERRARI 'Scrittura e biblioteche,' in *Milano e la Lombardia in età comunale (secoli XI-XIII)* (Milan, 1993) 131, n. 13; H. HOFFMANN, 'Das Fragment einer karolingischen oder ottonischen Briefsammlung,' *Deutsches Archiv* 50 (1994) 148, n. 7; R. KLIBANSKY and F. REGAN, *Die Handschriften der philosophischen Werke des Apuleius. Ein Beitrag zur Überlieferungsgeschichte (Abhandlungen der Akademie der Wissenschaften in Göttingen. Philologisch-Historische Kl. 3. Folge :* Göttingen, 1993) 40; J.-M. MARTIN, 'Le rôle de l'Église de Naples dans le Midi. À propos de deux assemblées ecclésiastiques du IXe siècle et de leurs actes,' in *Mélanges de l'École française de Rome. Moyen Âge — temps modernes* 107 (1995) 39 n. 3, and 40; G. OROFINO, *Codici decorati dell'Archivio di Montecassino I, Il secoli VIII-X* (Rome, 1994) 30, 37, n. 181; G. OROFINO, 'Miniatura in Capitanata. Bilancio e prospettive di un ricerca,' in *Capitanata medievale*, ed. M. STELLA, C. MARRIANI (Foggia, 1998) 203; G. OROFINO, 'Miniatura in Puglia agli inizi dell'XI secolo : l'Omiliario VI B 2 della Biblioteca Nazionale di Napoli,' *Miniatura* 3-4 (1991) 21 n. 4; M. PALMA, 'Ausilio Prete,' 'Flosculi,' 'Glossari latini' and 'Glossario latino' in *Virgilio e il chiostro. Manoscritti dei autori classici e civiltà monastica*, ed. M. DELL'OMO (Rome, 1996) 136, 139; P. RADICIOTTI, 'Manoscritti digrafici grecolatini e latinogreci nell'alto medioevo,' in *Römische historische Mitteilungen* 40 (1998) 101, n. 110; M. REUTER, *Metodi illustrativi nel medioevo. Testo e immagine nel codice 132 di Montecassino « Liber Rabani de originibus rerum »* (Naples, 1993) 42, n. 103; A. STRAMAGLIA, 'Apuleio come auctor : premesse tardoantiche di un uso umanistico,' *Studi umanistici piceni* 16 (1996) 146; and the forthcoming descriptions by B. M. TARQUINI, *I codici grammaticali in Scrittura Beneventana* (Montecassino) 45-54 (dependent on the present article for canonistic citations); and G. N. VERRANDO, *Bibliotheca Hagiographica Latina Manuscriptorum Bibliothecae Casinensis* (Montecassino).

25. pp. 186-88, PL 21.472-75.

26. pp. 240-44. On this text see my 'The « Isidorian » *Epistula ad Massonam* on Lapsed Clerics : Notes on the Early Manuscript and Textual Transmission,' in *Grundlagen des Rechts : Festschrift für Peter Landau,* eds. R. HELMHOLZ, P. MIKAT, J. MÜLLER, and M. STOLLEIS (Paderborn, 2000) 77-92.

27. pp. 203-208 : ed. in *Spicilegium Casinense* I. 377-81. On this text see H. MORDEK, *Kirchenrecht und Reform im Frankenreich : Die Collectio Vetus Gallica, die älteste*

Peter the Grammarian to Eusebius of Siponto with the texts of 22 canons,[28] texts of Roman synods of Gregory I and Gregory II;[29] the *De remediis peccatorum* attributed to Egbert of York;[30] a text attributed to pope Telesphorus on fasting during penitential seasons;[31] another reflecting the *Regula* of Chrodegang of Metz or the *Episcoporum ad Hludowicum imperatorem relatio* disapproving of a Mass said by a single priest;[32] a text from the Council of Vaison on excommunicates;[33] three canons annexed to the letters of Gregory;[34] a text attributed to Pope Stephan VI on foods and feastdays in a monastic community;[35] decretals of Innocent and Gelasius,[36] and a text on Jews and Christians in a letter of Gregory I to Bishop Fortunatus of Naples.[37]

---

systematische Kanonessammlung des fränkischen Gallien : Studien und Edition (*Beiträge zur Geschichte und Quellenkunde des Mittelalters* 1 : Berlin, New York, 1975) 105 n. 29, and W. HARTMANN, *Die Synoden der Karolingerzeit im Frankenreich und in Italien* (*Konziliengeschichte, Reihe A : Darstellung* : Paderborn, Munich, Vienna, Zürich, 1989) 356.

28. pp. 222-37; ed. AMELLI, *Spicilegium Casinense* I. 386-93 and lxxxviii, 390, where Amelli points out that c. 9 may pertain to the northern Apulian region, such as Siponto, that had been devastated by the Saracens in the ninth century. On this text see MORDEK, *Kirchenrecht*, pp. 205 f., nn. 35, 37, and HARTMANN, *Synoden*, p. 355.

29. pp. 213-17 and 217-222; on which see MGH Epist. I, Berlin 1891, pp. 362-66; and PL 67.341-44.

30. pp. 237-40; cf. H. WASSERSCHLEBEN, *Die Bußordnungen der abendländischen Kirche* (Halle, 1851, repr. Graz, 1958) 231-33 and 249 f., and H. J. SCHMITZ, *Die Bußbücher und die Bußdisciplin der Kirche*, 2 vols. (Mainz, 1883 and Düsseldorf, 1898; repr. Graz, 1958) 2.661-63.

31. p. 252; ed. *Spicilegium Casinense* I. 395-96, where a parallel text is printed from the Pseudo-Isidorian Decretals (cf. PL. 130.103 or P. HINSCHIUS, *Decretales Pseudo-Isidorianae et Capitula Angilramni* (Leipzig, 1863; repr. Aalen, 1963), 109. A closer parallel text is found in the *Collectio canonum Remedio Curiensi episcopo perperam ascripta* c. 28, ed. H. JOHN, (*Monumenta Iuris Canonici, ser. B : Corpus collectionum 2*; Vatican City, 1976) 152.

32. p. 254, cf. J.-B. PELT, *Étude sur la cathédrale de Metz*, IV.1 (Metz, 1937) c. 77; and *MGH, Legum Sectio II, Capitularia regum francorum*, eds. A. BORETIUS and V. KRAUSE (Hannover, 1890) II.1, p. 41 nr. (43) IX. Cf. PL 97.618.

33. p. 254; c. 6, CCSL 148.98 f.

34. pp. 248 f.; ed. *Spicilegium Casinense* I. 393 f. The first canon is c. 43 of the Council of Auxerre (561-605), CCSL 148A.270. The third canon can be found in the decretals of Innocent I, c. 19, PL 56.525, PL 84.648, and PL 88.880.

35. p. 209; ed. *Spicilegium Casinense* I. lxxxvii, 381 f. Amelli points out that the text mentioning 'nostro fideli episcopo Zacchariae' (bishop of Anagni) accords with the time of Stephan VI (885-91) and notes its affinity with a letter 'ad Lambertum Cenomanensem' by Stephan VI (887) (PL 129.807).

36. p. 210; ed. *Spicilegium Casinense*. I.382. Amelli printed these because he did not find the letter of Innocent. The second text is attributed to Felix pp. in the manuscript, although probably Gelasius was meant, as can be seen in PL 67.306.

37. p. 196. Gregory I to Fortunatus of Naples; see *Registrum* IX.105; CCSL 140A.657 f. This text finds a resonance in c. 3 of the council following the letter of Peter the Grammarian to Eusebius of Siponto on p. 228.

Of special interest as they touch on the CCH and the Coll 5L are three sections of the manuscript, the first two indirectly related to the CCH and Coll 5L, and the third containing texts clearly drawn from the CCH. The first section with canons is on pp. 191-92. These texts were published in the *Spicilegium Casinense* I.371-72 by Amelli, but he did not connect these texts specifically with the CCH or 5L :[38]

> (p. 191) <1> Scire nos oportet quia sex sunt sinodi. Primo in Nicea civitate trecentorum decem et octo patrum tempore Constantini maioris sub Iulio papa contra Arrium presbiterum Alexandrie, dicebat enim creaturam esse Filium Dei et quia fuit aliquando non erat Filius cum Patre et quia non consubstantialis Deo patri. Secunda synodus facta est in Constantinopolim sub Theodosio maiore imperatore centum quinquaginta patrum sub Damaso papa contra Macedonium patriarcham Constantinopolitanum, dicebat enim creaturam esse Spiritum sanctum et non consubstantialem Patri et Filio. Tertia sinodus in Efeso ducentorum patrum sub Theodosio iuniore imperatore et papa Celestino contra Nestorium impium patriarcham Constantynopolitanum, dicebat enim solummodo hominem dominum Iesum Christum et non Deum verum, unde nec Dei genitricem sanctam Mariam esse, et quaternitatem pro trinitatem colebat. Quarta synodus in Calcedona civitate sub Marciano imperatore dcxxx. patrum sub Leone papa contra Dioscorum patriarcham Alexandrie et Euticen archimandritam qui unam naturam per incarnationem dicebant habere dominum Iesum Christum addentes et Deitatem passam fuisset. Quinta synodus item Constantinopolim sub Iustiniano maiore imperatore centum quinquaginta patrum tempore Vigilii pape contra Originem et Evagrium et Didimum, impiissimum impiissimos et omnes ereticos, dicebant enim non resurget caro nostra et quia non est paradysus factus a Deo et finem habent pene impiorum et demones ut prius angeli existant. Sexta sinodus facta est Constantinopolim sub Constantino imperatore, patre Iustiniani novi imperatoris clxx. patrum contra Sergium, Pirrum, Paulum et Petrum patriarcham Constantinopolitanum et Cirum patriarcham Alexandrie et eorum similes, dicebant enim unam voluntatem et unam operationem habere Dominum nostrum Iesum Christum post incarnationem. Hec est sexta synodus universalis Constantinopolim celebrata et greco sermone conscripta tempore pape Agathonis exequente hac residente piissimo principe Constantino intra palatium suum simulque legatis apostolice sedis et episcopis clxx. residentibus. (*in marg.* vii. sub adri// et pp. et consta//no he//filio proi//im//nibus.)
> <2> Sinodus Romana. Si quis semedipsum abscidit, id est si quis suo consilio sibi amputavit, non fiat episcopus set etiam nec clericus qui sui homocida est et Dei condic<t>ionis inimicus.
> <3> Innocenti pp. Quidam aut tormenta sola exercuerunt aut etiam capitalem sententiom (sic) protulerunt a Deo enim scimus potestate

38. The texts are here numbered with < > for later reference.

concessas et propterea vindicatam noxiet hac omniumque fuisse pro missum et Dei esse ministrum vindicem huiusmodi dictum datum. Debemus ergo observare ne aut disciplinam evertere aut contra auctoritatem Domini venisse videamur. Ipsi autem in ratione reddenda gesta sua conservabunt omnia apostolatus et episcopatus primo per apostolum cepit Petrum. Sicut penitentiam (p. 192) agere cuiquam non conceditur clericorum, ita et post penitudinem nonnulli umquam laico liceat honorem clericatus adipisci, quia quamvis sint omnium peccatorum contagione mundati, nulla tamen debent sacramentorum instrumenta suscipere, qui dudum fuerint vasa vitiorum.
<4> Sancti Leonis pape. Secundum grecos in quarta propinquitate carnis licet nubere sicut in lege scriptum est. Secundum Romanos in quinta tamen in quarta non solvunt coniugium postquam factum fuerit. In tertia propinquitate non licet uxorem alterius accipere post eius obitum. Idem. Alienum est a consuetudine ecclesiastica ut qui in presbyteralem honorem aut diaconii gradum fuerint consecrati, manus impositionem remedium accipiant penitendi, qui sine dubio ex apostolica traditione descendit. Secundum quod scriptum est : Sacerdos si peccaverit, quis orabit pro illo? Unde huiusmodi lapsis ad promerendam misericordiam Dei privata est expetenda secessio, illa satisfactio si fuerit digna sit etiam fructuosa.
<5> Gelasius papa ad Faustum. Sancta Romana sedes de omni ecclesia iudicat et ipsa a nemine iudicatur. Duo sunt quippe quibus principaliter mundus hic regitur, auctoritas sacrata pontificum et regalis potestas, in quibus tanto gravius pondus est sacerdotum quando etiam pro ipsis regibus redditura est rationem.
<6> Sinodus Anthiocena ait propter utilitates ecclesiasticas et absolutiones earum rerum, que dubietatem controversiamque recipiunt, optime placuit, ut pro singulas quasque provincias, bis in anno episcoporum concilia celebrentur. Semel quidem post tertiam septimanam festi Paschalis, ita ut quarta septimana Pentecostes conveniat synodus, metropolitano provinciales episcopos ammonente. Secunda vero synodus fiad (sic) idibus octimbribus (sic), idest quinto decimo die mensis octimbris (sic). In ipsis autem conciliis assint presbiteri, diacones, et omnes qui se lesos existimant et synodi experiatur examen. Nullis vero liceat aput se celebrare concilia preter eos quibus metropolitana iura videntur esse commissa, inter cetera concilia quattuor esse, venerabiles synodos comperimus, que totam principaliter fidem complectuntur, quasi quattuor evangelia, vel todidem paradysi flumina. Harum prior Nicena synodus, secunda Constantinopolitana, tertia Ephesina, quarta Calcedonensis.

The first of these texts resembles the description of the early ecumenical councils found in the CCH and the Coll 5L.[39] There they are based on the *Etymologies* of Isidore, but here there are six councils de-

39. Rome, *Biblioteca Vallicelliana* Tom. XVIII, fol. 58v; Montecassino, *Archivio dell'Abbazia* 125, p. 4.

scribed reflecting the description of the councils in Bede's *De ratione temporum.*[40] In the Montecassino codex it is interesting that in the margin there is a description of the seventh ecumenical council, although this had been mutilated when the pages of the manuscript were trimmed in rebinding. The second text, attributed to a Sinodus Romana, is in both the CCH 1.22 and the Coll 5L 1.81(F.139).[41] The third text is attributed to Pope Innocent, although the latter part of the canon, anonymous but issuing from Pope Siricius, is found in canonical collections known in southern Italy.[42] The fourth text attributed to Pope Leo contains two disparate subjects, one of which is not related directly to the CCH or Coll 5L, but the second reflecting the Coll 5L. The first part, on degrees of consanguinity in marriage and the difference in the Greek and Roman positions on this subject, reflects the Penitential of Theodore of Canterbury.[43] The second part, a text of Leo I on the penance of clerics, is reflected in the Coll 5L 2.81.[44] The fifth text, *Duo sunt quippe*, of Gelasius I is here said to be addressed to Faustus, not the emperor Anastasius, and is not found in the CCH or Coll 5L. The incorrect attribution to Faustus may have arisen from the proximity of texts of Gelasius to Faustus and to Anastasius in various collections. [45] The sixth and final text in this florilegium of canonical material on pp. 191-192 is very closely related to the CCH and Coll 5L. The text of the Antiochene synod is found in the preface to the CCH in Vallicelliana Tom. XVIII and in the Coll 5L

---

40. Bede's *De temporum ratione* c. 66, CCSL 123B.528.

41. ROME, *Biblioteca Vallicelliana* Tom. XVIII, fol. 61v; and MONTECASSINO, *Archivio dell'Abbazia* 125, p. 41.

42. The first part of the canon is found in Innocent's Epistula ad Exsuperium Tolosanum in the *Collectio Dionysiana*, PL 67.247 and the *Decretales Pseudo-Isidorianae*, Hinschius, p. 532. The second part of the canon, 'omnia apostolatus .. cepit Petrum » resembles a canon of Innocent, Epistula ad Victoricum Rotomagensis in the *Collectio Dionysiana*, PL 67.241 or Siricius's Epistle to the African bishops in the *Decretales Pseudo-Isidorianae*, PL 130.687. The third part of the canon is from Siricius, Epistula ad Eumerium Tarraconensem, c. 14, in the *Collectio Dionysiana*, PL 67.837 and the *Decretales Pseudo-Isidorianae*, Hinschius, p. 522. On manuscripts of these collections in southern Italy, see my « *Canonistica Beneventana,* » *Proceedings of the Ninth International Congress of Medieval Canon Law, Munich, 13-18 Juli 1992,* eds. P. LANDAU and J. MÜLLER (*Monumenta Iuris Canonici, Ser. C, Subsidia* : Vatican, 1997), 21-40.

43. See PL 99.934. The concern with consanguinity is reflected in c. 15 of the canons following the letter of Peter the Grammarian to Eusebius of Siponto on p. 233 of the codex. The canon from Leo I, Epistula ad Rusticum Narbonensem, c. 2, is found in the *Collectio Dionysiana*, PL 67.288, and the *Decretales Pseudo-Isidorianae*, HINSCHIUS, p. 616

44. MONTECASSINO, *Archivio dell'Abbazia* 125, p. 41.

45. PL 56.634. The canon is actually directed to Anastasius Imperator but in the first line is the name of Faustus, and this canon is preceded by on 'Cuius supra Fausto magistro,' on which see the *Decretales Pseudo-Isidorianae*, HINSCHIUS, pp. 637, 639.

2.5.[46] The text following this on the four ecumenical synods is drawn from Isidore's *Etymologies* and is found in part in the preface to the CCH in Vallicelliana Tom. XVIII.[47]

The second section of the manuscript with a canon related to the CCH is on p. 194. The text is written in a hand of the first half of the eleventh century that is Beneventan but that does not follow all of the Beneventan-script rules :

> Dixit abbas pastor : Qui querellosus est monachus non est; qui fratri suo detraut (sic) monachus non est; qui malum pro malo redit monachus non est; qui <i>racundus est monachus non est; qui elatus est aut verbosus monachus non est. Qui autem vere est monachus semper est humilis et quietus et caritate plenus, e<t> timorem Dei semper pre oculis habet etiam in corde suo custodit.

The text itself is a form of one found in the *Vitas patrum*,[48] but it is interesting that portions of the same text are used in the B version of the CCH and are found in the excerpta of the CCH in the third section of the manuscript drawn more directly from the CCH.

This third section of the Montecassino manuscript often cited as containing excerpts of the CCH appears on the palimpsested pp. 256-260.[49] It follows a portion of a homily of Gregory I on Ezechiel on p. 255[50] and is written above the lower text of a glossary in two columns.[51] Again, the texts on pp. 256-260 were published by Amelli in the *Spicilegium Casinense* I.397-98, as an 'Excerpta ex patribus et conciliis de monacis,' but again, like Inguanez in his later catalogue, he did not comment on its relation to the CCH.[52] Since the excerpts are rather short, it is appropriate to print them here because of their rela-

46. Rome, *Biblioteca Vallicelliana* Tom. XVIII, 59r; Montecassino, *Archivio dell'Abbazia* 125, p. 41.
47. Rome, *Biblioteca Vallicelliana* Tom. XVIII, fol. 59r.
48. Cf. PL 73.922 and 74.391.
49. The complete latter section of the quaternion, including pp. 254-60 numbered as quire XVIII, has been erased. The fact that the conjugate pages earlier in the quire have not been palimpsested suggests the palimpsesting of the latter part of the quire took place after the quaternion was bound either as a quire or into a manuscript. This further suggests that the text on monks from the CCH was important enough to the users of the manuscript to have led to the time-consuming task of erasing of the lower text. The manuscript, now bound in an early modern off-white parchment binding of saec. XVII/XVIII, has been bound at least twice to judge by the two sets of binding holes in the quires.
50. Lib. I, hom. 9. CCSL 142.134, Hii namque ... auditu iustus erat ha...
51. The glossary begins with the words 'Incipit summule? Daniehelis prophete...' with a short introduction. There then follow in two columns words beginning with A and B, after each of which is 'sig' (=significat?). On p. 257 words beginning with Q appear and on p. 259 words with S.
52. Inguanez, p. 54.

tion to the CCH and the Coll 5L. The first thing one notices about the texts is that they are clearly drawn from the B version of the CCH, such as is found in Vallicelliana Tom. XVIII. The texts with their parallels in the Vallicelliana codex can be found in the first column of the table below. A comparison of this text with the A recension edited by Wasserschleben from St. Gall, *Stiftsbibliothek*, 243 (saec.IX[1]; St. Gall) and found below in the third column, clearly illustrates the substantial difference between the two recensions. But the texts in the Montecassino codex obviously do not follow the arrangement of the CCH in either the B or A versions of that collection. This may lead one to think that it is not the CCH itself that is being used but another collection from which canons of the CCH are being extracted. But if one looks to other collections whose canons from the CCH are included, there are only two known possibilities, the Coll 9L and the Coll 5L. Although the former is written in a Beneventan hand of the mid eleventh century, the contents of the collection could have been compiled in the tenth century.[53] As for the Coll 5L, the latest canons are those of the Emperor Henry II,[54] which makes the collection as we have it now post-date our Montecassino manuscript. There is a possibility, however, that the Coll 5L was compiled earlier and that the canons of Henry II were added to make what is now the Coll 5L as it has been transmitted in the known manuscripts. If one compares the texts found in our Montecassino manuscript with similar texts in the Coll 5L and Coll 9L, it is surprising to find that the arrangement is almost the same :[55]

MC 439	Coll 5L	Coll 9L
I. (40.3)		4.3
II. (40.4)	2.62 [2.109]	4.4
III. (40.10)	2.64 [2.113]	
IV. (40.5)		
V. (40.9)	2.64 [2.112]	4.7
VI. (40.11)	2.64 [2.114]	4.8
VII. (40.19)	cf. 2.64	4.9
VIII. (40.17)	2.67 [2.116]	4.13

53. On this see my 'South and Central Italian Canonical Collections of the Tenth and Eleventh Centuries (non-Gregorian).'

54. On these canons see my *The Collectio canonum Casinensis duodecim saeculi (Codex terscriptus). A Derivative of the South-Italian Collection in Five Books : An Incipit-Explicit Edition with an Introductory Study* (*Monumenta Liturgica Beneventana* III, *Studies and Texts,* 127; Toronto, 2001), pp. 4 f.

55. In the following comparison, ( ) in the first column = number of the canon in the CCH of Rome, *Biblioteca Vallicelliana* Tom. XVIII; and in the second column the first number is that of the Coll 5L as found in Montecassino 125 and [ ] = number of canon of the Coll 5L in Fornasari's edition.

Nonetheless there are significant differences. Neither the Coll 5L nor the Coll 9L has all of the canons that appear in the Montecassino monastic florilegium. While the Coll 9L has the first canon, which the Coll 5L lacks, neither collection has canon IV. Also, where there are parallels in the texts, the CCH at times has material not contained in the other collections and vice versa. But the arrangement of the canons in the Montecassino codex, not following the sequence of the CCH as it is known in either the A or B recensions, suggests that the florilegium does 'look to' or is an intermediary between the florilegium of monastic canons found in the Coll 9L or the Coll 5L, although clearly the sequence is not perfect. In other words, by the tenth century canons from the CCH were being arranged in florilegia that would eventually be reflected or used in the best-known south Italian collections of the tenth and early eleventh centuries. Hence, what is represented in the Montecassino florilegium of monastic texts consists, as always has been said, of excerpta from the CCH, but, as has not been said before, in a form looking to later compilations based on such collections of excerpta.

In the following table, the first column presents the text of the monastic florilegium in MONTECASSINO 439, noting in [ ] its parallels to the B recension of the CCH as found in the codex, ROME, *Biblioteca Vallicelliana* Tom. XVIII. In the text of the first column the order of canons, orthography, and grammar of the Montecassino manuscript has been maintained, 'ae' has been transcribed as 'e,' and < > represent missing letters in the mutilated manuscript. For ease of citation each canon in the Montecassino florilegium has been assigned a Roman numeral in [ ]. The second column contains the parallel text of the Coll 5L as found in the best manuscript of the collection, MONTECASSINO, *Archivio dell'Abbazia* 125, written at Montecassino in a Beneventan hand of the mid-eleventh century. Parallels with the Coll 9L are also noted in [ ] this column. The third column contains the parallel canons from the CCH as found in the A recension of the text of Wasserschleben's edition.[56]

56. H. WASSERSCHLEBEN, *Die irische Kanonensammlung* (2nd ed. Leipzig, 1885; repr. Aalen 1966) 147-52.

Montecassino 439 [p. 256]	**Text of the Collection in 5 Books With parallels in the Collection in 9 Books**	**CCH Recension A**
[=CCH Recension B; Vall. XL.3]	[cf. 9L 4.3]	[CCH 39.2 b]
[I.] De tribus maculis monachis.		De tribus maculis monachi.
In vita sanctorum : Abbas pastor, qui querellosus est, monachus non est, qui malum pro malo re<d>dit, monachus non est, qui iracundus est, monachus non est.		In uita sanctorum : Dicit abbas pastor, qui querellosus est, monachus non est, qui malum pro malo reddit, monachus non est, qui iracundus est, monachus non est.
[=Vall. XL.4] [II.] De variis generibus monachorum.	[Coll 5L 2.62; MC p. 101] [cf. 9L 4.4] De variis generibus monachorum.	[CCH 39.3] De uariis generibus monachorum.
Hysidorus : Sex genera monachorum sunt, quorum tria optima, reliqua vero deteriora atque omnibus modis evitanda. Primum genus est cenovitarum, id est in commune viventium, ad instar sanctorum illorum, qui tempore apostolorum in Hierusolimis venditis distributisque omnibus indigentibus habitabant in sancta communione vite, non dicentes vel habentes proprium aliquid nihil sed erant illis omnia communia et anima una et cor unum in Deum. Horum institutione sumpsere principia. Secundum genus heremitarum, qui procul ab hominibus recedentes deserta loca et vastas solitudines sequi atque habitare per<hi>bentur, ad imitationem,	Ysidorus. Sex genera monachorum sunt, quorum tria optima, reliqua vero deteriora atque omnimodis evitanda. Primum genus est cenobitarum, id est in communione viventium ad instar sanctorum illorum qui tempore apostolorum Hyerosolimis venditis distributisque omnibus indigentibus habitabant in sancta communi vita, non dicentes vel habentes aliquid proprium, sed erant illis omnia communia et omnia una et cor unum in Deo. Horum institutione monasteria supsere principia. Secundum genus heremitarum qui cum ab hominibus recederent deserta loca atque uastas solitudines sequi atque habitare perhibentur ad imitationem scilicet Helie atque Iohan-	Isidorus ait : Sex genera monachorum sunt, quorum tria optima, reliqua uero deteriora atque omnibus modis euitanda. Primum genus est coenobitarum, id est in commune uiuentium, ad instar sanctorum illorum, qui in tempore apostolorum in Hierusalem uenditis distributisque omnibus indigentibus in sancta communione uitae habitabant, nihil proprium sibi dicentes; sed erant illis omnia communia et anima una et cor unum in Deum. Horum autem institutione monasterica sumpsere principia. Secundum genus est heremitarum, qui procul ab hominibus recedentes deserta loca et uasta solitudinis sequi atque habitare perhibentur, ad imitationem

scilicet Elie atque Iohannis baptiste, qui recessus <her>emi penetraverunt. Hi quippe incredivili mundi contemptu solitudine delectantur, erbis tantum agrestibus victitantes aut pane solo vel aqua contenti, qui eis preceptus per intervalla temporum defertur, sicque secretissimi penitus et ab omnium hominum conspectu remati divino tantum colloquio perfruuntur, cui puris mentibus ineserunt, et propter cuius amorem non solum mundi, sed etiam hominum reliquerunt consortia. Tertium genus est anachoritarum, quia cenoviali conversatione perfecti includunt semetipsos procul in cellulis ab hominum conspectu remotis, nulli ad se prebentes accessum, sed in sola contemplationem viventes perseverant theoria, sed istis de examinatione cenobiorum probati, in omnibus disciplinis monasterii per triginta annos ad hanc contemplationem per obedientiam eliguntur. Quartum genus est eorum, qui anachoritarum imagine blandiuntur, qui, ut Cassianus : Brevi quodam [p. 257] fervore in primordiis suis cenobii perfectionem videntur expetere, sed continuo tepefacti, dum pristinos mores ac vitam resecare contempnunt, nec iugum humilitatis sustinere contenti sunt, subdique maiorum imperio dedignantur, separatas expetunt cellulas et solitarie sedere desiderant, ut a nemine lacessiti mansueti vel humiles estimentur. Quintum ge-

nis baptiste qui recessus heremi penetraverunt.
Hi quippe mundo contempto solitudines delectantur, herbis tantum agrestibus victitantes aut pane solo vel aqua contenti qui eis preceptum per intervalla temporum defertur, sicque secretissimi penitus et ab omni hominum conspectu remoti divino tantum colloquio perfruuntur, cui patri mentibus inheserunt et propter cuius amorem non solum mundi sed etiam hominum reliquerunt consortia. Tertium genus est anachoretarum quia cenobiali conversatione perfecti includunt semetipso procul in cellulis ab omnium conspectu remoti nullius ad se prebentes accessum sed in sole contemplationis viventes perseverantes theorica. Sed isti de examine cenobiorum probati in omnibus disciplinis monasteriorum per XXX annos ad hanc contemplationem per obedientiam eliguntur. Quartum genus est qui anachoritarum imagine blandiuntur qui ut Cassianus brevi quodam fervore in primordiis suis cenobium perfectionis videntur expetere, sed continuo tepefacti dum pristinos mores ac vitia resecare contempnunt nec iugum humilitatis sustinere contenti sunt subdique maiorum imperio dedignantur separatam expetunt cellulam et solitarie sedere desiderant ut a neminem lacessiti, mansueti vel humiles estimentur. Quintum genus est circillionum qui sub habitu monacho-

Helie et Iohannis, qui recessus heremi penetrauerunt. Hi quidem incredibili mundi contemptu sola solitudine delectantur, herbis tantum agrestibus uictitantes aut solo pane et aqua contenti, quod eis per certa interualla temporum defertur, sicque secretissimi penitus et ab omnium hominum conspectibus remoti diuino tantum conloquio perfruuntur, cui puris mentibus inheserunt. Et pro huius amore non solum mundum, sed etiam hominum relinquerunt consortia. Tertium genus est anachoretarum, qui iam coenobiali conuersatione perfecti semetipsos includunt in cellulis, procul a conspectu hominum remotis, nemini ad se prebentes accessum, sed in sola contemplatione theorica uiuentes perseuerant; sed isti de examinatione coenobiorum probati, in omnibus monasterii disciplinis per triginta annos ad hanc contemplationem per oboedientiam eleguntur. Quartum genus est eorum, qui anachoretarum imagine blandiuntur, qui, ut Cassianus dicit, breui quodam feruore in primordiis suis coenobii perfectionem uidentur expetere, sed continuo tepefacti, dum pristinos mores ac uitia recusare contempnunt, nec iugum humilitatis sustinere contenti sunt, subdereque se maiorum imperio dedignantur; separatas expetunt cellulas et solitarie sedere desiderant, ut a nemine lacessiti, mansueti uel humiles aestimentur. Quintum genus

nus est circumcellionum, qui sub habitu monachorum vagantur, circumferentes ypocrisin, circumeuntes provincias, nusquam fixi, nusquam stantes, nusquam sedentes; alii, que non viderunt, confingunt, opiniones sua<s> habentes pro Deo, alii membra martirum et filacteria sua magnificant, gloriam captantes ab hominibus, alii criniti incedunt, ut vilior habeatur tonsa sanctitas, quam comata. Unde videlicet, qui eos viderit, antiquos illos, quos legimus, cogitet, Samuhelem et Heliam et ceteros; alii honores, quos non acceperunt, habere protestantur, alii parentes et consanguineos in illa regione se audisse et venire et pergere mentiuntur. Omnes petunt, omnes exigunt aut sumptum lucro egestatis aut simulate pretium sanctitatis. Sextum genus est et ipsum deterrimum adque neglectum, quod per Ananiam et Safiram in exordio ecclesie pululavit, et apostoli Petri severitate succisum est, quique sarabaite vel rennuite nuncupati sunt. In catalogo : Quattuor genera monachorum dicuntur : Primum heremite, qui nichil commune cum mundo habent, set suum victum suis manibus exquirunt et dona iniquiorum non accipiunt; hi theoricam et actualem vitam continent, alii vero horum [p. 258] victum ab aliis sperant, orationi tantum vacantes. Secundum cenovite qui in commune vivunt ad instar apostolorum fami-

rum vagantur circumferentes hypocrisin, circumientes provincias nusquam missi nusquam fixi, nusquam stantes, nusquam sedentes, [p. 102] alii que non viderunt confingunt opiniones suas habentes pro Deo. Alii membranas martyrum et philacterias suas magnificantes gloriam captantes ab hominibus, alii criniti incedunt ut vilior habeatur tonsura quam comata, unde videlicet qui eos viderint antiquos illos, quos legimus cogitent, Samuhelem scilicet et Heliam et ceteros. Alii honores quos non acceperunt habere protestantur. Alii parentes et consanguineos in illa regione se audisse venire et pergere mentiuntur, omnes petunt omnes exigunt aut sumptu lucro egestatis aut simulatae pretium sanctitatis. Sextum genus est et ipsum teterrimum atque neglectum quod per Ananiam et Saphiram in exordio ecclesie pullulavit et apostoli Petri severitate succisum est, qui sarabaite vel rennuitae nuncupati sunt. In catalogo quattuor genera monachorum dicuntur : Primum heremitae qui nichil commune cum mundo habent, sed suum victum suis manibus exquirunt et dona iniquorum non accipiunt. Hi theoricam et actualem vitam continent. Alii vero horum victum ab aliis sperant, orationi tantum vacantes. Secundum cenobite qui in commune vivunt instar apostolorum familie duplicibus non induuntur, numquam horam vacuam relin-

est circumcellionum, qui sub habitu monachorum usque quaque uagantur, circumferentes hypocrisin, circumeuntes prouincias, nusquam missi, nusquam fixi, nusquam stantes, nusquam sedentes; alii, quae non uiderunt, confingunt, opiniones suas habentes pro Deo, alii membra martyrum uenditant, alii fimbrias et philacteria sua magnificant, gloriam captantes ab hominibus, alii criniti incedunt, ne uilior habeatur tonsa sanctitas, quam comata. Unde uidelicet, qui eos uiderint, antiquos illos, quos legimus, cogitet, Samuhelem et Heliam et ceteros; alii honores, quos non acceperunt, habere se protestantur, alii parentes et consanguineos suos in illa regione se audisse et ad eos pergere mentiuntur. Omnes petunt, omnes exigunt aut sumptum lucrum se egestant aut simulantes sanctitatis pretium. Sextum genus est et ipsum deterrimum atque uitandum, quod per Ananiam et Saphiram in ecclesiae exordio pullulauit, et apostoli Petri seueritate succisum est, quique ab eo, quod semetipsos a coenobii disciplina sequestrant, suas que libere appetunt uoluntates Aegyptiorum lingua "Sarabaite" siue "Rennuite" nuncupati sunt. In catalogo : Quatuor genera monachorum dicuntur : Primum. Heremitae, qui nihil commune cum mundo habent, sed suum uictum manibus suis exquirunt et dona aliorum non recipiunt; hi theoricam ui-

lie duplicibus non induuntur. Numquam horam vacuam relinquunt, sed sive legunt sive orant sive utilitatem proximi faciunt. Tertium genus vagabundi, qui nomen monachi desiderant habere, sed mores abnegant, inter mulierculas discurrunt, fabulas monasteriorum narrant, nullo sub regimine vivunt negotiis secularibus occupati, his magis periculum imminet, quam premium et cavendum his, quod alius dicit : Ve michi peccatori, qui nomen monachi fero. Quartum genus est sarabaite, qui necessaria sua sibi servant; domum in castello in monasterio faciunt, semper honerosi adveniunt, hortum constitutum oleribus habent, quadraginta dies vel ebdomadem in commune monastirii faciunt, totum reliquum tempus suo servitio exigentes; hi graves sermonibus, nichil sibi nisi quod ipsi statuunt placentes; nulli gradui iunguntur, neque monachi neque clerici neque plebiles neque laici. Hieronimus in epistula ad Benedictum : Quattuor genera monachorum dicuntur : Primum cenovitarum, militantium sub regula vel abbate, hoc est optimum genus; Sec...

quunt sed sive legunt sive orant sive utilitatem proximi faciunt. Tertium genus est vagabundi qui nomen monachi desiderant habere sed mores abnegant, inter mulierculas discurrunt, fabulas monasteriorum narrant, nullo sub regimine vivunt, negotiis secularibus occupati his magis periculum imminet quam premium. Et cavendum his quod alius dicit : Ve mihi peccatori qui nomen monachi fero. Quartum genus sarabaite qui necessarie suam sibi servant domum, in castello, in monasterio hoc faciunt, semper onerosi adveniunt, hortum constitutum oleribus habent, XL dies vel ebdomadem in commune monasterio faciunt totum reliquum tempus suo servitio exigente; hi graves sermonibus nichil sibi nisi quod ipsi statuunt placent, nulli gradui iunguntur, neque monachis neque clericis, neque plebeis, neque laicis. Hieronimus in epistola ad Benedictum. Quattuor genera monachorum dicuntur. Primum cenobitarum militantium sub regula vel abbate, hoc genus est optimum. Secundum anachoritarum qui solo brachio vivunt nec favorem plebis accipiunt. Tertium genus qui bini vel quaterni vel qui sine pastore nec accipiunt exemplum seniorum sed dicunt lex Dei est quod videtur illis, hoc genus non parvum criminis habet. Quartum genus girovagum qui hospitantur per provincias de quibus melius est tacere quam loqui. Revertamur ad opti-

tam et actualem continent, alii uero horum uictum ab aliis sperant, orationi tantum uacantes. Secundum, Coenobitae sunt, qui in commune uiuunt in instar apostolorum familiae duplicibus non induuntur. Nunquam horam uacuam relinquunt, sed siue legunt siue orant siue utilitatem proximi faciunt. Tertium genus est uagabundi, qui nomen monachi desiderant habere, sed mores abnegant, inter mulierculas discurrunt, fabulas monasteriorum narrant, sub nullo regimine uiuunt, negotiis saecularibus occupati, his periculum magis imminet, quam praemium et cauendum his, quod alius dicit : Vae mihi peccatori, quia nomen falsi monachi fero. Quartum genus est Sarabaite, qui necessaria sua sibi seruant; domum in castello siue in monasterio faciunt, semper onerosi adueniunt, ortum holeribus consitum habent, quadraginta uel ebdomadam in communione monasterii faciunt, totum reliquum tempus suo seruitio exigentes; hi graues sermonibus, nihil sibi placet, nisi quod ipsi statuunt; nulli gradui iunguntur, neque monachi neque clerici neque plebiles neque laici.

Hieronimus in epistola ad Benedictum dicit : Quatuor genera monachorum sunt : Primum coenobitarum, militans sub regula et abbate, hoc est optimum genus; Secundum anachoretarum, qui solo brachio uiuunt, nec fauorem plebis accipiunt. Ter-

mum genus quod militat sub regula vel abbate.

tium genus, qui bini uel terni uel quaterni uel quini sine pastore, nec accipiunt exemplum seniorum, sed dicunt, quod Lex Dei est, quod prouidetur illis; malum autem hoc genus est. Quartum genus et girouagum, qui hospitantur per prouincias, peius quam loqui est. Reuertamur ad optimum genus, quod militans sub regula uel abbate.

[= Vall. XL.10]
[III.] De suscipiendis monachis vitando malos principes.

Sinodus : Definimus monachos fugientes malos principes suscipi ab alia ecclesia ut sciatur causa. Gelasius : Monachos suscipite qui veniunt ad vos de loco viliore ad perfectio[p. 259]nem quorum abba ita degeneravit ab opere Dei ut mereatur ad mensam sanctorum no[n] recipi et fornicationis crimine non suspicionis set mali evidentis onerari, sine ullo scrupulo vel esitatione tales monachos suscipite ad vos velut flammam inferni confugientes nequaquam eorum consulente abbate. Item : Navi fracta qui potest natare natet. Sinodus Arelatensis decrevit ut exules vitia principum vitantes et incommodum loci non recusemus. Scimus quia Petrus suscepit fugientes de Hierusalem, Paulus suscepit Onesimum servum Philemonis.

[CCH 2.64; MC 125, p. 103]
De suscipiendis monachis vitandos malos principes.

Synodus. Definimus monachos fugientes malos principes suscipi ab alia ecclesia ut sciatur causa. Gelasius papa. Monachos suscipite qui veniunt ad vos de loco viliori ad perfectiorem quorum abbas ita degeneravit ab opere Dei ut mereatur ad mensam sanctorum non recipi et fornicationis crimine non suspicionis sed malitie videntes onerare. Sine ullo scrupulo vel esitatione tales monachos suscipite ad vos velut flammam inferni confugientes, nequaquam eorum consulentes abbatem.
Synodus Arelatensis decrevit ut exules vitia principum vitantes et incommodum loci non recusemus.

Ita Dominus duos filos Zebedei relicto patre suo suscepit. Gregorius : Quisquis mala mundi et vitia et incommodum ecclesie vitat suscipiendus magis quam eiciendus.	Gregorius. Quisquis mala mundi et incommodum ecclesie vitat, suscipiendus est magis quam eiciendus.	
[=Vall. XL.5] [IV.] De eo quod non oportet monachum fieri sine abbate.		[CCH 39.4] De eo, quod non oportet monachum fieri sine abbate.
Sinodus : Non oportet monachos fieri sine gubernatione, nisi tantum una ora, ne bentus discordie et dissensionis disperdat ecclesia. Gregorius : Tamquam piscis in terra vivere sine aqua non potest, ita monachus sine abbate vibere non debet. Augustinus : Quis navem agit, vel iacit si gubernator abscedat? Quis ab insidiis luporum custodit oves, si pastoris cura non vigilet? Quis latronibus et furibus resistit, si speculatorem non habeat? [p. 260]		Gregorius Romanus : Tamquam in terra piscis sine aqua non potest uiuere, ita monachus sine abbate uiuere non potest. Augustinus : Quis nauem agit, si gubernator abscedat, quis ab insidiis luporum custodit oues, si pastoris cura non uigilet, quis latronibus et furibus resistit, si speculatorem non habuerit? Sinodus : Non oportet monachos fieri sine gubernatione, nisi tantum una hora, ne uentus discordiae et dissensionis disperdat ecclesiam.
[=Vall. XL.9] [V.] <D>e monacho non retinendo ab abbate suo.	[Coll EL 2.64; MC p. 103] [cf. 9L 4.7] De monacho remisso non retinendo.	[CCH 39.6] De monacho non retinendo ab abbate suo.
Gelasius : Abbas remissius non retineat monachum suum ad districtiora se tendentem.	Gregorius : Abbas remissus non retineat monachum suum ad districtiora tendentem.	Gildas dicit : Abbas remissus non retineat monachum suum ad districtiora se tendentem.

[Vall. XL.11] [VI.] De eo quod monachus abbatem pessimum deserere debet.	[Coll. 5L 2.64, MC p. 103] [cf. 9L 4.8] De eo quod monachus abbatem pessimum deserere debet.	[CCH 39.12] De eo, quod debet monachus abbatem ualde malum deserere.
Hieronimus : Lupus vitandus, pastor bonus adeundus, spelunca latronis deserenda, ovile ovium petendum. Augustinus : Fugiunt oves vocem pastoris, quem non agnoscunt et deserta petunt, ita mali principis ovilia vitanda sunt et deserta abita petenda.	Hieronimus : Lupus vitandus, pastor bonus adeundus, speculunca deserenda ovile ovium petendum. Augustinus : Fugiunt oves vocem pastoris quem non cognoscunt et deserta petunt. Item : mali principis ovilia vitanda sunt et deserta vita petenda.	Hieronimus : Lupus uitandus est, pastor bonus adeundus, spelunca latronis deserenda, ouile ouium petendum. Agustinus : Fugiunt oues uocem pastoris, quem non agnoscunt et deserta petunt, ita mali principis ouilia.
[=Vall. XL.19] [VII.] De monacho paulo remissioris regule non ammittendo.	[9L 4.9] (not in 5L; but last section of text in 1349 is like the above)	[CCH 39.9] De monacho paulo remissioris regulae non admittendo.
Gelasius : Abba districtioris regule non ammittat monachum alterius abbatis paulo remissioris, et qui remissior est, non retineat monachum suum ad districtiora tendentem.		Gildas ait : Abbas districtioris regulae non admittat monachum alterius abbatis paulo remissioris, et qui remissior est, non retineat monachum suum ad districtiora tendentem.
[=Vall. XL.17] [VIII.] De eo quod non oporteat monachum a congregatione secedere.	[Coll 5L 2.67; MC p. 103] [cf. 9L 4.13] Quod non oporteat ad solitarias cellulas a congregatione discedere nisi probati post meritos labores.	[CCH 39.15,16] De eo, quod non oportet monachos a congregatione secedere.
Sinodus Agathensis : Monachis ad solitarias cellas non liceat a congregatione secedere, nisi forte probatis qui post emeritos labores ab abbatibus permittuntur,	Synodus Agatense : Servandum quoque de monachis ne quis ad solitarias cellulas liceat congregatione discedere, nisi forte probatis post emeritos labores aut propter	Sinodus Agathensis : Monachis ad solitarias cellulas non liceat a congregatione secedere, nisi forte probatis post meritos labores ab abbatibus permittatur, ita

ita tamen, ut intra eadem monasterii septa manentes separatas habeant cellulas.	infirmitatis necessitatem asperioris abbatis regula mittatur. Quod ita demum non fiat ut intra eadem monasterii septa manentes tamen sub abbatis potestate separatas habere cellulas permittatur.	tamen, ut intra eadem monasterii septa manentes separatas habeant cellulas. De eo, quod non oportet monacho cellam construere sine abbatis permissu.
Sinodus Aurelitana: Nullus monachus ambitionis et vanitatis impulsu cellam sine abbatis sui voluntate construere presumat.	Synodus Aurelianensis. Nullus monachus ambitionis et vanitatis impulsu cellam sine abbatis sui voluntate construere presumat.	Sinodus Auriliensis: Nullus monachus ambitionis et uanitatis impulsu cellam sine abbatis sui permissione construere praesumat.

XV

Further Evidence for the Influence of the *Hibernensis* in Southern Italy: an Early Eleventh-Century Canonistic Florilegium at Montecassino[1]

Of the thirty-seven manuscripts or fragments containing canonistic texts in Beneventan script, the bold and beautiful writing of southern Italy and Dalmatia, thirteen or over a third are now found in the Archivio della Badia at Montecassino.[2] The variety and chronological range of canonistic texts within

1. Research for this article was conducted for the program Monumenta Liturgica Beneventana supported by the Social Sciences and Humanities Research Council of Canada. I am grateful for the help of Don Faustino Avagliano OSB, who kindly gave permission to publish material from the Montecassino manuscripts cited in this article.

2. For all the manuscripts, except MSS 205 and 402, see my 'Canonistica Beneventana', in P. Landau & J. Müller (ed), *Proceedings of the ninth international congress of medieval canon law, Munich, 13–18 July 1992,* Monumenta Iuris Canonici, Ser. C, Subsidia (Vatican 1997) 21–40. The canonistic glosses in MSS 205, 384, and 402 (the last probably copied in Naples, according to Virginia Brown and Francis Newton) on texts of the early councils and popes are printed from MS 205 in Ambrosius Amelli (ed), *Spicilegium casinense, complectens analecta sacra et profana e. codd. casinensibus aliarumque bibliothecarum collecta atque edita cura et studio monachorum S. Benedicti archicoenobii Montis Casini* i (Montecassino 1888) 354–63. On the canonistic manuscripts see also Giuseppe Motta, 'Collezione canoniche dell'area cassinese nella'età dell'abate Desiderio', in Faustino Avagliano & Oronzo Pecere (ed), *L'età dell'abate Desiderio III, 1: storia arte e cultura,* Atti del IV Convegno di studi sul medioevo meridionale (Montecassino, 4–8 ottobre, 1987), *Miscellanea Cassinese* 67 (Montecassino 1992) 363–72; H. E. J. Cowdrey, *The age of abbot Desiderius: Montecassino, the papacy, and the Normans in the eleventh and early twelfth centuries* (Oxford 1983)

these manuscripts is surprisingly wide, including many major and minor collections of canons and penitentials spanning from the fifth or sixth centuries to the twelfth. These include the ancient *Collectio Dionysio-Hadriana* in MS 522 (s. xii [s. xii]); the ancient *Collectio Cresconius* and *Breviatio canonum* in MS 541 (s. xii½ [s. xi, Theobaldian]); the eighth-century *Collectio canonum hibernensis* in MS 297 (s. xi^{in} [s. xi^{med}]); miscellaneous *canones* and parts of the *Collectio canonum hibernensis* in MS 439 (s. x); the ninth-century *Collectio Dacheriana* in MSS 554 (s. x [s. xi½) and 541 (s. xi½ [s. xi, Theobaldian]); the ninth-century *Quadripartitus* in MS 541 (s. xi½ [s. xi, Theobaldian]); the ninth-century *Decretales Ps-Isidorianae* in MS 1 (s. xi$^{3/4}$ [Desiderian]); the *Penitentiale in II libris* in MS 554 (s. x [s. xi^{2}]); the *Decretum Burchardi* in MSS 44 and 45 (s. xi; [s. xi^{ex}]); the *Collection in five books* in MS 125 (s. xi^{med} [s. xi½]); extracts of the *Collection in five books* and the *Collection in 74 titles* in MS 522 (s. xii [s. xii]); miscellaneous canons and canonistic glosses in MS 384 (s. x^{in}) [s. x^{in}]; MS 402 (s. x); and MS 205 (s. xi^{in} [probably s. xi^{1}]); canonistic glosses in Latin and German in MS 541 (s. xi½ [s. xi, Theobaldian]); papal letters in MS 220 (s. xii); and the twelfth-century *Collectio canonum casinensis* in MS 216 (s. xii^{ex})[s. xii^{ex}]. Beyond these, one of the most remarkable of the canonistic codices in the Archivio is MS 372.

For over a century this last manuscript has been well-known for its penitential, the so-called *Penitentiale casinense*.[3] This penitential, although based on earlier, mostly northern texts, has been recognised, nonetheless, as a distinctive southern Italian penitential in its own right as opposed to the *Dacheriana*, *Quadripartitus*,

esp. 26–27, 95–103; and Francis Newton, *The scriptorium and library at Montecassino 1058–1105* (Cambridge, 1999) 273 n 126. Dates assigned by Newton for many of the MSS listed below are given in [ ]. Newton (273, n 126) notes the paucity of canonistic manuscripts from the great period of abbots Desiderius and Oderisius and speculates that many must have been made during this period of beautiful and abundant copying of manuscripts but were taken away, one might suppose, precisely for their beauty and for their abundance in the abbey's collection. On what one might call an 'overabundance' of MSS of Augustine's works copied in this period at Montecassino, see Newton (80–84.) It is highly interesting that Montecassino and its surrounds seem to have been a centre for the copying in Beneventan script of the first major collection of the 'reform' papacy, the *Collection in 74 titles* (one of whose MSS remains at Montecassino, MS 522), on which see my 'The South Italian *Collection in five books* and its derivatives: the South Italian appendix to the *Collection in seventy-four titles*', *Miscellanea Beneventana, Mediaeval Studies* 63 (2001) 351–63; and Newton, *Scriptorium and library*, 133–14.

3. See H. J. Schmitz, *Die Bußbücher und die Bußdisciplin der Kirche* (2 vols, Mainz 1883, Düsseldorf 1898; repr. Graz, 1958), i 397–401. A new study of this penitential is being undertaken by A. Gaastra, a member of the équipe of young Dutch scholars studying Continental penitentials under Dr Rob Meens in Utrecht.

and others representing a northern tradition.[4] More recently the manuscript has been cited and used for its readings of the *Collectio vetus gallica* in the monumental edition of that text by Hubert Mordek.[5] In his study, Mordek emphasised the fact that although the *Collectio vetus gallica* was compiled in the seventh century and was widespread in manuscripts especially from the eighth and ninth centuries in northern Europe, its youngest full witness is in the Montecassino codex.[6] Why this ancient Gallican systematic collection of canon law was copied so late and in a location so distant from its origin has puzzled scholars. Was it that wealthy libraries such as Montecassino wanted to have as broad a range of canon law collections as possible, the *Collectio vetus gallica* being the major systematic collection of the early Gallican Church, just as the *Collectio canonum hibernensis,* also represented in its holdings, was the 'national' collection of the ancient Irish church? Was it because it contained important canons touching monasteries, especially those under the Rule of St. Benedict? Or was it simply happenstance that the collection was copied at Montecassino? One will probably never know. Beyond the presence of the well-known *Penitentiale casinense* and *Collectio vetus gallica* in the manuscript, there is another interesting short canonistic compilation that has not received from scholars the attention it deserves, and it is the purpose of this note to redress this.

4. In 'Canonistica Beneventana', 23, it was pointed out that there are cases in which a Beneventan scribe or scribes added material to an older codex written in Carolingian script. For example, the codex, Vatican, BAV, Vat. lat. 1347, containing the *Collectiones Cresconii* and *Dacheriana* and the *Quadripartitus,* was written in Rheims in the third quarter of the ninth century, but by the early eleventh century it had travelled to southern Italy, where it was augmented by a Beneventan scribe and then was perhaps used as a model for another codex with like texts written completely in Beneventan script, Montecassino MS 541. It is interesting, also, that the tenth-century Montecassino MS 554 containing the *Dacheriana* is written in two or three hands. The major hand is Romanesca, but from p 15–30, this hand and two Beneventan hands alternate canons, the first probably a Romanesca scribe trying to write Beneventan but failing to follow all of the Beneventan rules. It is also interesting that from p 35–46, and 125–26 a Beneventan hand has glossed canons with glosses like those found in the same canons in the *Collection in five books.* The Beneventan 'gloss' in a darker hand on p 147 is not really a gloss, but the added conclusion to a canon of the *Collectio Dacheriana*, iii 26 (cf. MS 541, p 214).

5. Hubert Mordek, *Kirchenrecht und Reform im Frankenreich: Die Collectio vetus gallica, die älteste systematische Kanonessammlung des fränkischen Gallien: Studien und Edition,* Beiträge zur Geschichte und Quellenkunde des Mittelalters 1 (Berlin & New York 1975) esp. 280–81.

6. There were, as Mordek shows, many derivatives of the collection, and its influence on later collections was astonishingly wide. For a south Italian excerpt see my 'Beneventan monastic excerptum from the *Collectio vetus gallica*', *Revue Bénédictine* 102 (1992) 298–308.

Although the manuscript is at present within the holdings of the Archivio della Badia of Montecassino, the provenance of MS 372 was a little dependency of the great abbey called San Nicola della Cicogna, a small house whose ruins can be found some two kilometres northwest of the mother house on a small footpath leading past Albaneta, another dependency of Montecassino.[7] Whether it was written at San Nicola or in the mother house is unknown. Perhaps the latter, and when its texts were seen to be obsolete it was given to the small dependency for use there. Or it may have been that the manuscript was written elsewhere in the Beneventan zone of central southern Italy and taken to Montecassino or San Nicola.[8] In any event, the codex is one of three known whose provenance is San Nicola.[9]

The script of the codex has been dated by palaeographical specialists to the early eleventh century.[10] This is significant because it likely antedates the importation of manuscripts to Montecassino and the intense copying of codices there under abbot Theobald from the mid 1020s and beyond.[11] Further, it antedates by several decades the earliest manuscript of the major south Italian *Collection in five books*, several of whose texts are like those in our codex.

The *Collection in five books* itself is one of the great early medieval canonical collections compiled in southern Italy.[12] Its earliest extant appearance is in a manuscript written in the scriptorium of Montecassino in approximately the middle of the eleventh century and still kept in the Archivio della Badia, MS 125.[13] The latest canons in the collection are five attributed to the emperor, St

7. An ex libris on p 1 of the codex reads 'Liber s. Nicolai de cico<ni>a'.

8. Against this and for a Montecassino/San Nicola origin is the fact that the ink on many of the flesh sides of the folios is flaking. It is a characteristic of codices written in Beneventan script at Montecassino in the eleventh century that there is rubbing or flaking of the text on the flesh sides, on which see Newton, *Scriptorium and library,* 120–21. Of course it is not impossible that this same phenomenon occurred elsewhere in the Beneventan zone.

9. Montecassino, Archivio della Badia, 179 (martyrology/necrology); 191 (gospel lectionary); and our 372. On these see C. Hilken, *The necrology of San Nicola della Cicogna: Montecassino, Archivio della Badia, cod. 179, pp. 1–64,* Monumenta Liturgica Beneventana 2 (Toronto 2000) 4.

10. E. A. Loew, *The Beneventan script. a history of the south Italian minuscule* (2nd enlarged edition prepared by Virginia Brown), Sussidi eruditi 33–34 (2 vols, Rome 1980), ii 84.

11. On Theobald and his MSS see Newton, *Scriptorium and library,* 11–12, 32–34.

12. On the collection see my 'South-Italian canon law *Collection in five books* and its derivatives: new evidence on its origins, diffusion, and use', *Mediaeval Studies* 52 (1990) 278–95; and the much fuller 'South and central Italian canonical collections of the tenth and eleventh centuries (non-Gregorian)', in W. Hartmann & K. Pennington (ed). *The history of canon law in the age of reform, 1000–1140* (Washington D C, in press since 1993).

13. As to the location and dating of the MS, first, there is the characteristic flaking of the text on

Henry II, thus making the compilation of the collection as we have it now sometime after 1014.

Whether the *Collection in five books* was compiled at Montecassino itself or perhaps in San Liberatore and taken to Montecassino by Theobald in a now lost manuscript cannot at this point be demonstrated conclusively.[14] Also, there is a

the flesh sides of the folios in MS 125. Then, there are the hands in which the text was written. They are clearly not of the 'classic' age of abbot Desiderius in the later eleventh century, but neither are they of the age of Theobald. Of the five major hands responsible for the codex only one, hand 3, uses abbreviations characteristic of the Theobaldian epoch. For example, the use of the double macron as an abbreviation sign is found on p 259, 270, 289, 293, 297, and 298 as it is in the Theobaldian MS 541, p 255–56 and elsewhere. But, as Newton (*Scriptorium and library*, 168, n 226) points out, this usage, characteristic at Montecassino of the Theobaldian era, continued on, and in our MS these are not frequent enough to push the hand back to the age of Theobald. Thus, a date nearer the middle of the eleventh century rather than the 1020s is to be preferred. This may still mean, of course, that a copy or copies of the *Collection in five books* were made at San Liberatore alla Maiella or at Montecassino in the 1020s or before, on which see the next footnote.

14. Hubert Mordek (*Kirchenrecht und Reform im Frankenreich*, 100 n 14–15) and Theo Kölzer (*Collectio canonum Regesto Farfensi inserta*, Monumenta iuris canonici, Ser. B, Corpus collectionum 5 (Vatican City 1982) 50, 54) have made several important observations about the codex from Montecassino and its relation to documents of the second two decades of the eleventh century. Mordek drew attention to the *Chronicon casinensis* of 1023, which said that the abbot Theobald had made a *Liber canonum* for the poorly stocked library at Montecassino. (MS 125, p 1, begins with 'In Christi nomine. Incipit Liber canonum …'.) But most important was Mordek's reference to the *Commemoratorium* of 1019 mentioning a *Liber canonum* that Theobald had copied for the monastery of San Liberatore near Chieti before coming to Montecassino as abbot. Kölzer then tentatively suggested that Theobald's *Liber canonum* copied at San Liberatore may even have been a copy of the *Collection in five books*, which was carried to Montecassino and was used there as the exemplar for the extant Montecassino MS 125.

That the MS 125 was copied from earlier exemplars is suggested by several features in the codex. First, scribes seem to have been copying independently from separated quires; on p 208, for example, a scribe has stretched his last text to match the text of the next quire. But more important evidence for the use of exemplars lies in the construction of the codex, a misnumbering of canons in book 4, and a 'mis-placement' of the final quire of the codex. The text of the Montecassino codex is largely the product of five major hands: hand 1 wrote p 1–176; hand 2 p 177–256; hand 3 p 257–304; hand 4 (perhaps with some help) p 305–48; and hand 5 p 349–68. The 'youngest' of the hands palaeographically are hands 1 and 2; hand 3 is the 'oldest'. On p 187–88 hand 2 correctly copied the *capitulationes* and first part of the text of book 4. The Roman numbers assigned to the *capitulationes* and texts of canons match through p 252. Caps. clxxiiii through ccvi, however, are then copied not where they belong, but on a separate quire written by hand 5 and now bound at the back of the codex.

This strange circumstance suggests a number of scenarios. First, hand 2 correctly copied the *capitulationes* in correct order and the first texts of book 4 with numbers corresponding to those for the *capitulationes*. When he finished the text of cap. 'clxxiii De donis iniquiorum quae nihil a

possibility that the collection itself was compiled earlier, even in the tenth century, and the five canons attributed to Henry II were added at a later stage as *canones extravagantes* after 1014.[15]

sacerdote eis predicantes suscipienda sunt' from p 250–52 he looked for the next quire of the exemplar he was using. This quire may have been removed, away from the scriptorium for some reason or simply misplaced among the quaternia being copied. Thus, hand 2 copied a text without number from a quaternion beginning with the rubric 'De eo quod sola haelymosina non liberat sine alia virtute'. This text was, in reality, the last section of cap. ccvi and hence as one of the 'subtexts' of that cap. did not need a number. He then continued to copy from this exemplar numbering the next canon not 'cvii' but 'clxxiiii De helymosina et de propriis danda' and thereafter used his own numbers consecutively for the further canons. Eventually the scribe reached the end of the quire (p 256) with the word 'impu–' of a canon he had numbered clxxx. The next quire beginning on p 257 with 'denter' matching the previous 'impu' has several features distinguishing it from earlier quires: there is a different and cruder pricking and ruling system; there is a different decorative technique for the initials; and the 'oldest' hand in the codex, hand 3, begins. This scribe continues with '–denter' but numbers the canons copied thereafter correctly, according to the *capitulationes*. This may suggest that the quires of the MS written by hand 3 were themselves from the exemplar hand 2 was using. In this case, when hand 2 reached the word 'impu–' at the foot of p 256, he simply attached his exemplar beginning with 'denter' as the following text. Then later, when by comparing the *capitulationes* and the text of book 4 it was discovered that the texts of caps. clxxxiiii through ccvi were missing, these were copied by hand 5 into what is now the final quire of the manuscript, assigning them the correct (for the most part) numbers of the *capitulationes*. The last of these is on p 368 '<ccvi—number missing> De eo quod haelymosinas adiuvat peccatores licet non salvet', and the text is copied down to the section just before that appearing on p 252 without number 'De eo quod sola haelymosina non liberat sine alia virtute'. Hand 5 seems to have been conscious that the remainder of the cap. was on p 252 or on a quire that began with this text and started to stretch his text, but he failed and left blank a full column and a half on his final quire. It is, of course, possible that even this quire, which is unusual for its five-bifolia construction, its pricking and ruling, and the different hand 5 was itself the exemplar temporarily missing or misplaced when hand 2 'skipped' caps. clxxiiii through ccvi.

In any event, the quire with the missing canons from book 4 may then have been bound at the end of the MS. This may explain why the quire number for p 241–56 is 'xvi' and that for p 257–72 is 'xvii.' (The quire numbers for I–XI are ancient in a large bold hand, and those for xii–xxi are in a small different or later hand.) On the other hand, the quire at the end of the volume (without quire number) may have been intruded at some time between p 256 and 257 close to where the missing texts should have been. That this is so is because at some point a much later scribe wrote in the lower right-hand corner of p 256 what appears to be 'denter,' perhaps a reference to the 'denter' beginning p 257, which at that time was separated from p 256 by the intruded quire. This 'denter' is likely not a catchword, because there are none elsewhere in the MS, but a direction to the user to skip to 'denter' after the intruded quire. Whatever the case, the complexity of the writing and construction of the Montecassino MS of the *Collection in five books* suggests one or more exemplars being used in its copying.

15. This is suggested by the awkward placement of some of these texts after sections that dealt with subjects other than these canons. In the Vatican codex of the *Collection in five books*, Vat. lat. 1339, there are blank spaces left throughout the texts, almost as an invitation to further additions.

We return to codex 372. Our florilegium of canonistic texts appears on p 149–160 in two sections. In the first section the eight texts[16] clearly resemble many from the *Collection in five books*, as can be seen in the apparatus below accompanying the texts. But there are several differences from those now in MS 125. First, there are capitula rubrics in MS 372 that are lacking in MS 125. Second, the readings of several canons are unlike those in MS 125.[17] Third, there are no interlinear glosses as there are in the *Collection in five books*. But most important, several of the texts are not in MS 125, but are found in southern Italian *excerpta* from the *Collectio canonum hibernensis*, which enjoyed considerable diffusion in southern Italy at least from the tenth century and beyond.[18] For example, canon <8> is present in both the *Hibernensis* and the *Hibernensis* extract in MS 439, a manuscript written in the late tenth century in Siponto or northern Apulia.[19] But even here, the texts in our manuscript are spliced together in an order unlike those of the *Hibernensis*. Again, the sequence of passages in canon <6>, not contained in the *Collection in five books*, is found neither in the *Hibernensis* nor MS 439. All of this suggests that the compiler of our florilegium was using not the *Collection in five books* itself but a similar compilation antedating the *Collection in five books*. One immediately thinks of a collection like the *Collection in nine books*, compiled probably in the tenth century in the Beneventan zone but found now only in an eleventh century MS, Vatican, Vat. lat. 1349.[20] But this collection, with some of the canons of our florilegium, does not contain them all. Nor does the *Collectio canonum hibernensis* contain all of our texts. Hence, either the compiler was using a combination of collections similar to the *Collection in five books* or *Collection in nine books* plus the *Hibernensis*, or more likely a now lost compilation with texts like all of these. In short, this section of the florilegium suggests a rich store of canonistic texts, now lost, like those in these three collec-

Whether these blank spaces were the doing of the scribes of the Vatican codex or were in an exemplar being used is difficult to ascertain. But the addition of texts, *canones extravagantes*, to sections of the *Collection in five books* where they are inappropriate might be explained by just such blank spaces, since filled in, within an exemplar of the Vatican manuscript.

16. The texts in the edition below have been numbered in < > for convenience of citation.

17. For example, the first text in canon <4> reads in the *Collection in five books* in MS 125: 'Salomon. Verba oris insipientis grata et labia sapientis precipitabunt eum'.

18. See my 'Transmission of the *Collectio canonum hibernensis* in Italy from the tenth to the twelfth century', *Peritia* 14 (2001) 20–50.

19. See my 'Monastic florilegium from the *Collectio canonum hibernensis* at Montecassino', *Revue Bénédictine* 114 (2004) 92–111; and information supplied from this article in Barbara Maria Tarquini, *I codici grammaticali in scrittura beneventana* (Montecassino 2002) 49–58.

20. On this collection see my 'South and Central Italian canonical collections'.

tions circulating in southern Italy in the late tenth and early eleventh century.

One of the more interesting aspects of the first section of the florilegium is the concentration of monastic texts, resembling those in the northern Apulian MS 439, a tenth-century codex also containing traces of the *Collectio vetus gallica.*[21] Normally manuscripts of the *Collectio vetus gallica* had a long section xlvi, De monachis, with many monastic canons, including xlvi.12 (Autun, c. 15, mentioning the Rule of St Benedict), xlvi.33–37 *(Regula Benedicti)* as well as several other monastic canons. But in the *Collectio vetus gallica* of MS 372 this is strangely absent,[22] something noteworthy for a manuscript presumably made for, and certainly kept in, a Benedictine house. In the *Collectio vetus gallica* of MS 372, p 170, in the list of *capitulationes,* there are entries: xliii 'De clericis, abbatibus, monachiis non manentes in suo propositoriis'; xlv 'De monachis'; but in the text itself of the *Collectio vetus gallica,* p 207–8, the wealth of material on monks in other versions of the *Collectio* is missing. One wonders, therefore, whether the exemplar of the *Collectio vetus gallica* used in the making of MS 372 was lacking the usual monastic texts, and to make up for this the compilers of the codex as a whole included monastic texts in our florilegium from a collection like the *Collectio canonum hibernensis,* the *Collection in nine books,* or *Collection in five books* circulating in southern Italy.

The second section of the canonistic florilegium of MS 372, canons <9> through <26>, is fully as interesting as the first. It begins with the *capitulum,* 'Incipit epistula sancti Clementi ad sanctum Iacobum fratrem domini'. Next to this Don Mauro Inguanez wrote in pencil, 'Epis. II, M.P.G. 1, 483–90, breviter in cod.', an obvious reference to the pseudonymous Second Epistle of Clement to James.[23] In MS 372 this letter is divided into individual canons and before each there is a rubricated *capitulum.* Since most of the texts in this section are found in the *Collection in five books*[24] and often follow the readings of those canons in that collection, one might suspect that this collection was the source of the second section of our florilegium. But the sequence of texts is clearly that found in the Epistle itself, not in the *Collection in five books,* where they are scattered throughout LL. 2 and 3.

21. Mordek, *Kirchenrecht,* 100, 104–6.

22. ibid. 325–6.

23. On Don Mauro's work at Montecassino, especially his study of the codices, see Carol Jaccarini, *Dom Mauro Inguanez, 1887–1955: Benedictine of Montecassino,* tr. Victor Buhagiar (Medina 1987) 30–42; see also Joseph Flask, *Dom Mauro Inguanez, O.S.B.: Bibliotekarju Ewlieni (1947–1955)* (Valletta 1985).

24. Here noted in the apparatus to each canon.

Whence came these texts to our florilegium? The Epistle did have a circulation of its own,[25] but a major canonistic source would have been the *Decretales Ps-Isidorianae* found now in a later eleventh-century MS which was at Montecassino, MS 1. If the texts in MS 372 are compared with those in MS 1, the similarities and especially the sequence are obvious, but the inserted *capitula* and readings of the texts are clearly different and often reflect the texts in the *Collection in five books* of MS 125. It is clear that our compiler was excerpting from the Epistle, and hence he was perhaps also modifying the text as he went. But the similarities of the readings to those in the *Collection in five books* remains striking, suggesting that the compiler of that collection was also working from a text of the Epistle unlike that found in the *Decretales Ps-Isidorianae.*

The Clementine Epistle in it first part deals especially with liturgical subjects, particularly the eucharist, its care, and the maintenance of eucharistic paraphernalia. Most surprising, following these texts of the Clementine Epistle, the compiler intrudes as canons <21> to <24> four texts dealing especially with baptism, the water used in baptism, and holy oil. He then returns to the Clementine Epistle itself to conclude with warnings to follow the directives it gives. The source of these four intrusions is not that found in the southern Italian version of the *Decretales Ps-Isidorianae.* Thus, one must look to another interpolated version of the Epistle or postulate that the compiler either composed these intrusions on his own or borrowed them from an independent source. In any event, the second section of the florilegium presents a most interesting abbreviated and intruded version of the Second Epistle of Clement to James.

In the edition of the florilegium that follows, the orthography of the manuscript, faulty as it is,[26] is retained. Numbers for the canons have been added in angle brackets for ease of citation. Rubricated words have been placed in bold, and the capitula, whether rubricated or not, are in *italics.* After each canon or part thereof, possible sources or parallels are given in square brackets.

25. In southern Italian manuscripts alone written in Beneventan script the letter or fragments thereof appear in: (a) a tiny fragment from Goslar, Stadtarchiv, s.n. (s. xi), containing a text of the *Second Epistle of Clement* in an unusual recension related to a similar text (b) the Beneventan-script miscellany, London, British Library, Addit. 16413 (on which see Roger E. Reynolds, 'A South Italian liturgico-canonical mass commentary', *Mediaeval Studies* 50 (1988) 633 n 21); and (c) Rome, Biblioteca Vallicelliana B.32 (the Collection of Veroli).

26. On this see R. Jacobsson, 'Short reflexions on Beneventan Easter sequence texts', in A. Ziino (ed), *La sequenza medievale, Atti del Convegno Internazionale Milano 7–8 aprile 1984* (Lucca 1992) 129–30.

ABBREVIATIONS

5L *Collection in five books*
C parallels in MS 125
F parallels from Mario Fornasari (ed), *Collectio canonum in V libris (Lib. i–iii)* (CCCM 6, Turnhout 1970)
9L *Collection in nine books* of Vatican, Vat. lat. 1349
H *Collectio canonum hibernensis:* Hermann Wasserschleben (ed), *Die irische Kanonensammlung* (2nd ed. Leipzig, 1885; repr. Aalen 1966)
M *Decretales Ps-Isidorianae* as in Montecassino MS 1.

[p 149]

<1> *DE EO QUOD MELIOR EST DOCTA IUSTITIA QUAM SANCTA RUSTICITAS*

[incipit = 5L]

Hieronimus. Sancta quippe rusticitas sola sibi prodest et quantum edificat ex vitae merito aecclesiam Christi, tantum nocet si contradicentibus non resistat.

[5L C 3.105, p 147; F. 3.165; cf. H 38.7a, and 9L 2.134]

Augustinus. Melior est docta sapientia non minus erudiens, quam sancta rusticitas.

Danihel dicit: iustos fulgere sicut stellas id est doctos et intelligentes inter indoctos quasi firmamentum.

Vides quantum distat inter hos, licet iuxta hebraicam veritatem aliter legimus et reliqua.

[5L C 3.105, p 147; F 3.165 (2); cf. H 38.7b]

<2> *DE EO QUOD SANCTA RUSTICITAS DISCRETIONEM NON HABET*

[capitulum not in 5L]

Augustinus. In rusticitate sancta cavendum est ne aut minuat aut augeat.

In his enim dum mens rustici satiatur periculum incurrit. Et dum putat iustum esse quod facit, mens elevatur et in superbiam ruit et verba scripturarum contemnit.

[5L C 3.106, p 147; F 3.166.1; cf. H 38.8 and 9L 2.135]

<3> *DE EO QUOD SANCTA RUSTICITAS DEBET SUBICI NON PRAEESSE*

[capitulum not in 5L]

Hieronimus. Tunc sancta rusticitas bene utitur cum sub regimine monasterii et abbatis ex verbis scripture doceatur.

[5L C 3.147; F 3.166.2; cf. H 38.10 and 9L 2.136]

<4> *DE RUSTICITATE CERTANTES CONTRA SAPIENTIAM*

Salomon. Verba oris sapientis grata et labia insipientis precipitabunt eum.

[5L C 3.106, p 147; F 3.167.1; cf. H 38.9 and 9L 2.137]

Hieronimus in commentariis AEcclesiasticis. Stultitia, si sui rusticitate contenta esset, minus aliquid haberet mali. Nunc autem contra sapientiam bellum gerit et gurgite verborum suorum gratiam eloquii sapientiae indocto viro [p 150] viderit zelo stimulata non recipit.

[5L C 3.106, p 148; F 3.167.2; cf. H 38.9b]

<5> DE NOMINE MONACHORUM

[capitulum not in 5L]

In libro thimologiarum [*sic*]. Monachus greca ethimologia vocatus est eo quod singularis. Monos enim grecae singularitas dicitur. Ergo si singularius interpretatur vocabulum monachi, quid facit in turba qui solus est? Idcirco dicitur ergo monachus sive quia in hac vita solus, etsi inter multos habitet sive solus versetur sive quia solus in heremo vitam solitariam ducit.

[5L C 2.60, p 101; F 1.107; H 40.1, Vallic. t. xviii, f 108r]

De prepositi principes Helias et Heliseus discipulus eius fuerunt et alii prophetarum qui relictis urbibus iuxta fluenta Iordanis habitabant. Huius prepositi etiam in evangelio Iohannes Baptista extitit auctor qui heremum incoluit, locusta tantum et agresti melle nutritus. Iam denuo progeniti sunt conversationis huius novilissimi principes, Paulus et Antonius, Hilarion, Macharius, ceterique auctores quorum exemplis per universum mundum adolevit sancta institutio monachorum.

[5L C 2.61, p 111; F 2.108; cf. H 39.2 and 9L 4.2]

<6> *DE TRIBUS MACULIS MONACHIS*

In vita sanctorum: Abbas pastor, qui querellosus est, monachus non est. Qui iracundus est, monachus non est. Qui malum pro malo reddit, monachus non est.

[cf. MC 439.[I], p 256; and H 39.2b]

<7> *DE VARIIS GENERIBUS MONACHORUM*

Ysidorus. Sex genera monachorum sunt, quorum tria optima, reliqua vero deteriora atque omnibus modis aevitanda. Primum genus est cenovitarum, id est in commune viventium ad instar sanctorum illorum qui tempore apostolorum Hierosolimis venditis distributisque omnibus indigentibus [p 151] habitabant in sancta communionem vite, sed erant illis omnia communia et anima una et cor unum in Deum. Horum institutione monasteria sumpsere principia. Secundum genus eremitarum qui procul ab hominibus recedentibus deserta loca et vasta solitudines sequi atque habitare perhibentur ad imitationem scilicet Helie atque Iohannis Babtiste qui recesus heremi penetraverunt. Hi quippe incredibili mundi contemptu solitudine delectantur, herbis tantum agrestibus victitantes aut pane solo vel aqua contenti qui eis precaeptus per intervalla temporum defertur, sicque secretissimi penitus et ab omni hominum conspectu remoti divino tantum colloquio perfruuntur, cui puris mentibus ineserunt et propter cuius amorem non solum mundi sed etiam hominum reliquerunt consortia. Tertium genus est anachoretarum qui cenobiali conversatione perfecti includunt semetipsos procul in cellulis ab hominum conspectu remotis nullis ad se preventes accessum sed in sola contemplationem viventes perseverant theoria, sed isti de examinatione caenobiorum provati, in omnibus disciplinis monasterii per triginta annos ad hanc contemplationem per obaedientia eliguntur. Quartum genus est eorum qui anachoritarum imagine blandiuntur qui ut Cassianus: Brevi quodam fervore in primordiis suis caenovii perfectionem videntur expetere, sed continuo tepefacti dum pristinum mores ac vita resecare contempnunt, iugum humilitatis sustinere contenti non sunt, subdique maiorum imperio dedig[p 252]nantur separatas expetunt cellulas et solitarie sedere desiderant ut a nemine lacessiti, mansueti vel humiles extimentur. Quintum genus est circumcellionum qui sub habitu monachorum vagantur circumferentes ypocrisin, circumientes provincias nusquam missi, nusquam fixi, nusquam stantes, nusquam sedentes. Alii quae non viderunt confingunt opiniones suas habentes pro Deo. Alii membra martyrum et filacteria sua magnificant gloriam captantes ab hominibus. Alii criniti incedunt ut vilior habeatur tonsa sanctitas quam comata, unde videlicet qui eos viderint antiquos illos quos legimus cogitet, Samuhelem et Heliam et ceteros. Alii honores quos non acceperunt habere protestantur. Alii parentes consanguineos in illa regione se audisse et ideo venire et pergere mentiuntur. Omnes petunt omnes exigunt aut sumptum lucrum egestatis aut simulate pretium sanctitatis. Sextum genus est et ipsum teterrimum atque neglectum quod per Ananiam et Saphiram in exordio ecclesiae pullulavit et apostoli Petri severitate succisus est, qui sarabaite vel regni vite nuncupati sunt. In catalogo quattuor genera monachorum dicuntur: Primum eremite qui nihil commune cum mundo habent, sed suum victum suis manibus exquirunt et dona iniquorum non accipiunt. Hi theoricam et actualem vitam continent. Alii vero horum victum ab aliis sperant, orationi tantum vacantes. Secundum caenovite qui in commune vivunt in instar apostolorum familie duplicibus non induuntur, numquam ora vacuam relinquunt [p 153] sed sive legunt sive orant sive utilitatem proximi faciunt. Tertium genus est vagabundi qui nomen monachi desiderant habere sed mores abnegant, inter mulierculas discurrunt, fabulas monasteriorum narrant, nullo sub regimine vivunt, negotiis secularibus occupati his magis periculum imminet quam premium. Et cavendum his quod alius dicit: Ve michi peccatori qui nomen monachi fero. Quartums [sic] genum sarabaite qui necessaria sua sibi servant semper onerati adveniunt, hortum constitutum oleribus habent, quadraginta dies vel ebdomadem in commune monasterii faciunt totum relinquum tempus suo servitio exigentes; hi graves sermonibus nichil sibi nisi quod ipsi statuunt placentes, nulli gradui iunguntur, neque monachi neque clerici, neque pleviles, neque laici. Hieronimus in epistola ad Benedictum. Quattuor genera monachorum dicuntur. Primum cenobitarum militantium sub regula vel abbate, hoc est optimum genus. Secundum anachoritarum qui solo brachio vivunt nec favorem plevis accipiunt. Tertium genus qui bini vel terni vel quaterni vel quini sine pastore nec accipiunt exemplum seniorum sed dicunt lex Dei est quod videtur illis, hoc genus non parvum criminis habet. Quartum genus gyrovagum qui hospitantur per provincias peius quam loqui. Revertamur ad optimum genus quod militans sub regulam vel abbate.

[5L C 2.62, p 101–2; F 2.109; cf. H 39.3 and cf. 9L 4.4]

<8> *DE EO QUOD NON OPORTET MONACHUM FIERI SINE ABBATE*

Sinodus. Non oportet monachos fieri sine gubernatione, [p 154] nisi tantum una hora, ne venditus discordie et dissensiones disperdat aecclesia.

Gregorius: Tamquam piscis in terra vivere sine aqua non potest, ita monachus sine abbate non debet.

Augustinus: Quis navem agit vel iacit si gubernator abscedat? Quis ab insidiis luporum custodit oves si pastoris cura non vigilet? Quis latronibus et furibus resistet si speculatorem non habeat?

[M 439 [IV]; and cf. H 39.4]

<9> INCIPIT EPISTULA SANCTI CLEMENTI AD SANCTUM IACOBUM FRATREM DOMINI

Clemens Iacobo clarissimo. Quoniam sicuti a beatissimo Petro accepimus omnium apostolorum patre, qui claves regni celorum accepit, equaliter tenere debemus quae geruntur in sanctis. Nos te ex ordine docuit instruere.

[cf. M, p 14; cf. 5L C 3.137, p 157; F 3.218]

<10> DE GRADIBUS AECCLESIAE

Tribus enim gradibus divinorum commissa secretorum sunt sacramenta, id est presbiteris, diaconibus et ministris. Hii cum timore et tremore reliquias corporis Domini debent custodire fragmentorum ne aliquibus inusitata in sacrario inveniantur, et cum neglegenter aguntur, portione corporis Domini gravis inferatur iniuria. Communicatio enim corporis Domini Ihesu Christi, si neglegenter agatur et presbiter non curet ammonere officia graviori anathemate percussus iudicio digna humiliationis plaga feriatur. Certe tanta in sacrario holocausta offerantur, quanta populum sufficere debeant. Quod si remanserit, in crastinum non reserventur, sed cum timore et tremore clericorum cautela et diligentia consumatur.

[cf. M, p 14; cf. 5L C 3.141, p 157–8; F 3.218]

<11> QUALITER SE OBSERVENT QUI RESIDUA COMEDERINT CORPUS DOMINI

Qui autem residua corporis Domini quae in sacrario relicta sunt, consument non statim ad communes accipiendos cibos conveniant. Nec putent sancte portionis esse commiscendos [p 155] cibos qui per aque liquores egestus in secessum fundantur. Si igitur manet dominica portio in sacrario edatur et usque in sexta ieiunent ministri qui hec consumpserint. Et si est tertia vel quarta hora quando hoc consumunt, ieiunent usque ad vesperum. Sic in pavore sanctificationis eterne custodienda sunt.

[cf. M, p 14; cf. 5L C 3.141, p 158; F 3.218]

<12> QUALITER VEL QUOMODO VASA SACRARII STUDENDA SINT CU[sic] DILIGENTIA ET DISCRETIONE

De vasis sacrarii ita gerendum est altare, candelabrum, cathedra, palla, et velum, si vetuste senuerint incendio dentur. Quoniam ea quae in sacrario sancto fuerint ministerio et veteraverint, mala tractari non debent, sed incendio universe tradantur, cineresque eorum in baptisterio mittantur, ubi nullus transitus fuerit, aut in pariete aut in fossa cavimentorum conspersa iactentur, ne introeuntum pedibus inquinentur.

[M, p 14–5; cf. 5L C 3.148, p 161; F 3.229]

Nemo per ignorantiam clericus pallam mortuum crediderit obvoluendum, aut diaconum scapulas operire vel que iam fuit in altario aut certe quae data est in futura in mensa Domini proferatur.

[M, p 15; cf. 5L C 3.147, p 160; F. 3.228]

Qui hec fecerit vel leviter sue neglegenter habuerit divina misteria. Si diacono triennio, et sex mensibus alienus erit ab altario gravi percussus anathemate. Quod si clericus presbiter non ammoverit decem annos et mensibus quinque excommunicentur, pro quod de domini sacramentis subieciti ora sibi non amoverit ministeria et postea cum grandi humilitate matri reconcilietur aecclesie.

[M, p 15; cf. 5L C 3.141, p 158 and F. 3.218]

<13> DE LAVACRIS LINTEAMINUM AECCLESIAE

Pallas vero et vela quae in sacrario fuerint inferta, diaconus cum humilibus ministris in sacrario lavent, non eiciant foras extra sacrario ne vela domini corporis [p 156] male decidant aut sindonis foris abluta et erit haec operanti peccato; idcirco intra secretario a ministris precepimus diligentia custodiri. Sane pelvis nova comparetur et preter hi nichil aliud tangat, sed non in ipsa pelvis velis apponatur lavandis, sed tantum quae ad dominici altaris pertinent. Palle in alia pelve laventur et alia vela etiam ianuarum; cura sint idem hostiario ex ammonitione maiorum, ne quis neglegenter aut ignarus ad velum ianue domus Domini manus incondite tergat, sed statim cohercitur discat homo quae vela altarii domus Domini sancta sunt.

[M, p 15; cf. 5L C 3.147, p 160; F 3.228]

<14> DE OMNIBUS OBLATIONIBUS QUAE IN ECCLESIIS INTRAT

Precipimus etiam nec vi extero ab aecclesia vel laico de fragmentis Domini ponatur in mensam. Unde scis tu cui passim sacrarii panes impendis, unde nosti si a mulieribus mundi sunt. Sic et David Abimelech interrogatus cum panem sibi ad comedendum poscere si mundus esse a muliere, et cum se mundum ante triduum profiteretur, panis propositionis manducavit.

[M, p 15; cf. 5L C 3.179, p 167; F 3.273]

<15> QUALES DEBENT MINISTRI SANCTAE AECCLESIE

Ministri altaris dominici tales eligantur qui ante ordinationes coniuges noverunt. Quod si post ordinatione contigerit ministrum proprie invadere cubilem uxoris, secretarii non intret limina nec sacrificii portitor fiat nec altario contingat nec ab offerentibus holocausta oblationes suscipiant nec ad dominici corporis portionem accedat. Aqua sacerdotum porrigat manibus, hostium forinsecus claudat, minora gerat officia, [p 157] urceum sane ad altare non suggerat.

[M, p 15; cf. 5L C 3.138, p 157; F 3.215]

<16> SI QUISLIBET DE ORDINATIS DE VELAMENTIS AECLESIAE SUSTULE PER ALIQUID AD VENDENDUM

Si forte quispiam presbiter sine archidiaconus sacrarii sindonem sive velum subtracta vendiderit, Iude similis estimabitur Scariothis; qui propter avaritiam fecit hoc opus, noverit se supradicti Iude suscepturum penam.

[M, p 15]

<17> *DE CAUTELA CLERICORUM*

Clericus ad femine tabernaculum non properet aut accedat sed neque si maioris principis iussione. Aut presbyter solus cum sola fabulas ammisceat, sed duobus aut tribus adductis testibus, visitet infirma.

[M, p 15; cf. 5L C 2.15, p 77; F 2.37]

<18> QUIBUS LICITUM EST HABITARE DE ORDINATIS CUM CAUTELA

Nemo tamen cum extranea habitet, nisi soror aut proxima fuerit. Et cum magna cautela et sollicitudine fiat. Non ignoramus malitiam serpentis, sane universa haec cum mansuetudine aecclesiastica implenda sunt misteria. Negotium enim Domini non decet neglegenter impleri.

[M, p 15; cf. 5L C 2.13, p 75; F 2.31]

<19> *DE STUDIO ERGA CALICEM SANCTUM*

Iterum atque iterum de fragmentis dominicis demandamus. Calicem vero ad offerendum sanguinem Domini preparatum, cum tota ministri munditia preparent. Ne non bene lotum calicem peccatum diaconi fiat offerenti, cum tota honestate, cum toto quoque timore supra quae exposuimus ordinentur. Talesque ad ministerium eligantur.

[M, p 15; cf. 5L C 3.141, p 158; F 3.218]

<20> *DE QUIBUS VEL QUOD MINISTROS HABEAT SACERDOS*

Oportet enim Domini sacerdotem paucos habere ministros et tales qui possint digne opus Domini exercere quam multos inutiles qui onus grave ordinatori adducat.

[MC 1, p 15; cf. 5L C 3.141, p 158; F 3.218]

<21> *QUALITER CUSTODIENDA VEL CAVENDA OBSERVANDAQUE SIT AQUA QUAE IN BAPTISMATE CONSECRATUR PRECEPTUM APOSTOLICUM*

Inter quae etiam de aqua baptismatis ex iussione apostolica contestamus et precipimus: Ne quis iam baptizatus ex ea tan[p158]gere presumat aut aspargere nisi illi pro quibus consecrata cernitur esse. Hoc est illi pro quibus baptizandi sunt ut per manus sacerdotum hi baptizentur et fidem percipiant sancte trinitatis. Nam quicumque baptizatus huius aque tinctione fuerit quasi pro benedictione aspersus decem mensibus alienus maneat a corpore et sanguine Domini preter sacerdotes a quorum manibus tinguendi sunt hi qui necdum fidem baptismatis perceperunt quia in symbolo nostre professionis baptisma non duo confitemur et credimus, hoc ideo precipe ut nemo baptizatus ex aqua fontis baptismati se se aut domum suam tinguat ne talia faciendo, inter hereticorum numeretur dogmata. Inter gravissima heresis dogmata numerandus est indoctus atque impudens episcopus seu presbiter, in cuius plebe tale perseveraverit nephas scelus. Inspiciatur ergo aperitissimis sacerdotibus ab inchoatione et usque in finem omni sensu huius fontis consecratio et tunc repperiet utrum baptizatis? An baptizandis est a sanctis predicatoribus edita atque firmata? Ideoque discretus antistes discretos ordinet sacerdotes ut discrete plebem suam unusquisque quaeat instruere. Quicumque itaque episcopus seu sacerdos huius communionem non cum diligentia custodiendo observaverit radicitus a suo gradu evellatur. Evangelica firmante sententia: Si oculus tua aut manus vel pes tuus scandalizat te erue eum et proiece abste [sic]. Bonum est ergo abscidere et proicere indoctos sacerdotes de aecclesia quam plebs erroribus diruatur. Plebs audit errorem et manet in eo penitudentem dissolvere potest predicator predicantem errorem abscidere precipimus. [p 159] a plebe.

<22> *UT ALIA AQUA QUAE A SANCTIS VIRIS INSTITUTUM EST QUERAMUS PRO REMEDIUM INFIRMITATIS ET PRO BENEDICTIONEM NON EA QUAE PRO BAPTISMO CUM CHRISMA CONSECRATUR UT FIRMITAS FIDEI SUPER BRUTIS ANIMALIBUS VEL ELEMENTIS TINGUATUR*

Cum itaque quisque Christianus se suamque domum aut animalia, agros vel iumenta aqua exorcizata aspergi voluerit, requirat in alia institutione patrum et plenius inveniet. Nam de aqua baptismatis et sacre chrismatis, nemo bis et ter aut deinceps tinguendus est, aut unguendus, nisi tantum semel. Qui hec fecerit, omnimodis hereticus comprobari potest.

<23> *ITEM DE ALIA AQUA EXORCIZATA QUID ET QUOD AGI DEBEAT*

De aqua vero exorcizata ubi sal exorcizatum mixtum fuerit, omnibus infirmis et fidem iam perceptis omnibus et animaliis et iumentis agrisque et domibus aspergendum sive gustandum precipimus.

<24>*DE OLEO SANCTO QUE PRO INFIRMIS SANCTIFICATUR, QUOD SINE CHRISMATE ESSE DEBEAT SOLUMMODO, NAM CUM ALIIS SANCTIFICATIONIBUS*

Oleo vero sanctificatum similiter ordinamus quod pro infirmis cernitur consecratum dicente apostolo: Infirmatur quis in vobis inducat presbiteros aecclesie et orent super eum et unguent eum oleo et cetera Nam non chrismate liniatur. His ergo sententiis bene preparate, nequis haec praecepta minime credant implenda et in iudicium ignis eterni deveniant?

<25> *QUI ECCLESIASTICIS OPERIS SACRAMENTA NEGLEXERINT*

Haec igitur pater Iacobe de ore sancti Petri iuventis audivi a principio epistole huius usque ad hunc locum et sacramentis deligavit. Bene tuenda ubi non murium stercosa in fragmentis dominice portionis appareant, neque esiatata per clericorum neglegen[p 160]tia et convenientes qui accipere sibi medicinam desiderant et esitata cum viderint, non medicinam accipere, sed ridiculum aliquid cum fastidio sumant.

[M 1, p 15; cf. 5L C 3.141, p 158; F 3.218]

<26> DE OBSERVANDA IN TOTO HAEC OMNIA CUM MAXIMA DILIGENTIA

Si quis haec praecepta non integra custodierit sit anathema ei usque in adventum Domini nostri Ihesu Christi. Haec precepta a predicto beato Petro apostolo accepi et tibi pater karissime insinuare curavi, ut servare omnia precipias sine macula. Si quis ergo audierit te et servaberit haec, erit utile erit minister Christi Ihesu. Qui autem non audierit te, immo Dominum loquentem per te ipse sibi damnatione acquirit.

[M, p 17; cf. 5L C 3.146, p 160; F 3.228]

THE SOUTH ITALIAN *COLLECTION IN FIVE BOOKS* AND ITS DERIVATIVES: A SOUTH ITALIAN APPENDIX TO THE *COLLECTION IN SEVENTY-FOUR TITLES**

IT is perhaps surprising that Beneventan-script codices, which were the primary vehicle for the south Italian *Collection in Five Books* and its derivatives, should also be a vehicle for one of the earliest and most popular collections of the Gregorian reform period, the *Collection in Seventy-Four Titles*. Indeed, four of the codices of this collection are written in Beneventan script.[1] In past research on canonical collections there has been a tendency to separate "papally-oriented" collections from others, especially those with monastic features.[2] Although scholars have been aware of the fact that several of these early manuscripts of the "papal" *Collection in Seventy-Four Titles*[3]

* Research for this article was undertaken as part of the programme *Monumenta liturgica beneventana*, supported by a grant from the Social Sciences and Humanities Research Council of Canada. I am grateful to Don Faustino Avagliano of Montecassino and the authorities of the Biblioteca Medicea Laurenziana in Florence for allowing me to consult the manuscripts of the south Italian Appendix to the *Collection in Seventy-Four Titles*. I am also grateful to the late John Gilchrist for use of his microfilm of these manuscripts, and to the Institute for Advanced Study, Princeton, for the George William Cottrell Jr. Membership in the School of Historical Studies.

[1] El Escorial, Real Biblioteca de San Lorenzo Z.III.19 (s. XI ex.) and L.III.19 (s. XII); Rome, Biblioteca Vallicelliana F 54 (s. XII); and Montecassino, Archivio dell'Abbazia 522 (s. XII).

[2] See, e.g., Theo Kölzer, "Die Farfenser Kanonessammlung des Cod. Vat. lat. 8487 (Collectio Farfensis)," *Bulletin of Medieval Canon Law*, n.s., 7 (1977): 97, and "Mönchtum und Kirchenrecht: Bermerkungen zu monastischen Kanonessammlung der vorgratianischen Zeit," *Zeitschrift der Savigny-Stiftung für Rechtsgeschichte, kanonistische Abteilung* 69 (1983): 123–42. Also see Giorgio Picasso, "Sacri canones et monastica regula nella cultura del monachesimo subalpino (sec. XI)," in *Dal Piemonte all'Europa: Esperienze monastiche nella società medievale. Relazioni e comunicazioni presentate al XXXIV Congresso storico subalpino (Torino 27–29 maggio 1985)* (Turin, 1988), 199–211.

[3] The classic description of the *Collection in Seventy-Four Titles* as a "papal" collection is in Paul Fournier and Gabriel Le Bras, *Histoire des collections canoniques en Occident depuis les Fausses Décrétales jusqu'au Décret de Gratien*, 2 vols. (Paris, 1931–32; rpt. Aalen, 1972), 2:14–19. But Horst Fuhrmann, *Einfluß und Verbreitung der pseudoisidorischen Fälschungen von ihrem Auftachen bis in die neuere Zeit*, 3 vols., Schriften der Monumenta Germaniae Historica 24.1–3 (Stuttgart, 1972–74), 2:486–509, has modified this description by emphasizing other than papal objectives in the collection.

were in Beneventan script, they have ignored the fact that Beneventan script was primarily a monastic one.[4] This is one indication that the connection between papally sponsored reform movements and monasteries was much closer than one might think. In fact, in recent historical, liturgical, and artistic scholarship the connections between Montecassino itself, Rome, and the papacy have been shown to be close indeed. John Cowdrey has stressed the relation between Gregory VII and Montecassino.[5] Numerous monks of the abbey were cardinals, and two popes of the period had been monks there, Victor III and Gelasius II. Under the former, the abbot Desiderius, Beneventan script reached its classical apogee.[6] On the liturgical side Richard Gyug has made the important discovery that the famous Casinese manuscript of the *Pontificale Romano-Germanicum,* Montecassino, Archivio dell'Abbazia 451, was an exemplar used to make the first "Roman" pontifical, the *Pontificale Romanum XII saeculi,* of the Desiderian pontifical, Vatican, Biblioteca Apostolica Vaticana Barb. lat. 631.[7] And art historians are now discovering the impact the architecture, decoration, and fresco painting of Montecassino had in Rome in the late eleventh and early twelfth centuries.[8] Hence, it is perhaps not unexpected that papal reforming measures epitomized in the *Collection in Seventy-Four Titles* were written in the Beneventan script of south Italian monasteries.

One of the primary manuscript witnesses used by John Gilchrist in his edition of the *Collection in Seventy-Four Titles* was Montecassino 522, a codex written in the twelfth century most probably at Montecassino.[9] Its contents have been described by John Gilchrist, including canons from a great variety of sources beyond the *Collection in Seventy-Four Titles.* Immediately following the *Collection in Seventy-Four Titles* there is a florilegium that consists of thirty-seven chapters deriving, as Gilchrist notes, from the *Collectio Dionysio-Hadriana,* the *Pseudo-Isidorian Decretals,* Burchard's *Decretum,* and even

[4] See my article, "Monumenta Liturgica Beneventana: Un Programa Superior de Investigacion de Historia Liturgica Medieval en el Pontificio Instituto de Estudios Medievales de Toronto (Canadá)," *Oriente – Occidente: Revista de Investigaciones Comparades* 16 (1999): 101–15.

[5] H. E. J. Cowdrey, *Pope Gregory VII, 1073–1085* (Oxford, 1998), esp. chap. 11.

[6] See E. A. Loew, *The Beneventan Script: A History of the South Italian Minuscule,* second edition prepared and enlarged by Virginia Brown, Sussidi eruditi 34 (Rome, 1980), 124–25.

[7] Richard F. Gyug, "The Pontificals of Monte Cassino," in *Miscellanea cassinese: L'Età dell'Abate Desiderio. Atti del IV Convegno di studi sul medioevo meridionale, Montecassino e Cassino 4–8 ottobre 1987* (Montecassino, 1992), 413–39.

[8] This has been emphasized most recently by John Osborne, "Framing Sacred Space: Eleventh-Century Mural Pointing in the Churches of Rome," to be published in the transactions of the Fordham University symposium, *The Liturgy of Rome in the Eleventh Century* (New York, 1998).

[9] J. T. Gilchrist, *Diuersorum patrum sententie siue Collectio in LXXIV titulos digesta,* Monumenta iuris canonici, Ser. B: Corpus collectionum 1 (Vatican, 1973), xxxii, dates the manuscript s. XI/XII, whereas Loew, *Beneventan Script* 2:89, dates it s. XII.

Gregory VII.[10] The florilegium also contains texts deriving from the *Collection in Five Books*. That this source has not been noted is understandable, since most of the canons deriving from the *Collection in Five Books* are from the as yet unedited books 4 and 5 of this collection.[11] Yet their presence in this florilegium is further evidence of the widespread influence of the *Collection in Five Books* in its many derivatives.[12]

The second major manuscript witness to the *Collection in Seventy-Four Titles* treated by Gilchrist is Florence, Biblioteca Medicea Laurenziana 16.15, a manuscript also written in the twelfth century, not in Beneventan but in a Carolingian script.[13] Again, there are numerous texts in addition to the *Collection in Seventy-Four Titles*, including many patristic texts, an Ordinal of Christ,[14] texts of eleventh-century popes including Alexander II, Gregory VII, and Urban II, and a list of popes reaching from Peter through Paschal II. But what is most unusual is that the same texts used as a continuation of the *Collection in Seventy-Four Titles* in Montecassino 522 follow the collection in the Florence manuscript (fols. 98r–103v) and that *capitulationes* for them, which are lacking in the Montecassino codex, are placed after the *capitulationes* preceding the *Collection in Seventy-Four Titles*. That is, the scribe of the Florence codex considered the Appendix as an integral part of the *Collection in Seventy-Four Titles*. In a sense, then, these additional texts are a parallel, albeit a shorter parallel, to the south German so-called Swabian Appendix to the *Collection in Seventy-Four Titles* studied by Johanne Autenrieth and edited by Gilchrist.[15]

[10] Gilchrist, *Diversorum patrum sententie*, 179–95.

[11] For the edition of books 1–3 of the collection, see Mario Fornasari, *Collectio canonum in v libris (Lib. i–iii)*, CCCM 6 (Turnhout, 1970).

[12] See my "The South-Italian Canon Law *Collection in Five Books* and Its Derivatives: New Evidence on Its Origins, Diffusion, and Use," *Mediaeval Studies* 52 (1990): 278–95, "The South-Italian *Collection in Five Books* and Its Derivatives: The *Collection of Vallicelliana Tome XXI*," in *Proceedings of the Eighth International Congress of Medieval Canon Law: San Diego, University of California at La Jolla, 21–27 August 1988*, ed. S. Chodorow, Monumenta iuris canonici, Ser. C, Subsidia 9 (Vatican, 1991), 77–92, "The South Italian *Collection in Five Books* and Its Derivatives: Maastricht Excerpta," *Mediaeval Studies* 58 (1996): 273–28, and "South and Central Italian Canonical Collections of the Tenth and Eleventh Centuries (non-Gregorian)," in *Studies in Medieval and Early Modern Canon Law*, ed. W. Hartmann and K. Pennington (Washington, D.C., in press since 1993).

[13] Gilchrist, *Diversorum patrum sententie*, xxxiv.

[14] See my *The Ordinals of Christ from Their Origins to the Twelfth Century*, Beiträge zur Geschichte und Quellenkunde des Mittelalters 7 (Berlin and New York, 1978), 75 n. 95, and "Christ as Cleric: The Ordinals of Christ," in my *Clerics in the Early Middle Ages: Hierarchy and Image* (Aldershot, 1999), II, 17.

[15] Johanne Autenrieth, "Bernold von Konstanz und die erweiterte 74-Titelsammlung," *Deutsches Archiv* 14 (1958): 375–94; and Gilchrist, *Diversorum patrum sententie*, 180–96.

Among the concerns expressed in the canons of the Appendix are liturgical matters involving baptism, the Eucharist, confirmation, and requirements for those to be ordained; protection of the abbey of Montecassino from the depredations of the Normans and others; condemnation of lay investiture; false penitence; Sabbath abstinence; regulations regarding tithes and offerings; simony; married clergy; clerical and monastic immunity from lay jurisdiction; matrimony and marital regulations; burial; the power of bishops; false testimony; and theft of ecclesiastical property. While many of the canons might apply to clerics of any kind, secular or monastic, there is definitely a monastic bent to several of the canons. This is seen, for example, in the immunities given to Montecassino itself and her monks and in canons relating to abbots.

Particularly interesting are the sources of the canons: Burchard's *Decretum*, the *Collectio Dionysio-Hadriana*, texts from the councils of Gregory VII, a text resembling one of Henry II, the *Pseudo-Isidorian Decretals*, the *Collection in Five Books*, and even the *Collection in Seventy-Four Titles* itself. Virtually all of these texts were available at Montecassino: Burchard's *Decretum* in Montecassino 44 and 45, the *Collectio Dionysiana* and *Collectio Dionysio-Hadriana* in Vatican City, Biblioteca Apostolica Vaticana Vat. lat. 5845 and Montecassino 522; texts from the councils of Gregory VII in Montecassino 216;[16] texts of Henry II in Montecassino 125; the *Pseudo-Isidorian Decretals* in Montecassino 1; the *Collection in Five Books* in Montecassino 125;[17] and the *Collection in Seventy-Four Titles* in Montecassino 522 and perhaps El Escorial, Real Biblioteca de San Lorenzo Z.III.19 and L.III.19.[18]

The place of composition of this Appendix to the *Collection in Seventy-Four Titles* was almost certainly Montecassino. The Florence manuscript is in Carolingian script and was probably written in central Italy, while the Montecassino codex is in Beneventan script of the twelfth century and was likely written at Montecassino. Also, it is interesting that in the canon of Gregory

[16] On this collection, see my *The Collectio canonum casinensis duodecimi saeculi (Codex terscriptus): A Derivative of the South-Italian Collection in Five Books. An Implicit Edition with Introductory Study*, Monumenta Liturgica Beneventana 3, Studies and Texts 137 (Toronto, 2001).

[17] It is, of course, possible that the canons found in the *Collection in Five Books* and the South Italian Appendix came to the latter from other sources compiled before the former, but this is unlikely because of these possible previous sources, such as the *Collection in Nine Books* or *Collections of Vatican, San Pietro H-58* (Vatican City, Biblioteca Apostolica Vaticana Vat. lat. 1349 and San Pietro H-58 respectively), there is no evidence that these existed at Montecassino, while there was at Montecassino a manuscript of the *Collection in Five Books*. On the other hand, there could have been other earlier sources now lost for the canons found in the *Collection in Five Books*. It is also possible that the canons found in the *Collection in Five Books* were drawn from other later derivatives of that collection, but until all of these are edited, it seems preferable to cite the canons as they appear in the *Collection in Five Books*.

[18] Gilchrist, *Diversorum patrum sententie*, xxxv, xlvii.

VII dealing with depredations of monastic property, the references to the Normans and to Montecassino have been omitted in the Florence text. Canons dealing with Montecassino itself and abbots have already been noted, and there is one canon that does not specifically mention Montecassino but can be tied to it. This is canon 20 regarding clerical immunity from lay jurisdiction:

> Ut nullus sacerdos vel diaconus seu subdiaconus vel de qualicumque gradu clericorum presumat facere legem nisi ante presentiam episcopi sui, per quattuor domini evangelia finienda sine guadia et sine fideiussore. Quod si interventum fuerit et guadiam dederit et fideiussorem posuerit, et ad seculare iudicium sine voluntate episcopi sui iterit excommunicetur et ipse iudex qui eum sine episcopi sui iussione receperit sit anathema. Si resipuerit tres carinas cum septem sequentibus annis peniteat.

Where and when this canon originated is not certain, but later in the twelfth century the text of this canon is reflected in a privilege given to the church of San Germano (the previous name of the present city of Cassino) by Pope Clement III (1188):

> sane quia sacris canonibus cautum est ut nullus sacerdos, seu diaconus, vel subdiaconus, aut de qualicunque gradu clericorum ad forum judicis saecularis trahatur, sancimus et apostolica auctoritate statuimus, ut sicut bonae memoriae Gerardus quondam Cassinensis abbas cum assensu fratrum suorum decrevit, ut nullus clericorum in toto territorio Sancti Benedicti habitantium saeculari judicio constringatur, nec ab aliqua persona laica judicetur, vel purgationem facere, aut legem subire, sive gaudium aut fidejussorem praestare cogatur.[19]

The *abbas* mentioned here is Gerard, who was abbot of Montecassino from 1118 to 1123, almost precisely the time in which the Montecassino manuscript was written.

In the following implicit edition of the Appendix,[20] the text found in the Montecassino manuscript is used inasmuch as the text was most likely compiled there. In the Florence manuscript canons are at times ordered differently from those in the Montecassino manuscript, and several canons appearing in the latter are omitted in the former. The Florence manuscript, however, contains rubrics for the canons that the Montecassino manuscript lacks, and in the cases where this happens the rubrics from the Florence manuscript are inserted in boldface. Also, there are rubrics and numbers for the canons in the Florence manuscript following those for the *Collection in Seventy-Four Titles*, and hence, before the text of the Appendix itself is given below, these rubrics

[19] Quoted from PL 204:1344–45; see canon 20 of the Appendix in the edition below.
[20] On "implicit" editions, see the preface to my *Collectio canonum casinensis.*

and the canon numbers in the Florence manuscript are printed in boldface. It must be noted, however, that in the text of the Appendix itself in both manuscripts no numbers are assigned to the canons.

In this implicit edition of the canons, *capitulatio* numbers in brackets 〈 〉 have been added to facilitate consultation. They correspond to the rubrics or separation of units in the Montecassino manuscript. These brackets have also been used where readings are illegible in the manuscripts.

Spelling, grammar, and syntax in Beneventan-script codices are notoriously inconsistent and faulty.[21] In this incipit-explicit edition these peculiarities in the manuscript have been maintained since they may suggest relationships with other derivative collections based on the *Collection in Five Books* or other canonical collections used by the compilers of the Cassino collection.

Following the lead of the CD Rom program by Linda Fowler-Magerl, *Kanones. A Selection of Canon Law Collections Compiled Outside Italy Between 1000 and 1140* (Piesenkofen in the Oberpfalz, 1998), the incipits and explicits reported here consist of a minimum of six words.

Sources for the canons are assigned as follows. Canons taken from Burchard's *Decretum* (= Burchard) are cited not from the superior edition of M. de Neuss (Novesianus) (Cologne, 1548; rpt. with introductory essays by T. Kölzer and G. Fransen [Aalen, 1992]), but according to the Migne "edition" (PL 140) for ease of consultation. Canons from books 1–3 of the *Collection in Five Books* (= 5L) are cited from Fornasari's edition (CCCM 6); canons from books 4–5 of are cited from Montecassino 125 (= C), since the Vatican and Vallicelliana manuscripts of the collection (Vat. lat 1339 and Rome, Biblioteca Vallicelliana B 11) are defective. For ease of consultation, canons from the *Collectio Dionysio-Hadriana* are cited from the edition of the *Collectio Dionysiana* (*Redactio II*) in PL 67:137–316. Canons included in the *Pseudo-Isidorian Decretals* are cited from *Decretales pseudo-Isidorianae et capitula Angilramni*, ed. P. Hinschius (Leipzig, 1863) (= Hinschius). Canons from the Roman council of 1078 are cited from book 6 of *Das Register Gregors VII*, ed. E. Caspar, MGH Epistolae Selectae 2 (Berlin, 1920–23), 400–406 (= Caspar). It would be possible to cite parallels given in Fowler-Magerl's *Kanones* for many of the canons, but such citations would clutter the *apparatus fontium* unnecessarily and can easily be found by consulting *Kanones*. Sources of the canons found in Burchard's *Decretum* can easily be found in Hartmut Hoffman and Rudolf Pokorny, *Das Dekret des Bischofs Burchard von Worms: Textstufen, frühe Verbreitung, Vorlagen*, MGH Hilfsmittel 12 (Munich, 1991).

[21] On this, see R. Jacobsson, "Short Reflexions on Beneventan Easter Sequence Texts," in *La Sequenza Medievale. Atti del Convegno Internazionale Milano 7–8 aprile 1984*, ed. A. Ziino (Lucca, 1992), 129–30.

CONTINUATION OF *CAPITULATIONES* FOR THE *COLLECTION IN SEVENTY-FOUR TITLES* IN FLORENCE 16.15

(fol. 55v) **cccxvi. Ut diaconi mensuram propriam iuxta patrum decreta custodiant. Ex decreta Gelasii generali.**

cccxvii. Quod diaconibus nec offere nec presbyteris corpus tradere nec ante eos communicare nec sedere sit licitum. Ex concilio Niceno cap. xviii.

cccxviii. De his que omnino prohibentur presbiteris. Ex decreta Gelasii generali cap. viii.

cccxviiii. De presbiteris ut nichil super episcopos presumant. De presbiteris.

[blank space]

ccxx [*sic, et infra ccxxi–ccxxiiii*]. **De suscipiendis his qui persecutionem patiuntur.**

ccxxi. De investitura ecclesiarum a laicis non accipenda.

ccxxii. De ordinationibus pretio precibus aut obsequio non faciendis.

ccxxiii. De his qui monasteriorum 〈. . .〉 deripiunt 〈. . .〉. In decretis Gregorii.

ccxxiiii. Quod episcopi 〈debeant augere numerum ordinatorum si de ordinando episcopo fuerit contradictum.〉

(fol. 56r) **cccxxv. De falsa penitentia ha** [*sic*] **de falsis penitentibus similis.**

cccxxvi. De abstinentia sabbati.

cccxxvii. De decimis a laicis non accipiendis.

cccxxviii. Quod decime in potestate debeant esse episcoporum.

cccxxviiii. Ut nullus presbiter ecclesiam per precium obtineat.

cccxxx. Ut nullus clericus audeat legem facere vel sacramentum iurare coram laica potestate absque presentia vel iussione episcopi sui.

cccxxxi. De his qui matrimonio iuncti sunt vel nubere non possunt. Gregorius Iohanni Ravennani episcopo.

cccxxxii. De clericis sepulcrorum violatoribus.

cccxxxiii. De clericis apostantibus.

cccxxxiiii. Ut res ecclesie permaneant in episcopi potestate.

cccxxxv. Ut nullus clericus alicui laico super evangelia iuret. Ex concilio Remensi.

cccxxxvi. Justinanus Augustus Iohanni prefecto. De eadem re in primo libro Codicis.

cccxxxvii. Quod non liceat clerico ante laicum iudicem stare et quod iudicare non debeat.

cccxxxviii. Clericus sine presentia episcopi sui et quod de nullo crimine accusari possit iuste sine vii. legalibus ac idoneis testibus.

cccxxxviiii. De periurio sponte perpetrato.
cccxxxx. De periurio non sponte perpetrato.
cccxxxxi. De falso testimonio.
cccxxxxii. De is qui consentiunt falso testimonio.
cccxxxxiii. De eadem re.
cccxxxxiv. Interrogatio Augustini anglici episcopi de his qui in ecclesia furantur.
cccxxxxv. Responsio beati Gregorii papae. De eadem re.
cccxxxxvi. De homine qui pro mortis necessitate filium suum baptizavit.
cccxxxxvii. De his qui proprios filios a fonte baptismatis aliquo negligentie modo suscipiunt.
EXPLICIUNT CAPITULA

TEXT OF THE SOUTH ITALIAN APPENDIX FROM MONTECASSINO 522

(p. 180) ⟨1⟩ EX DECRETO GELASII GENERALI UT DIACONI MENSURAM PROPRIAM IUXTA PATRUM DECRETA CUSTODIANT.
Diacones quoque propriam constituimus observare mensuram . . . quod et facere laycis christianis plerumque conceditur.
(Gelasius, *Decretum generale,* cap. 9; Hinschius, 650–51; and cf. Burchard 4.57 [PL 140:738])

⟨2⟩ EX CONCILIO NICENO. CAP. XIIII. QUOD DIACONIBUS NEC OFFERE NEC PRESBITERIS CORPUS TRADERE NEC ANTE EOS COMMUNICARE NEC SEDERE SIT LICITUM.
Pervenit ad sanctum concilium quod in locis quibusdam et civitatibus presbiteris sacramentum . . . (p. 181) . . . post hanc diffinitionem cesset esse diaconus.
(Conc. Nic., c. 14; Hinschius, 250; and cf. Montecassino 522, p. 257)

⟨3⟩ EX DECRETO GELASII PAPAE GENERALI. CAP. VIII. DE HIS QUE OMNINO PROHIBENTUR PRESBITERIS.
De his que omnino prohibentur presbiteris que si presumpserint . . . vacabit si talia facientem dissimulare iudicaverit.
(*Fons non invenitur; vide infra* ⟨4⟩)

⟨4⟩ DE PRESBITERIS UT NICHIL SUPER EPISCOPOS PRESUMANT.
Nec minus etiam presbiteros ultra suum modum . . . (p. 182) . . . vacuatur si immoderate facientem dissimulaverit vindicare.
(Gelasius, *Decretum generale,* cap. 8; Hinschius, 651)

⟨5⟩ IN DECRETIS GREGORII.
Gregorius episcopus servus servorum dei. Si quis Normannorum vel quorum-

libet hominum predia monasteria beati Benedicti montis casinensis invaserit . . . suibiaceat donec resipiscat et ecclesie satisfaciat.

(Conc. Rom. [1078], cap. 2; Caspar, 403; and *Italia pontificia* 8, ed. P. F. Kehr [Berlin, 1935], 147)

(p. 183) ⟨6⟩ CANONE APOSTOLORUM QUO IN QUI NON SPONTE EUNUCHIZATI SUNT SUSCIPIANTUR AD CLERUM.

Eunuchus si per insidias hominum factus . . . natus est et dignus efficiatur episcopus.

(*Canones apostolorum,* c. 21; Hinschius, 28; cf. Montecassino 522, p. 242; 5L 1.139 [CCCM 6:97]; and Montecassino 541, p. 40])

⟨7⟩ DE ORDINATIS EPISCOPIS NEC RECEPTIS.

Si quis episcopus non susceperit officium et curam . . . eruditores in obedientis populi non fuerunt.

(*Canones apostolorum,* c. 37; Hinschius, 29; cf. Montecassino 522, p. 246; and 5L 1.169 [CCCM 6:112])

⟨8⟩ DE HIS QUI AD EPISCOPATUM VOCANTUR ET VITANT.

Si quis episcopus manus impositionem acceperit episcopatus . . . integra decreverit eiusdem provincie synodus sacerdotum.

(Conc. Antioch., c. 17; *Collectio Dionysio-Hadriana,* PL 67:162; cf. Montecassino 541, p. 283)

⟨9⟩ DE SUSCIPIENDIS HIS QUI PERSECUTIONEM PATIUNTUR.

Osius episcopus dixit: Suggerente fratre et coepiscopo nostro Olimpio etiam hoc placuit ut si aliquis vim perpessus est et inique expulsus . . . (p. 184) . . . benevolentia et humanitas ei est exhibenda. Omnis synodus dixit: Universa que constituta sunt catholica ecclesia in universo orbe diffusa custodiet.

(Cf. Burchard 1.119 [PL 140:584]; Montecassino 522, p. 324; and Conc. Sard., c. 21, *Collectio Dionysio-Hadriana,* PL 67:182)

⟨10⟩ QUOD ADHIBEANT EPISCOPI NUMERO ORDINATORUM SI DE ORDINANDO EPISCOPO FUERIT CONTRADICTUM.

Sed illud est statuendum ut quando ad eligendum episcopum convenerimus . . . dignationis responsione. Ab universis episcopis dictum est, Satis placet.

(Conc. Afric. c. 17; *Collectio Dionysio-Hadriana,* PL 67:196; cf. Burchard 1.6 [PL 140:551])

⟨11⟩ DE INVESTITURA ECCLESIARUM A LAYCIS NON ACCIPIENDIS.

(p. 185) Quoniam investituras ecclesiarum contra statuta sanctorum patrum a laycis personis . . . usque ad dignam satisfactionem excommunicationi subiacere.

(Conc. Rom. [1078], cap. 3; Caspar, 403)

⟨12⟩ DE ORDINATIONIBUS PRETIO PRECIBUS AUT OBSEQUIO NON FACIENDIS.
Ordinationes que interveniente pretio vel precibus vel obsequio alicui persone . . . veritas testatur fures sunt et latrones.
(Conc. Rom. [1078], cap. 5; Caspar, 403)

⟨13⟩ DE FALSIS PENITENTIBUS.
Falsas penitentias dicimus que non secundum auctoritatem sanctorum patrum pro qualitate . . . (p. 186) . . . ut omnipotens deus cor illius illustret ad penitentiam.
(Conc. Rom. [1078], cap. 6; Caspar, 404)

⟨14⟩ DE ABSTINENTIA SABBATI.
Quia dies sabbati apud sanctos patres nostros in abstinentia . . . festivitate interveniente vel infirmitate impediente abstineat.
(Conc. Rom. [1078], cap. 8; Caspar, 405)

⟨15⟩ DE DECIMIS A LAYCIS NON ACCIPIENDIS.
Decimas quas in usum pietatis concessas esse . . . (p. 187) . . . commitere et eterne damnationis periculum incurrere.
(Conc. Rom. [1078], cap. 7; Caspar, 404)

⟨16⟩ QUOD DECIME IN POTESTATE ESSE DEBEANT EPISCOPORUM.
Ut nullus abbas decimas et primitias et reliqua . . . in cuius diocesi habitat detineat apostolica sanctione firmamus.
(Conc. Rom. [1078], cap. 9; Caspar, 405)

⟨17⟩ Si quis episcopus aut presbiter aut diaconus vel subdiaconus per pecuniam . . . et sit anathema sicut Symon Magus a Petro.
(*Canones apostolorum,* c. 30; *Collectio Dionysio-Hadriana,* PL 67:144; and Hinschius, 29)

⟨18⟩ **UT NULLUS PRESBITER ECCLESIAM PER PRECIUM OBTINEAT.**
Quicumque presbiter per pretium ecclesiam fuerit adeptus . . .. eamque sibi taliter vindicaverit omnimodo deponatur.
(Burchard 3.110 [PL 140:695])

⟨19⟩ Si presbiter uxorem acceperit deponatur. Si vero (p. 188) . . . fornicator proicite eum de medio vestri.
(Cf. Burchard 2.108 [PL 140:645]; Conc. Neoceasar., c. 1; *Collectio Dionysio-Hadriana,* PL 67:155)

⟨20⟩ **UT NULLUS CLERICUS AUDEAT LEGEM FACERE ET SACRAMENTUM IURARE CORAM LAICA POTESTATE ABSQUE PRESENTIA EPISCOPI SUI.**
Ut nullus sacerdos vel diaconus seu subdiaconus vel de qualicumque gradu

clericorum presumat facere legem nisi ante presentiam episcopi sui, per quattuor domini evangelia finienda sine guadia et sine fideiussore. Quod si interventum fuerit et guadiam dederit et fideiussorem posuerit, et ad seculare iudicium sine voluntate episcopi sui iterit excommunicetur et ipse iudex qui eum sine episcopi sui iussione receperit sit anathema. Si resipuerit tres carinas cum septem sequentibus annis peniteat.

(*Fons non invenitur; vide* Montecassino 216, pp. 130–131; cf. PL 204:1344–45; and *Italia pontificia* 8:194)

⟨21⟩ **DE HIS QUI MATRIMONIO IUNCTI SUNT ET NUBERE NON POSSUNT.**

GREGORIUS JOHANNI RAVENNATI EPISCOPO.

Quod autem interrogasti de his qui in matrimonio iuncti sunt et nubere non possunt . . . Si autem ille aliam acceperit separentur.

(Burchard 9.40 [PL 140:821])

(p. 189) ⟨22⟩ **DE CLERICIS SEPULCHRORUM FRACTORIBUS.**

Si quis clericus in demoliendis sepulchris fuit . . . submovere sed et penitentie triennio deputari.

(Burchard 11.63 [PL 140:871]; and 5L 4.133b [C, p. 235, attributed to Gregory])

⟨23⟩ **DE CLERICIS APOSTANTIBUS.**

Clericus tonsura dimissa si uxorem acceperit. . . . Uxorem si usurpaverit cum penitentia dimittere compellatur.

(Burchard 8.97 [PL 140:811])

⟨24⟩ Karissimi monemus ut intelligatis potestatem episcoporum vestrorum in eisque . . . quod tamen eum summopere precavere oportet.

(*Coll. in LXXIV titulos* 225 [Gilchrist, *Diversorum patrum sententie,* 141])

⟨25⟩ **UT RES ECCLESIE PERMANEAT IN EPISCOPI POTESTATE.**

In sancto concilio decretum est et a sanctis patribus et sancitum ut omnes ecclesie cum (p. 190) dotibus suis . . . ad ordinationem vel dispositionem suam semper pertineant.

(Burchard 3.146 [PL 140:702])

⟨26⟩ **EX CONCILIO REMENSI. UT NULLUS CLERICUS ALICUI LAICO SUPER EVANGELIA IURET.**

Ut nullus ex ecclesiastico ordine cuiquam layco quicquid supra sacrosancta evangelia iuret. . . . causa fuerit persummissam sibi personam expurgetur.

(Cf. Burchard 2.188 [PL 140:657])

⟨27⟩ **IUSTINIANUS AUGUSTUS IOHANNI PREFECTO IN PRIMO LIBRO CODICIS. DE EADEM RE.**

Dignum est ut totus clericalis ordo a prestando iureiurando immunis esse . . .

persummissam personam hoc officium liceat delegare.
(Cf. Henricus II: *Constitutio nova Ariminensis* [PL 140:231–32])

(p. 191) ⟨28⟩ **NON LICEAT CLERICUS ANTE LAICUM IUDICEM STARE ET QUOD IUDICARI DEBEAT IN PRESENTIA EPISCOPI SUI.**
Non liceat sacerdoti vel clerico vel monacho succinctus ante laycum iudicem stare . . . idoneos si hoc non fecerit sub anathemate sit.
(Cf. Sylvester, *Ex synodalibus gestis*, cap. 5; Hinschius, 449)

⟨29⟩ Si quis iniuriam dereliquerit hoc est statim passus et ad animum . . . penitentia remissa iniuria non poterit recolere.
(*Fons non invenitur*)

⟨30⟩ **DE PERIURIO SPONTE PERPETRATO.**
Si quis periurium fecerit episcopus xii^{m}. annis peniteat, iii^{s}. ex his in pane et aqua. . . . Laycus iii^{s} i^{m} in pane et aqua.
(Cf. *Liber sacramentorum Augustodunensis*, ed. O. Heiming, CCL 159B [Turnhout, 1984], 298, no. 2187; and *Paenitentialia minora franciae et italiae saeculi VIII–IX*, ed. R. Kottje et al., CCL 156 [Turnhout, 1994], 63 [BU 5] and 127 [ME 5,6])

⟨31⟩ **DE PERIURIO NON SPONTE PERPETRATO.**
Si quis coactus qualibet necessitate aut nesciens periuraverit . . . (p. 192) . . . et post vii. annos iudicio sacerdotis communicet.
(5L 4.145 [C, p. 239])

⟨32⟩ **DE FALSO TESTIMONIO.**
Si quis falsum testimonium dixerit episcopus vii. annis peniteat. . . . laycus iii^{s} i^{m} in pane et aqua.
(5L 4.94 [C, p. 223])

⟨33⟩ **DE HIS QUI CONSENTIUNT FALSO TESTIMONIO.**
Qui consentiunt ad falsum testimonium ii. annis peniteat. Si quis iuraverit in manu hominis apud grecos nichil est . . . in periurium ducitur tamen iurat perconsensum ii. annis peniteat.
(5L 4.94 [C, p. 223])

⟨34⟩ **DE FALSO TESTIMONIO.**
Si quis falsum testimonium dicens ut placeat proximo suo qualeque fratri . . . intulit tali iudicio damnetur iudice sacerdote.
(5L 4.94 [C, p. 223])

(p. 193) ⟨35⟩ **AUGUSTINUS ANGLICUS EPISCOPUS. DE FURANTIBUS IN ECCLESIA.**
Obsecro quid pati debeat qui dei ecclesia aliquid furto abstulerit?

RESPONSIO BEATI GREGORII.
Gregorius. Hoc tua fraternitas ex persona furis pensare. . . . Sed absit ut ecclesia cum augmento recipiat quod detur reus rebus videtur ammittere.
(*Interrogatio Augustini et Responsio Gregorii,* cap. 4; Hinschius, 738)

⟨36⟩ **DE HOMINE QUI PRO NECESSITATE MORTIS FILIUM SUUM BAPTIZAVIT.**
Iohannes episcopus Anselmo Lemonecine ecclesie. Ad limina beatorum Petri ac Pauli apostolorum principum. Hic presens homo nomine Stephanus orationis (p. 194) causa veniens . . . (p. 195) . . . prefatas auctoritates divinas aliquatenus separari debere.
(5L 5.114a [C, p. 333]; cf. Montecassino 372, p. 45)

⟨37⟩ **DE HIS QUI PROPRIOS FILIOS A FONTE BAPTISMATIS ALIQUO NEGLIGENTIE MODO SUSCIPIUNT.**
Deusdedit sancte Romane et apostolice ecclesie episcopus Gurdiano Hispaniensis ecclesie coepiscopo et fratri dilecto. Pervenit ad nos diaconus vester vestre sanctitatis epistolam ferens quod quidam viri etiam et mulieres . . . (p. 196) . . . recipiant alterum virum si voluerint. Similiter et viri uxorem.
(Burchard 17.44 [PL 140:928])

XVII

THE SOUTH ITALIAN *COLLECTION IN FIVE BOOKS* AND ITS DERIVATIVES: MAASTRICHT EXCERPTA

WHEN E. A. Lowe undertook his research for his classic *The Beneventan Script,*[1] his hunt for manuscripts written in the distinctive hand of south Italy and Dalmatia rarely lead him into archives that may have had examples of his script. Rather, he concentrated with good reason on libraries with their collections of manuscripts containing non-diplomatic materials. Lowe explored archives only in a few cases, such as Dalmatia, yet as the search for further items written in Beneventan continues, it has been discovered that the archive, ecclesiastical or secular, is one of the most fruitful venues.[2] Codices written in this script were largely

[1] E. A. Loew, *The Beneventan Script: A History of the South Italian Minuscule* (Oxford, 1914).

[2] The following archives are noted in Loew, *The Beneventan Script* and *The Beneventan Script: A History of the South Italian Minuscule,* Second edition prepared and enlarged by Virginia Brown, vol. 2: *Hand List of Beneventan MSS.,* Sussidi eruditi 34 (Rome, 1980); E. A. Lowe, "A New List of Beneventan Manuscripts," in *Collectanea vaticana in honorem Anselmi M. Card. Albareda a Bibliotheca Apostolica edita,* 2 vols., Studi e testi 219–20 (Vatican City, 1962), 2:211–44; Virginia Brown, "A Second New List of Beneventan Manuscripts (I)," *Mediaeval Studies* 40 (1978): 239–89, "A Second New List of Beneventan Manuscripts (II)," *Mediaeval Studies* 50 (1988): 584–625, and "A Second New List of Beneventan Manuscripts (III)," *Mediaeval Studies* 56 (1994): 299–350. Some depositories called archives are also libraries.

Altamura, Archivio Biblioteca Museo Civico, Archivio Capitolare; Ascoli Piceno, Archivio di Stato, Fondo notarile Ascoli Piceno; Augsburg, Stadtarchiv; Avellino, Archivio di Stato; Aversa, Archivio Capitolare della Chiesa Cattedrale S. Paolo, Archivio Storico Diocesano; Avezzano, Archivio Diocesano dei Marsi; Bamberg, Staatsarchiv; Barcelona, Archivo de la Corona de Aragon; Bari, Archivio del Duomo, Archivio di S. Nicola, Archivio di Stato; Benevento, Archivio di Stato, Commissione Diocesana per i Beni Culturali; Bisceglie, Archivio Capitolare del Duomo, Archivio del Duomo, Archivio parrocchiale della Collegiata dei SS. Matteo e Niccolò, Archivio Storico Diocesano; Bologna, Archivio di Stato; Caiazzo, Archivio Capitolare; Camerino, Archivio Arcivescovile, Archivio di Stato; Cava, Archivio della Badia della Santissima Trinità; Cologne, Historisches Archiv; Corfinio, Archivio Capitolare della Cattedrale S. Pelino; Corinaldo, Archivio Storico Comunale; Cremona, Archivio di Stato; Ferentino, Archivio Storico e Notarile; Foggia, Archivio di Stato; Foligno, Archivio di Stato; Frosinone, Archivio di Stato; Gaeta, Archivio del Capitolo Cattedrale, Archivio del Duomo; Gerona, Arxiu de la Catedral; Giovinazzo, Archivio Capitolare; Goslar, Stadtarchiv; Koblenz, Landeshauptarchiv; Latina, Archivio di Stato; Lucca, Archivio di Stato; Lucerne, Stiftsarchiv S. Leodegar; Macerata, Archivio di Stato; Matera, Archivio di Stato; Mirabella Eclano, Archivio della Chiesa Collegiata; Monopoli, Archivio Unico Diocesano; Montecassino, Archivio della Badia; Naples, Archivio di

liturgical and hence usually had heavy wear. As liturgical rites copied in Beneventan became obsolete or outmoded, the folios of the manuscripts in which they were written might be palimpsested or reused for other purposes.[3] When "retired," the manuscripts were often dismembered and the membra disiecta used as binding covers for archival material or for pastedowns and flyleaves in other manuscripts or printed books. To a lesser extent, this was also the case with legal manuscripts, be they of secular or ecclesiastical law.[4] The manuscript fragments that are the subject of this note once belonged to a book of canon law related to the eleventh-century *Collection in Five Books.*

The excerpta are written on two parchment bifolia now found in the Rijksarchief Limburg of Maastricht in the Netherlands.[5] The blue-grey folder in which they are found bears the call number "R.A. Limburg 18.A. Collectie Handschriften Cat. nr. 196." The old manuscript number was 167.I.27. The recent catalogue of the 543 manuscripts and fragments in the Rijksarchief edited by G. J. M. Jägers describes the bifolia as follows: "[Fragment uit een verhandeling over kerkelijk recht.] Handschrift; perkament; ongedateerd. 8° (onregelmatig van formaat); 1 katern (membrum disjectum), ongepagineerd (8 p.), geglosseerd, initialen (in rood en groen), in omslag. / Latijnse tekst. Delen van de tekst in rood./"[6] The two bifolia are of medium-quality parchment of a yellow-tan colour. As bifolia they

Stato, Archivio Storico Diocesano; Northampton, Northamptonshire Record Office; Orvieto, Archivio di Stato; Parma, Archivio di Stato; Peterlingen, Stadtarchiv; Ravenna, Archivio Storico Arcivescovile; Rieti, Archivio Capitolare; Rome, Archivio di Stato; St. Petersburg, Arkhiv . . . Instituta Istorii Akademii; Sala Consilina, Archivio Parrocchiale di S. Pietro Apostolo; Salerno, Archivio di Stato; San Giovanni in Fiore, Archivio parrocchiale della Chiesa Matrice di San Giovanni in Fiore; Split, Arheološki Muzej, Nadbiskupski Arhiv, Riznica Katedrale, Kaptolski Arhiv; Teramo, Archivio della Curia Vescovile; Trani, Archivio Capitolare; Trogir, Kaptolski Arhiv; Troia, Archivio del Duomo; Udine, Archivio di Stato; Vatican City, Archivio Segreto Vaticano; Venice, Archivio di Stato; Zadar, Archives of the Convent of St. Mary, Archiepiscopal Archives, Historijski Arhiv; Zagreb, Arhiv Hrvatske, Arhiv Jugoslavenske Akademije; Zürich, Staatsarchiv.

[3] A classic example of this are the Boccaccio autographs, on which see Virginia Brown, "Boccaccio in Naples: The Beneventan Liturgical Palimpsest of the Laurentian Autographs (MSS. 29.8 and 33.31)," *Italia medioevale e umanistica* 34 (1991): 41–126.

[4] See, e.g., Toni Schmid, "Canon Law in Manuscripts from Medieval Sweden," *Traditio* 7 (1949–51): 444–49; and *Helgeränet: Från Mässböcker till Munkepärmar,* ed. Kerstin Abukhanfusa, Jan Brunius, and Solbritt Benneth (Stockholm, 1993), 72, 79–80, 164–65, 179.

[5] I am grateful to Dr. Rudolf Pokorny for originally drawing my attention to these folios. Research has been supported by a grant from the Social Sciences and Humanities Research Council of Canada for the project Monumenta Liturgica Beneventana.

[6] *Catalogus van de handschriftencollectie van het Rijksarchief in Limburg,* ed. G. J. M. Jägers (Maastricht, 1991), 70–71.

are unnumbered and bear no foliation or pagination; hence for ease of description they can be called here Bifolium A and Bifolium B.

The measurements of Bifolium A are 280 mm. (wide) × 206 mm. (high), the extending tabs at the top reaching to 223 mm. Bifolium B measures 270 × 201 mm., the extending tabs at the top reaching to 214 mm. No pricking is visible, but on Bifolium A marginal rules and lines have been made by drypoint from hair to flesh side. The vertical rulings for margins, from left to right across Bifolium A, fols. 2v–1r, are (first rule cropped) 4, 101, 105, 136, 141, 237, and 243 mm. The three middle and lowest lines continue through the center of the bifolium. On each folio there are twenty-six lines of text, 6/7 mm. apart, in one column. The writing space is approximately 170 × 96 mm.

Originally the folding of Bifolium A was the reverse of its current folding, as can be seen in the continuity of text from the present folio 2v to 1r. Bifolium B is still folded in its original direction, although there are two center folds, one original, the other more recent. Still visible on both bifolia are the original four binding holes whose measurements from the top of the bifolia are 26/29 mm., 83/85 mm., 133/134 mm., and 179/180 mm.

After the manuscript from which the bifolia were taken was dismembered, Bifolium A appears to have been folded inside out. Bifolium B was placed within Bifolium A and the two stitched together, as can be seen when three sets of stitching holes appearing on both sides of the folded bifolia are placed together and carefully examined. It was probably at the time of stitching that two tabs were made at the tops of each folio and were reinforced with bits of parchment. Presumably all this had to do with creating a "binder" for other pieces of parchment or paper, be they diplomatic or otherwise. The folder must have appeared somewhat ragged inasmuch as the bifolia were carelessly folded and stitched together.

By the later Middle Ages the binder with or without its contents seems to have reached Limburg, because in the outer margins of Bifolium A and inner margins of Bifolium B there are cursive texts in Dutch which date probably to the fifteenth or sixteenth century.[7] In the latter one can make out the words "kloster," "Jan van Mechelen," "Smeets" (?), "Thomas," "Van Soo" (?), and twice the year "anno 98," and in the former the name of "Jan van Gugning/Gruying/Gruyning" (?) and his wife. Also on the former there is a little prayer written "A mon premier commencement, soit

[7] Dr. J. Hermans of the Rijksuniversiteit Groningen has kindly dated the writing to the fifteenth century.

Dieu le père omnipotents."[8]

Later the two bifolia were unstitched and took on an afterlife as pastedowns for a book, which the modern catalogue of the Rijksarchief does not identify. Visible on both bifolia are stains left by the turned-in covers which once held them fast to the boards of the volume.

The hand of the Latin text is of a distinctive central Italian type, the romanesca, of the later eleventh century.[9] Many other manuscripts containing collections deriving from the *Collection in Five Books* are also in romanesca.[10] In our fragments the text-ink is brown; minims measure 3 mm., descenders 4.5 mm., and ascenders 4/4.5 mm. Rubrics are in reddish-orange; larger initials, which are in the left-hand margin, are also in reddish-orange; and small rubricated initials are found throughout the text. There is one incipit of a canon on Bifolium B, fol. 2r, in large decorative letters beginning with a large *C* with acanthus-leaf motifs.

As with the manuscripts of the *Collection in Five Books* and many of its derivative collections, words throughout the text are glossed, usually with single simple synonyms. These glosses are in a small hand contemporary with the main text. In some instances there is no word separation, and a later hand has made light slash marks to assist the reader or another copyist.

As to the text of the canons themselves, they are generally arranged in blocks taken in order from the *Collection in Five Books,* books 1 and 2 (Bifolium A, fols. 2r–2v–1r–1v) and, after a lacuna, book 4 (Bifolium B, fols. 1r–1v and, after another lacuna, 2r–2v). The major topics dealt with are ecclesiastical judges and judgements, monks, infanticide, and swearing and oaths. There is one canon on monks that is not drawn from the *Collection in Five Books* (at least in its known witnesses). This canon, <XVI> *Placuit communi,* forbidding certain duties to monks, is also found in the *Collectio canonum* of Anselm of Lucca and in Gratian's *Decretum,* and it is attributed to Pope Eugenius in these collections.[11] Strangely, in the Maas-

8 Dr. Rob Meens of the Universiteit Utrecht has suggested that words in the marginal entries such as "coram" and "item noch" might point to someone writing on behalf of some judicial procedure, like a local court of *scabini.*

9 On this script, see Paola Supino Martini, *Roma e l'area grafica romanesca (secoli x–xii),* Biblioteca di Scrittura e civiltà 1 (Alessandria, 1987).

10 On these, see Roger E. Reynolds, "The South-Italian Canon Law *Collection in Five Books* and Its Derivatives: New Evidence on Its Origins, Diffusion, and Use," *Mediaeval Studies* 52 (1990): 278–95.

11 Gratian, *Decretum* C.16 q.1 c.8. I am grateful to Professor Robert Somerville for drawing this parallel to my attention. He notes that Friedberg in his edition of the *Decretum* used a conglomerate form of the collection of Anselm of Lucca that does not give an indication of the eleventh- and twelfth-century forms of Anselm. In any event, the text can be found in the A1 and C forms of Anselm's collection: A1 5.68 and C 5.65. On the various recensions of Anselm's col-

tricht excerpta it is attributed to both Eugenius and *Karolus imperator*. This is notable for two reasons: (1) Charlemagne had died before Eugenius became pope, and (2) in the *Collection in Five Books* Charlemagne is referred to not as *imperator* but as *rex*. It is possible that the canon came from Carolingian times inasmuch as some of its terminology, such as "pro lucro terreno," has a Caroline ring to it,[12] and it fits into the Carolingian efforts to assert the distinctive character of monks. On the other hand, the canon includes the term *ecclesia secularis*, which may point to a later date, and the canon could be an eleventh-century forgery fitting into the efforts of conservatives to keep monks in their monasteries.[13] As to the reasons for the unusual attribution, one can only speculate. If the canon did originate in Carolingian times, it is possible that Charlemagne in his years as emperor and Pope Eugenius later both legislated on this matter. In this respect it is telling that in Carolingian times both secular and clerical rulers legislated on ecclesiastical matters and that there were attempts, such as those in the Pseudo-Isidorian Benedictus Levita, to demonstrate the coincidence of secular and canon law. If the Maastricht canon is an eleventh-century forgery, the presence of Charlemagne's name and his position as emperor, not king, is more difficult to explain. It may be that the attribution in this canon arose from textual confusion in a source like the *Collection in Five Books*. In the collection and its relatives, such as the *Collectio Angelica*, there is occasional confusion in the attribution of canons to secular rulers such as Charlemagne or Henry II.[14] Moreover, there are in the *Collection in Five Books* separate canons attributed to both Charlemagne and Eugenius, one of the latter regarding monks.[15] As to why both Charlemagne and Eugenius are cited in the Maastricht text, while only the latter is cited in Anselm of Lucca's collection, is also a matter for speculation. It may be that the compiler of the Maastricht text took it from Anselm or one of his sources and added the name of Charlemagne. On the other hand, it may have been Anselm or one of his sources who was borrowing from a text like that of Maastricht and recognizing that Charlemagne and Eugenius did not rule at the same time simply omitted the former's name. In any event, the origins of the canon and its attibution are unclear.

lection, see Peter Landau, "Die Rezension C der Sammlung des Anselm von Lucca," *Bulletin of Medieval Canon Law*, n.s., 16 (1986): 17–54.

[12] Professor Hubert Mordek has kindly made this observation to me.

[13] Professor Giles Constable has kindly pointed this out to me.

[14] See Reynolds, "South-Italian Canon Law *Collection in Five Books*," 289.

[15] See *Collectio canonum in v libris (lib. i–iii)*, ed. M. Fornasari, CCCM 6 (Turnhout, 1970), 260.

If the texts in the Maastricht excerpta drawn from the *Collection in Five Books* are compared with the manuscripts of that collection, it is clear that they are closest to those in the romanesca manuscript from Narni, Vatican City, Biblioteca Apostolica Vaticana Vat. lat. 1339. Because of variants in both texts and glosses the Maastricht texts cannot be based on a manuscript such as Rome, Biblioteca Vallicelliana B 11 from San Eutizio presso Norcia, although in canon <XI> both the Maastricht and Vallicelliana texts are alike in omitting the words "a clero" from the end of the canon.

In the Maastricht texts there are several deviations from similar texts in the *Collection in Five Books*. First, the number of glosses on words is reduced in the Maastricht excerpta, usually to one. Second, in some instances, notably canons <XI>, <XII>, and <XIII>, a reference to the original number of the canon is given. Possibly the compiler of the Maastricht excerpta added these to his model or he was using a source other than the *Collection in Five Books*.

Following is an incipit-explicit edition of the Maastricht excerpta. In several instances, where the texts are short, the complete text has been given. Italicized words and letters represent those rubricized in the manuscript. Letters and words in boldface are decorated in the manuscript in some way. Within braces { } are the glosses over the prior word. Numbers in pointed brackets < > have been added to each canon for ease of citation. Words or letters supplied in < > are illegible or are missing in the manuscript. The orthography of the manuscript has been maintained. Where a canon appears in Fornasari's partial edition of the *Collection in Five Books*,[16] the canon number (preceded by 5L) and page from that edition (= F) are cited. His numbers, however, are found in no manuscript of the collection, and so the page number in the best manuscript of the collection, Montecassino, Archivio della Badia 125 (= MC), is also given. Where a canon is drawn from the unedited book 4 of the *Collection in Five Books*, the number and page of the canon in MC is given.

// bifol. A, fol. 2r //

<I> <occidunt . . . malum exemplum> praebendo; an frustra dictum est . . . in ipso est eum a quo attenditur {videtur} occidit.

5L 1.192; F, p. 121; MC, p. 50.

[16] See preceding note.

<II> *De his qui praepositorum culpas in publico produnt.*

Sententia dampnantur Cham filii Noe qui suorum praepositorum ... facta non diligant, nec nudent sed tantum operiant.

5L 1.205; F, p. 126; MC, pp. 52–53.

<III> *Qualiter praepositis oboedire conveni<t>.*

Predicator omnipotentis domini Apostolus dicit: Obedite praepositis vestris ... non gementes. Hoc enim non expedit {non convenit} vobis.

5L 1.207; F, pp. 126–27; MC, p. 53.

<IV> Itemque.

Rogamus vos fratres // bifol. A, fol. 2v // ut noveritis eos qui laborant inter vos ... horum intuentes exitum {initium et finis} conversationis.

5L 1.207; F, p. 127; MC, p. 53.

<V> *De iudicibus ecclesiae quales fieri debent.*

Paterius.

Non oportet iudices ecclesiae habere timorem humanum ... cautelitatem {studium} secularem habere, sed exempla divina.

5L 1.223.1; F, p. 137; MC, pp. 57–58.

<VI> Ihesus filius Syrach.

Quia non oportet servum dei cautum esse. ... Quia in quocumque iudicio iudicaveritis, iudicabitur de vobis.

5L 1.223.2; F, pp. 137–38; MC, p. 58.

<VII> *De iudicio clericorum ut non sit apud iniquos.* // bifol. A, fol. 1r //

Paulus.

Auferte malu<m> ex vobis ipsis. Audet aliquis vestrum negotium habens iudicari ... An nescitis quoniam angelos {episcopos. presbiteros} iudicabimus? Numquid non magis quam vos?

5L 1.224.1; F, p. 138; MC, p. 58.

<VIII> ***P***aterius.

Indigni sunt huius{isti}modi qui etiam de minimis iudicent. ... contemptibiles {reprehensibiles} sunt in ecclesia illos constituite ad iudicandum.

5L 1.224.2; F, p. 138; MC, p. 58.

<IX> *S*ynodus Cartaginenses.

Clericus qui causam suam sive iustam sive iniustam ad iudicium . . . illud est, dirimetur {abscidetur} et omnimodo oboediant statutis {legibus} eorum.

5L 1.224.3; F, p. 138; MC, p. 58.

<X> *P*aterius.

Omnis mundialis {secularis} etiam si sapiens sit, non iudicet iudicia ecclesiae.

5L 1.224.4; F, p. 138; MC, p. 58.

<XI> *Clericum fidemiussorem esse non oportet.*
In canonibus apostolorum. Titulo xx.

*C*lericus fideiussionibus inserviens abiciatur.

5L 1.230; F, p. 140; MC, p. 67.

<XII> *Ex decretis Celestini pp. Titulo vicesimo.*

*N*ulli sacerdotum liceat suos canones ignorare {nescire} nec quicquam {aliquid} . . . aliquorum libitu {voluntate} licentia populis permissa {concessa} frangatur?

5L 2.1; F, p. 179; MC, p. 67.

<XIII> *De synodis quae ab episcopis suis debentur temporibus in provincia celebrari.*
Ex concilio Anthioceno. Cap. xx. // bifol. A, fol. 1v //

Propter utilitates ecclesiasticas et absolutiones earum rerum {causarum} . . . praeter eos quibus metropolitana iura {potestates} videntur esse commissa.

5L 2.5; F, pp. 181–82; MC, p. 68.

<XIV> *De eo quod monachus abbatem pessimum deserere debet.*

*H*ieronimus.

Lupus vitandus pastor bonus adeundus. Spelunca latronis deserenda ovile ovium petendum.

5L 2.114.1; F, p. 258; MC, p. 103.

<XV> *Augustinus.*

Fugiunt oves vocem pastoris quem non cognoscunt et deserta petunt. Ita mali principes [*sic*] ovilia vitanda sunt et deserta vita petenda.

5L 2.114.2; F, p. 258; MC, p. 103.

<XVI> ***Ex decretis Eugenii pp. et Karoli imperatoris.***

*P*lacuit communi nostro consilio ut nullus monachorum pro lucro terreno de monasterio suo exire nefandissimo ausu praesumat . . . neque qualibetcumque [*sic*] negotiis sese implicare sit suo claustro contemptus [*sic*]. Quia <. . . .>

Anselm of Lucca, *Collectio canonum,* Version A1, 5.68, Version C, 5.65 (cf. Gratian, *Decretum* C.16 q.1 c.8).

// bifol. B, fol. 1r //

<XVII> <. . . qua mu. . . .> consuetudinem sive incuna sive in alio loco ubi . . . si non baptizatus .i. an. pen. Si vero <bap>tizatus .ii^{as}. qua dicitur.

5L 4.84.3; MC, p. 220.

<XVIII> *Iudicium Comeani.*

*S*i mulier fidelis parit infantem et si possit non nu<trit> eum sed proicit. . . . Sed tamen propter purificandam animam s<uam> iudicium sacerdotis peniteat.

5L 4.85.1; MC, p. 220.

<XIX> *Iudicium Comm<eani>.*

*S*iqua mulier ebria aut per aliquam crapula<m> {superfluitat<em>} infantem suum oppresserit. . . . Si vero per aliquam ebitudin<em> {debilitate<m>} mentis aliquantulum venie praebeatur.

5L 4.85.2; MC, p. 220.

<XX> *De mu<lie>ribus conceptos suos natos necantibus et de consent<ientibus eis>*

*H*ieronimus.

Quae mulier hanc detestatione {contradictione} . . . et parricida in filium suum. <I>nde definimus ei // bifol. B, fol. 1v // <ut usque in finem vi>tae <su>ae peniteat.

5L 4.85.3; MC, p. 220.

<XXI> *Augustinus.*

Quae mulier aut laborat {operatur} ut non concipiat aut partum . . . tantorum homicidiorum ream esse cognoverit.

5L 4.85.3; MC, pp. 220–21.

<XXII> *Concilio Ancyrano.*

<Si qu>am mulier fornicaverit <et in>fantem qui exinde fuerit natus occiderit . . . conscias {consentientes} scelerum ipsarum .x. annis <ager>e penitentiam iudicamus.

5L 4.86.1; MC, p. 221.

<XXIII> *In eodem concilio.*

<Si quis c>onceptum mulieris deceperit {destruxerit} si ante .xl^{a}. dies .xl^{a}. <die>s penit. Si autem post .xl. dies ut homicida pen.

5L 4.87.1; MC, p. 221.

<XXIV> *Iudicium canonicum.*

<Pater> aut mater si sciens uo<lunt>arie necat filium suum ante baptismum . . . per capta {perdita} mente inscius {nescius} et <. . .>

5L 4.88; MC, p. 221. // bifol. B, fol. 2r //

<XXV> <. . .> salutem et brevietur penitentia eius. Si autem non potuerit ut homidica peniteat. Si potuerit et noluerit ut impius iudicetur.

5L 4.136; MC, pp. 235–36.

<XXVI> *De coniuratione vel conspiratione.*
Ex concilio Calcedonensi.

CONIURATIONIS {coadunationis} ***VEL CONSPIRA***tionis crimen ab exteris {extraneis} . . . episcopis aut clericis a gradu proprio penitus {per omnia} abiciantur.

5L 4.137.1; MC, p. 236.

<XXVII> *De clericis per creaturam iurantibus.*
Concilio Cartagensi.

Clericum per creaturam {celum et terram} iurantem accerrime {durissime} obiurgandum {increpandum} si persisterit {perseveraverit} in vitio excommunicandum.

5L 4.137.2; MC, p. 236.

<XXVIII> *De tria iuramenta que solvenda sunt.*

*H*ieronimus.

Tria iuramenta solvenda {destruenda} sunt. Primo cum quis male facere iurat. . . . Omne nodum {ligatura} iniquitatis dissolve.

5L 4.139.1; MC, p. 236.

<XXIX> Item.

Iuramentum perversum retro . . . non putans esse peccatum.

5L 4.139.2; MC, p. 236.

<XXX> *ORIGEN.*

Alii frustra {invanum} iurant nec se ipsos adiuvant nec alios ut melius solvere {rumpere} videatur quam implere.

5L 4.139.3; MC, p. 236.

<XXXI> *S*ynodus defini- // bifol. B, fol. 2v // tio.

Intanta [*sic*] {inordinata} laudabiliter solvenda nec praevaricatio sed est temeritatis {perversitatis} emendatio.

5L 4.139.4; MC, p. 236.

<XXXII> *In libro <Regum>.*

*S*aul iuravit Ionathan occidere et non occisus est nec in hoc iuramentum culpatus . . . irrita {vana} erunt nec tenebitur obnoxia {culpabile}.

5L, 4.139.5; MC, p. 236.

<XXXII> *S*ynodus hibernensis.

Iuramentum filii et filiae nescientes [*sic*] patre, iuramentum monachi nesciente abbate, iuramentum servi non permittente domino irrita erunt.

5L 4.139.6; MC, p. 236.

<XXXIV> *H*isidorus.

In malis autem promissis resinde {abside} fidem in turpi uoto muta. . . . Bonum igitur est malum quod pellit {expellit} pessimum.

5L 4.139.7; MC, p. 236.

<XXXIII> *GREGORIUS.*

Quod latenter {absconse} et per vim {virtute} et illicite {iniuste} introductum est. . . . Scriptum est enim omnia bona erunt in comparatione {assimilatione} peiorum.

5L 4.139.8; MC, p. 236.

In recent studies it has been shown that the *Collection in Five Books,* which survives in only three manuscripts and perhaps a fragmentary folio, had become very popular in southern and central Italy in the late eleventh and early twelfth centuries and gave rise to many abridgements and derivative collections—over twenty thus far identified.[17] Almost all of these derivatives are found in libraries in central and southern Italy. The only exceptions thus far have been those in Spain: the *Collectio Toletana,* found in a central Italian manuscript taken to Toledo by Cardinal Zelada; the collection in Madrid, Biblioteca Nacional 373, in Beneventan script; and the excerpta in El Escorial, Real Biblioteca de San Lorenzo Z III 19, also in Beneventan and written possibly at Montecassino. The Maastricht fragments copied in central Italy now show that a derivative collection, either in whole or in part, also travelled to the Low Countries.

[17] See Reynolds, "South-Italian Canon Law *Collection in Five Books,*" 278–95.

XVIII

GRATIAN'S *DECRETUM* AND THE *CODE* OF JUSTINIAN IN BENEVENTAN SCRIPT

A recently published article, entitled "Canonistica Beneventana," was devoted to studying the appearance of canon law collections in Beneventan script.[1] The number of these collections represented and the volume of manuscripts in Beneventan is surprisingly large. The ages of the manuscripts range from the late eighth century to the late twelfth or early thirteenth centuries. The earliest collection represented is a version of the ancient fifth- or sixth-century *Collectio Dionysiana* and the latest is an excerpt from the late eleventh-century *Tripartita* of Ivo of Chartres. Between these chronological limits, virtually all of the major early medieval canon law collections are represented in Beneventan script: the *Concordia Cresconii, Collectio vetus gallica, Collectio canonum hibernensis, Collectio Dionysio-Hadriana, Collectio Dacheriana, Pseudo-Isidorian Decretales,* Burchard's *Decretum,* the *Collection in Five Books,* and the *Collection in Seventy-Four Titles.* The only major collections conspicuous for their absence are the *Collectio canonum hispana,* Regino's *Libri duo de synodalibus,* the *Collectio canonum* of Anselm of Lucca, and Ivo's other collections. The origins of the collections themselves, from Germany and France down to southern Italy, are a reflection of the wide cultural ties in the areas where Beneventan script was written.

Surprisingly, there has been no evidence that any collection from the time of Gratian and beyond was copied in Beneventan script. To explain this anomaly several reasons were adduced in "Canonistica Beneventana." First, there is the well-known prohibition by the Emperor Frederick II at Melfi in 1231 forbidding the use of Beneventan for legal documents. Thereafter, Beneventan was used almost exclusively for liturgical texts. More important, the study of law from the time of Gratian and beyond was centered in the universities. Prior to this time ecclesiastical law had been a preoccupation not only outside monasteries but within, as witnessed by the

[1] Roger E. Reynolds, "Canonistica Beneventana," *Proceedings of the Ninth International Congress of Medieval Canon Law, Munich 13–18 Juli 1992,* ed. Peter Landau, Monumenta Iuris Canonici, Ser. C (Vatican, 1996), 21–40.

many canonical collections written in the monasteries. When legal training moved to the universities, Beneventan could not have been a script of choice. It was primarily a monastic one, slow to write and difficult to read if one were not accustomed to its peculiarities. Law professors and students from outside the Beneventan zone would not have looked favorably on the script, and hence, it is not surprising that no witnesses to Gratian's *Decretum* and canonical compilations beyond him have been reported in Beneventan script.

Now, however, a fragment of Gratian's *Decretum* has been identified. MS 9 of the Biblioteca dell'Abbazia at Montevergine is a miscellaneous theological manuscript written in a Gothic cursive hand of the fifteenth century. On fol. 1r there is a cropped ex libris, "Iste liber est domus . . . ," and on fol. 1v in a sixteenth-century hand in black ink is ". . . beati francisci sub. . . ." On fol. 70v in the Gothic hand of the scribe is "Iste liber est monasterii Sancti laurencii de padula ordinis cartusiensis . 66 ."[2] In December of 1992, when the manuscript was examined, there was pasted into the back inside cover a part of a folio in Beneventan script with the hair-side uppermost. The folio had been partially unglued with the result that traces of the script could also be seen on the inside back cover. As of May 1993, the fragment had been detached from the book and assigned the shelfmark Perg. 6518. At the bottom of the Beneventan fragment is written in a clumsy, non-expert hand (ordinary minuscule of the sixteenth century), "Ego frati colubanum del patula mociro e santula . . . de la Padula(?)." The fragment itself measures 270 × 202 (184 × 176) mm. and is written in two columns, each with forty-three lines surviving. The width of column a is 82.4 mm. and column b 85.5 mm. The distance between columns is 10 mm. and the distance between lines is 3–5 mm. Binding holes are visible, and from top to bottom they measure 6, 12.5, 28.5, 78, 82, 33, and 20 mm. Ruling is from hair to flesh side and seems not to have been a direct impression. Brown ink is used for the text with red for chapter headings. Alternating red and blue initials are used at the beginning of chapters. On the side of the folio that was glued to the back cover, there is a large initial, 55 × ca. 40 mm. The letter is formed of white and red vinestem and is infilled with blue and red. The interior of the letter is filled with white and yellow vinestem terminating in blue or yellow flowers with the full body of a springing pink dog. The tail of a *Q* is composed of similar vinestem and flowers and terminates in two flowers, one red, the other blue. The script itself appears to be of the thirteenth century; the initials

[2] See G. Mongelli, "I codici dell'Abbazia di Montevergine," *Archivi: Archivi d'Italia e rassegna internazionale degli archivi,* 2d ser., 26 (1959): 177–78.

and color blue also suggest a date at least of the late twelfth century and beyond. The text from Gratian's *Decretum* is C.2 q.7 c.58–q.8 c.3, C.2 q.8 c.5–C.3, C.3 q.1 c.2–c.5, C.3 q.1 c.6–q.2 c.5. Glosses in a non-Beneventan hand can be seen in both margins.

* * *

Among texts written in Beneventan script, liturgical ones far outnumber all others,[3] but legal texts are also well represented. These are primarily canon law: there are no less than twenty-one canonical collections known to have been written in the script and, as noted above, they range from the most ancient of collections down to the *Decretum* of Gratian. Other types of legal texts in Beneventan are far fewer, but they do exist. Inasmuch as Beneventan was written primarily in the southern duchy of the Lombards, one would expect there to be manuscripts of the *Leges Langobardorum,* and indeed there are five such manuscripts: Cava, Archivio della Badia della Santissima Trinità 4; Madrid, Biblioteca Nacional 413; Montecassino, Archivio della Badia 246; Naples, Biblioteca Nazionale, Branc. I.B.12; and Vienna, Österreichische Nationalbibliothek 394.[4] Because Beneventan was also written where Roman law prevailed in antiquity, one might also expect to find as many Roman law texts in the script. Thus far, this has not been the case. Only three manuscripts have been reported: Leipzig, Universitätsbibliothek Hänel 6 contains the *Epitome latina Novellarum Iustiniani;* Vienna, Österreichische Nationalbibliothek 395 + Ser. n. 11928 contains the *Institutiones Iustiniani;* and in the renowned *Codex Pisanus* of Justinian's *Digest,* Florence, Biblioteca Medicea Laurenziana, s.n., written in uncials of the sixth century, a Beneventan hand has written a few texts, demonstrating that the codex was in southern Italy, probably Montecassino, before travelling to Amalfi, Pisa, and Florence. Beyond these manuscripts, there are also excerpts from the *Epitome Iuliani* scattered through several south Italian canonical collections written in Beneventan, such as the *Collection of Vallicelliana Tome XVIII,* and the *Collection in Five Books* and its derivatives.[5] Hence, it is possible that the *Epitome* at one

[3] Approximately seventy percent, and as further manuscripts and fragments are found, that proportion grows higher; see Virginia Brown, "A Second New List of Beneventan Manuscripts (III)," *Mediaeval Studies* 56 (1994): 299.

[4] In *Leges Langobardorum,* ed. F. Bluhme, MGH Leges 4 (Hannover, 1868), lxi, it is reported that Naples, Biblioteca Nazionale Brancatiana II.B.28 containing the *Liber Papiensis* is in Lombardic or Beneventan. There exists no such manuscript by that number in Naples.

[5] See *Collectio canonum in v libris (lib. i–iii),* ed. M. Fornasari, CCCM 6 (Turnhout, 1970), xiv–xv.

time circulated in manuscripts written in Beneventan, although the canonistic compilers may have drawn their texts from manuscripts written in other hands.

That Roman law texts are rarely found in Beneventan script may be due to a number of factors. First, Roman and Lombard law were at times seen to be competitive,[6] and hence, there might have been some hesitation to copy Roman law in Beneventan, a script particularly associated with the Lombards even the Middle Ages. Moreover, it is significant that aside from liturgical manuscripts in Beneventan, the majority of Beneventan codices date to the twelfth century and before, and in this period Roman law was known in Europe primarily in its "tribal" versions such as the *Lex Romana Visigothorum* or *Lex Romana Burgundionum.* The revival of Roman law studies from the twelfth century and beyond took place largely in university contexts, and Beneventan, primarily a monastic script slow to write and difficult to read, appears not to have been used for university purposes, as noted above in the case of canon law: apart from the single fragment of the *Decretum* of Gratian, all the canon law collections written in Beneventan antedate Gratian.

Thus far, no manuscripts in Beneventan of the *Code* of Justinian have been reported. Now, however, an example has appeared in the Biblioteca Vallicelliana in Rome, Carte vallicelliane XII, 3.[7] When a seventeenth-century paper manuscript, Vallicelliana P 63, containing the *Adagia graeca latine atque italice explicata,* was restored in 1982 by Angelo Pandiniglio in Rome, a bifolium containing the *Code* was detached from it. The Beneventan text is written on a bifolium cropped at the top, outer margins, and bottom so that parts of it are missing on three sides. The bifolium measures 282 × 205 mm. with two columns of text, each 91 mm. wide with and interlinear margin of 38 mm. The ruling of the twenty-three or twenty-four lines, 13/14 mm. apart, was done from hair to flesh side, perhaps after folding. The ink is dark brown with traces of black, and with the exception of a rubric in orange on fol. 2rb, there is no illumination. The script is of the eleventh century, and the text of the *Code* includes 7.64.2–9 and 7.71.8.4 through 72.6.

N.B. Please see additional information in the Addenda.

[6] On this see Francesco Calasso, *Introduzione al diritto comune* (Milan, 1970), 294–302.

[7] See V. D'Urso, *Carte vallicelliane. Catalogo* (Rome, 1986) (typescript, unnumbered pp.).

ADDENDA

In a preface to a series of short notes in *Miscellanea Beneventana* published in *Mediaeval Studies* 58 (1996) entitled 'Parerga Beneventana' the importance of collecting and reporting significant fragments of manuscripts discovered in our search for Beneventan items was emphasized. 'Colligite fragmenta ne pereant.' The value of reporting such items can be justified on several grounds. For example, our colleague in musicology, Thomas Forrest Kelly, has pointed out that if the many fragments of graduals and antiphonaries in Beneventan script were not known, we would have little idea as to how common the full volumes of these manuscripts were in the Middle Ages. Another reason for reporting significant fragments of manuscripts is demonstrated in the following addenda.

IV. Visigothic-script remains of a pandect Bible and the *Collectio canonum hispana* in Lucca

Sometime after completing this article on the Lucca pandect Visigothic fragments I learned of what appeared to be another fragment of this Bible owned by my late friend and colleague, Domenico Maffei. Since the fragment was in private hands, I hesitated to report it. But now it has been briefly described in the catalogue by Enzo Mecacci of the manuscripts belonging to Professor Maffei. It is described there as dating to the late ninth or early tenth century, somewhat later than the dating assigned to it in my article and by E.A. Lowe in the *Codices Latini Antiquiores*. This new dating is based on the somewhat insecure grounds of the use of the assibilated or unassibilated 'ti', so Lowe's earlier date is still to be preferred. Professor Maffei's daughter, Dr Paola Maffei, has since very generously written me about the provenance of the fragment:

'This fragment was used for the binding of a not common edition containing the consilia of the French jurist Barthélemy Chasseneuz [Barthélemy Chasseneuz, *Repertorium Consiliorum*, Lyon, Iacopo Giunta, 1535]. The book was owned by the Paitelli family, who lived in Sant'Angelo in Vado in the area of Urbino [see Rutilio Paitelli, Expeditiones causarum civilium ... annotationibus ... Ludovici Paitelli eiusdem auctoris filii, Sant'Angelo in Vado 1629]. My father [Professor Maffei] bought it in 1984 from the antiquarian library Brocchi in Ravenna, and then decided (not immediately: the file-card I typed still says: manuscript pergament) to bind it again in order to recover the fragment. My father owns other books coming from the Paitellis, bought elsewhere, but they have other bindings. It could be of some interest the fact that the Chasseneuz consilia, once having arrived in that part of Italy do not seem to have moved far away (Urbino and Ravenna are quite nearby).'

XVIII. Gratian's *Decretum* and the *Code* of Justinian in Beneventan script

The fragments of the Justinian's *Code,* which I briefly described, have now been expanded in a brilliant article by Dr Simon Corcoran 'New subscripts for old rescripts: the Vallicelliana fragments of Justinian Code Book VII,' to appear in *Zeitschrift der Savigny Stiftung für Rechtsgeschichte: Romanistische Abteilung* 126 (2009), pp. 401–22. There he demonstrates that the fragments, copied in the late eleventh century, possibly at Montecassino, are a bridge between the original and later versions of the *Code* and provide eleven new or revised rescripts.

INDEX OF MANUSCRIPTS

GENERAL INDEX